Construction Morphology

For Herry

Construction Morphology

GEERT BOOIJ

OXFORD
UNIVERSITY PRESS

This book has been printed digitally and produced in a standard specification
in order to ensure its continuing availability

OXFORD
UNIVERSITY PRESS

Great Clarendon Street, Oxford OX2 6DP
United Kingdom

Oxford University Press is a department of the University of Oxford.
It furthers the University's objective of excellence in research, scholarship,
and education by publishing worldwide.
Oxford is a registered trade mark of Oxford University Press in the UK
and in certain other countries

© Geert Booij 2010

The moral rights of the author have been asserted

Reprinted 2012

British Library Cataloguing in Publication Data
Data available

Library of Congress Cataloging in Publication Data
Data available

ISBN 978-0-19-957191-8

Contents

Abbreviations and symbols

´	main stress, high tone
`	secondary stress, low tone
=	clitic boundary
-	affix boundary
↔	corresponds with
≈	is paradigmatically related to
·	syllable boundary
<	left edge of schema
>	right edge of schema
<	derives from
*	ungrammatical
α	variable for + or −
ω	phonological word
σ	syllable
Ø	zero
A	adjective
Acc	accusative
aci	accusativus-cum-infinitivo
Adj	adjective
Adv	adverb
Aff	affix
AP	adjectival phrase
CM	Construction Morphology
Comp	completive aspect
Cop	copula
D	determiner
Dat	dative
Def	definite
Dem	demonstrative
Det	determiner

Dig	digital
Dim	diminutive
DP	determiner phrase
Excl	exclusive
F	feminine, feature
Fem	feminine
Gen	genitive
Inf	infinitive
Inst	instrumental
Loc	locative
m	minimal number, non-plural
M	masculine, measure noun
Masc	masculine
MWE	multi-word expression
N	noun
Neg	negative
Neut	neuter
Nom	nominative, nominalization
NP	noun phrase
Num	numeral
Obj	object
Obl	oblique argument
Ord	ordinal
P	preposition, person, particle
pers	person
PHON	phonological representation
Pl	plural
Poss	possessive
PP	prepositional phrase
Pref	prefix
Pres	present tense
Progr	progressive
Ptcp	participle
R	relation
Refl	reflexive

RHR	right-hand head rule
SBJ	subject
SC	small clause
SCV	separable complex verb
SEM	semantic representation
Sg	singular
SOV	subject–object–verb
Subj	subject
Suff	suffix
SVO	subject–verb–object
SYN	syntactic representation
t	trace
TNS	tense
tr	transitive
V	verb
VN	verbal noun
VP	verb phrase
x,y	variable

Figures and Tables

Acknowledgements

This book is a synthesis of a number of ideas on and arguments for the use of the notion 'construction' in morphological analysis that I developed in recent years. In writing this book I have made use of some of my published articles on Construction Morphology. Some sections of Chapter 3 are taken from 'Compound construction: schemas or analogy? A Construction Morphology perspective', published in *Cross-disciplinary issues in compounding*, edited by Sergio Scalise and Irene Vogel, Amsterdam / Philadelphia: John Benjamins, 2010, 93–107. Chapter 4 is based on 'A constructional analysis of quasi-incorporation in Dutch', *Gengo Kenkyu* 135 (2009) 5–28, a journal published by The Linguistic Society of Japan. For Chapter 6, I have made use of my article 'Constructional idioms as products of language change: the *aan het* + INFINITIVE construction in Dutch', in Alexander Bergs and Gabriele Diewald (eds.) (2008), *Constructions and language change*, Berlin / New York: Mouton de Gruyter, 79–104. Chapter 7 is based on my article 'Phrasal names: a constructionist analysis' in *Word Structure* 2 (2009), 219–240, a journal published by Edinburgh University Press (www.eupjournals.com/jbctv). Chapter 8 has been written as a text for this book, but an adapted version has appeared as 'Constructions and lexical units: an analysis of Dutch numerals' in *Linguistische Berichte*, Sonderheft 19, 2010, 1–14, published by Helmut Buske Verlag, Hamburg. Finally, some of the data in Chapter 10 are from an article published in 2002, 'The balance between storage and computation in phonology' in Sieb Nooteboom, Fred Weerman, and Frank Weijnen (eds.), *Storage and computation in the language faculty*, Dordrecht: Kluwer, 115–138. The permission of each of the publishers to re-use this material is hereby gratefully acknowledged.

In preparing this book, I profited from the comments by anonymous reviewers on drafts of the publications mentioned above, and from those by my audiences on the occasions that I presented parts of this work.

Last but not least I would like to thank my colleagues who were kind enough to comment on a draft of the text of this book: Farrell Ackerman (San Diego), Kristel van Goethem (Leuven), Franz Rainer (Vienna), and Teresa Vallès (Barcelona). Their remarks led to various improvements, but of course the responsibility for this text is entirely my own.

Geert Booij
Leiden, January 2010

1

Morphology and construction grammar

1.1 Introduction

The title of this book, *Construction Morphology* (henceforth *CM*), promises a theory of linguistic morphology in which the notion 'construction' plays a central role. The theory of *CM* aims at a better understanding of the relation between syntax, morphology, and the lexicon, and at providing a framework in which both the differences and the commonalities of word level constructs and phrase level constructs can be accounted for.

In this chapter, I outline the main ingredients of this theory: a theory of word structure, a theory of the notion 'construction', and a theory of the lexicon. These are the topics of sections 1.2 and 1.3. In section 1.4 I discuss how the notion 'construction' can be made fruitful for morphological analysis and theorizing. A specific advantage of the notion 'construction' is that it can be used both at the level of word structure and that of syntactic structure without obliterating the differences between these two domains. This is shown in section 1.5 where phrasal units with word-like properties are introduced. Although this book focuses on word formation, inflectional phenomena also provide strong evidence for the correctness of a constructional approach, as briefly discussed in section 1.6. Section 1.7 provides a survey of the issues and phenomena that are discussed in the chapters that follow.

1.2 Word-based morphology

There are two basic approaches to the linguistic analysis of complex words. In the morpheme-based approach which was dominant in post-Bloomfieldian American linguistics, a complex word is seen as a concatenation of morphemes. In this approach, morphological analysis can be defined as the 'syntax of morphemes'. For instance, the English word *walker* can be seen as a concatenation of the verbal morpheme *walk* and the nominalizing suffix *-er* that carries the meaning 'agent'. This is the way in which English morphology is often taught in textbooks, for example in Harley (2007). In a more radical form, the morpheme-based approach has even led to the claim that 'morphologically complex words are the outcome of the manipulation of morphemes that takes place in syntax' (Julien 2002: 297). Alternatively, we might take a word-based perspective in which words are the starting points of morphological analysis (Aronoff 2007). This is done by comparing sets of words like:

(1)   buy   buyer
      eat   eater
      shout   shouter
      walk   walker

We then conclude to a formal difference between the words in the left column and those in the right column. This difference correlates systematically with a meaning difference: the words on the right in (1) have an additional sequence -er compared to those on the left, and denote the agents of the actions expressed by the verbs on the left. Words like *buy* and *buyer* stand in a paradigmatic relationship, as opposed to the syntagmatic relationship that holds for words that are combined in a phrase or a sentence. This paradigmatic relationship between pairs of words like *buy* and *buyer* can be projected onto the word *buyer* in the form of word-internal morphological structure:

(2) $[[buy]_V er]_N$

In the mind of the speaker of English, the set of words listed in (1) may give rise to an abstract schema of the following (provisional) form:

(3) $[[x]_V er]_N$ 'one who Vs'

This schema expresses a generalization about the form and meaning of existing deverbal nouns in -er listed in the lexicon, and can also function as the starting point for coining new English nouns in -er from verbs. That is, new deverbal nouns in -er are not necessarily coined on analogy with a specific existing deverbal word in -er, but may be formed on the basis of this abstract schema. A new word is formed by replacing the variable *x* in the schema with a concrete verb. This is the operation of 'unification'. For instance, the recently coined English verb *to skype* 'to communicate by means of Skype' can be unified with schema (3), resulting in the new noun *skyper*. As Tomasello (2000: 238) points out, language acquisition starts with storing mental representations of concrete cases of language use. Gradually, the language learner will make abstractions across sets of linguistic constructs with similar properties, thus acquiring the abstract system underlying these linguistic constructs.

The idea that word formation patterns can be seen as abstractions over sets of related words is rooted in a venerable tradition. For instance, the German linguist and Junggrammatiker Hermann Paul wrote in his famous *Prinzipien der Sprachgeschichte*, published in 1880, that the language learner will start with learning individual words and word forms, but gradually (s)he will abstract away from the concrete words (s)he has learned, and coin new words and word forms according to abstract schemas. This enables the language user to be creative in word formation and inflection (Paul 1880 [3rd edition 1898]: 102). This tradition is continued in the paradigmatic approach to word formation in the European tradition of word formation research (Schultink 1962; Van Marle 1985, 2000), in recent work in various varieties of non-transformational generative grammar such as Head-driven Phrase Structure Grammar (Riehemann 1998, 2001), and in the theoretical framework of Cognitive Linguistics (Croft and Cruse 2004; Langacker 1987, 1991; Taylor 2002).

Since such schemas depend on relationships between words, this morphological model has been called the network model (Bybee 1995), and the notion 'network' is indeed a proper term for conceptualizing the set of relationships between words in a lexicon (Bochner 1993). This approach may also be qualified as the 'abstractive' approach (Blevins 2006) because the coinage of new words depends on abstractions over sets of existing words and word forms in the lexicon of a language.

Schema (3) may be said to license the individual deverbal nouns in *-er* in the English lexicon. Complex words, once they have been coined, will be stored in the lexicon of a language (which generalizes over the lexical memories of the individual speakers of that language), if they have idiosyncratic properties and/or they have become conventionalized. A word is conventionalized if it has become the word to be chosen in a language community to denote a particular concept. For instance, the English compound *cash dispenser* is a word used to denote a machine from which one can take cash money. This machine can also be denoted by *cash machine* and *automatic teller machine* (*ATM*), but the word *money machine*, though well-formed and transparent as to its meaning, is not a conventional term for this device. Hence, words like *cash dispenser* must be stored in the lexicon.

This very short sketch of the analysis of a morphological pattern makes two assumptions. First, it assumes that there are specifically morphological generalizations or rules that cannot be reduced to either syntax or phonology. That is, this book takes the lexicalist position that the grammars of natural languages have a relatively autonomous morphological sub-grammar. Secondly, it assumes that complex words, i.e. the outputs of morphological operations, can be listed in the lexicon.

Morphological schemas have the following functions: they express predict-able properties of existing complex words, they indicate how new ones can be coined (Jackendoff 1975), and they give structure to the lexicon since complex words do not form an unstructured list but are grouped into subsets. This conception of the grammar avoids the well-known rule versus list fallacy (Langacker 1987), the unwarranted assumption that linguistic constructs are either generated by rule or listed, and that being listed excludes a linguistic construct from being linked to a rule at the same time.

The relation between schema (3) and the individual words that conform to this schema is that of 'instantiation': each of the nouns in -er listed in (1) instantiates the schema in (3). Schema (3) provides a direct account of the fact that -er is a bound morpheme that does not occur as a word by itself, since this morpheme is not listed in the lexicon as an autonomous lexical item. Its existence is bound to its occurrence in schema (3). The same sequence of sounds /ər/ is used in other morphological schemas as well, for instance in the schema for the comparative form of English adjectives.

The use of constructional schemas like (3) looks similar to the use of word formation rules, as proposed in Aronoff (1976). The equivalent Aronovian rule is:

(4) $[x]_V \rightarrow [[x]_V \, er]_N$ Semantics: 'one who Vs habitually, professionally'

The similarity between the two approaches is that they are both word-based (and hence affixes are not lexical items themselves), and both assume the coexistence of abstract patterns (rules/schemas) and complex words instan-tiating these rules/schemas listed in the lexicon. Yet, there are a number of advantages of schemas over rules that will be discussed in more detail in the next chapter. One difference that can already be mentioned here is that, whereas rules are always source-oriented (you take a base word, and perform some morphological operation on that base word), schemas can also be product- or output-oriented (Bybee 1995; Haspelmath 1989). For example, in Ngiti, a Central-Sudanic language of Zaire, the plural forms of nouns that are kinship terms or denote other inalienable possession are always character-ized by a Mid-High tone pattern whereas the corresponding singular forms have a number of different tone patterns (Kutsch Lojenga 1994: 135) (Low tone is marked by `, High tone by ´, and Mid tone is unmarked):

(5)   *singular*   *plural*
      àba 'father'   abá
      abhu 'grandfather'   abhú
      adhà 'co-wife'   adhá

Hence, the plural forms can only be characterized uniformly in terms of an output-oriented schema that specifies the Mid-High tone pattern of all these plural forms. The following schema is output-oriented, and expresses the relevant generalization:

(6) $[\text{Mid High}]_{\text{Ni}}$ 'plural N_i' (where N_i is inalienable)

The notion 'schema' is a very general notion from cognitive science. It is 'a data structure for representing the generic concepts stored in memory' (Rumelhart 1980: 34). That is, it can be used for making generalizations across all sorts of linguistic levels and types of (linguistic and non-linguistic) information. In Chapter 2 I discuss the properties of schemas in more detail in relation to the structure of the lexicon.

What is the implication of word-based morphology as outlined very briefly above for our conception of the architecture of the grammar? How does morphology fit into that architecture? My starting point is that each word is a linguistic sign, a pairing of form and meaning. The form of a word in its turn comprises two dimensions, its phonological form, and its morphosyntactic properties. Hence, each word is a pairing of three types of information which will be labelled as PHON, SYN, and SEM respectively. Its meaning (SEM) may have both strictly semantic and pragmatic components (McConnell-Ginet 2008). Morphology affects all three dimensions of words. That is why we need a 'tripartite parallel architecture' of the grammar (as advocated by Culicover and Jackendoff 2005, 2006; Jackendoff 2002a, 2007 on the basis of primarily syntactic considerations). The essence of this model is that each level of representation is governed by rules and principles of its own, and that there are interface modules that specify the links between types of information on the different levels (Jackendoff 2002a: 125).

In Figure 1.1, Jackendoff uses the term 'rules' for regularities on a particular level of linguistic description, such as phonology or syntax. However, nothing hinges on this term, and one could use the term 'schema' here as well. For instance, for each language we need a phonological grammar that specifies how the sounds of a word are grouped into syllables and higher-level prosodic constituents such as the foot and the phonological word. The regularities in the phonological structure of words can be expressed by schemas for phonological structure, and the actual assignment of phonological structure to a word will then have the form of matching the sound sequence of that word with phonological schemas including those for prosodic structure. Hence, we might express the commonalities in the phonological properties of words as phonological schemas that generalize over the phonological properties of words. The notion 'schema' is a far more general notion than the notion

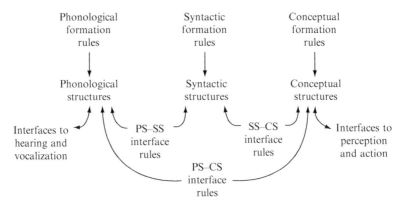

FIGURE 1.1. The tripartite parallel architecture

'construction' or 'constructional schema' which denotes a schematic pairing of form and meaning.

In sum, a word, like a sentence, is a complex piece of information. It links a particular sequence of sounds to a particular meaning, and it has formal properties such as a syntactic category label. The information contained in the English simplex word *dog*, for instance, can be represented in Figure 1.2, where the symbol ↔ stands for 'correspondence'.

The first piece of information in Figure 1.2 concerns the phonological properties of this word: it is a phonological word (ω) that consists of one syllable (σ) that in its turn consists of a sequence of three sounds. This phonological word bears the same index as the syntactic information about this word (that it is a noun), and is also co-indexed with the semantic information that it expresses the predicate DOG. Co-indexation is used to specify the correspondence between the three kinds of information involved in knowing a word. We thus see that a word has a tripartite parallel structure.[1]

---

[1] This is a traditional insight, formulated as follows by the linguist E. M. Uhlenbeck in his *dies* lecture for the University of Leiden in 1976: 'woorden zijn eenheden waaraan drie dimensies zijn te onderkennen. Zij vertonen een hoorbare vorm – dit is hun fonische dimensie –, zij leveren in het gebruik een kennisbijdrage tot het geheel waarvan zij deel uitmaken – dit is hun semantische dimensie –, en tenslotte hebben zij een grammatische dimensie waaronder allereerst moet worden verstaan dat zij over systematische verbindingsmogelijkheden beschikken ten opzichte van andere woorden' [words are units for which three dimensions can be distinguished. They exhibit an audible form – this is their phonic dimension –, they contribute knowledge to the expression as a whole – this is their semantic dimension –, and finally they have a grammatical dimension, which means first of all that they dispose of systematic possibilities of connection in relation to other words [my translation] (Uhlenbeck 1976)].

$$\omega_i \leftrightarrow N_i \leftrightarrow DOG_i$$

$$|$$

$$\sigma$$

$$|$$

dog

FIGURE 1.2. The lexical representation of *dog*

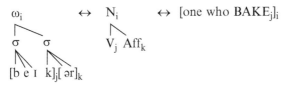

FIGURE 1.3. The lexical representation of *baker*

Jackendoff considers each word as a set of interface rules between the different levels of representation. Instead, I use the term 'correspondence' for denoting such relationships. The term 'interface' is used to denote the systematicity in the correspondence between the three types of information.

In many cases we need to specify more morpho-syntactic properties of words than their syntactic category. For instance, in many languages nouns belong to a particular gender or noun class, a property that is often only indirectly visible, through the behaviour of a noun in agreement processes (Corbett 2006).

Let us now look at a complex word such as the English word *baker*, a noun derived from the verb *bake* through suffixation with *-er*. The three kinds of information (phonological, morpho-syntactic, and semantic) concerning this word may be represented as in Figure 1.3.

The phonological structure of *baker* is that of a phonological word consisting of two syllables, (beɪ)$_\sigma$ and (kər)$_\sigma$. Its formal structure is that of a deverbal noun, as indicated by the tree that represents its morphological structure. The (informal) semantic representation expresses that *baker* is a subject noun that denotes the subject of the action of baking. The co-indexed pieces of information with the index *j* together form the information concerning the base word *bake* that recurs in the meaning of *baker*. That is, the relation between base word and derived word is expressed by co-indexation of the three pieces of information concerning the base word that recur in the derived word. Let us therefore assume that each word in the lexicon has a lexical index that is attached to the three pieces of information of a word. If the verb *bake* carries the lexical index 82, then we can refer to its properties as PHON$_{82}$, SYN$_{82}$, and SEM$_{82}$. Note that affixes do not have a lexical index since they are not words.

$$\begin{array}{ccccc}
\omega_i & \leftrightarrow & N_i & \leftrightarrow & [\text{one who PRED}_j]_i \\
| & & \diagdown & & \\
[\ ]_j[\text{ər}]_k & & V_j \quad \text{Aff}_k & &
\end{array}$$

FIGURE 1.4. The schema for deverbal -er

Hence, co-indexation for affixes is of restricted relevance, and is only used for correlating phonological information with a position in morpho-syntactic structure.

The representation in Figure 1.3 may be generalized into a schema for agentive subject nouns derived from verbs by means of the suffix -er, because there is a large set of such deverbal nouns in English. This is achieved by omitting the word-specific information. This morphological schema thus specifies that there is a systematic relation (shown in Figure 1.4) between the three kinds of linguistic information involved (this schema is a generalization of the lexical representation given in Figure 1.3).

In Figure 1.4 the level of the syllables has been omitted because the number of syllables of words ending in -er is not fixed but depends on the phonological make-up of the base verb. Hence it is a computable, predictable property of each individual deverbal noun in -er. Instead of the specific predicate BAKE, the general label PRED (Predicate) is used to refer to the semantics of the base verbs.

The operation on the PHON level specified in this schema is that of concatenation: the sound sequence corresponding to the affix is concatenated to the right of that of the base word. Thus, a particular sequence of sound segments is created. In addition, the general phonological algorithm of a language for prosodic structure, which is partially universal, will compute the prosodic structure of these nouns in -er, and predict the syllabification of baker as ba.ker (dots indicate syllable boundaries).

The systematic aspects of the correspondence relations between the three levels of information is accounted for by interface modules. The notion 'interface' refers to the fact that properties of one level may relate to those of another. An example of a relation between the phonological and the morpho-syntactic level is that the suffix -er is one of the so-called cohering suffixes of English. This means that this suffix forms one domain of syllabification with the stem to which it has been attached. The word baker is syllabified in the same way as the word father, in which the sequence -er is not a suffix. The sound sequence -er forms one syllable with the preceding consonant in both words: ba.ker, fa.ther. Thus, the morphological boundary between bak- and -er in baker is not respected in phonology, in the sense that it does not coincide with a syllable boundary. That is, morphological and prosodic structure are not necessarily isomorphic. In the default case, a word-internal suffix boundary is ignored in computing the prosodic structure of a complex word.

There are also suffixes that do influence the way that a complex word is syllabified. The English suffix -less, for example, is a non-cohering suffix. This means that this suffix forms its own domain of syllabification. The adjective *help-less*, for instance, is syllabified as *help.less*, with a syllable boundary coinciding with the internal morphological boundary. Compare the syllabification of this adjective to the syllabification of the word *staples*, which is *sta.ples*, with a syllable boundary before the consonant cluster /pl/. The distinction between cohering suffixes and non-cohering ones is therefore a theoretical distinction that we need for a proper account of the interface between morphology and phonology. This shows that there are two competing phonological subsystems or co-phonologies (Orgun and Inkelas 2002) for English complex words with suffixes: one subsystem for cohering suffixes such as -er, in which the suffix boundary is ignored in prosodic structure, and one subsystem for non-cohering suffixes such as -less in which the suffix boundary coincides with a syllable boundary.

Affixation and compounding are the most common but not the only two formal mechanisms for creating complex words. Other (forms of) words may also be created by vowel alternation (Umlaut or metaphony, as in German *Vater* 'father.SG' versus *Väter* 'father.PL', and Ablaut or apophony, as in *run-ran*), tone and stress alternations, and truncation processes (as in the formation of hypocoristics, for instance *Rebecca – Becky*). In those cases the morphological structure of a word cannot be represented in terms of constituent structure. Instead, we need to assign these words features such as [plural] or [+ hypocoristic] that trigger the application of specific phonological processes unique for words with that feature. Thus, each class of words may have its own co-phonology.

In sum, the interface module between morphology and phonology specifies which types of morphological information are accessible for the computation of the phonological properties of complex words, and how they influence these phonological properties. Inversely, morphological processes may make use of phonological information. For instance, the English word formation process that derives verbs from adjectives through the addition of the suffix -en only applies to monosyllabic bases. Hence, we find the verbs to *blacken* and to *redden*, but to *yellowen* is ill-formed.

Similarly, there is an interface module for the relation between morpho-syntax and semantics. The most general principle for the relation between the morpho-syntactic structure of a word and its semantics is the Compositionality Principle: the meaning of a complex word is a compositional function of the meaning contribution of its constituents, and its structure (Hoeksema 2000). An example of the role of the structure of words in the computation of the semantic interpretation of complex words is the following. In Germanic languages, the right constituent of a compound, that is, its formal head that determines its syntactic category, is its semantic head as well. Hence, we get a contrast in interpretation between the following pairs of compounds that consist of the same word constituents:

(7)   *Dutch*
     (de) geld-zak '(the) money bag'   (common gender)
     (het) zak-geld '(the) pocket money'   (neuter gender)
     German
     (die) Wasser-leitung '(the) waterpipe'   (feminine gender)
     (das) Leitung-s-wasser '(the) tap water'   (neuter gender)

The different definite articles indicate that the two compounds of each pair differ in gender as well: in the first example, *geldzak*, the head *zak* 'bag' has common gender, and hence the compound has common gender as well, whereas the head *geld* 'money' in the second compound *zakgeld* is a neuter noun that takes *het* as its DEF.SG. article, and thus the compound *zakgeld* is neuter as well. Similarly, the gender difference between the German compounds in (7) follows from a corresponding gender difference between *Leitung* 'pipe' (feminine) and *Wasser* 'water' (neuter). The compound construction as a whole provides a specific meaning contribution since it designates the right constituent as the head. As shown more extensively in Chapter 2, morphological constructions are the carriers of specific meaning components that are not derivable from the meaning of their constituents.

Another systematic relation between SYN and SEM of words concerns argument structure. For instance, in English a predicate with two semantic roles, an Agent and a Patient, will be a verb with the Agent expressed as subject, and the Patient as direct object. That is, there are systematic links between the semantic structure of predicates and their syntactic valency that can be expressed by linking rules. Morphological operations may create semantic properties of derived verbs in such a way that they systematically create transitive verbs (as in the case of causativization where a Causer-role is added). For instance, if we derive the Dutch causative verb *ver-duidelijk* 'to clarify' from the adjective *duidelijk* 'clear', this causative verb is predictably transitive.

In short, we need an interface module that computes predictable properties of words on the SYN and SEM levels. Note, however, that the syntactic valency of a verb may also depend on the specific construction in which it occurs, as discussed in section 1.3.

A direct interface between SEM and PHON is also possible. This applies to phenomena like the marking of focus, and the marking of questions by means of specific intonation patterns. Sound symbolism may be considered as a case of such interface at the word level (Marchand 1969: Chapter 7). For instance, English words that begin with the consonant sequence *spr-* tend to express the meaning of spreading, as in *sprawl, spread*, and *sprinkle*. Since *spr-* is not a morpheme, there is a direct interface between the level of the sounds and that of meaning here. However, this kind of symbolism is hard to capture in hard and fast rules.

The tripartite structure in Figure 1.4, an instance of a word formation schema, makes clear that morphology is not a module of grammar on a par with the phonological or the syntactic module that deal with one aspect of linguistic structure only. Morphology is word grammar and similar to sentence grammar in its dealing with the relationships between three kinds of information. It is only with respect to the domain of linguistic entities that morphology is different from sentence grammar since morphology has the word domain as its focus.

This architecture for morphology is the same as that for sentence grammar, but its domain is smaller, namely that of the word. However, this does not mean that the two sub-grammars are completely separate components, with lexical insertion as the only point of contact between them, as suggested in Ackema and Neeleman (2004). As argued in this book, there are various forms of interaction between these two domains, which will force us to reconsider how syntactic and morphological structures relate.

1.3 Constructions

The notion construction (defined as a pairing of form and meaning) is a traditional notion used in thousands of linguistic articles and books. In most cases it refers to a syntactic pattern in which particular formal properties correlate with specific semantics. For instance, many linguists of English speak of 'the passive construction' since the grammar of English possesses a specific sentence form in order to express this meaning.

A well-known example of a syntactic construction is the caused motion construction exemplified by sentence (8) (Goldberg 2006: 73):

(8)   Pat sneezed the foam off the cappuccino

In this sentence, the verb *to sneeze* is used as a transitive verb, although it is normally an intransitive verb. Its use as a transitive verb correlates with the presence of an object that moves along a path specified by a PP. The transitivity of the normally intransitive verb *to sneeze* and the meaning component that the sneezing caused the foam to move is therefore to be seen as a property of this construction as a whole. A similar example from Dutch is the resultative construction exemplified by the following sentence:

(9)   De nieuwe kok kookte twee Michelin-sterren bij elkaar
       The new cook cooked two Michelin-stars by each other
       'The new cook acquired two Michelin-stars by his way of cooking'

The verb *koken* 'to cook' does not select objects like stars but objects of the food type. Yet, in this resultative construction the object *Michelin-sterren* is possible.

Another example of a syntactic construction is the NPN-construction, exemplified by phrases like the following (Jackendoff 2008):

(10)   day by day, point for point, face to face, week after week, argument upon argument

The NPN construction consists of a bare singular count noun followed by one from a restricted set of prepositions and the same bare singular count noun. Jackendoff, following Culicover, refers to this construction as a 'syntactic nut', a non-canonical structure of English that is strongly entrenched in the grammar of English, and productive as well.

The individual instantiations of the construction as listed in (10) will be referred to as 'constructs'. Jackendoff does not specify a general meaning of this NPN construction; instead, he provides meaning specifications for each specific preposition choice, such as 'succession' for *by* and *after*, and 'matching/exchange' for *for*. This illustrates that not all linguists require a construction to always have a specific holistic, non-compositional meaning component.

The choice of words in a particular construction may be partially fixed. Consider the following phrases of Dutch, all instantiations of a particular construction:

(11)   een schat van een kind 'lit. a sweetheart of a child, a sweet child'
       een kast van een huis 'lit. a cupboard of a house, a big house'
       die boom van een kerel 'lit. that tree of a chap, that big chap'

The structure of these phrases and the corresponding semantic interpretation can be represented as follows:

(12) $[[x]_{Ni} [[van]_P [[een]_{Det} [x]_{Nj}]_{NP}]_{PP}]_{N'\ k} \leftrightarrow [SEM_j$ with SEM_i-like property$]_k$

That is, these phrases exemplify the general structure of Dutch NPs with an N as head, preceded by a determiner, and followed by a PP complement.

Semantically, however, it is the noun of the PP-complement that functions as the head, and it also determines the gender of the relative pronoun for which it is the antecedent as shown by the following example:

(13)   een kast van een huis, {*die / dat} nodig geverfd moet worden
       a cupboard of a house that urgently painted must be
       'a big house that has to be painted urgently'

The noun *kast* 'cupboard' is of common gender, whereas *huis* 'house' is neuter; the relative pronoun *dat* is the pronoun for antecedents with neuter gender, whereas *die* is used for antecedents of common gender. The two nouns have to agree in number. For instance, the plural of *een schat van een kind* is *schatten van kinderen*, with both nouns in their plural form and the zero plural indefinite article: both **schatten van een kind* and **een schat van kinderen* are ill-formed in the interpretation given here.

A schema like (12) is a constructional idiom, that is, a type of idiom in which not all positions are lexically fixed, and hence some are variable.[2] In (12) it is only the fillings of the determiner and the preposition slots of the PP complement that are lexically fixed. The set of constructs of the type (12) can be extended, and hence they do not form a fixed list of expressions. The first noun has to be a noun that expresses an evaluation of properties of the noun in the PP-complement. For instance, it is possible to coin the phrase *een godin van een vrouw* 'lit. a goddess of a woman, a ravishing woman' as a new instantiation of this constructional idiom. Nevertheless, this construction does not lend itself to unlimited extension, and the example *een godin van een vrouw* is experienced as a case of creative language use. That is, the notion 'restricted productivity' applies here, a notion that is normally used for describing the use of morphological patterns. Similar constructs are found in English (*a brute of a man*) (Aarts 1998), German (*ein Teufel von einem Mann* 'a devil of a man, a brute man') (Leys 1997), Spanish (*esa mierda de libro* 'that shit of book, that shitty book') and French (*ton phénomène de fille* 'your phenomenon of daughter, your amazing daughter') (Hulk and Tellier 1999).

The existence of such constructional idioms has implications for our view of the lexicon. Traditionally, the lexicon is conceived of as the list of conventional and fixed linguistic expressions, both words and larger idiomatic

---

[2] The idea of 'constructional idioms' can be found in the work of Langacker (1987), in Construction Grammar (Fillmore et al. 1988; Goldberg 1995, 2006; Kay and Fillmore 1999; Pitt and Katz 2000), and in work by Jackendoff (1997b, 2002a,b). Other terms used are 'lexical phrases with a generalized frame' (Nattinger and De Carrico 1992), and 'idiomatic pattern' (Everaert 1993).

phrasal units. However, the facts discussed here imply that the lexicon has to be extended with partially underspecified idioms, in the case of Dutch the type N_1 *van een* N_2 with the meaning 'N$_2$ who/which is like an N$_1$' and with similar constructional idioms in other languages.

In both Dutch and English (and in a number of other languages as well (Himmelmann 1998), we find PPs in which a preposition is followed by a bare count noun. That is, the determiner that is expected to precede a count noun is lacking. Examples are:

(14) *Dutch*   *English gloss*
      per trein   by train
      per vliegtuig   by plane
      per bus   by bus
      per auto   by car

The nouns do not denote specific entities, but are used generically to denote a particular means of transportation. The specific properties of this construction are the choice of the preposition (*by* in English, the preposition *per*, a Latin borrowing, in Dutch), and the bare count noun, which correlates with the specific meaning 'means of transportation' (Baldwin et al. 2003). Note that these phrases are in conformity with the general constraints on the form of Dutch and English PPs, and form a specific subset of these phrases. The constructional schema for these expressions is therefore:

(15) [[per /by]$_P$ [[x]$_{Ni}$]$_{NP}$]$_{PPj}$ ↔ [through transportation by SEM$_i$]$_j$

Recall that the symbol ↔ stands for the relation of correspondence between the different types of information. SEM stands for the meaning component of the noun. The choice of noun is semantically restricted to nouns that denote a means of transportation. This restriction will be imposed by the meaning of this construction. Hence, if we were to coin the Dutch phrase *per tapijt* 'by carpet', this implies that carpets can be used as a means of transportation. Schema (15) is also another example of a constructional idiom, since the slot for the preposition is lexically fixed, whereas the slot for the noun is occupied by a variable.

The notion 'construction' plays an important role in a number of recent linguistic models: Construction Grammar (Croft 2001; Fried and Östman 2004; Goldberg 1995, 2006), the Simpler Syntax Model (Culicover and Jackendoff 2005, 2006), Cognitive Linguistics (Langacker 1999), and Head-driven Phrase Structure Grammar (HPSG) (Sag 2007; Sag et al. 2003). The following features of the constructional approach are of significant relevance to the further articulation of *CM*:

(16) Pieces of syntactic structure can be listed in the lexicon with associated meanings, just as individual words are; these are the MEANINGFUL CONSTRUCTIONS of the language.

Construction grammar makes no principled distinction between words and rules: a lexical entry is more word-like to the extent that it is fully specified, and more rule-like to the extent that it contains variables [. . .]. [L]exical entries are arranged in an inheritance hierarchy. (Jackendoff 2008: 15)

Goldberg stresses the point that constructions can vary in size and complexity. She provides Table 1.1 to illustrate this point (Goldberg 2009: 94).

In a previous publication, Goldberg also listed the category morpheme in this list of constructions (Goldberg 2006: 5). However, the category 'morpheme' should not appear on this list because morphemes are not linguistic signs, i.e. independent pairings of form and meaning. The minimal linguistic sign is the word, and the occurrence of the category 'morpheme' in this list is to be seen as an infelicitous remnant of morpheme-based morphology. Instead, bound morphemes form part of morphological schemas, and their meaning contribution is only accessible through the meaning of the morphological construction of which they form a part. This insight is done justice in Table 1.1, and also in the sketch of the syntax–lexicon continuum by Croft (2001) in Table 1.2. Note that in this table we do not find the morpheme as a construction type.

Michaelis and Lambrecht (1996: 216) also mention the relevance of construction grammar for the analysis of words:

In Construction Grammar, the grammar represents an inventory of form-meaning-function complexes, in which words are distinguished from grammatical constructions only with regard to their internal complexity. The inventory of constructions is not unstructured; it is more like a map than a shopping list. Elements in this inventory are related through inheritance hierarchies, containing more or less general patterns.

TABLE 1.1. Examples of constructions varying in size and complexity

	example
Word	tentacle, gangster, the
Word (partially filled)	post-N, V-ing
Complex word	textbook, drive-in
Idiom (filled)	like a bat out of hell
Idiom (partially filled)	believe <one's> ears/eyes
Ditransitive	Subj V Obj$_1$ Obj$_2$ (e.g. he baked her a muffin)

TABLE 1.2. The syntax–lexicon continuum

Construction type	Traditional name	Examples
Complex and (mostly) schematic	syntax	[SBJ *be*-TNS VERB-*en by* OBL]
Complex and (mostly) specific	idiom	[*pull*-TNS NP's *leg*]
Complex but bound	morphology	[NOUN-s], VERB-TNS]
Atomic and schematic	syntactic category	[DEM], [ADJ]
Atomic and specific	word/lexicon	[*this*], [*green*]

Source: Croft 2001: 17

It should be clear by now that the notion 'construction' has relevance for the theory of word structure. Yet, the investigation of the constructional aspects of word structure is still in its beginnings. Culicover and Jackendoff (2006: 19) state: 'We take morphology to be the extension of the parallel architecture below the word level'. Although this is a good starting point, we also have to investigate to what extent morphology has principles of its own which makes it partially different from syntax. In their study Culicover and Jackendoff (2005) focus on the phrase level, and at the end of their book they observe: 'We have looked not at all at morphology. How does it integrate into the system? What are the implications for the structure of the lexicon?' (Culicover and Jackendoff 2005: 545). It is the aim of this book to contribute to answering these questions, and find out about the commonalities and differences of syntax and morphology.

1.4 Construction Morphology

The use of the notion 'morphological construction' is by no means a recent innovation. For instance, Bloomfield in his chapters on morphology, speaks of 'three types of morphologic constructions' (Bloomfield 1935: 227), and he remarks that a complex word reveals 'an outer layer of inflectional constructions, and then an inner layer of constructions of word formation' (Bloomfield 1935: 222). What is new, however, is the use of the notion 'construction' as developed in Construction Grammar for morphological analysis.[3]

---

[3] The view that complex words instantiate morphological constructions is also stated explicitly in Croft (2001: 17), in Goldberg (2006: 5), and in Inkelas and Zoll (2005: 11–16), which presents a cross-linguistic construction-morphological analysis of reduplication. An example of a constructional analysis of prefixed words is the analysis of English *be*-verbs in Petré and Cuyckens (2008).

Let us return to the schema for English deverbal nouns in (3). This schema can be qualified as a constructional idiom at the word level, that is, a word level construction with one fixed position, that of the suffix. The meaning of the constructional idiom is also specified. This meaning is a holistic property of the construction as a whole: the agent meaning cannot be derived from the suffix *-er* as such, since this meaning is only invoked when this suffix forms a noun together with a verbal base. In combination with an adjective, the bound morpheme *-er* evokes a completely different meaning, that of the comparative. The individual deverbal nouns in *-er* are morphological constructs that instantiate this construction. In schema (3) the two form levels, phonological form and morpho-syntactic form, are conflated into one representation. I will continue to do this, for ease of exposition, but these levels will be split when necessary for the purpose of analysis or argumentation.

Schema (3) is a case of derivation, word formation by means of an affix. Patterns of compounding, the other main type of word formation, can also be represented straightforwardly as constructions, as in schema (17) for the nominal compounds of Germanic languages which are normally right-headed:

(17) $[[a]_{Xk} [b]_{Ni}]_{Nj} \leftrightarrow [SEM_i$ with relation R to $SEM_k]_j$

The variable X stands for the major lexical categories (N, V, A, and P). The lower-case variables *a* and *b* in this schema stand for arbitrary sound sequences. The lower-case variables *i*, *j*, *k* stand for the lexical indexes on the PHON, SYN, and SEM properties of words. The use of phonological variables indicates that phonological information does not play a restrictive role in this type of word formation in Germanic languages. In (17) the general meaning contribution of the compound schema is specified, since morphology is about form–meaning pairs. The nature of R is not specified but is determined for each individual compound on the basis of the meaning of the compound constituents, and encyclopaedic and contextual knowledge (Downing 1977; Jackendoff 2009). The following English compounds exemplify the various options defined by schema (17):

(18)   NN   book shelf, desk top, towel rack
       VN   drawbridge, pull tab
       AN   hard disk, blackbird, blackboard
       PN   afterthought, overdose, inland

Schema (17) does not yet express that it is not only the syntactic category of the head that is identical to that of the whole compound, but that the two N-nodes are also identical with respect to properties such as gender and declension class. Hence, we elaborate schema (17) as (17') in which $[aF]$ stands for the set of relevant subclass features:

(17′) $[[a]_{Xk}\,[b]_{Ni}\,]_{Nj} \leftrightarrow [\text{SEM}_i \text{ with relation R to SEM}_k]_j$
$$[aF][aF]$$

Template (17′) thus specifies the category of right-headed nominal endo-centric compounds of Germanic languages. It specifies that the head is not only the formal head but also the semantic head: a compound with an N in the right position denotes a certain N, not a certain X. Each individual nominal compound is an instantiation of this constructional schema.

A clear advantage of this schematic description of nominal compounds is that we do not need an additional separate Right-hand Head Rule (Williams 1981) in order to express the generalization (that holds for Germanic languages, but is not a universal) that the category of a compound is determined by its right constituent.

New complex words can be coined through the unification of a schema with a lexical item. For instance, the unification of the verb $[skype]_V$ 'to communicate by means of Skype' with schema (3) results in the construct $[[skyp]_V er]_N$ 'one who SKYPEs' (where SKYPE stands for the meaning of the base verb). That is, through unification the variables in the formal structure and the semantic specification of the schema are turned into constants. Unification is the basic operation, both at the word level and the phrase level, to create well-formed linguistic expressions.

Prefixation can be analysed in the same way. Consider the following English prefixed words, verbs in which the word *out* is 'prefixed' to a verbal stem, as in

(19)   out-achieve, out-bid, out-class, out-dance, out-do, out-grow, out-jockey, out-perform

The common meaning of these verbs is that the subject of the action surpasses someone/something else in quality in the relevant domain of action.[4] If Mary outdances John, Mary dances better than John. All these *out*-verbs are transitive verbs, and the pattern is productive, as illustrated by the following sentence from the Internet with the verbs *outthink* and *outgun*:

(20)   Your success depends solely on your ability to out-gun and out-think your opposition

The word *out* can be used as a preposition and as an adverb. Hence, one may classify these *out*-verbs as compounds of the word *out* with a verb. Yet, these

---

[4] This does not mean that this is the only meaning of *out* in verbs, as shown by a verb like *outblaze* that has both the meaning 'to exceed in shining, to outshine', and the intransitive meaning 'to flare up'.

out-verbs are usually considered cases of prefixation. Although *out* is a polysemous item with quite a range of meanings, it has developed this special meaning of surpassing / exceeding in combination with verbs, and this is why it is looked upon as a prefix in many descriptions of the morphology of English. This specific meaning of *out* can still be related to the other ones because *out* can have the meaning 'away from, beyond', as in *outbuilding* and *outreach* which is related to the 'prefixal' use of *out*. That is, *out-V* exhibits a constructional semantic property since it implies the selection of a specific meaning of the constituent *out* that is tied to this class of verbs. This can be expressed directly by assuming the following morphological construction:

(21) $[[out]_{Adv} [x]_{Vi}]_{Vj} \leftrightarrow$ [to exceed someone/thing in SEM_i]$_j$

In this constructional schema we can still do justice to the property of *out* that it is not a bound morpheme *stricto sensu*, but a word with a specific meaning in a specific construction. This morphological construction thus has a 'configurative meaning', in line with a Gestalt view of pattern-based morphology. We do not need to classify *out* as a prefix, with the unwanted implication that it is just homophonous by coincidence with the word *out*.

1.5 Multi-word units

The lexicon is the repository of all simplex words and of all complex words that are idiosyncratic or conventionalized. In addition, the lexicon has to specify multi-word units that are idiomatic. Being idiomatic means for a linguistic construct that is has unpredictable properties that have to be learned and memorized by the speaker. The size of idiomatic constructs may vary from sentences (for instance, proverbs) to phrases consisting of two words, the minimal size for lexical phrases (for instance, the NP *red tape* as an idiom for bureaucracy, *urban legend* 'popular myth', or *black death* for 'pest'). Phrases may be stored in the lexicon for another reason as well. They might be completely regular but conventionalized expressions. For instance, the conventional name in Dutch for a decision made by the king or queen is the AN phrase *koninklijk besluit* 'royal decree'. The possible alternative expression for this meaning is the NN compound *koningsbesluit* 'king's decree', but this is not the conventional expression. Hence, the coinage of this NN compound is blocked by the existence of the conventional NP *koninklijk besluit*. The blocking effect can be used as a test for the conventionality of such expressions.[5]

---

[5]   See (Jackendoff 1997b: Chapter 7) for a discussion of the relevant English facts.

As has been pointed out in the recent literature, multi-word expressions (MWEs) are not just fixed sequences of words with an atomic meaning but differ in their degree of compositionality and syntactic flexibility (Pitt and Katz 2000; Sag et al. 2002). The notion 'constructional idiom' introduced above can be used to do justice to certain aspects of this flexibility, in particular to the fact that idiomatic constructions can receive new instantiations.

It is not my aim in this book to develop a complete analysis of MWEs. I focus on those MWEs that instantiate productive patterns, and that are functionally similar to complex words. A clear example is the class of phrasal verbs in Germanic languages that are usually referred to as particle verbs. Examples from English are *to put down* and *to phone up*. The Dutch equivalents of these particle verbs are *neer-leggen* and *op-bellen*, with the particle preceding the verb (written as one word, although they are phrasal and other words can come in between the particle and the verb). These particle verbs function as alternatives for prefixation in the coinage of complex predicates, and this explains the restricted productivity of deverbal prefixation in Germanic languages: there is strong competition from particle verb formation which is a functionally equivalent means of creating complex predicates. In Chapter 5 I argue that these particle verbs can be seen as instantiations of phrasal constructional idioms, whereas prefixed verbs are instantiations of constructional idioms at the word level. This is illustrated here by means of the following minimal pairs from Dutch, with different locations of the main stress:

(20)   *particle verb*   *prefixed verb*
       óver komen 'to come over'   over-kómen 'to happen to'
       dóor leven 'to continue living'   door-léven 'to live through'

These particle verbs are clearly lexical units, and we can do justice to their properties by analysing them as being formed according to phrasal constructions (Chapter 5). By using the notion 'constructional idiom' for the analysis of particle verbs, we can maintain the boundary between phrasal and morphological constructs, and yet do justice to the word-like (lexical) properties of particle verbs.

Another reason for dealing with phrase-sized constructs in a theory of Construction Morphology is the phenomenon of periphrasis. This notion is used to refer to the fact that cells in the inflectional paradigms of words may be filled by word combinations instead of words. For instance, in most European languages we find periphrastic tenses like the perfect, expressed by the combination of a specific verb (the auxiliary) and a participle. In Latin, the perfective passive is expressed by a combination of the verb *esse* 'to be', and the past participle:

(21) Paradigm of 3rd pers. sg. forms of *laudare* 'to praise'

IMPERFECTIVE	*Active*	*Passive*
Present	laudat	laudatur
Past	laudabat	laudabatur
Future	laudabit	laudabitur

PERFECTIVE	*Active*	*Passive*
Present	laudavit	laudatus/a/um est
Past	laudaverat	laudatus/a/um erat
Future	laudaverit	laudatus/a/um erit

The fact that this periphrastic form is the only possible form for expressing the perfect past shows that the form fills a cell in the inflectional paradigm. Moreover, in the case of deponent verbs (verbs with a passive form and an active meaning) such as *loquor* 'to speak', the periphrastic form has an active meaning, just like the other, synthetic, forms. For instance, *locutus est* means 'he has spoken' (Börjars et al. 1997).

This means that phrasal constructs may express morphological properties (Ackerman and Stump 2004; Ackerman and Webelhuth 1998; Börjars et al. 1997; Sadler and Spencer 2001). Therefore, we have to investigate how such phrasal constructs with a morphological function can be accounted for in morphology. In *CM* such an account is readily available because these periphrastic expressions can be analysed in terms of constructional idioms. In English, for instance, the passive construction consists of a form of a lexically fixed verb *be* with a participle. This specific pattern expresses the passive meaning, which cannot be derived from the meaning of one of the constituent words: neither the verb *to be*, nor the participle itself is the carrier of the passive meaning.

A special class of lexical constructs is formed by complex numerals. Compare the form of the following complex numerals in Spanish and Dutch:

(22)

number	*Spanish*	*Dutch*
31	treinta y un/uno/una	een-en-dertig
32	treinta y dos	twee-en-dertig
33	treinta y tres	drie-en-dertig

The construction of these numerals is similar in that in both languages the mechanism of coordination is used: the two constituent numbers are linked by the conjunction for 'and': *y* and *en* respectively. Hence, these number names look like syntactic constructs. Moreover, they cannot be considered as lexically fixed idioms because the formation of number names is, for obvious reasons, productive. Yet, this is not syntactic coordination *tout court* since in these languages the order of the two constituents is fixed differently: in

Spanish the smaller addend has to follow the larger one, whereas in Dutch the smaller addend precedes the larger one. In both languages, the order of the coordinated constituents is not free, as is normally the case in coordination (as in Dutch *dertig koeien en twee paarden* 'thirty cows and two horses', or *twee paarden en dertig koeien* 'two horses and thirty cows'). An additional observation is that the vowel of the Dutch constituent *en* is [ə], whereas normally *en* is pronounced as [ɛn]. Does this mean that these complex number names are to be considered as word constructs? In other words, such lexical constructs raise the question of how to demarcate word constructs from phrasal constructs. We can do justice to the intermediate status of such constructs in *CM*, by assuming specific constructional schemas for such number names in the lexicon, as argued in detail in Chapter 8.

In sum, the use of the notion 'construction' in morphological analysis is also motivated by the fact that lexical phrasal constructions with word-like functions must be dealt with as well, and can receive an insightful analysis in *CM*.

1.6 Inflectional patterns as constructions

Inflectional systems are a classical problem for a morpheme-based analysis of word-internal structure because in many languages there is no one-to-one correspondence between the building blocks of inflected words and their morpho-syntactic and morpho-semantic properties. The phenomena involved are described in terms of notions like cumulative exponence, extended exponence, stem allomorphy, inflectional classes, thematic vowels, syncretism, suppletion, and periphrasis. This is why morphologists have proposed variants of realizational morphology in which there are rules that spell out the phonological form of each word form, a word with a particular array of features (Ackerman and Stump 2004; Anderson 1992; Spencer 2004; Stump 2001). The crucial observation from a constructionist point of view is that it is the specific array of building blocks like stem allomorph, thematic vowel, ending, etc. that as a whole evokes a specific set of morpho-syntactic and morpho-semantic properties. That is, this set of properties is a holistic property of the inflectional construction. The thematic vowels in the conjugations of various Indo-European languages do not contribute a particular property directly but only as part of the array of morphological building blocks in a verb form. Indeed, Spencer (2004) explicitly concludes that for these reasons we have to consider morphologically complex words as constructions. As an example of such a holistic property, Spencer observes that the Spanish future conditional verbal word forms consist of the infinitival stem followed by the inflectional ending for the imperfect indicative of the 2nd and 3rd conjugation, as in *cantar-ía* 'sing, future conditional, 1sg'. It is the combination of the two building blocks that provides this specific interpretation. Similarly, in Dutch present participles are derived from the infinitival form by adding the suffix -*d*, without an infinitival meaning being involved. Consider the following examples. There is a small set of verbs (23b) that have an infinitival form in -*n* instead of the regular -*en*. The same difference is found in the present participle:

(23) a. lop-en 'to walk'   lop-en-d 'walking'
         hei-en 'to drive piles'   hei-en-d 'driving piles'
      b. doe-n 'to do'   doe-n-d 'doing'
         slaa-n 'to hit'   slaa-n-d 'hitting'

Hence we should derive the present participle from the infinitival form even though the infinitival 'meaning' is not involved.

Therefore, inflectional phenomena provide direct evidence for the idea that morphologically complex words should be seen as constructions with holistic properties. However, this book will focus on constructional properties of word formation because it is for this domain that I want to present a number of in-depth analyses that flesh out the theory of Construction Morphology.

1.7 Outlook

In this chapter some initial considerations for the use of the notion 'construction' in the analysis of morphological and lexical phrasal constructs have been presented. In the following chapters, these analyses will be fleshed out.

In Chapter 2 I give a more detailed analysis of the nature of the lexicon, and of the advantages of using constructional schemas to express morphological generalizations. Chapter 3 discusses the advantages of a hierarchical conception of the lexicon in more detail.

Chapters 4–8 deal with specific phrasal lexical constructs that support *CM*: quasi-incorporation (Chapter 4), particle verbs (Chapter 5), progressive constructions (Chapter 6), phrasal names (Chapter 7), and numeral expressions (Chapter 8).

In Chapter 9 I deal with construction-dependent morphology, the phenomenon that the occurrence of bound morphemes is linked to specific syntactic constructions.

Chapter 10 deals with some phonological issues related to Construction Morphology, in particular the nature of lexical phonological representations,

and the question whether lexically encoded allomorphy affects the identifica-
tion of morphological relations between words.

Chapter 11 discusses what the findings of this book imply for our view of
the architecture of the grammar, and their implications for models of language processing. In this chapter I also identify some issues that have not been
broached in detail in this book, thus suggesting topics for further research.

2

The lexicon as a network
of relations

2.1 The hierarchical lexicon

In a number of recent grammatical models the lexicon is represented as a hierarchy of types (Flickinger 1987; Kilbury et al. 2006; Krieger and Nerbonne 1993; Sag et al. 2003; Sag 2007). For instance, we may classify the words of a language according to the syntactic category to which they belong, and then further subclassify these different word types. At the bottom of the hierarchy we find the individual words. Part of the English lexicon may thus look as follows:

(1)

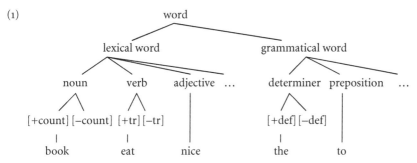

This hierarchy can be interpreted as an inheritance tree. That is, each node inherits the properties of its dominating nodes. Thus, the hierarchy states that *book* is a word, a lexical word (=word of a lexical category), a noun, and a count noun. The word *eat* is characterized as a transitive verb, and *the* as a definite determiner. This hierarchy expresses what properties are shared by subclasses of words.

The formal implication of using 'inheritance' is that for individual words only those properties need to be specified that are not inherited from dominating nodes.

Each individual word may form the end node of a number of such hierarchies. For instance, we may also assume a semantic hierarchy in which words are classified according to their semantic type, as names for objects, properties, and events. A noun like *book* is an object name, whereas the noun *boldness* denotes a property. Hence, a semantic classification may cross-classify with a formal syntactic classification. The word *boldness* will thus inherit properties from at least two hierarchies, a formal one (it is a noun), and a semantic one (it denotes a property). The idea of an inheritance hierarchy may also be used for morphological purposes (Hippisley 2001; König 1999; Krieger and Nerbonne 1993; Riehemann 1998, 2001).[1] For instance, we may divide the class of nouns into simplex nouns and complex nouns, and divide the latter class into a number of morphological subclasses, each with a specific morphological structure. Thus, a subpart of that (morphological) hierarchy would look as follows:

(2)

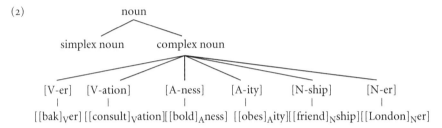

The schemas that directly dominate the individual words are (the abbreviated versions of) the constructional word formation schemas introduced in Chapter 1. They specify the relevant properties of each subclass, and each word inherits the PHON, SYN, and SEM properties specified by that schema.

   A second way in which information about a complex word can be inherited is that the information concerning its base word is also part of the information concerning the complex word. That is, in addition to inheritance of information in a lexical entry from the schemas that dominate it, there is also inheritance of information from the base word. The word *skyper*, coined through unification of the verb *skype* with the schema for deverbal nouns in *-er* (schema 3 in Chapter 1), inherits the information concerning *skype*. The relation between *skype* and *skyper* can be represented as follows:

(3)   [skype]$_{Vi}$ [V-er]$_{Nj}$

         [[skyp]$_{Vi}$-er]$_{Nj}$

The relation between base word and derived word can be specified through co-indexation: the lexical index of the PHON, SYN, and SEM properties of

---

[1] An example of the use of such hierarchies for the analysis of inflection can be found in Corbett and Fraser (1993).

the base word appears as part of the PHON, SYN, and SEM information concerning the derived word as well.

There are two possible interpretations of inheritance. In one interpretation, all inheritable information is omitted from the lexical entry of a word. This is the 'impoverished entry theory'. In the case of a completely regular complex word this means that the only information left to be specified is that the word exists. That is, there is an empty lexical entry, with a lexical index as the only non-predictable information. This is the interpretation assumed in Sag (2007). In another interpretation, the individual lexical entries are fully specified, and the inheritance mechanism serves to compute which of this information is redundant information; this is the 'full entry theory' defended in Jackendoff (1975, 1997b: 129). I assume the latter theory. In this interpretation, a specific morphological construct (that is, a complex word) is licensed by the schema of which it is an instantiation together with the base word with which it is unified. The schemas thus provide a basis for computing the informational cost of each lexical entry by indicating which information is predictable, hence redundant (Bochner 1993; Jackendoff 1975).

2.1.1 Default inheritance

A crucial notion in our model of the hierarchical lexicon is the notion of 'default inheritance' (Briscoe et al. 1993; Evans and Gazdar 1996; Kilbury et al. 2006; Lascarides and Copestake 1999): the specification of a word for a particular property is inherited from the dominating node, unless the actual lexical entry has another specification for that property. The mechanism of default inheritance is necessary because we want to be able to express that a word has an exceptional property, although it is regular in most respects. Consider, for instance, the deverbal adjectives in -baar '-able' in Dutch. Like its German counterpart (Krieger and Nerbonne 1993; Riehemann 1998, 2001), this suffix is normally attached to transitive verbs. Yet, there are exceptional adjectives in Dutch such as werk-baar 'feasible, practicable', an adjective that is derived from the intransitive verbs werk 'to work'. Apart from this single exceptional fact, this is a regular adjective. Hence, this adjective will have an exceptional subcategorization (co-occurring with an intransitive verb), which overrules the subcategorization for transitive verbs in the relevant schema. In other words, the unification of the schema with the intransitive verb werk 'to work' is not blocked. 'The effect of default unification is that incompatible values for attributes are ignored, rather than causing unification failure' (Copestake 1993: 226). The effect of default inheritance is that information on a higher node may be superseded by information concerning the relevant property on a lower node. Hence, this system of computing properties of words is non-monotonic. This means that not all information that is derived from higher nodes is necessarily preserved.

A second example of the need for default inheritance has to do with inheritance in the 'part-of'-hierarchy: a property of a base word may not recur in the complex word of which it forms a part. Dutch nominal compounds usually inherit their gender specification from their nominal heads. There are two genders in modern Dutch, common and neuter. In a few cases, the gender of the compound is (sometimes optionally) different from that of its head noun, as illustrated in (4):

(4)   *common gender*   *neuter gender*
      spleet-oog 'lit. split-eye, Asian person'   oog 'eye'
      appel-moes 'apple sauce'   moes 'pulp'

The first example is a bahuvrihi-compound that denotes a person with the property mentioned by the compound; hence, the gender shift has to do with the semantics of the compound noun. In these compounds, the specification for gender thus overrules the gender specification of the head noun which is normally imposed on compounds through the compound schema (17') in Chapter 1.

Default inheritance can also be used to express abstract generalizations about a morphological system. In Germanic languages derivational suffixes usually determine the syntactic category of the derived word, whereas derivational prefixes such as *re-* and *un-* tend to be category-neutral. This is part of the motivation behind Williams' Right-hand Head Rule (RHR) (Williams 1981). However, a number of prefixes do determine the category of the derived word, and hence conflict with the RHR. Examples from English are the prefixes *be-* and *en-*, as in the denominal verb *to behead* and the deadjectival verb *to enlarge*. We may therefore assume the general schema for English category-neutral prefixation:

(5) $[a\ [b]_{Yj}]_{Yi} \leftrightarrow [SEM\ [SEM_j]]_i$

where *a* and *b* are phonological variables, and Y stands for the syntactic category of the base word. Recall that affixes do not have lexical indexes since they are not words. Their meaning contribution, indicated by the non-indexed SEM in schema (5), will have to be further specified for each individual prefixation pattern. This schema expresses that in prefixation, the base word shares its syntactic category with the prefixed derivative. The meaning of the prefix construction is a semantic operator on the meaning of the base word. This schema is a generalization about a number of morphological constructions, and hence it is a meta-construction.

Schema (5) dominates the schema for words with the English prefix *be-* (which is an instantiation of the variable *a*) that is productively attached to base nouns:

(6) $[a \, [b]_{Yj}]_{Yi}$ $\leftrightarrow$ $[\text{SEM} \, [\text{SEM}_j]]_i$

   $[be[b]_{Nj}]_{Vi}$ $\leftrightarrow$ $[\text{SEM} \, [\text{SEM}_j]]_i$

The category specification V of the *be*-verbs will overrule the specification Noun of the derived words that is predicted by the general schema, as desired, in conformity with the idea of default inheritance. The specific meaning contribution of the *be*-construction is specified by spelling out the non-indexed SEM on the lowest line. The meaning contributed by the morphological construction with the prefix *be-* varies. In *to behead*, the meaning is that of removal (of the head), in *to bejewel* it is the meaning of furnishing (with jewels).

   The same mechanism can be used for making the relevant generalizations about certain aspects of Italian word formation. In Italian, derivational suffixes are category-determining, except evaluative suffixes such as diminutive and augmentative suffixes which preserve the syntactic category of the base word (Scalise 1988):

(7) N   tavolo 'table'   tavol-ino 'small table'
    A   giallo 'yellow'   giall-ino 'yellowish'
    Adv   bene 'well'   ben-ino 'reasonably well'

Hence, we assume a general schema for Italian category-determining suffixes, which states that the category of the derived word (Y) may differ from that of the base word (X). This schema dominates a subschema for words with evaluative suffixes that inherit their syntactic category from their base word. This subschema will specify that in diminutives and augmentatives, the category of the derived word is identical to that of the base word, that is: X and Y have the same value.

   These examples illustrate the necessity of a hierarchical lexicon, with different levels of abstractions (individual words, morphological constructions, and morphological meta-constructions). In this way it is possible to express generalizations and subgeneralizations about the properties of sets of (complex) words in the lexicon.

   The need for morphological schemas in a hierarchical lexicon is confirmed by observations concerning 'base-less' complex words. In the non-native layer of its lexicon, English has thousands of complex words in which an affix is recognizable, but that do not have a corresponding base word. Here are some examples of such nouns ending in -*ism*:

(8)   anachron-ism, anglic-ism, aut-ism, bapt-ism, bolshev-ism, metabol-
      ism, pacif-ism

These words are all predictably nouns that denote some abstract phenomenon
(ideology, movement, disposition, etc.). Yet, their meaning is not fully predictable because they have no corresponding base words. That is, the
corresponding schema that dominates these words is:

(9)   [x – *ism*]$_{Ni}$ ↔ [PHENOMENON, IDEOLOGY, DISPOSITION, ...]$_i$

This schema specifies that words of this form are predictably nouns and
express one of the semantic categories mentioned; yet their semantics is
opaque as far as the meaning of the part before the suffix is concerned.
There is a formal base (*x*), but this *x* has no label for a lexical category, and
has therefore no lexical entry of its own. It is a root, only recognizable as part
of a complex word. In this respect such roots are identical to affixes which do
not have independent existence either outside complex words. The same
observation, the lack of a base word, holds for many nouns ending in *-ist*,
words like *anglic-ist, aut-ist, bapt-ist, bolshev-ist*, and *pacif-ist*, which are both
English and Dutch words. They always denote persons involved in something,
but that is often the only predictable property (Y is the semantic variable for
the specific nature of the ability, ideology, or disposition):

(10)   [x – *ist*]$_{Ni}$ ↔ [PERSON WITH ABILITY, IDEOLOGY, DISPOSITION Y]$_i$

An interesting property of these schemas is that they are output-oriented.
Such schemas cannot be formulated as rules, which are by definition input-
oriented because there is no input element available in these cases. Thus, these
generalizations form an argument in favour of schemas instead of rules (cf.
section 1.2).

   It is not the case that all nouns in *-ist* have a root as their base. There are
also cases in which an existing noun or adjective functions as base word, as
shown here for Dutch:

(11)   *with N as base*
       accordeon 'accordion'   accordeon-ist 'accordionist'
       alcohol 'id.'   alcohol-ist 'alcoholic'
       Marx 'id.'   Marx-ist 'id.'

       with A as base
       actief 'active'   activ-ist 'id.'
       fundamenteel 'fundamental'   fundamental-ist 'id.'
       sociaal 'social'   social-ist 'id.'

As the glosses show, the same observation holds for English.

This array of facts concerning these nouns in -*ist* can be accounted for by assuming two subschemas of (10).

(12) $[[x]_{Nj} - ist]_{Ni} \leftrightarrow$ [PERSON WITH ABILITY, IDEOLOGY, DISPOSITION Y RELATED TO SEM$_j$]$_i$

$[[x]_{Aj} - ist]_{Ni} \leftrightarrow$ [PERSON WITH ABILITY, IDEOLOGY, DISPOSITION Y RELATED TO SEM$_j$]$_i$

Thus it is expressed that the variable *x* in schema (10) may assume the value of a noun or an adjective, but this is not required, as shown by words like *aut-ist*. The same holds for schema (9) in which *x* may also have the value noun or adjective, as in the English words *Marxism* and *socialism* respectively. In the case of words in -*ist* we thus get the following schema:

(10') $[x - ist]_{Ni} \leftrightarrow$ [PERSON WITH ABILITY, IDEOLOGY, DISPOSITION Y]$_i$
         If x = N$_j$, A$_j$, then Y is related to SEM$_j$

which expresses that if X is a noun or an adjective, the meaning of the base word plays a role in the meaning of the word in -*ist*. In some cases the semantic analysis is quite straightforward: an *accordionist* is a person with the ability to play the accordion, and the word *alcoholist* denotes a person with the disposition to drink too much alcohol. However, if the noun in -*ist* denotes a person with a particular disposition or ideology, the semantic description might be more complicated. A socialist, for instance, is not a person who is social or has social abilities but a person who adheres to *socialism*. Hence, the meaning of the word *socialist* can only be properly described by referring to the meaning of the corresponding deadjectival noun *socialism*. In section 2.2 I discuss what this implies for word formation schemas.

2.2 Paradigmatic relations

The relations of 'instantiation' and 'part of' are the two basic types of relationship in the lexicon as far as complex words and their bases are concerned. However, there are more relevant relationships, which are paradigmatic in nature (Koefoed and Van Marle 1980). An important one is that between two sets of words with the same degree of complexity, derived from the same base word. For instance, Dutch has two sets of deverbal agent nouns, sex-neutral ones in -*er*, and a class of nouns in -*ster* that denote female agents (Van Marle 1985; Van Santen and De Vries 1981):

(13) *verb*   *deverbal noun*   *deverbal noun*
      arbeid 'to labour'   arbeid-er 'labourer'   arbeid-ster 'female labourer'
      spreek 'to speak'   sprek-er 'speaker'   spreek-ster 'female speaker'
      werk 'to work'   werk-er 'worker'   werk-ster 'female worker'
      zwem 'to swim'   zwemm-er 'swimmer'   zwem-ster 'female swimmer'

Based on these three sets of words, the language user can establish the following paradigmatic relationships (indicated by the symbol ≈) between the three sets of words and the corresponding schemas:

(14) $< V_i \leftrightarrow \text{ACTION}_i > \approx < [V_i\text{-er}]_{Nk} \leftrightarrow [\text{SUBJ OF ACTION}_i]_k > \approx$
      $< [V_i\text{-ster}]_{Nj} \leftrightarrow [\text{FEMALE SUBJ OF ACTION}_i]_j >$

The symbols < and > demarcate a construction. Words with the same base word can form a word family, and (14) is a generalization about word families with shared verbal bases. The reality of word families has been confirmed by so-called family size effects. In lexical decision tasks the speed of the decision correlates positively with the size of the word family of a word (Schreuder and Baayen 1997).

The paradigmatic relationship between the two schemas for deverbal nouns in (14) makes it possible to coin a noun in -*ster* directly from a word in -*er*, by replacing the suffix -*er* with -*ster*. One argument for assuming that this analysis is sometimes the more adequate one is that when a deverbal noun in -*er* has a particular semantic idiosyncrasy, this semantic property recurs in the corresponding female noun, as illustrated by the following examples (Booij 2002b: 6–7, based on Van Marle 1985):

(15) betwet-er 'lit. better knower, pedant'   betweet-ster 'female pedant'
      oproerkraai-er 'revolution crower, ring   oproerkraai-ster 'female ring
      leader'   leader'
      padvind-er 'lit. path finder, boy scout'   padvind-ster 'girl scout'
      strooplikk-er 'lit. syrup licker, toady'   strooplik-ster 'female toady'

Note that the common semantic idiosyncrasy of these word pairs cannot be explained in terms of a common verbal base because Dutch does not have the verbs *betweten, oproerkraaien, padvinden* or *strooplikken* (the infinitive form of these verbs, which is the citation form, ends in -*en*).

The type of paradigmatic relationship in (14), a correlation between two sets of words of the same degree of morphological complexity, can also be observed in cases where there is no base word that is shared by the word pairs, as discussed above. Consider the following English word pairs in -*ism* and -*ist*:

(16) altru-ism   altru-ist
      aut-ism   aut-ist
      bapt-ism   bapt-ist
      commun-ism commun-ist
      pacif-ism   pacif-ist

Even though they have no corresponding base word, the meaning of one member of a pair can be defined in terms of that of the other member. In particular, the meaning of the word in -*ist* can often be paraphrased as 'person with the ability, disposition, or ideology denoted by the word in -*ism*'. Hence, the following paradigmatic relationship can be defined for these two schemas:

(17) $< [x\text{-ism}]_{N_i} \leftrightarrow \text{SEM}_i > \approx < [x\text{-ist}]_{N_j} \leftrightarrow$ [person with property Y related to $\text{SEM}_i]_j >$

where SEM_i represents the meaning of the word in -*ism*. Thus, an altruist has a disposition for altruism, and a pacifist adheres to the ideology of pacifism. The paradigmatic relationship between these two schemas may lead to the coining of new words. For instance, if we know what *determinism* is, we can easily coin the word *determinist*, and then we know that this word denotes a person adhering to determinism. The same holds for nouns in -*ist* with a lexeme as their base, such as *Marxist* and *socialist*. A Marxist is an adherent of Marxism and not necessarily a follower of Marx, since Marxism as a doctrine encompasses more than the ideas of Marx (in fact, Marx himself declared that he was not a Marxist). Similarly, a socialist is not necessarily a social person but an adherent of the ideology of socialism.

Even though semantically the word in -*ism* is the starting point for the word in -*ist*, this does not mean that the actual order of derivation necessarily reflect this semantic asymmetry. For instance, the word *abolitionist* may have been coined before *abolitionism*. Paradigmatic relationships like that in (17) allow for word formation in both directions.

Hence, we need relationships such as those in (17) for an adequate account of the semantics of certain sets of words in -*ist*. The meaning of these nouns in -*ist* is not simply a compositional function of their constituent parts but contains the meaning of a related word with the same degree of complexity.

We find such systematic paradigmatic relationships across Germanic and Romance languages (Vallès 2003). In a rule-based framework such relationships require an operation of affix replacement instead of affix concatenation. In a schema-based analysis, it suffices to state the precise semantic correlation between two classes of words with the same degree of morphological complexity. Thus, the assumption of paradigmatic relations between constructional schemas provides the flexibility that we need for expressing generalizations about the semantic interpretation of complex words.

Such 'mismatches' between the form and the meaning of complex words may arise through borrowing of sets of complex words from other languages. Consider the following Dutch word pairs and their English glosses:

(18)   alloc-eer 'to allocate'   alloc-atie 'allocation'
        communic-eer 'to communicate'   communic-atie 'communication'
        reden-eer 'to reason'   reden-atie 'reasoning'
        stabil-is-eer 'to stabilize'   stabil-is-atie 'stabilization'

The nouns in -atie '-ation' are semantically the nominalizations of the verbs on the left, just like their English counterparts. Yet, the part before -atie is not identical to the corresponding verb, which has an additional morpheme -eer. This mismatch between form and meaning is due to the historical fact that the inflectional ending -er of French infinitives has been reinterpreted in Dutch as a derivational suffix -eer. In combination with the massive borrowing of the corresponding nouns in -atie, this led to the following productive paradigmatic pattern:

(19) $< [\text{x-eer}]_{Vi} \leftrightarrow [\text{SEM}]_i> \approx <[\text{x-atie}]_{Nj} \leftrightarrow [\text{action of SEM}_i]_j >$

New Dutch nouns in -atie can readily be formed on the basis of verbs in -eer. For instance, once the verb implement-eer 'to implement' has been coined, the corresponding noun implement-atie 'implementation' is its derived nominal.

Elaborate patterns of paradigmatic relationships can be found in the Dutch system for coining geographical names (Booij 1997a). Consider the following data concerning inhabitative nouns and toponymic adjectives in Dutch:[2]

(20)   *toponym*   *inhabitative*   *toponymic adjective*
        Provençe   Provenç-aal   Provenç-aal-s
        Amerika   Amerik-aan   Amerik-aan-s
        Catalonië   Catal-aan   Catal-aan-s
        Guatemala   Guatemalt-eek   Guatemalt-eek-s
        Chili   Chil-een   Chil-een-s
        Madrid   Madril-een   Madril-een-s
        Portugal   Portug-ees   Portug-ees
        Ambon   Ambon-ees   Ambon-ees
        Rome   Rom-ein   Rom-ein-s

---

[2] Similar patterns in the coining of German toponymic adjectives are observed by Becker (1990: 42).

Palestina	Palest-ijn	Palest-ijn-s
Azië	Azi-aat	Azi-at-isch
Monaco	Moneg-ask	Moneg-ask-isch
Israel	Israel-iet	Israel-it-isch
Moskou	Moskov-iet	Moskov-it-isch

There is quite a lot of unpredictable variation in the form of the inhabitant names as to the form of the stem and the choice of a particular suffix. The choice between -s and -isch /is/ in the toponymic adjectives is determined by the suffix of the inhabitant name. The form of the toponymic adjective always correlates with that of the inhabitant name, even though the meaning of the toponymic adjective does not encompass inhabitance. For instance, the adjective *Amerikaans* does not mean 'pertaining to inhabitants of America' but 'pertaining to America'. That is, the adjective is a relational adjective that expresses a relation to a geographical entity. The formal analysis of the toponymic adjectives has to be one in which the suffixes -s and -isch are attached to corresponding inhabitative nouns, even though this is not the base word from the semantic point of view. Thus, the two relevant schemas are paradigmatically related as follows:

(21) $< [x]_{Ni} \leftrightarrow [\text{inhabitant of } j]_i > \approx < [[x]_{Ni\text{-}(i)s}]_{Ak} \leftrightarrow [\text{relating to } j]_k >$

A related morphological pattern with similar properties is that of female inhabitant names: they are formally derived through attachment of the female suffix -e to the toponymic adjective, even though they express the meaning 'female inhabitant of':

(22)

inhabitative	*toponymic adjective*	*female inhabitative*
Provençaal	Provençaal-s	Provençaal-s-e
Amerikaan	Amerikaan-s	Amerikaan-s-e
Guatemalteek	Guatemalteek-s	Guatemalteek-s-e
Chileen	Chileen-s	Chileen-s-e
Portugees	Portugees	Portuge-s-e
Ambonees	Ambonees	Ambone-s-e
Romein	Romein-s	Romein-s-e
Palestijn	Palestijn-s	Palestijn-s-e
Breton	Breton-s	Breton-s-e
Aziaat	Aziat-isch	Aziat-isch-e
Monegask	Monegask-isch	Monegask-isch-e
Israeliet	Israelit-isch	Israelit-isch-e
Moskoviet	Moskovit-isch	Moskovit-isch-e

The following schema expresses this paradigmatic relationship between the relevant sets of complex words:

(23) $< [[x]_{Ni\text{-}(i)s}]_{Ak} \leftrightarrow [\text{relating to } j]_k > \approx < [[[x]_{Ni\text{-}(i)s}]_{Ak}e]_{Nm} \leftrightarrow [\text{female inhabitant of } j]_m$

where *j* is the index for the geographical entity involved that is also mentioned in (21).

In conclusion, the part-of relationship between a base word and a word derived from that base word is only one of the possible paradigmatic relationships between words in the lexicon. There are also paradigmatic relationships between derived words with the same degree of morphological complexity. These relationships make the lexicon a structured whole, a multi-dimensional network of individual words and sets of words, that is, a 'web of words'. The schemas form a hierarchy of layers of different degrees of abstraction across sets of words. The importance of subschemas is discussed in more detail in Chapter 3.

2.3 Constructional properties

An important argument for using the notion 'morphological construction' is that it enables us to specify properties of sets of derived words that cannot be deduced from the properties of their constituent parts. A first example comes from Romance languages. French, Italian, and Spanish have nominal compounds of the form VN such as:

(24)   *French*
      a. chauffe-eau
         heat-water
         'water heater'
      b. coupe-ongle
         clip-nail
         'nail clipper'
      c. garde-barrière
         guard-gate
         'gate keeper'
      d. grille-pain
         toast-bread
         'toaster'

Italian

e. lava-piatti
   wash-dishes
   'dish washer'
f. mangia-patate
   eat-potatoes
   'potato eater'
g. porta-lettere
   carry-letters
   'postman'
h. rompi-capo
   break-head
   'brain teaser, puzzle'

Spanish

i. lanza-cohetes
   launch-rockets
   'rocket launcher'
j. come-curas
   eat-priests
   'anti-clerical'
k. mata-sanos
   kill-healthy.people
   'quack doctor'
l. limpia-botas
   clean-boots
   'boot black'

These VN compounds are all nominal compounds, consisting of a verbal stem followed by a noun in either the singular or the plural form (Rainer 2001). These are exocentric compounds since the noun on the right is not the head of the compound. For instance, Italian *lava-piatti* does not denote a certain type of *piatti* 'dishes' but a machine that washes dishes. So there is no constituent to which the meaning component 'agent/instrument' of these compounds can be assigned. This is why one finds analyses in which a nominalizing zero-suffix is postulated on analogy with overt agentive/instrumental suffixes such as English deverbal *-er*. The problem of such analyses is that there is no other motivation for such zero-elements than the agent/instrument meaning, and the fact that the relevant complex words are nouns.

The notion 'construction' implies that there may be meaning aspects of the construction as a whole that do not derive from its constituents. That is, there is room for holistic properties. In the case discussed here, the two holistic properties are the agent/instrument meaning, and the word class of the compounds. Thus, the following schema can be assumed for such Romance VN compounds with agent or instrument meaning:

(25) $[[V_k][N_i]]_{Nj} \leftrightarrow$ [AGENT / INSTRUMENT$_j$ OF ACTION$_k$ ON OBJECT$_i$]$_j$

Schema (25) is a morphological construction in which a specific morphological form (a subtype of exocentric compounds) correlates with a specific (non-compositional) meaning. In addition to these constructional properties, the exocentric VN-compounds of French have masculine gender as default gender.[3]

A second example of exocentric compounding can be observed in the following set of Spanish adjectives which can be qualified as bahuvrihi-adjectives, a type found in many languages (Bauer 2008), for instance in Spanish and Slovak:

(26)   *Spanish*
    a. pel-i-rroj-o
       hair-LINKING VOWEL-red-MASC.SG
       'red-haired'
    b. cabiz-baj-o
       head-low-MASC.SG
       'with low head, crest-fallen'

    Slovak
    c. dlh-o-krk-á
       long-LINKING VOWEL-neck-NOM.SG.FEM
       'long-necked'
    d. mal-o-list-ý
       small-LINKING VOWEL-leaf-NOM.SG.MASC.
       'small-leafed'

In (26b) the linking vowel of the first stem is dropped because there is a phonological requirement of bisyllabicity on the first constituent (including the linking vowel). These Spanish compounds are adjectives, but their adjectival constituent is not the head of the compound; instead, it modifies the left constituent. Hence, we need the following morphological schema for these Spanish adjectives:

(27) $[[x]_{Ni} [y]_{Aj}]_{Ak} \leftrightarrow$ [PROPERTY OF HAVING OBJECT$_i$ WITH PROPERTY$_j$]$_k$

---

[3] The range of interpretation of these VN compounds is larger since some denote locations or events (Franz Rainer, pers. comm.). For a more elaborate discussion of the properties and analysis of the Romance exocentric compounds, see Fradin (2009) and Kornfeld (2009).

To this schema we should add the phonological restriction that *x* is bisyllabic. Hence, the addition of a linking vowel to the stem *pel-*. Moreover, this schema applies only to nouns that denote body parts (Rainer and Varela 1992: 134). It will be clear that the meaning of *cabizbajo* is metaphorical and hence idiosyncratic. Schema (27) holds mutatis mutandis for Slovak as well, with the difference that in the Slovak possessive adjectives the order of adjective and noun is reversed, and there is a linking vowel *o* between the adjective and the noun.

Exocentric compounding is a widespread phenomenon.[4] In English, there are just a few of such compounds, like *cut-throat* and *pick-pocket*. In Chinese, on the other hand, there are lots of exocentric compounds (Ceccagno and Basciano 2009). Japanese also has a large set of exocentric compounds (Kageyama 2009). Italian has a productive category of VV-compounds that are nouns, such as *fuggi-fuggi* 'run.away-run.away 'rush, stampede'. They form a category of action nouns performed by a plurality of agents (Masini and Thornton 2008). French features lots of nominal exocentric compounds of the form PN such as *après-guerre* 'lit. after-war, period after the war', *entre-colonne* 'lit. between-column, distance between two columns', *sans-papiers* 'lit. without-papers, person without legal papers', and *sous-tasse* 'lit. under-cup, saucer'.

An excellent case for a constructional analysis of morphology is the phenomenon of reduplication (Inkelas and Zoll 2005). Reduplication is in essence a morphological operation, the doubling of pieces of information encapsulated in lexemes (in the simplest case, that of complete reduplication, the doubling of a word). Additionally, a phonological operation, triggered by the reduplicative doubling structure may apply, in case the reduplicant constituent is phonologically not identical to the base constituent. The doubled structure conveys a meaning that is not reducible to the meaning of its constituents. It is the reduplication structure itself that evokes particular meanings, such as plurality for reduplicated nouns, and intensity for reduplicated verbs. The evoked meanings may differ across languages (Inkelas and Zoll 2005: 14–15).

A simple example may serve to illustrate the constructional analysis of reduplication. In Afrikaans, a daughter language of Dutch, complete reduplication is a productive process, borrowed from Malay. All lexical categories can be reduplicated. The shared meaning of reduplication in all cases of Afrikaans reduplication is that of 'increase' (Botha 1988). However, it has to be specified for each subcase what exactly has increased. An example of a semantic

---

[4] Surveys and discussion of exocentric compounds can be found in Bauer (2008), Guevara and Scalise (2009), and Scalise and Guevara (2006).

regularity is that when plural nouns are reduplicated, the meaning of reduplication is 'considerable number' (Botha 1988: 92):

(28) a. Die kinder drink bottels-bottels limonade
         The children drink bottels-bottels lemonade
         'The children drink bottles and bottles of lemonade'
      b. Bakke-bakke veld-blomme versier die tafels
         Bowls-bowls wild-flowers decorate the tables
         'The tables are decorated with wild flowers by the bowlful'

Hence, the following (sub)schema for reduplication of plural nouns can be
assumed (pl = plural):

(29) $[[x]_{Npl,i}\ [x]_{Npl,i}]_{Nj} \leftrightarrow [\text{CONSIDERABLE NUMBER OF OBJECTS}_i]_j$

In this schema the two subconstituents are co-indexed, which indicates their
identity. In this case, the phonological make up of the two constituents is also
identical but there are lots of cases in which reduplication triggers an additional phonological operation of truncation, resulting in partial reduplication
(Inkelas and Zoll 2005).

   Analyses of word formation in which use is made of zero-affixes can be seen
as indications that a constructional analysis is in order, as pointed out above.
This can also be illustrated with the phenomenon of conversion of verbal
stems into nouns in Dutch. Conversion is also labelled 'zero-derivation' since
the change in word class cannot be linked to an overt affix. This word
formation process applies to Dutch simplex verbs, and the gender of the
converted noun is always common:

(30) *verb stem*   *noun with common gender*
      bouw 'to build'   bouw 'building'
      loop 'to walk'   loop 'walk'
      trap 'to kick'   trap 'kick'
      val 'to fall'   val 'fall'
      was 'to wash'   was 'wash'
      zet 'to put'   zet 'move'

In Dutch the gender of suffixed nouns is predictable from the nominalizing
suffix. For instance, all deverbal nouns ending in the suffix -*ing* have a
common gender. The problem is that in the words in (30) there is no overt
suffix that we can assign a gender property to. Hence, the gender feature value
[−neuter] must be seen as a property of the construction as a whole. The
following schema expresses this generalization:

(31) $[[x]_{Vj}]_{N[-neuter],i} \leftrightarrow [\text{ACTION}_j]_i$

The examples of conversion given so far were all conversions of simplex verbs, and simplicity of the base verb is indeed a condition on this word formation process. Derived verbs with suffixes do not lend themselves to conversion. However, verbs with prefixes like *be-*, *ge-*, *ont-*, and *ver-* do allow for conversion, but in this case the converted noun has neuter gender:

(32)   *verb*   *derived neuter noun*
     a. be-derf 'to spoil'   bederf 'decay'
        be-gin 'to begin'   begin 'beginning'
        be-heer 'to manage'   beheer 'management'
     b. ge-bruik 'to use'   gebruik 'use'
        ge-loof 'to believe'   geloof 'belief'
     c. ont-bijt 'to breakfast'   ontbijt 'breakfast'
        ont-werp 'to design'   ontwerp 'design'
        ont-zet 'to relieve'   ontzet 'relief'
     d. ver-bruik 'to consume' verbruik 'consumption'
        ver-zuim 'to omit'   verzuim 'omission'
        ver-lang 'to desire'   verlangen 'desire'

It is not the prefix that determines the gender since these prefixes are not nominalizing but verbalizing. Hence, the relevant schema has to refer to the internal morphological make-up of the verbal stem:

(33) $[[\text{Prefix-x}]_{Vj}]_{N[+\text{neuter}], i} \leftrightarrow [\text{ACTION}_j]_i$ (Prefix = *be-*, *ge-*, *ont-*, *ver-*)

Since this schema is more specific than schema (31), it will overrule this more general schema in the formation of new nouns through conversion, in line with Panini's principle that when two rules compete, the most specific one wins.

In conclusion, the gender of derived nouns may be a property of the morphological construction as a whole instead of being derivable from a base constituent. By making use of the notion 'morphological construction' we avoid making use of arbitrary zero-affixes with a gender feature for the statement of the gender regularities involved.

2.4 Schema unification

Rumelhart (1980: 40–41) mentions six general properties of schemas, four of which are of immediate relevance for our discussion of the importance of constructional schemas for morphology:

(34)   1. Schemata have variables.
       2. Schemata can embed, one within another.

3. Schemata represent knowledge at all levels of abstraction.
4. Schemata are active processes.

Properties 1, 2, and 4 have already been discussed above: morphological constructions are schemas with variables, they have various degrees of abstractness, and they are also the recipes for coining new words. The second property, the 'embeddability' of schemas is interesting for morphological analysis. The relevant phenomenon is that possible complex words may form intermediate steps in coining new words. That is, in a word-based morphology, morphological operations may not only apply to existing, listed words but also to non-conventionalized but possible complex words (Booij 1977: Chapter 1). Given the existence of word formation schemas as abstractions over sets of complex words, such schema can be unified into more complex schemas. For instance, the following two (formal parts of the) schemas of English derivational morphology can be unified:

(35) $[un\text{-}A]_A + [V\text{-}able]_A = [un[V\text{-}able]_A]_A$

On the basis of this complex schema we may derive multiply complex adjectives of this type in one step from a verbal base, for instance, the adjective *unbeatable* from the verb *beat*, without an intermediate adjective *beatable* that is a possible but not existing complex adjective of English. Such unified schemas thus specify the co-occurrence of word formation patterns in the coining of complex words.

Dutch deverbal adjectives in *-baar* '-able' form a productive derivational category, which can be subsequently prefixed with the negative prefix *on-* 'un-'. The negative prefix *on-* attaches productively to all kinds of adjectives, both simplex and complex ones, to form adjectives that express a negative property, as in *on-gewoon* 'un-common' and *on-beleefd* 'impolite'. In many cases, the intermediate adjective is only a possible word, and not listed. This is the case for, among many others, the following adjectives:

(36) | *verb* | *deverbal adjective* | *on-adjective* |
|---|---|---|
| bedwing 'suppress' | bedwing-baar 'suppressable' | on-bedwing-baar 'unsuppressable' |
| bestel 'deliver' | bestel-baar 'deliverable' | on-bestel-baar 'undeliverable' |
| blus 'extinguish' | blus-baar 'extinguishable' | on-blus-baar 'unextinguishable' |
| verwoest 'destroy' | verwoest-baar 'destroyable' | on-verwoest-baar 'undestroyable' |

The same observation can be made for another class of deverbal adjectives of Dutch, those ending in the unproductive suffix *-elijk*. A few examples are listed in (37); again, the intermediate adjectives are possible but non-existing words:

(37) *verb*   *deverbal adjective*   *on-adjective*
      beschrijf 'describe'   beschrijf-elijk 'describable'   on-beschrijf-elijk
                                                                        'undescribable'
      herroep 'revoke'   herroep-elijk 'revocable'   on-herroep-elijk
                                                                        'irrevocable'
      meet 'measure'   met-elijk 'measurable'   on-met-elijk
                                                                        'immeasurable'

Both patterns (36) and (37) suggest that word formation schemas can be unified into a complex schema that licenses such multiply complex adjectives without the existence of the intermediate positive adjective being required. That is, the following unifications appear to have taken place:

(38) $[on\text{-}A]_A + [V\text{-}baar]_A = [on[V\text{-}baar]_A]_A$
       $[on\text{-}A]_A + [V\text{-}elijk]_A = [on[V\text{-}elijk]_A]_A$

The unification of word formation schemas accounts for the possibility of simultaneous use of two or more word formation patterns (in the examples above the formation of deverbal adjectives and *on*-adjectives). If we described word formation processes as word formation rules, it would be impossible to give a straightforward formal account of the co-occurrence of two or more word formation rules. The assumption of a unified schema, on the other hand, in addition to the basic schemas, gives direct expression of the generalization that the two word formation processes may co-occur and apply simultaneously. Therefore, these observations support the use of word formation schemas instead of word formation rules.

   The actual rise of such unified schemas is the result of the language user's ability to establish a direct relation between a base word and a complex word that is two or more derivational steps away from that base word. The theoretical point is that the rise of such schemas does not imply a formal complication of the grammar because the properties of such schemas follow from the unification of independently established word formation schemas. Thus, language users may coin a new multiply complex negative adjective directly from a verbal base without an intermediate step. The unified schema is productive if the affixes involved are productive. This is the case for words with *on-* and *-baar*, but not for *on-* in combination with the unproductive *-elijk*.

This analysis implies that we are not forced to assume discontinuous affixes *on-baar* and *on-elijk* for the derivation of these Dutch *on*-adjectives, in addition to the affixes *on-*, *-baar*, and *-elijk*. The properties of the schemas with these seemingly discontinuous affixes follow from the two underlying word formation schemas. The nested structure of these schemas is also essential: the prefix *on-* does not attach to verbal bases, only to adjectival and nominal bases (the Dutch negative prefix for verbal bases is *ont-* 'un-').

An example of a unified schema for English is the attachment of the combination of the prefix *de(s)-* with the verbalizing suffixes *-ate* and *-ize* to nouns, as in:

(39) *noun*   *verb*
      caffeine   de-caffein-ate
      moral   de-moral-ize
      mythology   de-mytholog-ize
      nuclear   de-nuclear-ize

An intermediate verb like *to nuclearize* is certainly a possible verb. Yet, we should not require the existence of these verbs as a necessary intermediate step since the use of the verb *denuclearize* does not require that the object involved has first been subject to a process of nuclearization. That is, we assume unified templates of the following (simplified) form:

(40) $[de\,[[x]_N\,ate]_V]_V$ $[de\,[[x]_N\,ize]_V]_V$ $[de\,[[x]_A\,ize]_V]_V$

Co-occurrence of word formation patterns is also found on a large scale in Slavonic languages where compounding and derivation are often combined. In Polish, for instance, both complex nouns and complex adjectives are created according to the pattern [stem$_1$ – interfix – stem$_2$ – suffix – (inflectional ending)] (Szymanek 2009). This is illustrated in (41):

(41) a. obc-o-kraj-owiec
         foreign-INTERFIX-country-SUFFIX 'foreigner'
      b. drug-o-klas-ist-a
         second-INTERFIX-form-SUFFIX-INFLECTION 'second form pupil'
      c. dw-u-maszt-ow-y
         two-INTERFIX-mast-SUFFIX-INFLECTION 'two-masted'
      d. wiel-o-barw-n-y
         multi-INTERFIX-colour-SUFFIX-INFLECTION 'multi-coloured'

The derivational suffixes can also be attached to simplex stems, and hence there is motivation for a separate morphological schema for these denominal suffixes. The same applies to compounding: there are also right-headed compounds in Polish without a derivational suffix and with an interfix (an intermediate linking vowel). Yet, the building blocks of the words in (41) may not exist by themselves. For instance, the compound *dw-u-mast* 'two-mast' does not exist as such, but only shows up as part of the denominal adjective (41c). Therefore, the complex words in (41) should indeed be considered to be formed according to a unified complex schema.

Unified schemas are constructions themselves, and hence they may possess specific constructional properties of their own. This can be observed in Dutch complex words of the following type:

(42) a. tand 'tooth'   ge-tand 'toothed'
         tak 'branch'   ge-tak-t 'branched'
         spits 'point'   ge-spits-t 'pointed'
      b. rok 'skirt'   kort-ge-rok-t 'short-skirted'
         jas 'coat'   wit-ge-jas-t 'white-coated'
         schouder 'shoulder'   breed-ge-schouder-d 'broad-shouldered'

The derived words in (42a) and the right constituent of the derived words in (42b) have the form of a past participle. Dutch past participles are formed by prefixing the verbal stem with *ge-*, and by simultaneously suffixing the stem with *-t* or *-d* (*-t* after a stem-final voiceless segment, *-d* otherwise). Participles can be converted to adjectives, and thus participate in AA compounding. As we noted before, possible words may form intermediate stages in word formation. The head constituents of these words presuppose a verbal stem. However, denominal verbs such as *spits, tand, tak, rok, jas,* or *schouder* do not exist as words in Dutch. Therefore, such adjectives with participial form are traditionally referred to as *participia praeverbalia* 'pre-verbal participles' (Van Haeringen 1949*b*). That is, these participles came into being without the actual verb being coined. Moreover, the words *gerokt, gejast,* and *geschouderd* do not exist by themselves, but only in AA compounds, that is in combination with a modifying adjective.

These adjectivalized participles may be seen as a case in which the conversion of nouns into verbs is triggered by other morphological processes. Moreover, they exhibit a specific semantic property. The semantic relation between a converted verb and its base noun can be quite diverse in Dutch (Booij 1979). However, in the morphological construction under discussion here, the relation between the base N and the derived V is always that V means 'to provide with N'. For instance, the meaning of *getand* is 'provided with teeth, having teeth'. This semantic specialization underscores the construction status of this complex morphological schema.

An adjective like *breedgeschouderd* is thus an instantiation of a multiply complex schema, the unification of the following schemas:

(43)   N to V conversion $[[x]_N]_V$
      Past participle formation $[ge \ [x]_V \ d]_V$
      Participle to A conversion $[[ge \ [x]_V \ d]_V]_A$
      AA compounding $[[x]_A[y]_A]_A$

These schemas can be unified into the following complex template, and the morphological structure of *getakt* and *breedgeschouderd* will be as follows:

(44)   a. (i) $[[ge[[y]_N]_V \ t]_V]_A$ (ii) $[[x]_A[[ge[[y]_N]_V \ d]_V]_A]_A$
     b. (i) $[[ge[[tak]_N]_V \ t]_V]_A$ (ii) $[[breed]_A[[ge[[schouder]_N]_V \ d]_V]_A]_A$

That is, the coinage of *breedgeschouderd* may be conceived of as the unification of template (44a ii) with the adjective *breed* and the noun *schouder*. As we may expect for a construction, the unified AA schema has an additional specific semantic property as well: the scope of the modifying adjective is not the whole head constituent but only its nominal base: this compound does not mean 'having shoulders in a broad way' but 'having broad shoulders'. This specific scope property of the derived words in (42b) can thus be specified as a property of template (44a ii). In this way we can do justice to both the idiosyncrasies of this construction and to the fact that the existence of this word formation schema follows from independently established word formation schemas of Dutch.

The same phenomenon can be observed for *participia praeverbalia* beginning with the prefix *be-*:

(45)   haar 'hair'   be-haar-d 'having hair, hairy'
     klant 'client'   be-klant 'having clients, patronized'
     jaar 'year'   be-jaar-d 'having years, old'
     mos 'moss'   be-mos-t 'having moss, moss-covered'

The prefix *be-* can be used for deriving verbs from nouns, with the meaning 'to provide with N'. Yet, there are no *be*-verbs *behaar*, *beklant*, etc. in Dutch. Thus, these adjectives have been coined by unification of a noun with the following unified complex morphological schema:

(46) $[[[be[x]_N]_V d]_V]_A$

Such schemas could be simplified in the course of time, with omission of the verbal intermediate step. This simplification results in new morphological schemas such as (47), with a discontinuous affix *be-...-d*:

(47) $[be[x]_{Ni}d]_{Aj} \leftrightarrow [\text{provided with SEM}_i]_j$

Thus, a language may acquire new morphological schemas as an effect of schema unification and subsequent simplification. The existence of English adjectives such as *bejewelled, bespectacled,* and *bewigged* that also miss a corresponding verb (although such a verb may be coined) may be explained in the same way. Missing verbs can also be observed in Italian privative adjectives like *s-famigli-ato* 'without family, single' (Mayo et al. 1995). This adjective has the form of a prefix followed by an adjective which has the shape of the participle of the non-existing verb *famigiliare* (the part *famigliato* may also be analysed as a denominal adjective with the suffix *-ato*). Hence, at least two simultaneous derivational steps are involved in the coining of this adjective. This leads to the conclusion these complex adjectives with prefix *s-* are derived by means of a generalized schema that is the unification of more basic schemas of word formation.

2.4.1 Embedded productivity

The term 'embedded productivity' denotes the phenomenon that a word formation process is normally unproductive, but is productive when it co-occurs with another word formation process. That is, schema unification may result in a productive schema even though one of its building blocks is unproductive. This is the case for verbal compounding in Dutch, which is unproductive, as in most other Germanic languages (Harbert 2007). What we do find for Dutch are the following classes of verbal compounds:

(i) conversions of nominal compounds such as $[[[voet]_N[bal]_N]_N]_V$, 'to play football';

(ii) isolated cases of back formation: $[[beeld]_N[houw]_V]_V$ 'to sculpture' back-formed from *beeld-houw-er* 'lit. statue-cutter, sculpturer'; $[[woord]_N[speel]_V]_V$ 'to play with words' from *woord-spel-ing* 'word-play, pun';

(iii) quasi-compound verbs that mainly occur in the infinitival form, such as $[worst]_N[hap]_V$ 'sausage eat'; these verbs have finite forms but only in embedded clauses where the two parts are linearly adjacent (... *dat Jan worst-hap-te* 'that John sausage ate'). These NV verbs are discussed in Chapter 4.

Embedded in nominal compounds, however, NV compounds appear to be quite productive (Booij 2002b: 150); the following examples illustrate this pattern:

(48) a. $[[[aardappel]_N[schil]_V]_V[mesje]_N]_N$
          potato peel knife
          'potato peeler'

   b. [[[brand]_N[blus]_V]_V[installatie]_N]_N
      fire extinguish installation
      'fire extinguisher'
   c. [[[koffie]_N[zet]_V]_V[apparaat]_N]_N
      coffee make machine
      'coffee maker'

In these nominal compounds the left constituent is a NV compound in which the N functions as the Patient of the verb. Dutch does not have the corresponding compound verbs *aardappelschil*, *brandblus*, and *koffiezet* as NV compounds (*koffiezet* does occur, however, but as a phrasal, separable verb, cf. Chapter 4).

   [NV]_V compounding is not only increased by VN compounding but also by suffixation with the deverbal suffixes *-er*, *-ster*, *-ing*, and *-erij* and by the present participle ending *-end* used to form adjectives:

(49) a. aandacht-trekk-er
       attention-draw-er
       'person who draws attention'
    b. brand-bluss-er
       fire-extinguish-er
       'fire extinguisher'
    c. kinder-verzorg-ster
       child-care-FEM SUFFIX
       'children's caretaker (fem.)'
    d. kranten-bezorg-ster
       newspapers-deliver-FEM SUFFIX
       'newspaper woman'
    e. evangelie-verkondig-ing
       gospel-preach-ing
       'gospel preaching'
    f. hand-oplegg-ing
       hand-impos-ition
       'imposition of hands'
    g. bijen-houd-erij
       bees-keep-ing
       'bee-keeping'
    h. bloem-kwek-erij
       flower-grow-ing
       'flower nursery'

    i. haat-drag-end
       hate-bear-ing
       'resentful'
    j. ijzer-houd-end
       iron-contain-ing
       'iron containing'

The proper account of complex words of the type $[NV\text{-}er]_N$ has provoked a lot of discussion in the morphological literature on English and Dutch (Booij 1988; Hoekstra and Van der Putten 1988; Lieber 1983). The main objection to assuming NV compounds as bases for these kinds of derivation (the hypothesis put forward by Lieber for English) is that, both in English and Dutch, NV compounding is not productive (Lieber 2004: 48). On the other hand, semantically the assumption of NV bases is attractive because the N in these examples functions as the Patient of the V. Therefore, two other analytical options have been considered in the literature.

First, a word such as *brand-bluss-er* 'fire extinguisher' may be analysed as a case of NN compounding in which the head noun is a deverbal N, *bluss-er* 'extinguisher' that takes the noun *brand* 'fire' as its semantic argument. That is, the semantic unit corresponding with the NV sequence *brand blus* 'fire extinguish' is not reflected by a structural unit NV. Instead, the notion 'inheritance of argument structure' is invoked: the deverbal noun inherits the Patient argument of its base verb, and the left constituent satisfies this Patient role (Booij 1988).

In an alternative analysis, proposed by Hoekstra and Van der Putten (1988), the structural analysis of these compounds as NN compounds is maintained, but the Patient role is not assigned through inheritance. Instead, this role is assigned to the noun by the general principle for interpretation of the relation between the two parts of a compound ('give a sensible interpretation, in line with your conceptual and encyclopaedic knowledge').

Once we accept the idea that the productivity of a certain word formation pattern may be linked to its occurrence in specific morphological constructions, another analytical option is available: these words are suffixed NV compounds, that is, derived words with an NV compound as their verbal base. This structure $[[NV]_V\ er]_N$ gives direct expression to the generalization that the noun and the verb belong together from the semantic point of view. A *grappen-mak-er* 'lit. jokes maker, comedian', for instance, is someone who makes jokes, and an *aandacht-trek-ker* 'lit. attention drawer' is someone who draws attention. Therefore, we can opt for this analysis, now that we have a way of overcoming the problem that NV compounding in isolation is unproductive. This structural analysis is the same as that proposed by Lieber (1983).

Through unification of the schemas $[NV]_V$ and $[V\ er]_N$ we get the schema $[[NV]_V\ er]_N$. This latter, unified schema can be qualified as productive, unlike the NV template itself. Thus, we meet with another type of holistic property of morphological constructions, productivity.

The observed productivity boost of NV compounding in deverbal word formation can be expressed by unification of the relevant schemas. Hence, the following productive unified schemas can be postulated for Dutch:

(50) $[[[N][V]]_V\ er]_N$
      $[[[N][V]]_V\ ster]_N$
      $[[[N][V]]_V\ ing]_N$
      $[[[N][V]]_V\ erij]_N$

These templates will be linked to two different word formation schemas, one for NV compounding and one for deverbal nouns in -*er*. The schemas will be instantiated by complex words such as those listed in (49).

The words in (49) have often been called synthetic compounds since they seem to be cases of compounding and derivation at the same time. The account outlined above makes this notion of simultaneity more precise: structurally there is a hierarchy in that the compound is part of a derived word. The systematic co-occurrence of the two word formation processes is expressed by schema unification.

2.5 A web of words

In this chapter we have seen that a lexicon has to be conceived of as a web of words (and phrasal lexical units), a module of the grammar that contains a network of relationships between individual words and morphological schemas. In addition, the schemas themselves are also related in three ways: in terms of instantiation (a schema can be instantiated by subschemas), unification (creating derived schemas), and paradigmatically (with systematic asymmetries between form and meaning). Furthermore, morphological schemas are to be seen as constructions, since they exhibit holistic properties (both formal and semantic ones) that do not derive from their constituents.

The importance of subschemas in a hierarchical lexicon is discussed in more detail in Chapter 3.

3

Schemas and subschemas in the lexicon

3.1 Schemas and subschemas

As discussed in section 1.4, nominal compounding in Germanic languages can be represented by the following schema, repeated here for convenience:

(1) $[[a]_{Xk} [b]_{Ni}]_{Nj} \leftrightarrow [\text{SEM}_i \text{ with relation R to SEM}_k]_j$

This schema is a subcase of the more general schema for all right-headed compounds:

(2) $[[a]_{Xk} [b]_{Yi}]_{Yj} \leftrightarrow [\text{SEM}_i \text{ with relation R to SEM}_k]_j$
$\qquad\quad | \quad |$
$\qquad [aF] [aF]$

In schema (2) we express that the compound as a whole shares all word class properties and subclass properties (indicated by $[aF]$) of the right constituent. For instance, the gender of the head noun is identical to that of the corresponding nominal compound as a whole. In addition, the formal head of the compound also functions as its semantic head, as expressed on the right of the double arrow in schema (2). Schema (2) is the most abstract generalization that one can make about compounds in Germanic languages. However, it has to be supplemented with more specific information in order to do justice to the properties of the various subclasses of compounds. For instance, if Y is assumed to stand for the three lexical categories N, A, and V, this seems to imply that nominal, adjectival, and verbal compounds have the same status in Germanic languages. This is not correct, however. Verbal compounds do not form a productive category in Germanic languages (Harbert 2007). A verbal compound like English *to baby-sit* is a well-known exception to this rule, and its coining can be explained as a case of back formation from the NN compound *babysitter*. This lack of productivity of the morphological category of NV compounds can be expressed by not having a subschema for verbal compounds. Instead, the few existing cases of back formation are linked directly to the general schema. This reflects the idea that generalizations are bottom-up. If there are just a few words of a certain type, the language user may not appeal to the corresponding subschema. However, we should realize that the cue for productivity of a pattern, and hence the existence of the corresponding subschema is not type frequency alone. Crucial for productivity is that the language user comes across new types from time to time. This is operationalized in the productivity measure proposed by Baayen (1992), which is based on the number of hapaxes in a corpus. Hence, we might consider the option that subschemas are enriched with information on their degree of productivity. Here, I leave this issue open.

Another property that distinguishes subsets of compounds is that of the degree of recursivity. Nominal compounding in Germanic languages exhibits recursivity: both the head constituent and the non-head constituent can be compounds themselves, as illustrated here by some Dutch examples:

(3) *left constituent recursive*:
     a. $[[[[ziekte]_N[verzuim]_N]_N[bestrijdings]_N]_N[programma]_N]_N$
        illness absence fight program 'program for reducing absence due to illness'
     b. $[[[aardappel]_N [schil]_V]_V[mesje]_N]_N$
        potato peel knife 'knife for peeling potatoes'

     right constituent recursive:
     c. $[[zomer]_N [[broed]_V[gebied]_N]_N]_N$
        summer breed area 'breeding area for the summer'

     both constituents recursive:
     d. $[[[grond]_N[water]_N]_N[[over]_P[last]_N]_N]_N$
        ground water over burden 'groundwater problems'

However, recursivity is not allowed in all kinds of Dutch compounding. In AN compounding, neither the modifier A nor the head N can be a compound itself. That is, for both parts recursivity is not allowed. For Dutch adjectival compounds similar restrictions hold: the parts cannot be compounds themselves (De Haas and Trommelen 1993). In sum, it is only in NN compounding that the process of compounding is recursive in Dutch, thus making long and complex compounds possible. This can be expressed by stating the following property of the subschema for NN compounds: 'N can be a compound itself'. Thus, we get compound structures like the following which are unifications of the NN schema with itself, and with $[VN]_N$ compounds:

(4) a. $[[NN]_N N]_N$
  b. $[N [NN]_N]_N$
  c. $[[NN]_N [NN]_N]_N$
  d. $[N [VN]_N]_N$

Dutch AN compounds are subject to the even stronger restriction on the A-constituents that they are simplex, underived adjectives.[1] Thus, we have to impose the following restriction on the class of possible fillers of the $[AN]_N$ subschema: 'A is simplex'. As a consequence of this restriction, Dutch AN sequences with derived adjectives have phrasal status (Chapter 7).

Differences in subsets of complex words with respect to productivity can also be observed in the domain of derivation. For example, Dutch features a large set of verbs with the verbalizing prefix *ver-* that belong to a number of semantic subclasses. In present-day Dutch, it is only a restricted number of subsets that can be expanded. The prefix *ver-* is productive with adjectives for coining verbs with the meaning 'to become/make A' (5a), and with verbs to express the meaning 'to waste by V-ing' (5b), but its use for creating new verbs that indicate a removal through the action denoted by the base verb is not possible in present-day Dutch although there are some such verbs in the lexicon (5c):

(5) a. *productive*: geel 'yellow'; ver-geel 'to become yellow', ver-rood 'to become redder';
  b. *productive*: drink 'to drink'; ver-drink 'to waste by drinking', ver-rook 'to waste by smoking';
  c. *unproductive*: jaag 'to hunt'; ver-jaag 'to chase away', *ver-smijt 'to smash away'.

The differences in productivity can be accounted for assuming subschemas for the productive cases, dominated by a general schema for all *ver*-verbs that expresses that this prefix always creates verbs. Such subschemas identify the regions of productivity of a word formation process (Heyvaert 2003).

The fact that sets of complex words may have both common and distinctive properties justifies a model of the lexicon in which the individual existing complex words of a language are dominated by a hierarchy of schemas that represent different levels of abstraction at which generalizations concerning subsets of complex words can be made.[2]

---

[1] An exception is the word *speciaalzaak* 'specialist shop' in which *special* 'special' is a (formally) complex adjective.

[2] Subschemas may also pertain to the semantic dimension of compounds. For instance, there is a subset of compounds where the two constituents have a part–whole relation (as in *flower bed*), an origin–entity relation, as in *hay fever*, etc. (Ungerer 2007: 667).

The use of schemas for expressing generalizations about word formation patterns has other advantages as well. The idea that category-determining affixes are heads of complex words, just like the right constituents of compounds, raises conceptual and empirical problems (König 1999: 166–167). First of all, it forces us to assign a lexical category label to bound morphemes without this property being accessible in other constructions than complex words. Furthermore, unlike the right constituents of compounds, category-determining suffixes do not always function as the semantic heads of the words they create, and hence, it is a happy consequence of the approach outlined so far that we can do without the RHR without missing the relevant generalizations. For instance, the Dutch diminutive suffix, which is category-determining and creates neuter nouns, has the semantic role of modifying the meaning of its base when added to a noun:

(6)   boek 'book'   boek-je 'booklet'
      hond 'dog'   hond-je 'doggy'
      muis 'mouse'   muis-je 'little mouse'

Hence, the suffix is not the head of these diminutive nouns from the semantic point of view but a modifier. Yet, this suffix is category-determining since its uniform output category is that of Noun, whatever the category of the base word.

The diminutive suffix can also be added to a number of adjectives, some verbs, and even adpositions, and then creates nouns as well:

(7)   blond 'blond'   blond-je 'blond girl'
      zwart 'black'   zwart-je 'black child/girl'
      zit 'to sit'   zit-je 'seat'
      bedank 'to thank'   bedank-je 'thanks'
      uit 'out'   uit-je 'outing'

In this case, the diminutive suffix still has the modifier meaning 'small', but at the same time its nominalizing nature evokes entities related to what is denoted by the base word. Hence, the meaning 'small entity' is invoked. That is, in a way the suffix seems to function as both a semantic head and a semantic modifier. This complicated mix of semantic headedness and modification finds a natural account in the constructional schema (8a) for diminutives that expresses both the formal and the semantic properties of diminutive nouns:

(8)   a. $[[x]_{Yi}\text{-je}]_{Nj} \leftrightarrow [\text{SMALL } [\text{ENTITY RELATED TO SEM}_i]]_j$
      b. $[[x]_{Ni}\text{-je}]_{Nj} \leftrightarrow [\text{SMALL } [\text{SEM}_i]]_j$

Schema (8a) expresses that the diminutive suffix is category-determining, and at the same time a modifier from the semantic point of view: it adds the meaning 'small' to the base word. Schema (8b) applies to denominal diminutives only, and can be seen as a subschema of (8a). An additional property that has to be added to schemas (8) is that these nouns are always neuter.

The Italian evaluative suffixes are exceptional compared to the other non-inflectional suffixes of this language in that they are not category-determining, but transparent to the category of their base words, as mentioned in section 2.1.1 and repeated here for convenience (Scalise 1984: 184):

(9) N   tavolo 'table'   tavol-ino 'small table'
     A   giallo 'yellow'   giall-ino 'yellowish'
     Adv   bene 'well'   ben-ino 'more or less well'

Scalise proposed to account for this exceptional behaviour of Italian suffixes by assuming a special level for Italian morphology, a level in between derivational morphology and inflectional morphology at which the RHR does not apply (Scalise 1984). However, we can do away with this additional machinery of level ordering by making use of the idea of the hierarchical lexicon. What we need is a template for evaluative suffixes dominated by the general suffixation template, in which it is specified additionally that the categories of base and output word are identical:

(10) $[[a]_X \, b]_Y$
        |
       $[[a]_{Xj} \, ino]_{Xk} \leftrightarrow$ [HAVING PROPERTY$_j$ TO A LESSER DEGREE]$_k$

We thus conclude that subschemas are an empirically necessary and theoretically advantageous part of the description of patterns of word formation, in order to make generalizations about subsets of words within a particular morphological category. In the next section, I will discuss semantic phenomena that provide evidence for subschemas.

3.2 Semantic subgeneralizations require subschemas

In many compounds, one of its constituents corresponds to a word that also occurs independently but assumes a specific meaning when part of a compound. An example of this phenomenon is the set of words with intensifying meaning that occur as the left constituents of Dutch XA compounds, where X = N, A, or V (Van der Sijs 2001):

(11)   Intensifying lexemes in Dutch XA compounds

noun	*example*
ber-e 'bear'	bere-sterk 'very strong', bere-gezellig 'very cosy'
bloed 'blood'	bloed-serieus 'very serious', bloed-link 'very risky'
dood 'death'	dood-eng 'very scary', dood-gewoon 'very ordinary'
kei 'boulder'	kei-goed 'very good', kei-gaaf 'very nice'
pis 'piss'	pis-nijdig 'very angry', pis-woedend 'very angry'
poep 'shit'	poep-heet 'very hot', poep-lekker 'very pleasant'
ret-e 'ass'	rete-leuk 'very nice', rete-spannend 'very exciting'
reuz-e 'giant'	reuze-leuk 'very nice', reuze-tof 'very good'
steen 'stone'	steen-goed 'very good', steen-koud 'very cold'
stok 'stick'	stok-oud 'very old', stok-doof 'very deaf'
stront 'shit'	stront-vervelend 'very boring', stront-eigenwijs 'very conceited'
adjective	
dol 'mad'	dol-blij 'very happy', dol-gelukkig 'very happy'
stom 'stupid'	stom-toevallig 'completely coincidental', stom-verbaasd 'very surprised'
verb	
kots 'vomit'	kots-misselijk 'very sick', kots-beu 'very tired of'
loei 'sizzle'	loei-hard 'very hard', loei-goed 'very good'
piep 'squeak'	piep-jong 'very young', piep-klein 'very small'
scharrel 'potter'	scharrel-ei 'free range egg', scharrel-vlees 'free range meat'
snoei 'prune'	snoei-hard 'very hard', snoei-heet 'very hot'

In these words, the first constituent no longer carries its literal meaning as specified in the left column, and functions as a word with an intensifier meaning. In a few cases there might still be a semantic explanation for the intensifier interpretation of the modifying noun and the head: *bere-sterk*, for instance, can be interpreted as 'as strong as a bear'. However, there is no obvious way in which the word *gezellig* 'cosy' can be related to a typical property of bears. This semantic reanalysis of such words as intensifiers is made overt by the fact that they can be attached productively with this specific intensifier meaning to form new adjectives. In this connection, a noteworthy point concerning the intensifiers *bere-*, *rete-*, and *reuze-* is that they consist of a consonant-final stem followed by a linking element *-e* [ə]. They appear without schwa when used as independent words. This linking element is a necessary part of these nouns when used as intensifiers.

A similar productive use of noun modifiers is found in Dutch NN compounds such as:

(12) bliksem   bliksem-actie 'fast action', bliksem-bezoek 'fast visit'
      'lightning'
      kak 'shit'   kak-buurt 'posh neigbourhood', kak-madam 'posh
                       lady'
      pracht 'beauty' pracht-stoel 'beautiful chair, pracht-vent 'great guy'
      wereld 'world'   wereld-vrouw 'fantastic woman', wereld-kans 'great
                       chance'

In all these compounds, the original meaning of the lexeme has acquired a more general and abstract meaning of intensification. In a few cases, there is an additional pejorative meaning as well. Such words are sometimes called affixoids because they have become similar to affixes in having a specialized meaning when embedded in compounds. They are not yet affixes because they correspond to lexemes, that is, unbound forms, but their meaning differs from that when used as independent lexemes.

We can formally express the affixoid nature of these compound-initial lexemes by specifying them in constructional idioms of the following form:

(13) $[[\text{bere}]_N [x]_{Ai}]_{Aj} \leftrightarrow [\text{very SEM}_i]_j$
      $[[\text{dol}]_A [x]_{Ai}]_{Aj} \leftrightarrow [\text{very SEM}_i]_j$
      $[[\text{loei}]_V [x]_{Ai}]_{Aj} \leftrightarrow [\text{very SEM}_i]_j$
      $[[\text{wereld}]_N [x]_{Ni}]_{Nj} \leftrightarrow [\text{excellent SEM}_i]_j$

Constructional idioms are morphological or syntactic schemas in which one or more positions are lexically fixed, whereas other positions are open slots, represented by variables (Jackendoff 2002a). Being embedded in constructional schemas makes these words similar to affixes. The difference is that affixes do not carry a lexical category label, and hence cannot be related to independent lexemes in the lexicon.

The existence of such schemas does not block the coining of compounds according to the general schema for NN compounds, in which the specified words still have their lexical meaning. For instance, the Dutch NN compound *wereldreis* 'world journey' has an interpretation based on the literal meaning of *wereld* 'world'.

One may wonder whether these 'affixoids' should be considered as still being related to the corresponding lexeme. An argument in favour of that position is that part of the lexeme's meaning may still be present. For instance, the lexical meaning of *dol* 'mad' is reflected by the fact that, as a modifier, it is used primarily with words denoting a psychological mood, and *pis-* carries a pejorative connotation (just as *pis* 'piss'), and is used for denoting high intensity of bad psychological moods. The prefixoid *dood-* may have the meaning of 'very serious, almost leading to death', as in *doodziek*, but also occurs with a more neutral meaning of intensity, as in *doodleuk* 'coolly'. The noun *poep* 'shit' has lost its negative connotation almost completely, and can be used for positive qualifications, as in *poep-lekker* 'very pleasant'. So in the case of these affixoids, there is variation as to the extent to which the meaning of the corresponding lexeme still plays a role. The risk of assuming a connection between the semantic content of the bound constituent and the corresponding lexeme is that of etymologizing. The historical relation between the bound and the independent use of these words is obvious, but to what extent is it also a synchronic relationship? I will not decide this issue here because it requires more extensive research and analysis, but there is probably a cline of relatedness between such lexemes used as independent words and their bound use.

We can consider these changes in the meaning of 'bound lexemes' as being cases of grammaticalization (Hopper and Traugott 2003; Ramat 2001) since these prefixoids have lost their original lexical meaning more or less, and have acquired a more general and abstract meaning of intensification. However, this does not mean that the lexical meaning of these prefixoids has become completely irrelevant, as noted above: there are cases in which the lexical meaning is still relevant, a phenomenon referred to as 'persistence' (Hopper 1991). The extension of the use of these prefixoids to new classes of host words (for instance, *poep* 'shit' being attached to *lekker* 'nice') might be taken as a manifestation of grammaticalization, which is defined as follows:

Grammaticalization is the change whereby in certain linguistic contexts speakers use parts of a construction with a grammatical function. Over time the resulting grammatical item may become more grammatical by acquiring more grammatical functions and expanding its host-classes. (Brinton and Traugott 2005: 99)

In this definition of grammaticalization, the expansion to new host words is taken as a symptom of grammaticalization, and this can be used as an argument in favour of a grammaticalization interpretation for the changes discussed above. We may speak here of new host words in the sense that new semantic classes of host words have become available, such as a positive adjective *lekker* 'nice' for an inherently negative word *poep* 'shit'. Therefore, we conclude that this is a form of grammaticalization.

As may be the case for regular affixes as well, these affixoids do not exhibit unrestricted productivity. For instance, the use of *dol-* is mainly used in combination with an adjectival head that expresses a positive feeling, as in:

(14)   dol-begerig   'very greedy'
       dol-blij   'very glad'
       dol-gelukkig   'very happy'
       dol-verliefd   'deeply in love'

The point to be noted here is that XA compounding is a productive word formation process in Dutch, but that there are restrictions on specific subcases of this general pattern. For instance, with *dol* 'very' as its first constituent, the head adjective has to denote a particular psychological mood. This can be specified in a subschema for [*dol*-A] adjectives. The observation that there may be such lexically governed differences in productivity supports a model of the grammar and the lexicon in which generalizations can be stated at different levels of abstraction (Jackendoff 2008).

The specific meaning of intensification of compound constituents illustrated in (11) correlates with these affixoids being usable in repetitive coordination, which expresses an emphatic meaning. This appears to be a systematic option for all prefixoids with intensifier meaning, as a Google search (13 May 2008) reveals:

(15)   a.   bere- en bere-goed 'very, very good'
            bloed- en bloed-mooi 'very, very beautiful'
            dood- en dood-ziek 'very, very ill'
            kei- en kei-leuk 'very, very nice'
            pis- en pis-nijdig 'very, very angry'
            poep- en poep-arm 'very, very poor'
            rete- en rete-stabiel 'very, very stable'
            reuze- en reuze-tevreden 'very, very pleased'
            steen- en steen-rijk 'very, very rich'
            stok- en stok-kreupel 'very, very crippled'
            stront- en stront-lazerus 'very, very drunk'
       b.   dol- en dol-komisch 'very, very comical'
            stom- en stom-dronken 'very, very drunken'
       c.   kots- en kots-beu 'very, very tired of'
            loei- en loei-heet 'very, very hot'
            piep- en piep-klein 'very, very small'
            snoei- en snoei-lelijk 'very, very ugly'

The same kind of repetitive coordination is possible with Dutch intensifiers that correspond to prepositions such as *door* 'through' and *in* 'in':

(16)   a.   door- en door-nat
            through and through-wet
            'wet through and through'

  b. in- en in-triest
     in- and in-sad
     'very, very sad'

If we want to make a generalization as to which elements can occur in such repetitive coordination, we need to be able to refer to the class of compound-initial words with intensifier meaning. This is possible thanks to constructional idioms like those in (13). Note, by the way, that the intensifier meaning of the word *in* 'in' is tied to its occurrence in adjectival compounds, thus providing additional evidence for the necessity of a constructional idiom representation of such sets of compounds.

Repetition of adjectives for emphatic purposes is found in other languages as well. Examples are Italian *grande grande* 'very big' and Finnish *mukava mukava* 'very comfortable' (Guevara et al. 2009). Note, however, that in Dutch, this emphatic pattern is restricted to complex adjectives with an intensifying modifier, and with obligatory gapping. For instance, one cannot say *doornat en doornat* 'wet-through and wet through, very wet', instead the gapped form in (16a) has to be used. This implies that there is a specific construction, an instantiation of coordination of adjectives with the formal property of gapping, and the corresponding semantic property of emphasis of the modifier constituent.[3]

The reality of the generalizations expressed in (13) is confirmed by the observation that in Dutch some of these prefixoids have been reanalysed as adverbs or adjectives. This is the case for *kut* and *reuze*:

(17) [kut- x]_N 'cunt-'   > kut (A) 'bad, worthless'
      [reuze- x]_N 'giant-' > reuze (A) 'fantastic'

The following sentences illustrate the adjectival use of these words:

(18) a. Ik vind dat helemaal kut
         I find that completely cunt
         'I consider that completely worthless'
      b. Het uitstapje was reuze
         The outing was giant
         'The outing has been great'

---

[3] Phrases such as *dol- en dolblij* may be derived from *dolblij and dolblij* through the rule of prosodic gapping that deletes one of two identical prosodic words (Booij 1985). However, the rule of prosodic gapping is normally optional, whereas omission of the first of two identical constituent is obligatory in these cases of emphatic repetitive coordination. This implies that this instantiation of gapping is to be considered as a subconstruction of gapping; the obligatoriness of the gapping and the formal identity of the corresponding adjectives corresponds with an emphatic meaning.

The nominal origin of *reuze* 'fantastic' is reflected by its final schwa which is a linking element, the noun when used as an independent word being *reus*. Such a development can only be understood if we assume subpatterns like $[[reuze]_N A]_A$ in the hierarchical lexicon of Dutch. The meaning of intensification that is connected to these nouns is a type of meaning expressed prototypically by adjectives, and hence the categorial reinterpretation of these nouns as adjectives in this context is a natural development. The reinterpretation of *kut* as an adjective has also led to this word having a comparative and a superlative form: *kutt-er, kut-st*, as in *Dit was het kutst van alles* 'This was the worst of all'.

Similar productive patterns have been observed for German and Swedish. In Swedish, for instance, we find *skit-bra* 'shit-good, very good' and *jätte-vinst* 'giant-profit, very high profit'. The word *jätte* can also be used as an adjective, parallel to the Dutch word *reuze*. German examples are *Klasse-film* 'class-film' and *Spitzen-film* 'top-film', both meaning 'excellent film' (Ascoop 2005; Ascoop and Leuschner 2006). In German, *klasse* 'class' can therefore also be used as a predicative adjective.

The rise of such subpatterns of compounding in which one of the constituents is lexically specified does not necessarily coincide with the meaning of the specified constituent becoming completely detached from its original lexical meaning, and vaguer. Words may acquire new and quite specific 'bound' meanings when embedded in complex words. Consider the interpretations of the Dutch noun *hoofd* 'head' when functioning as the modifier noun in NN compounds. This word has a number of related meanings, and mainly three interpretations when used as the first part of compounds:

a. (physical sense) head of a body, as in *hoofd-pijn* 'headache';
b. abstract (metaphorical) meaning 'uppermost', referring to a hierarchy, as in *hoofd-kwartier* 'headquarters';
c. abstract (metaphorical) meaning 'most important, main', as in *hoofd-ingang* 'main entrance'.

These three meanings can be observed in the following compounds:

(19) a. hoofd-haar 'head-hair, hair of the head'
          hoofd-kussen 'head cushion, pillow'
          hoofd-pijn 'head-pain, headache'
      b. hoofd-afdeling 'head-department'
          hoofd-agent 'head-agent, senior officer'
          hoofd-bestuur 'head-board, central board'
          hoofd-directie 'head-directorate, central directorate'

c. hoofd-altaar 'head-altar, main altar'
   hoofd-bezwaar 'head-objection, main objection'
   hoofd-doel 'head-goal, main goal'
   hoofd-verdachte 'head-suspect, main suspect'

It is in particular the third meaning that is typical for the compound context: a *hoofdaltaar*, for instance, is not an altar that functions as the head of all altars in the church but it is the main altar of a church. The lexemes *head* in English and *hoofd* in Dutch have a comparable range of related meanings. Yet, the meaning of *hoofd* as 'main' in compounds does not hold for English, where other words have to be used such as *main, major, chief, central, principal,* and the like. The interpretation 'main' for *hoofd* 'head' is certainly not unexpected, and a natural interpretation for this polysemous word. Yet, this meaning is not available for the word in isolation. For instance, speakers of Dutch cannot refer to a *hoofdaltaar* as *het hoofd van de altaren* 'the head of the altars' which shows that the meaning 'main' of this noun is a bound meaning. This compound-conditioned and productive interpretation of *hoofd* forms part of the linguistic knowledge of Dutch language users. Such knowledge can be expressed by subschemas, as part of the hierarchical lexicon:

(20) $[[x]_N [y]_N]_N$ (schema for NN compounds)

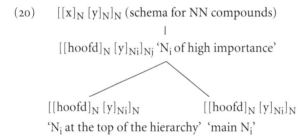

$[[hoofd]_N [y]_{Ni}]_{Nj}$ 'N$_i$ of high importance'

$[[hoofd]_N [y]_{Ni}]_N$ $[[hoofd]_N [y]_{Ni}]_N$
'N$_i$ at the top of the hierarchy' 'main N$_i$'

What the rightmost subschema expresses is that the use of *hoofd* in a compound with the meaning 'main' is a productive pattern of Dutch word formation. Again, note that this schema does not block the formation of compounds with other interpretations of the noun *hoofd*, since these can be formed in accordance with the highest schema in (20).

Similar observations as to the 'bound' interpretation of nouns in compound constructions can be made for the Dutch noun *kunst* 'art' which has acquired a productive meaning 'artificial' in NN compounds such as:

(21)   kunst-bont 'art-fur, artificial fur'
        kunst-boter 'art-butter, artificial butter, margarine'
        kunst-koe 'art-cow, artificial cow'
        kunst-mest 'art-manure, artificial manure, fertilizer'

besides compounds with the literal interpretation, as in *kunst-collectie* 'art collection'.

The phenomenon of bound interpretations for polysemous words has been noted for other languages as well. For instance, Packard observed that in Mandarin Chinese some polysemous lexemes have 'bound' meanings that are only available when they are embedded in compounds. 'The morpheme *gōng* means many things ('labour, art, industry, work, job') and it is bound in certain of these meanings ('labour, art, industry') and free in others' (Packard 2000: 68). It is a cross-linguistic phenomenon that specific interpretations of polysemous lexical items are bound to particular constructions, morphological or syntactic ones. This phenomenon is referred to as heterosemy (Lichtenberk 1991).

Dutch has AN compounds with a productive bound meaning for the adjective. An example is the use of the adjectives *oud* 'old' and *nieuw* 'new' which have acquired the meanings 'former' and 'modern, recent' respectively when part of a compound. The meanings of *nieuw-* in (22b) correspond with that of the prefix *neo-* in many European languages. The specific uses of *nieuw* in Dutch are found with language names, and with substantivized participial adjectives (Van Goethem 2008):

(22) a. oud-collega 'old-colleague, former colleague'
          oud-gevangene 'old-prisoner, ex-prisoner'
          oud-leerling 'old-pupil, former pupil'
      b. nieuw-Fries 'new-Frisian, modern Frisian'
          nieuw-Nederlands 'new Dutch, modern Dutch'
          nieuw-Zweeds 'new-Swedish, modern Swedish'
      c. nieuw-aangekomen-e 'new-arrived, newcomer, recent arrival'
          nieuw-bekeerd-e 'new-converted, neophyte, recent convert'
          nieuw-gedoopt-e 'new-baptized, recently baptized person'

Such semantic subschemas may be cases of what has been called semantic concentration (Meesters 2004). The Dutch noun *polder* 'polder' has acquired two new meanings when part of a compound. It may function as a synonym for 'typically Dutch' (the polder being a characteristic type of Dutch landscape), as in *polder-Islam* 'the Dutch variety of Islam', sometimes with negative connotations like 'narrow-minded' (23a). It is also used productively with the meaning 'ready to make compromises' (23b). This second meaning probably originated from the compound *poldermodel* 'model of organizational culture as developed in polders'. The idea is that Dutch political culture is characterized by cooperation and consensus rather than conflict. The historical background is that cooperation was necessary in order to fight the threat of water floods, and keep the dike protection in good order. This implied the acceptance of compromise solutions.

(23)   a. polder-gezeur 'polder-nagging, narrow-minded nagging'
           polder-gelul 'polder-bullshit, narow-minded bullshit'
       b. polder-cultuur 'polder-culture, consensus culture'
           polder-discussie 'polder-discussion, discussion aimed at consensus'
           polder-houding 'polder-attitude, consensus attitude'

The use of nouns in compounds as in (23b) has been qualified as 'semantic concentration' (Meesters 2004) since the meaning of the whole compound word *poldermodel* is projected ('concentrated') on the constituent word *polder*. This has also led to the coinage of the verb *polder* 'lit. to polder, to make compromises'.

   Semantic concentration can also be observed in the use of the verb *scharrel* 'to scratch' in the word *scharrel-kip* 'lit. scratch chicken, free-range chicken'. This word refers to chickens that can freely scratch the ground, and potter around. This use has been extended to other compounds:

(24)   a. scharrel-vlees
           scratch-meat
           'free-range meat'
       b. scharrel-ei
           scratch-egg
           'free-range egg'
       c. scharrel-melk
           scratch-milk
           'free-range milk'
       d. scharrel-wijn
           scratch-wine
           'eco-wine'

This use of the word *scharrel* is clearly a case of semantic concentration, the presence of the meaning of a word that is not a formal constituent, in this case 'free-range *animal*' (Meesters 2004: 52). As the last example *scharrelwijn* shows, even the notion of animal has disappeared as a necessary part of its meaning. That is, we have to assume an intermediate schema:

(25) $[[\text{scharrel}]_V[x]_{Ni}]_{Nj} \leftrightarrow [\text{ECO} [\text{SEM}_i]]_j$

which expresses this lexicalized yet productive meaning of *scharrel* when embedded in a compound. This schema correctly predicts the possibility of coining new compounds such as *scharrel-slager* 'free-range butcher, eco-butcher' (Google search 25 Oct., 2009).

Semantic concentration can also be observed in the use of *stief-* 'step' as the first part of a compound, as in *stief-moeder* 'step-mother'. The morpheme *stief* with this meaning is a bound root, like its English counterpart *step-*. It occurs in a number of established compounds with the head noun denoting a family relation such as *moeder* 'mother', or *zuster* 'sister'. We now also find it in the following compounds (from a Google search):

(26)   stief-gezin 'step-family, family with step-parents'
        stief-problemen 'step-problems, problems originating from being a step-family'
        stief-problematiek 'step-problems, problems originating from being a step-family'
        stief-informatie 'step-information, information about the problems of step-families'

Such semantic subgeneralizations are not restricted to words in compound-initial position; the phenomenon of semantic specialization can also be observed for the heads of Dutch compounds:

(27)   *nouns*
        baron 'baron' > rich dealer   afval-baron 'trash-baron, rich dealer in trash'
        boer 'farmer' > seller   sigaren-boer 'cigar-farmer, cigar seller'
        man 'man' > seller   bladen-man 'magazine-man, magazine seller'
        marathon 'marathon' >   jazz-marathon 'jazz-marathon'
        long session

        adjectives
        vol 'full, with high amount   betekenis-vol 'meaning-full, meaningful'
        of'
        vrij 'free, not being subject   belasting-vrij 'tax-free'
        to'
        ziek 'sick, excessively fond   familie-ziek 'family-sick, extremely fond
        of'   of one's family'

These Dutch words have developed more specialized meanings when embedded as heads of compounds. German and Swedish exhibit similar patterns (Ascoop 2005; Ascoop and Leuschner 2006).

    This type of lexicalization can be found cross-linguistically. A nice example comes from Maale, a North Omotic language spoken in Southern Ethiopia. The noun *nayi* 'child' has developed the general meaning 'cattle caretaker', as illustrated by the following complex words (Amha 2001: 78):

(28) a. bayi nayi
         cattle child
         'one who brings cattle to the grazing area'
      b. waari nayi
         goat child
         'one who takes care of goats'
      c. móótsi naya
         cattle.camp child
         'one who lives in a cattle camp and takes care of cattle there'

Because cattle herding is historically a task of children in the Maale-speaking society, the word for child has acquired a more general meaning.

   In Afrikaans, a daughter language of Dutch as spoken in South Africa, personal names can be compounded with the 3rd person plural pronoun *hulle*. The productive meaning of this constructional idiom is that of collectivity 'x and all others who belong to him':

(29) Jan-hulle 'John-they, John and all others belonging to him'
      Pa-hulle 'father-they, father and his relatives'
      Oom Jan-hulle 'Uncle John-they, Uncle John and his relatives'

In sum, we need subschemas for complex words in order to express the relevant semantic generalizations. In section 3.4 we will see that such subschemas may give rise to new derivational affixes.

3.3 Synchronic arguments for subschemas: headedness variation in compounding

It is clear that Williams' Right-hand Head Rule (Williams 1981) cannot be a rule in the sense of a universal since many languages have left-headed compounds. Hence, one might consider the position of the head as a morphological parameter. For instance, Germanic languages may be qualified as right-headed, and Romance languages such as Italian as left-headed (Scalise 1984, 1992). Another example of a left-headed language is Maori (Bauer 1993). The problem for such a parameter approach is that languages may have both left-headed and right-headed compounds. This is the case for Romance languages, and for Chinese and Japanese. Vietnamese has left-headed native compounds, and right-headed compounds borrowed from Chinese. In Javanese, compounds are left-headed except for some right-headed compounds of Sanskrit origin (Bauer 2009: 349).

Catalan, Italian, and Spanish also have sets of right-headed compounds, even though the default position of compound heads is the left position. Examples of such compounds in Catalan and Spanish are the following:

(30)   *Catalan*: eco-sociologia 'eco-sociology', euro-exèrcit 'European army', tele-porqueria 'TV rubbish';
       Spanish: auto-escuela 'driving school', cine-club 'cinema club', tele-novela 'TV soap opera', video-arte 'video art'.

Rainer and Varela (1992: 121) make the following remark with respect to these types of compound:

Such right-headed n-n compounds would have to be limited to a fixed number of first elements […] which is quite atypical since compound types can generally be defined at the categorial level. […] Another property which they share with prefixes is their form: they are typically bisyllabic and end in a vowel.

Therefore, they consider morphemes like *auto-* as prefixes. 'The alternative would consist in setting up an independent sub-type of word formation characterized by right-headedness, a purely pragmatically driven rule of interpretation, and severe restrictions on the number and form of elements that can serve as left constituents' (Rainer and Varela 1992: 121–122).

   In the framework of Construction Morphology we can analyse these words as right-headed compounds without losing the generalization that most Romance compounds are left-headed since we can assume constructional idioms such as:

(31) $[[\text{auto}]_{Ni}\ [x]_{Nj}]_{Nk} \leftrightarrow [\text{SEM}_j \text{ with relation R to SEM}_i]_k$

This schema states that right-headed compounds are possible with a number of specific, listed constituents. By lexically specifying the left constituent of these compound schemas we express that the class of right-headed compounds in Spanish is restricted to compounds that begin with a word from a closed set. The difference between *auto* and *tele* is that *tele* 'television' occurs as an independent word as well, unlike *auto*. Hence, the meaning of *auto* is only retrievable from the complex words in which it occurs, and in that sense it is a prefix.

   The same observation has been made for Italian. As Schwarze (2005: 149) pointed out, a restricted set of nouns can occur in right-headed compounds The best example is that of compounds beginning with *auto* 'car', as in:

(32)   auto-centro 'car center', auto-convoglio 'convoy', auto-dromo 'motor-racing circuit', auto-linea' bus route', auto-servizio 'car service', auto-stop 'hitch-hiking'

They contrast with the regular left-headed NN compounds such as *auto-ambulanza* 'ambulance', *auto-botte* 'tank truck', *auto-cisterna* 'tank truck', and *auto-pompa* 'fire truck'. Other types of right-headed compounds in Italian begin with words or roots such as *foto-*, *radio-*, and *tele-*.

The constructional idiom format can be used to account for Italian root compounds as well. For instance, the root *tele-* can be used in right-headed complex words such as *tele-spettatore* 'television watcher'. In Italian, the morpheme *tele* is not a word by itself but only occurs as part of complex words; hence, it is to be qualified as a root. It also lacks a syntactic category. The fact that *tele* is a root can be expressed by a constructional idiom $[tele[x]_N]_N$ which expresses that *tele* can only occur as part of a complex word, and does not determine the syntactic category of the compound in which it occurs.

Schwarze (2005: 317) used these data to argue that we must distinguish between rules and pattern-imitation:

Constructed words arise from a generative system which may be described in terms of rules. These rules operate on morphological segments and their semantic representations in such a way that the forms and meanings of possible words are defined. [...] Complex, non-constructed words, on the other hand, are brought about by "paragrammatical procedures" [such as univerbation and pattern-based word formation].

In the framework presented here we can avoid a dual mechanism model in which words are constructed according to two different procedures, as proposed by Schwarze. By making use of the concept of constructional schema these data receive a straightforward interpretation: these subsets of right-headed compounds can be accounted for by means of constructional idioms. Thus, we do not have to qualify this kind of compound formation as 'paragrammatical'.

Catalan provides examples of the same phenomenon (Pérez Saldanya and Vallès 2005). The noun *ràdio* 'id.' can be used as the head in constructions like *radio-despertador* 'radio alarm clock' and *ràdio pirata* 'pirate radio station'. It is also used productively as a prefixoid that functions as a modifier of the noun to which it is attached, as in *radio-pirata* 'illegal radio amateur' and *radio-novella* 'radio serial'. Pérez Saldanya and Vallès therefore rightly conclude that the Catalan lexicon has to contain a productive subschema for nouns of the structure $[radio-N]_N$ with the meaning 'N related to radio communication'.

Mandarin Chinese is reported to have both left-headed and right-headed compounds (Ceccagno and Basciano 2009; Packard 2000). Right-headed compounds have either a noun or a verb in head position. In the case of verbal compounds, the non-head functions as a modifier of the verb. Verbal compounds are left-headed, however, if the non-head functions as an argument of the verb. The following examples illustrate these patterns (Ceccagno and Basciano 2009: 485):

(33)   *right-headed*:
       $[[\text{dú}]_N[\text{fàn}]_N]_N$ drug-criminal 'drug criminal'
       $[[\text{hán}]_N[\text{shòu}]_V]_V$ letter-sell 'order by mail'

       left-headed:
       $[[\text{jìn}]_V[\text{dú}]_N]_V$ prohibit-poison 'ban sale and abuse of drugs'

In other words, generalizations about the position of the head must be made in terms of the corresponding semantic structure. In attributive compounds the head is on the right, whereas in compounds with a verb-argument structure the head is on the left. Such generalizations can be expressed by morphological schemas, which by definition express the correspondence between the form and meaning of complex words.

   In Japanese, compounds are usually right-headed. Yet, there is a class of Sino-Japanese compounds that is left-headed. These are bi-morphemic compounds with a verbal noun on the left, and an internal argument on the right. The morphemes involved are bound morphemes that do not occur as independent words (Kageyama 1982, 2009):

(34)   a. soo-kin
          send-money
          'remit'
       b. ki-koku
          return-country
          'return to one's country'
       c. syuk-ka
          go.out-fire
          'a fire breaking out'

Such left-headed compounds can be embedded in regular right-headed compounds:

(35) $[[\text{soo-kin}]_{VN} \ [\text{hoohoo}]_N]_N$
       $[[\text{send-money}]_{VN} \ [\text{method}]_N]_N$
       'way of remittance'

We can maintain the generalization that Japanese compounds tend to be right-headed by assuming an abstract schema for right-headed compounds. There will be an additional left-headed schema in the Japanese lexicon for this special class of Sino-Japanese compounds. This schema will then dominate constructional idioms of the following types:

(36)   [[*soo*]$_{VN}$ [x]$_N$]$_{VN}$ 'sending N' (where VN = verbal noun, and N is a Sino-Japanese noun)

Note that these morphemes are bound morphemes in the sense that they do not occur as words by themselves, only embedded in compounds. This is expressed by representing them as fillers of the slots of constructional idioms. Kageyama (1982: 233) pointed out that the productivity of these patterns varies. A very productive one is *rai-* 'come' that attaches to almost all names of cities and towns:

(37)   rai-han 'coming to Osaka', rai-sin 'coming to Kobe', rai-huku 'coming to Fukuoka'

'If a new city is born, a new *rai*-compound will most probably be made' (Kageyama 1982: 233). So there is a constructional idiom [[*rai*]$_{VN}$ [x]$_N$]$_{VN}$. Furthermore, a morpheme like *datu-* 'escape' has become productive to make similar VN compounds with non-Chinese nouns:

(38)   datu-sarariiman 'quit the job of an office worker'
       datu-sutoresu 'to get rid of stress'
       datu-tokai 'to get out of a big city'
       data-koogai 'get rid of environmental pollution'

In sum, the following hierarchy of compound schemas can be established for Japanese:

(39)

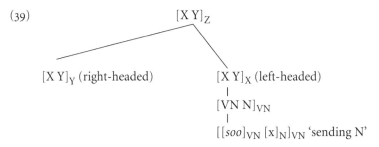

There are more languages whose compounds can be either right-headed or left-headed. Biak, an Austronesian language spoken on New Guinea, has left-headed NN compounds, in which the head position is filled by nouns like *man* 'man, bird-like entity' or *in* 'female person, fish-like entity'. There are also right-headed NN compounds, however. In that case, the compound expresses a specific semantic pattern, either 'N$_2$ is part of N$_1$', or 'N$_2$ is a product of N$_1$' (Van den Heuvel 2006: 91–93):

(40) a. randip-vukór
          pig-head
          'head of a pig'
      b. ai-snáw
          tree-branch
          'branch of a tree'

Thus, besides an abstract schema for Biak left-headed NN compounds, we
need an additional one for specific semantic types of right-headed compounds. In this respect, Biak is similar to Chinese, for which we also observed
a correlation between semantics and position of the head. Once more, we see
that the idea of a hierarchical lexicon with subschemas expressing intermediate generalizations is essential for a proper account of patterns of word
formation.

3.4 Diachronic arguments for subschemas: routes to affixhood

In section 3.2 we saw a number of cases in which words when embedded in
compounds have acquired a special meaning. This phenomenon may be
considered a case of grammaticalization. When a constituent of a compound
acquires a 'bound' meaning, this does not necessarily lead to that meaning
being an abstract, grammatical one, as we saw above, but clearly there is a
transition from a lexical to a less lexical meaning. This conclusion is supported by the existence of lexical affixes in some Amerindian languages
(Gerdts 1998; Mithun 1997, 1999). Salishan and Wakashan languages have
lexical suffixes, that is, suffixes with a specific, non-grammatical meaning
(Gerdts 1998). Mithun reports that Spokane, a Salishan language has about
100 lexical suffixes that are similar to noun roots except that they do not occur
as independent words. Yup'ik has more than 450 verb-like derivational suffixes. Most of the Yup'ik verbal suffixes have verbal roots as counterparts,
with differences in form correlating with differences in meaning (Mithun
1999: 48–56, 2010). The Amerindian language Bella Coola also has a set of
lexical suffixes (Saunders and Davis 1975).

    For the Athapaskan language Slave, Rice reports that some nouns only
appear as parts of compounds, not independently. Yet, such nouns can be
used productively for coining new compounds. This applies, for instance, to
the bound noun *teh* 'water' (Rice 2009: 544). This suggests a compound
schema with its head position filled lexically with the root *teh*. Similar facts
obtain for Mohawk (Mithun 2009: 580).

Mithun (1999: 55) points out that 'a historical origin in compounding accounts well for the special properties of lexical affixes' a position also defended by Carlson: 'productive compounding, particularly of nominal objects and locatives led to the set of bound morphemes referred to as lexical affixes' (Carlson 1990: 69). Lexical suffixes in Spokane developed from right members of compounds, and lexical prefixes from left members (Carlson 1990: 78). The compound origin of some of these Spokane suffixes is also supported by the fact that they begin with a linking element [ɬ] or a nominalizing element [s] that does not occur at the beginning of the corresponding independent root.

The Amazonian language Matses of the Panoan family also features lexical affixes: it has a set of 27 body part prefixes that denote various body parts but have some other meanings as well. For instance, the lexical prefix *an-* has meanings like 'mouth, tongue, (hand)palm, (foot)sole', like its independent word counterpart *ana*, but also additional meanings like 'cavity, concave surface, interior, centre'. Hence, synchronically, the prefix is not just a bound allomorph of the corresponding noun. Fleck proposes the hypothesis that 'Panoan (verbal) prefixation evolved from past noun incorporation that co-existed with noun-noun and noun-adjective compounding that involved synchronic reduction of body-part roots' (Fleck 2006: 93).

Lexical prefixes also occur in Japanese, and hence 'Japanese has a far richer stock of prefixes than English' (Kageyama 1982: 226). For instance, there is a substantial set of prefixes with adjectival meaning such as *dai-* 'big', *oo-* 'big', *tyuu-* 'middle', *syoo-* 'small', *ko-* 'small', *koo-* 'high', *tei-* 'low', *sin-* 'new', *ko-* 'old', *huru-* 'old', *zyuu-* 'heavy', *kei-* 'light', *tyoo-* 'long', *tan-* 'short', *kyuu-* 'sudden', *bi-* 'beautiful', *aku-* 'bad', and *koo-* 'good'.

The existence of 'bound' compound constituents or lexical affixes receives a straightforward interpretation in a lexicon with morphological schemas that express generalizations about subsets of compounds that share one of the constituents, that is constructional idioms (schemas with one position specified) at the compound level. The bound nature of the specified constituents is expressed by their not being co-indexed with independent lexemes in the lexicon. The origin of such lexical suffixes can thus be explained by the assumption that particular lexemes can 'survive' in compound schemas in which they occupy a slot, even though the corresponding lexeme got lost.

In short, many languages have compounds with bound stems that do not occur outside complex words. An interesting case of a language with lots of bound stems is the Australian language Ngalakgan (Baker 2008). Many of the stems in this language occur either as left, non-head constituent (that is, they are right-binding), or as right, head constituent (that is, they are left-binding). Right-binding and left-binding stems are hence similar to prefixes and suffixes respectively. Thus, the distinction between such stems and lexical affixes might be blurred: 'Left- and right-binding stems are synchronically at the border between stem- and affix-like behaviour' (Baker 2008: 139). Both these stems and disyllabic affixes form prosodic words of their own. Yet, there are also prosodic differences between these two categories as to their effect on the stress pattern of the complex words involved: with real suffixes main stress may be on the stem or the suffix, whereas in compounds with bound stems main stress is always on the head (Baker 2008: 149). In Baker's analysis, this follows from the fact that suffixes can be treated in two ways: either they form a prosodic word of their own, or they form one prosodic word with the preceding morpheme. A bound stem, on the other hand, always forms a prosodic word of its own and hence words with such stems are prosodic compounds. This contrast is illustrated in (41) (Baker 2008: 149):

(41)   *suffix* -pulu:
    acu-(jàppa)$_\omega$ (-púlu)$_\omega$ or   cu-(jáppa-pùlu)$_\omega$
    F-sister-PL   F-sister-PL
    'my sisters'   'my sisters'

    bound stem ŋini
    cu- (jàppa)$_\omega$ (ŋíni)$_\omega$
    F-sister-1.m.DAT
    'my sister'

Since the main stress is on the last prosodic word, words with bound stems always have main stress on that bound stem, whereas in the case of suffixes the main stress may be located on the first syllable of the single prosodic word.

The bound nature of a right-bound stem like *mala* 'group' that functions as a modifier can be represented lexically as $[[mala]_N[x]_N]_N$. That is, we need constructional idioms for the instantiations of the general productive pattern of NN compounding in Ngalakgan in which use is made of bound stems. These compound structures will then categorically correspond to prosodic compounds.

In section 1.4 a related problem of interpretation (compounding or affixation?) was discussed concerning the status of the morpheme *out* in English verbs such as *out-bid, out-perform, out-play, out-rank*, and *out-stay*. The morpheme *out* when combined with a verb has acquired the meaning of excess, or more precisely 'to exceed someone else in V-ing', where V denotes the base verb. The morpheme *out-* might be considered a prefix here because of this specific meaning of *out* when combined with verbs. Indeed it is often referred to as a prefix in the morphological literature. The same holds for a morpheme like *over* that has three meanings when combined with verbs among which is the meaning of excess (Lieber 2004: 130):

(42)   *locational*: over-lap, over-fly, over-turn
        completive: over-ride, over-run
        excess: over-bid, over-burden, over-indulge

Lieber observed that prefixes that correspond to a lexeme exhibit much more polysemy than derivational affixes, which do not have such a counterpart and tend to have one abstract meaning. Therefore, Lieber (2004: 129) proposed the hypothesis that 'prefixal *over-* is nothing more than a bound version of prepositional *over*'. This implies that such verbs are verbal compounds but that a specific subschema is necessary to express the specific meaning of *over* in combination with verbs.

In sum, what we see here, is that words may receive specific interpretations when embedded in complex words (Brinton and Traugott 2005: 129), and the recurrence of such lexicalized bound meanings in new words of the same type. This combination of being bound to specific constructions and productivity signals the existence of constructional idioms, schemas with partially pre-specified constituents and corresponding meanings. Thus, we may assume the following constructional idiom for verbs like *outbid* (repeated from section 1.4):

(43) $[[out]_{Adv}[x]_{Vi}]_{Vj} \leftrightarrow$ [to exceed someone/thing in SEM_i]$_j$

The advantage of assuming subschemas is that we do not have to introduce a formal morphological category like semi-affix or affixoid for these phenomena. Subschemas express that speakers are able to make subgeneralizations about subsets of compounds, and thus create new words in which the lexicalized meaning of a subconstituent of a complex word can be used productively.

The label of semi-affix is also used by Marchand (1969: 356) for the second part of words like the following:

(44)   a. man-like, praise-worthy, side-ways, clock-wise, hard-ware
        b. whore-monger, play-wright

The right constituents in the words (44a) do correspond to independent lexemes, but they have particular interpretations when embedded in complex words. The right constituents in (44b) do not occur independently anymore. Again, the productive patterns exemplified in (44a) can be expressed by sub-schemas for compounds with the right constituent specified.

Such subpatterns are a potential source of new derivational suffixes, if the relation with the corresponding independent lexeme is no longer felt due to semantic change, or if that lexeme gets lost. For instance, the English suffix *-ful*, as in *beautiful*, may no longer be perceived as related to the lexeme *full*. A suffix like *-hood* derives historically from a lexeme with the meaning 'quality'. The Dutch suffix *-lijk* and its English counterpart *-ly* derive from the noun *leik* 'body', and the suffix *-dom* (a suffix in both Dutch and English) derives from a lexeme for 'dominion'. It is well known that many derivational affixes derive historically from lexemes used as the first or second constituent of compounds. As Malkiel put it: 'Diachronically, the transmutation of a "blurred" compound into an affixal derivative is an almost trivial phenomenon' (Malkiel 1978: 128). The best known case for Romance languages is the adverbial suffix *-mente* (French form *-ment*) which derives from the Latin noun *mens* 'mind' in its ablative form, as in *clara mente* 'with a clear mind, in a clear way'.

This rise of derivational morphemes is rightly qualified as grammaticalization (Aikhenvald 2007: 58), since these morphemes have become affixes. If situated at the endpoint of grammaticalization, these morphemes have abstract grammatical properties, but such bound morphemes may still have a rather specific meaning, as we saw above. Hence, it seems that there is a cline for such bound morphemes ranging from a more lexical to a more grammatical meaning, a pattern characteristic of grammaticalization.

Other examples from Dutch and German of suffixes deriving from lexemes are the following:

(45)   *Dutch*
       -baar   draag-baar 'bearable'
       -gewijs   groeps-gewijs 'group by group'
       -heid   wijs-heid 'wisdom'
       -loos   vruchte-loos 'fruitless'
       -schap   vriend-schap 'friendship'

       German
       -bar   frucht-bar 'fruitful'
       -heit   Weis-heit 'wisdom'
       -los   arbeits-los 'without work, unemployed'
       -schaft   Freund-schaft 'friendship'
       -weise   ausnahms-weise 'exceptionally'

The lexical origin of such suffixes can still be seen in their phonological shape: they contain a full, unreduced vowel, form a phonological word of their own, and carry a secondary stress, just like the heads of compounds (Booij 1995; Dalton-Puffer and Plag 2000).

The Dutch adverb *weer* 'again' has a formally corresponding morpheme in initial position in complex verbs like:

(46) a. weer-leg
        again-lay
        'to refute'
     b. weer-staan
        again-stand
        'to resist'
     c. weer-spreek
        again-speech
        'to counter-argue'
     d. weer-kaats
        again-throw
        'to reflect, to re-echo'
     e. weer-klink
        again-sound
        'to resound'

The bound meaning of *weer* is 'in opposition to', or 'in inverse direction'. Hence, there is still some relation to the meaning of *weer* as an independent word, but this relation is pretty weak, and we might therefore consider *weer* a real prefix. This means in terms of representation that it is not co-indexed with the independent lexeme *weer* 'again'. Becoming an affix thus means loss of co-indexation with a separate lexeme.

The Dutch/English/German prefix *be-* developed from complex verbs beginning with the morpheme *bi* 'at'. This prefix has lost its lexical meaning completely, and in Dutch and German it now serves to create various sorts of transitive verbs. That is, it is now a purely grammatical morpheme.

Thus, the rise of bound meanings for lexemes embedded in complex words, and the change of lexemes into affixes shows the necessity of assuming morphological subschemas that account for the bound interpretations of lexemes, and for the possibility of such changes.

3.5 Semantic arguments for constructional schemas

The semantic variation in word formation processes has been a persistent topic of debate among morphologists. In this section I discuss how the patterns of polysemy in word formation provide evidence for different levels of generalization and degrees of abstractness in a hierarchical lexicon.

A well-known example of polysemy in the realm of word formation is the set of deverbal nouns ending in -er in Dutch, English, and German. This polysemy has been discussed widely in the literature. Such deverbal nouns can have a range of interpretations, as illustrated by the following Dutch examples (Booij 1986, 2002*b*: 123):

(47)   *animate agent*   bakk-er 'baker' < bak- 'to bake'
                            schrijv-er 'writer' < schrijv- 'to write'
       non-animate agent houd-er 'container' < houd- 'contain'
                            wijz-er 'pointer' < wijz- 'to point'
       instrument   maai-er 'mower' < maai- 'to mow'
                            zoem-er 'buzzer' < zoem- 'to buzz'
       object   voor-lader 'front-loader' < voor-laad- 'to front-
                            load'
                            rok-er-tje 'lit. smok-er-DIM, cigar/cigarette' <
                            rook- 'to smoke'
       event   miss-er 'failure' < mis- 'to fail'
                            treff-er 'hit' < tref- 'to hit'
       causer   af-knapp-er 'what makes you break down' < af-
                            knap- 'to break down'
                            gill-er 'what makes you scream' < gil- 'to scream'

Similar patterns of polysemy obtain for such agent nouns in English (Booij and Lieber 2004; Ryder 1999*a,b*), German (Meibauer et al. 2004), and Romance languages (Rainer 2005). Importantly, such deverbal nouns in -er often have more than one meaning. For instance, the Dutch deverbal noun *tell-er* 'lit. count-er' may denote both an agent (someone who counts) and an instrument.

There are three approaches to the problem of polysemy in word formation. The most radical option is taken by so called separationist morphologists: there is no systematic form–meaning correspondence in morphology, and therefore form and meaning should be accounted for by different modules of the grammar (Beard 1995). This, however, is an option that we should not take since it means that we give up the linguist's task of accounting for the cross-linguistic systematicity that we find in polysemy.

If we do assume systematicity in the relation between form and meaning, there are two options that do not necessarily exclude each other: monosemy and polysemy. In the monosemy approach we assign a very general and vague meaning (often referred to as *Gesamtbedeutung*, a term coined by Roman Jakobson) to a certain morphological pattern. This approach is a sensible first step in the analysis of compounds which exhibit a wide variety of meaning relations between their constituents. It also makes sense for the class of verbs derived from nouns through conversion in Dutch and English (Booij 1979). This is what Copestake and Briscoe (1995: 16–17) call 'constructional polysemy' or vagueness.

Is the monosemy approach applicable to the interpretational variation observed for the deverbal nouns listed in (47)? It has been argued that the different interpretations of at least a subset of these meanings might indeed be reduced to a general meaning: the deverbal suffix *-er* derives subject names (Booij 1986; Rappaport Hovav and Levin 1992). The subject (or external argument) of the base verb usually carries the semantic role of Agent, and hence we get deverbal *-er*-nouns with the corresponding semantic role. The notion Agent used here is a very general notion, and is meant to also encompass the semantic role of subjects of verbs of experience and belief. Thus, we account for nouns such as *hearer* and *believer* derived from verbs where the degree of agentivity is pretty low. In Dutch, we find deverbal nouns such as *stijger* 'riser' and *daler* 'dropper' both used for qualifying the behaviour of shares at the stock market, derived from verbs with a single argument with the semantic role of Theme, *stijgen* 'to rise', and *dalen* 'to drop'. These verbs are usually qualified as unaccusative verbs. By qualifying deverbal *-er*-nouns as subject names instead of Agent names we account for the existence of these nouns as well.

However, the monosemy approach cannot do justice to the whole range of interpretations. In particular, the object, event, and causer interpretations cannot be derived from the general characterization 'subject name'. Hence, we need a 'regular polysemy' approach in which a prototypical meaning forms the starting point for deriving other meanings through the semantic extension mechanisms of metaphor and metonymy. The Agent role is prototypically assigned to human beings, but non-human agents and even non-animate agents can also function as subjects of verbs: a movie can be said to thrill people and therefore be referred to as a *thriller*, and a *container* is a inanimate entity that contains something. Nouns such as *computer* and *printer* can be seen as Agent nouns with a personified Agent because a computer computes something, and a printer prints something (Booij 1986: 163; Heyvaert 2003). The driving force behind this ramification of the conceptual category of Agent is that of metaphor: we can conceive of devices that are able to perform certain actions as agents. This metaphorical interpretation of the notion Agent can be seen as the source of the rise of the instrumental meaning. The non-animate meaning of *printer*, for instance, can be circumscribed as 'instrument for printing', and such interpretations might have been the historical source for the development of an instrumental subschema. This kind of polysemy through metaphor is to be qualified as sense extension, the extension of the range of meanings of a word through conceptual mechanisms such as metaphor and metonymy. The conventionalized metaphorical interpretation of certain words leads to new senses of such words. Moreover, there are also instrument nouns for which the metaphorical interpretation 'personified agent' is not possible, as is illustrated by the following examples from Dutch:

(48)   klopp-er 'knock-er'
       krabb-er 'scrap-er'
       kurken-trekk-er 'cork-pull-er, cork screw'
       veg-er 'sweep-er, brush'

You cannot say, for instance, that a *veger* sweeps the floor, only that one sweeps the floor with a *veger*. Therefore, we have to conclude that synchronically the instrumental interpretation is not necessarily connected to an agentive interpretation of the same word. This implies that it is not only individual words but also the constructional schema for deverbal *-er*-nouns as such that has become polysemous: there is a separate subschema for instrumental deverbal nouns.

The rise of this instrumental subschema might also be interpreted as a case of metonymic sense extension: the word in *-er* is used for one of the participants in the event denoted by the base verb. We need this latter type of explanation anyway because the object, event, and causer interpretation cannot be related metaphorically to the Agent role of the subject. In general, then, we need some other explanation for these non-agentive types of meaning of deverbal *-er*-nouns (Booij 1986; Booij and Lieber 2004; Heyvaert 2003; Panther and Thornburg 2003). The basic generalization is that these nouns can denote another participant in the event denoted by the verb than the agent. These sense extensions can therefore be seen as resulting from metonymy. The existence of a number of semantic subschemas for a word formation process is also referred to as semantic fragmentation (Rainer 2003).

For each of the deverbal *-er*-nouns we have to specify their conventional interpretation(s) in the lexicon. As we saw above, many of these words can have more than one interpretation. In a hierarchical lexicon we can assume subschemas for the different interpretations such as Agent, Instrument, Object, etc. These subschemas express which of the options that are sanctioned by the general abstract schema are used productively, and function as the level at which new deverbal *-er*-nouns are coined. They specify in a direct fashion how a new word for an agent, an instrument, or an object involved in a certain type of action can be coined.

A first approximation of the specification of Dutch deverbal *er-* nouns is (49):

(49) $[V_i\text{-er}]_{Nj} \leftrightarrow$ [entity involved in SEM$_i$]$_j$

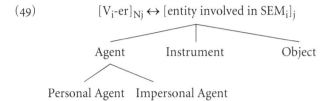

Individual deverbal *-er*-nouns may be linked to more than one of these subschemas because we also find this polysemy at the level of the individual word. For instance, the Dutch word *in-ruil-er* 'in-trad-er' denotes both someone who replaces his car for another one (agent name) and the object of the transaction (object name).

This hierarchy thus specifies the different meanings of deverbal *er*-nouns, and their common properties. It does not give direct expression to the nature of the semantic relationships between the (prototypical) Agent interpretation and the other ones. The semantic-conceptual extension mechanisms are to be taken as the driving forces behind this polysemy pattern that is specifiable in a hierarchical lexicon. The hierarchy of general schema and subschemas is a synchronic description of the relevant set of words, specifies the attested patterns, and the possibilities for coining new words of the different subtypes. It thus expresses how the conceptual extension mechanisms have been conventionalized in the lexicon of a particular language (Copestake and Briscoe 1996).

This interpretation of the role of subschemas as being directly involved in word formation is supported by historical evidence. As Rainer shows, there are a lot of Spanish deverbal nouns in *-dor* (the counterpart of English *-er*) for which either only instrumental interpretations are recorded or for which the agentive use is recorded much later than the instrumental use (Rainer 2005).

The role of convention in establishing semantic subpatterns of a morphological category can also be seen when we compare different word formation schemas for nouns that denote persons. Both in English and Dutch, for example, the nominalizing suffix *-ist* that attaches to adjectives and nouns can only be used to denote human beings with a certain ideology (*Marxist*) or profession (*violinist*), and never appears in nouns that denote non-animate agents or instruments, unlike nouns in *-er*. This means that the extension pattern is specifically linked to the morphological schema for *-er*-nouns, and thus leads to subschemas for this morphological category.

The necessity of a distinction between the actual polysemy patterns in a language-specific lexicon and the driving forces behind polysemy (metaphor, metonymy, conceptual extension schemas) is also clear from another well-known case of polysemy in word formation, the different meanings of deverbal words that end in the English suffix *-ery* (Lieber 2004: 41) and its counterparts *-erij* in Dutch (Hüning 1999) and *-erei* in German (Hüning 1996). These suffixes derive from French loans with the deverbal suffix *-erie*. German deverbal nouns with *-erie* exhibit three basic meanings: event, result of the event, and location of the event. More than one meaning may be found for one single word, as is the case for *Brauerei* 'brewery' which has both an action and a location meaning. The common driving force behind the polysemy of both types of deverbal nouns, those in *-er* and those in *-erie* is that the verbal base denotes an event with a number of entities involved. The deverbal noun therefore denotes one of the entities involved in the event. Yet, we have to specify the concomitant set of meanings for each morphological category because they may differ as to which of the set of potential meanings of a morphological category (as determined by general cognitive mechanisms) have become conventionalized. For instance, as Hüning (1996: 220) points out, the German nouns in *-erei* can never be used as instrument names, unlike *-er*-nouns, although instruments may be involved in the event denoted by the base verb of the *-erei*-noun.

Moreover, the polysemy of a morphological category may have other causes than conceptual extension schemas (Rainer 2005). Other factors that may be involved are ellipsis and homonymization. In French, the instrumental interpretation of nouns in *-eur* and *-euse* can often be interpreted as the result of ellipsis (omission of the noun) in the patterns *appareil* (masculine noun) + adjective in *-eur* or *machine* (feminine noun) + adjective in *-euse*, as in *(appareil) tondeuse* 'pair of clippers'. The different adjectival endings reflect the gender distinction between the two head nouns. In some Romance languages the descendant of the Latin locative suffix *-torium* became, due to phonetic change, identical to that of the Latin agentive suffix *-torem*, as in Catalan *-dor* that appears in both agent and locative nouns. This is a case of homonymization. Hence, patterns of polysemy do not necessarily follow from cognitive extension schemas but may also be due to historical coincidence. Consequently, the actual hierarchy of the set of deverbal *-er*-nouns is not necessarily completely isomorphic to the conceptual networks and extension mechanisms that lie behind these patterns of polysemy.

Another example of semantic fragmentation is the occurrence of a set of meanings for denominal *-er*-nouns in Dutch (Van Santen 1992: Chapter 7).

With a few exceptions such nouns denote persons. The general meaning of this morphological pattern can be circumscribed as 'person classified according to its relation with what is denoted by the base noun'. At least the following subclasses may be distinguished:

(50) a. *inhabitant of N*
          Amsterdam 'id.'   Amsterdamm-er 'inhabitant of A'.
          Hoogeveen 'id.'   Hoogeven-er 'inhabitant of H'
      b. *person with relation to N*
          VVD 'liberal party'   VVD-er 'member of VVD'
          AOW 'state pension'   AOW-er 'state pensioner'
          20e eeuw '20th century'   20e-eeuw-er '20th-century person'
          apotheek 'pharmacy'   apothek-er 'pharmacist'
          watersport 'water sports' watersport-er 'water sports enthusiast'
          rolstoel 'wheel chair'   rolstoel-er 'person using a wheel-chair'
          harde lijn 'hard line'   harde-lijn-er 'hard-liner'
          Rode Kruis 'Red Cross'   Rode-Kruis-er 'Red Cross-er'

Denominal *-er*-nouns also denote inanimate objects with a property mentioned by the base noun:

(51) [tien-pond]-er 'ten-pound-er'
      [dubbel-dekk]-er 'double-deck-er'
      [drie-wiel]-er 'three-wheel-er, tricycle'
      [twee-kapp]-er 'two-roof-er, semi-detached house'
      [twee-takk]-er 'two-branch-er, flower with two branches'

As these examples illustrate, the base constituent of these names for non-animate entities is a compound consisting of a quantifier and a noun.

How should we interpret the multiple use of these denominal *-er*-nouns? It is not sufficient to state that the meaning of such nouns is a Gesamtbedeutung, 'entity with some relation R to its base noun'. For instance, the specific use of the suffix *-er* for the formation of inhabitative names has been conventionalized into a productive subschema. This comes as no surprise given that the suffix *-er* in geographical names derives from the Germanic suffix *-warja*, whereas the agentive suffix *-er* derives historically from the Latin suffix *-arius* (Meibauer et al. 2004: 157). There is also synchronic evidence for the relative autonomy of this inhabitative subschema of denominal *-er*-nouns. For instance, these words have specific paradigmatic relations with the class of nouns for female inhabitatives marked with the suffix *-se*, whereas other personal nouns in *-er* have a female counterpart that ends in *-ster*:

(52) a. Amsterdamm-er 'inhabitant of A.'   Amsterdam-se 'fem. inhabitant
                                             of A.'
          Hoogeveen-er 'inhabitant of H.'   Hoogeveen-se 'fem. inhabitant
                                             of H.'
      b. VVD-er 'member of VVD'   VVD-ster 'fem. member of VVD'
          AOW-er 'state pensioner'   AOW-ster 'fem. state pensioner'
          wetenschapp-er 'scientist'   wetenschap-ster 'fem. scientist'

The female suffix -se replaces the inhabitative -er, whereas the suffix -ster
replaces -er in other personal nouns. Words such as *Amsterdam-ster or
*VVD-se are ill-formed. That is, the two subpatterns exhibit different para-
digmatic relationships within the lexicon. A second observation is that only
the inhabitative suffix -er has a competitor, the suffix -enaar, as in:

(53) Utrecht   Utrecht-enaar / Utrecht-er 'inhabitant of Utrecht'
      Heiloo   Heiloo-enaar / Heiloo-er 'inhabitant of Heiloo'

This option is not available in the case of the other type of personal noun:
VVD-enaar, for instance, is completely out. What we observe here is that the
denominal suffix -er is used productively for the creation of (at least) two
different kinds of denominal personal nouns in -er, classificatory names and
a specific subset thereof, inhabitant names. In addition, these nouns may
also denote inanimate entities. The following schemas account for the observations made above:[4]

(54) a. $[[x]_{Ni} er]_{Nj} \leftrightarrow$ [person with some relation to $SEM_i]_j$
      b. $[[x]_{Ni} er]_{Nj} \leftrightarrow$ [inhabitative of $SEM_i]_j$

The schema in (54b) is a subschema of (54a) because the two schemas are
identical except that the notion 'person' is made more specific, and specified
as 'inhabitative'. In addition, we have the following schema for the *tienponder*-
type of nouns:

(55) a. $[[QN]_{Ni} er]_{Nj} \leftrightarrow$ [object with property $SEM_i]_j$

Finally, this suffix is also used for creating nouns on the basis of numerals
such as *twintig-er* 'person in his twenties' or 'object with weight/measure 20',
and *dertig-er* 'person in his thirties':

(55) b. $[[x]_{Num,i} er]_{Nj} \leftrightarrow$ [entity with some relation to $SEM_i]_j$

---

[4] A word like *Amsterdamm-er* can receive other interpretations than that of inhabitative name, in
accordance with general schema (54a). For instance, it may also mean 'person born in Amsterdam', or
'person who plays for the soccer club of Amsterdam'.

These specific schemas can be assumed to be dominated by a general schema for nouns in -er:

(56) $[X_i\text{- er}]_{Nj}$ ↔ [entity with relation R to SEM_i]$_j$ (X = V, N, QN, Num)

This schema also generalizes over the deverbal nouns in -er discussed above. Relation R is underspecified, parallel to what is the case for compounds, and is filled in by specific subschemas and interpretation mechanisms based on the semantics of the base words. The subpatterns and their relations are given in the following tree, in which the subschemas are denoted by their numbers in the text above:

(56')

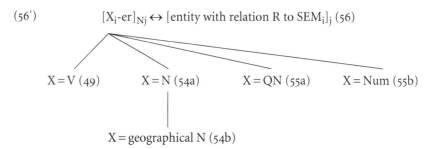

This analysis of Dutch derived nouns in -er leads again to the conclusion that we need morphological subschemas in order to account for the relevant subregularities. In a hierarchical lexicon, such subschemas can be specified without losing the possibility of expressing that they are instantiations of more general word formation schemas. Thus, these polysemy phenomena support the idea of analysing complex words by means of hierarchically ordered constructional schemas.

3.6 Subschemas for allomorphy patterns

Lexemes may exhibit systematic stem allomorphy when embedded in compounds. Such systematic stem allomorphy can be captured by means of schemas. An example of this type of allomorphy is found in the Athapaskan language Slave '[I]n many Slave dialects, the word for "eye" begins with [d], while as the first member of a compound, it begins with [n] or [r], depending on the dialect' (Rice 2009: 543–544).

(57)   independent form: *da* 'eye'
       right-hand member of compound: *da*
       sasó da 'metal-eye, glasses'
       left-hand member of compounds: *ra*
       ra tú 'eye-water, tears'

In Dutch compounds, a number of allomorphy patterns can be observed. A first example is the complex allomorphy involved in using the word *met* and its variants *mee* and *mede*. This word is used as a preposition, adverb, predicate, and particle. This raises the question whether we should consider it one lexeme, or a set of phonologically similar and semantically related lexemes. As an adverb it is used only as modifier of adverbial phrases, such as *mede om die reden* 'also for that reason' (it has an archaic flavour in that use). It is used as a predicate in a sentence like *Heb je geld mee?* 'Have you money with?, Have you got money with you?'. It is also used as part of a compound. Here are the different forms and their uses.

(58)   preposition: *met* [mɛt]
        adverb: *mede* [me:də]
        predicate: *mee* [me:]
        particle: *mede* or *mee*
        first part of a compound: *mede* [me:də]

Historically the three phonological forms are related as follows: the long and original form is *mede*. The short form *mee* is the effect of a historical phonological process of *de*-deletion. The form *met* is the effect of schwa apocope followed by word-final devoicing of obstruents and vowel shortening.

   The long form *mede* occurs in a few (archaic) particle verbs: *mede dingen* (but also *mee dingen*) 'to compete', and *mede delen/mee delen* 'to inform'. Otherwise, the particle form is *mee*. Hence, we may assume that the particle verb pattern arose through a kind of incorporation of the predicate *mee* (and its older form *mede* in a few cases) into the verb. The form *mede* is the form that has to be used within compounds, and has acquired the specific meaning 'shared with, co-, fellow-':

(59)   a. [[mede]$_{ADV}$ N$_i$]$_{Nj}$ ↔ [SEM$_i$ with others]$_j$
       b. mede-beslissing 'co-decision'
           mede-bewoner 'fellow occupant'
           mede-broeder 'fellow brother'
           mede-lander 'fellow countryman'
           mede-weten '(shared) knowledge'

We might consider qualifying *mede* as a prefix, but there is a clear lexical relation with the adverbial lexeme *mede* 'also, together with', both in form and meaning. Schema (59a) is therefore to be preferred to a prefixal interpretation: *mede* is an adverb that functions as the modifier in nominal compounds, with a specialized, compound-determined meaning. The historical explanation for this use of the archaic form *mede* is that this word was the regular form when the first compounds of this type were made. Hence, this archaic form could survive and be used productively once it had become part of a compound subschema.

The use of the word *mee* as a particle is illustrated by the following particle verbs; it is a productive category:

(60)   mee-bidden 'to join in praying'
       mee-denken 'to join in thinking'
       mee-drinken 'to join in drinking'
       mee-eten 'to join in eating'

The choice of *mee*, which is a 'comitative' predicate, reflects the origin of this type of particle verb: a number of particle predicates arose through incorporation of a predicate, as discussed in more detail in Chapter 5. A complex noun like *mee-eter* 'one who joins in eating' is well-formed since it is derived from the established particle verb *mee-eten* 'to join in eating', but it has a meaning different from that of the compound *mede-eter* 'fellow diner'. Prepositions do occur as parts of compounds, and adverbs can function as particles, as shown in (61):

(61)   compound: [[tussen]$_{Prep}$ [gerecht]$_N$]$_N$ 'lit. between-dish, intermediate course'
       particle verb: [neer]$_{Adv}$ [halen]$_V$ 'lit. down pull, to pull down'

Hence, we can only exclude the selection of *met* in compounds and *mede* in (newly coined) particle verbs by specifying the choice of the lexeme variant in a subschema. This will impede the use of the other word variants in compound and particle verb constructions. In short, the selection of a particular word form from the set of forms of a lexeme is governed by the construction in which these words appear.

The Dutch nouns *einde* [ɛɪndə] 'end' and *aarde* [aːrdə] 'earth' both have a short allomorph without final schwa: *eind* [ɛɪnt] and *aard* [aːrt]. This is the effect of the historical phonological process of schwa apocope mentioned above that has applied optionally to a number of Dutch nouns. Both *einde* and *eind* can be used as independent words, whereas the short allomorph *aard* occurs in compounds only. The regularity is that the short forms have to be used in compounding with these words as modifiers:

(62)   a. eind-examen/*einde-examen 'lit. end-exam, final exam'
          eind-gesprek/*einde-gesprek 'lit. end-interview, final interview'
          eind-station/*einde-station 'lit. end-station, final station'
          eind-spel/*einde-spel 'lit. end-game, final game'

b. aard-appel/*aarde-appel 'lit. earth-apple, potato'
   aard-atmosfeer/*aarde-atmosfeer 'earth-atmosphere'
   aard-schok/*aarde-schok 'earth-quake'
   aard-worm/*aarde-worm 'earth-worm'

The only exception to this generalization in standard Dutch is *aarde-werk* 'earthenware, pottery', in which *aarde* has a specialized meaning and denotes the material out of which the pottery is made.

In order to account for the distribution of these allomorphs we need schemas for compounds with these words in initial position:

(63) $[[eind]_N [x]_{Ni}]_{Nj} \leftrightarrow [final SEM_i]_j$
      $[[aard]_N[x]_{Ni}]_{Nj} \leftrightarrow [SEM_i \text{ related to earth}]_j$

As in the previous cases, these schemas will impede the use of *einde* and *aarde* in the general NN compounding schema, since the schemas in (63) contain more specific information, and hence will normally overrule the general $[NN]_N$ schema. The long form *aarde* is used in NA compounds like *aarde-duister* 'earth-dark, very dark'.

Stem allomorphy is also found for a few Dutch verbs. They have a long stem allomorph that ends in -*d*, and a short one without -*d*:

(64) glijd/glij   'to glide'
      rijd/rij   'to ride / drive'
      snijd/snij   'to cut'
      wijd/wij   'to dedicate'

Both allomorphs occur as independent words. The typical pattern for these words is that the long allomorph appears in derived words and the short allomorph is used in compounds. The effect of this selection is that derivation will not create word-internal onsetless syllables, although this could have been repaired in Dutch by means of glide insertion (Booij 1995). Occasionally, we might find derived forms with a glide like *glij-er* [ɣlɛi.jər]. But even with consonant-initial suffixes, the long form is chosen, as in *snijd-baar* 'slice-able'.

(65)   *compound*   *derived word*
     a. glij-baan 'slide-track, slide'   glijd-er 'slid-er' /ɣlɛi.dər/
        glij-middel 'slide-means, lubricant'
     b. rij-baan 'ride-track, lane'   rijd-er 'rid-er' /rɛi.dər/
        rij-bewijs 'ride-licence, driving licence'
        rij-wiel 'ride-wheel, bike'

c. snij-biet 'cut-beet, spinach beet'   snijd-er 'cutt-er' /snɛi.dər/
   snij-gras 'cut-grass, cutting gras'   snijd-baar 'slice-able' /snɛit.ba:r/
   snij-vlak 'cut-edge, cutting edge'   snijd-sel 'cutt-ing' /snɛit.səl/
d. wij-water 'holy water'   wijd-ing 'consecration' ʋɛi.dɪŋ/

This pattern of allomorph distribution can be captured by subschemas for VN compounds in which the form of the left verb is specified:

(66) $[[glij]_{Vi} [x]_{Nj}]_{Nk} \leftrightarrow [SEM_j$ related to $SEM_i]_k$
       $[[rij]_{Vi} [x]_{Nj}]_{Nk} \leftrightarrow [SEM_j$ related to $SEM_i]_k$
       $[[snij]_{Vi} [x]_{Nj}]_{Nk} \leftrightarrow [SEM_j$ related to $SEM_i]_k$
       $[[wij]_{Vi} [x]_{Nj}]_{Nk} \leftrightarrow [SEM_j$ related to $SEM_i]_k$

In some cases we find semantic differences between the allomorphs of a noun. The word *eer* [e:r] 'honour' has a long allomorph *ere* [e:rə] that has an archaic flavour when used as an independent word, being the original form without apocope. As the first constituent of a compound, we find both *eer* and *ere*. However, if the meaning to be expressed is 'honorary', one must always use the long form *ere*-:

(67)   a. eer-wraak 'honour-revenge, revenge for the protection of family honour'
          eer-betoon 'honour-show, tribute'
       b. ere-lid 'honorary member'/*eer-lid
          ere-voorzitter 'honorary chairman'/*eer-voorzitter
          ere-doctor 'honorary doctor'/*eer-doctor

This implies that the following schema has to be assumed:

(68) $[[ere]_N[x]_{Ni}]_{Nj} \leftrightarrow [$honorary $SEM_i]_j$

This schema will block the insertion of the short noun allomorph *eer* 'honour' in a general $[NN]_N$ schema with the specific 'honorary' meaning of the lexeme *eer* since schema (68) is more specific than the general schema for NN compounds. The survival of the old form *ere* in compounds with this particular meaning shows once more that language users make generalizations across subsets of compounds which are captured by subschemas. Allomorphy patterns thus provide additional evidence for the necessity of subschemas for the coinage of complex words.

3.7 Analogy or schema?

A widely and intensively debated issue in the analysis of complex words is whether the formation of new complex words has to be considered a matter of analogy, or as the result of using symbolic schemas that generalize across sets of existing complex words.[5] In analogical models, existing words or classes of words function as the examples for coining new words. In rule- or schema-based models, on the other hand, words are formed according to abstract patterns. Linguists such as Pinker have proposed that both ways of coining complex words co-exist, for instance in the formation of the past tense forms of English weak verbs (abstract rules) versus strong verbs (analogy or associative patterns) (Pinker 1999).[6]

The implication of assuming a hierarchical lexicon with different levels of abstraction is that the relation between these two options is not a matter of 'either/or'; there is both analogical word formation, based on an individual model word, and word formation based on abstract schemas. These schemas may differ in their degrees of abstractness, as argued above. Hence, specific sets of existing complex words may play a role in coining new complex words. Moreover, it is not necessarily the case that all language users make the same subgeneralizations. Schemas are based on lexical knowledge, and this type of knowledge varies from speaker to speaker. Hence, speakers may also differ in the number and types of schemas that they deduce from their lexical knowledge.

It is clear that analogical word formation in the strict sense, with individual words as models, does exist, as illustrated here by some examples from Dutch:

(69)   *existing word with idiosyncratic   analogically coined word
        meaning*
        angst-haas 'lit.' fear-hare, terrified   paniek-haas 'lit. panic-hare,
        person'   panicky person'
        moeder-taal 'lit. mother language,   vader-taal 'lit. father-language,
        native language'   native language of father'
        hand-vaardig 'lit. hand-able, with   muis-vaardig 'lit. mouse-able,
        manual skills'   with mouse-handling skills'
        nieuw-komer 'lit. new-comer, recent   oud-komer 'lit. old-comer, immi-
        immigrant'   grant who arrived a long time ago'

---

[5] A third type of approach not discussed here is the connectionist 'subsymbolic' approach, as proposed by Rumelhart and McClelland (1986), and discussed by Pinker (1999) and many others. For discussion of the notion 'analogy' with respect to word formation, see Becker (1990, 1994) and Hüning (1999).

[6] There are also models of morphology in which morphological rules (or schemas), that is symbolic abstract patterns, are assumed which reflect the distribution of morphological properties of the existing set of words in the lexicon. This is obtained by assigning rules or schemas a probability index, a measure of confidence that the rule provides the best choice for creating the required morphological form (Albright and Hayes 2003).

regel-neef 'lit. rule-nephew, busy-   regel-nicht 'lit. rule-niece, female
body'   busy-body'
oog-getuige 'eye-witness'   oor-getuige 'ear-witness'

For these words we can indeed point to one particular existing compound as the model for the formation of the new compound, and the meaning of this new compound is not retrievable without knowing the (idiomatic) meaning of the model compound.

Analogical word formation may develop, however, into a pattern that abstracts away from specific model words. In English, the word *Watergate* functioned as the model of a number of English compounds in *-gate* that all denote a particular political or personal scandal, and hence this looks like a clear case of analogical word formation. However, since a set of such words has been formed in the meantime, it is no longer obvious that it is always the word *Watergate* itself that functioned as the model word. Once a set of words in *-gate* has been formed, language users may discover the commonality of such words in *-gate*, and hence this kind of productive compound formation is now better characterized by the schema:

(70) $[[x]_{Ni} [gate]_N]_{Nj} \leftrightarrow$ [political scandal pertaining to SEM$_i$]$_j$

That is, the word *gate* has acquired the meaning 'political scandal' when embedded in compounds. This schema expresses that it is no longer necessarily the case that language users model their new *gate*-compound after the word *Watergate* (which does not exclude that individual speakers used a particular word in *-gate* as their model for a new word). Dutch speakers have extended this use of *-gate* to Dutch, as illustrated by the following examples (Hüning 2000):

(71)   kippen-gate 'chicken-gate, scandal concerning chickens'
       Stadion-gate 'financial problems concerning renovation of the Olympic Stadium'
       Zuid-Holland-gate 'financial scandal concerning the province of Zuid-Holland'

Hüning concluded that the rise of such a set of *-gate* words has given rise to a new morphological process in Dutch. This use of *-gate* is comparable to that of endings like *-burger*, *-holic*, *-tainment*, and *-zine* in English: a new type of compound constituent with a specific meaning is created, with the structural reinterpretation of an existing complex word being the first step. The rise of *-burger* is due to morphological reanalysis: *hamburg-er* > *ham-burger*, whereas in the case of -*gate*, the compound structure of *Water-gate* is maintained, but with a different interpretation of *gate*.

A similar example from Italian is the emergence of compounds with -*o-poli* 'scandal' (Ramat 2001). This use emerged from the word *tangent-o-poli* 'town where the bribery system is dominant', from the root *poli* 'town'. New coinages are *sanit-o-poli* 'the affair of the health ministry' and *banc-o-poli* 'bank scandal'. Thus, like -*gate*, (-*o*)-*poli* has acquired a new meaning, 'bribery scandal'.

Yet, the emergence of a symbolic schema for words in -*gate* does not mean that the link with the word *Watergate* is no longer present: this word is still linked to the subschema and reinforces its entrenchment. That is, analogy-based account and schema-based accounts of word formation are not to be seen as distinct alternatives, but can co-exist (Tuggy 2007: 100–102).

The use of schemas for word formation patterns presupposes a symbolic approach to representing linguistic knowledge. There are also models of morphology that try to do away with symbolic representation of abstract morphological knowledge, models in which analogy to existing words and memory-based learning plays a central role (Daelemans 2002; Keuleers and Daelemans 2007; Keuleers et al. 2007). In such models the notion 'analogy' has received sophisticated elaborations. These analogical models have been developed for inflectional processes of Dutch in which a choice has to be made between different inflectional endings, as in the case of plural nouns. The correct inflectional endings are computed by measuring the degree of similarity between the input word and the set of words in the lexicon, and by selecting the inflectional form that corresponds to that of the most similar word(s) found.

Similar selection problems must be solved when selecting the proper linking element in a newly coined Dutch compound with a noun as first constituent. There are three linking elements: -*s*, -*en*, and Ø, the absence of a linking element. The problem is that there are no categorical rules for choosing one of the three options. The linking element to be selected is that of those existing compounds to which the new compound is most similar. In a study of Dutch compounding, Krott (2001) showed that analogical modelling can account for the selection of linking elements in an adequate way. Similarly, Plag (2006) has argued that analogy plays a crucial role in computing the correct stress pattern of English compounds, where a choice has to be made between main stress on the first or on the second part of the compound. If a lexeme has more than one form when embedded in a compound – for instance since it may combine with different linking elements – the selection of a particular form may be modelled analogically since it is clear that the language user has access to existing compounds that share properties such as the initial constituent lexeme with the new compound. The language user who wants to speak about the food that a sheep is provided with may first decide to use a Noun-Noun compound for that purpose that begins with the lexeme SCHAAP 'sheep' as its modifier noun, and the lexeme VOER 'feed' as the head lexeme. At this stage, use is made of the abstract schema for NN compounds that specifies that the right N is the head, or a relevant subschema thereof. Next, the question arises whether the correct form of the lexeme SCHAAP is *schaap, schapen-, or schaaps-* (as in *schaap-herder* 'shepherd, *schap-en-kaas* 'sheep's cheese' and *schaap-s-kooi* 'sheep fold' respectively). It is at that stage that analogical modelling can make predictions as to which allomorph is preferably chosen (the form *schapenvoer* should be predicted as being the most probable one since *schapen* is the most frequently used allomorph). Similarly, the choice of the correct stress pattern for a new English compound may be modelled analogically, since the location of main stress in English compounds is partially governed by the presence of specific words. Compounds ending in *street* carry initial stress, compounds with *avenue* have final stress: *Háste strèet* vs. *Hàste Ávenue*. Hence, if a new compound in *street* is coined, it will also carry secondary stress.

However, it may as well be the case that (some) language users have developed subschemas for compounds with *street* and *avenue* that express these stress regularities, in particular if all words of a certain subtype exhibit the same stress pattern. That is, we might assume schemas like $[X [str\grave{e}et]_N]_N$ and $[X [\acute{a}venue]_N]_N$. Similarly, if, as pointed out above, the choice of one particular allomorph of a word is systematic within compounds, language users are able to abstract the relevant subschema, although not every individual may do this.

The analogical model of compounding as developed by Krott (2001) deals with one aspect of compound formation only, the selection of the proper form of the compound, in particular the linking element. The creation of a new word involves two stages, however. First, it has to be decided how a particular semantic content is going to be expressed, the stage of lexical selection (Levelt 1989), and then the proper forms of the selected lexical items have to be computed. One of the options for expressing a particular semantic content is to use a complex word for that content. The range of possible morphological forms for the expression of semantic content in a language can be specified by a set of hierarchically ordered constructional schemas in the lexicon. One of these schemas might be selected, and open positions in such schemas filled in with lexemes. For instance, if we want to express the concept 'main entity' in Dutch, speakers of Dutch may know that they can use the schema $[[hoofd]_N N_i]_N$ with the meaning 'main entity$_i$' for this purpose. This kind of abstract knowledge might therefore be assumed to be available, in addition to a set of existing compounds of that form.

In an analogical account of the lexical selection stage of language production, based on similarity to existing words, the model will first have to identify the set of nouns with a modifier constituent that expresses the notion 'main', and then construct the new *hoofd*-compound in an analogical fashion. In a psycholinguistic interpretation of this model, this means that language users do not have the morphological subschema for 'main entity' at their disposal beforehand. Instead, the model for morphological expression of 'main N' must be constructed as part of the lexical selection process.

I consider it an empirical question to what extent speakers make the necessary computation by means of a pre-established subschema, or by means of analogy to individual words. There are certainly unambiguous cases of word formation by analogy, as argued above. On the other hand, language users are able to discover abstract patterns. The rise of affixes from compound constituents is a clear illustration of the reality of this abstraction. It is possible that individual language users differ considerably in the degree to which they develop subschemas for the coinage of complex words, since they differ in their lexical knowledge and in the degree to which they create new complex words.

A hierarchical lexicon with different levels of abstractness and generalization, as outlined in this book, defines constituent families, sets of words that share a particular morpheme as building block. The existence of constituent families is confirmed by psycholinguistic evidence, in particular through the family size effect: the larger the size of a constituent family of a word, the faster it will be retrieved (Baayen 2003; Schreuder and Baayen 1997). Subschemas thus represent the paradigmatic structure of the lexicon that is so important for understanding language production (Baayen 2003: 63).

In sum, the concept of a hierarchical lexicon with constructional idioms for subsets of complex words provides an enlightening framework for modelling the regularities in the semantic interpretation and formal composition of complex words.

4

Quasi-Noun Incorporation

4.1 Morphological and syntactic constructions

In the previous chapters it was argued that the notion 'construction' is an essential tool for the analysis of morphological phenomena and the structure of the lexicon. In this and the following chapters, I focus on the analysis of lexical constructs that are not words in the morphological sense but are very similar to complex words: tight syntactic units that function as lexical units that are names for concepts. Such syntactic units and their similarities to complex words are sometimes seen as problematic for a well-defined boundary between morphology and syntax. I will argue that this is not the case. We can make a clear distinction between morphologically complex words and syntactic lexical units, and yet express their similarities as well, by using the notion 'construction' for the analysis of both complex words and such phrasal units.

This chapter deals with lexical constructs, mainly in Dutch, of the type *piano spelen* 'lit. piano play, to play the piano', combinations of a bare noun and a verb. Such N + V sequences look like verbal compounds, that is, as cases of noun incorporation, but they are not cases of incorporation in the morphological sense, since the two words can be split and cannot occur as one (complex) verb in second position in root clauses; witness the ungrammaticality of a sentence like *Jan piano speelt* 'John plays the piano'. It will be argued that such N + V sequences form phrases or syntactic compounds with a specific constructional meaning, that of 'nameworthy activity'.

4.2 Forms of noun incorporation

In many languages nouns can be combined with verbs into verbal compounds with the structure $[N\ V]_V$ or $[V\ N]_V$. This word formation process is referred to as noun incorporation (Sapir 1911) and has been studied extensively (Baker 1988, 1996; Carlson 2006; Gerdts 1998; Haugen 2008; Mithun 1984, 2000, 2010; Mithun and Corbett 1999; Riehl and Kilian-Hatz 2005). In prototypical incorporating verbal compounds the noun saturates a thematic role of the verb, often that of Patient. In some languages, nouns with other semantic roles can be incorporated (Creissels 2008). Noun incorporation is used primarily to form verbs that express a nameworthy and often conventional activity (Mithun 1984). These incorporated nouns do not denote specific entities, and receive a generic interpretation.[1]

The difference between a sentence with a noun that projects an independent Noun Phrase and a sentence with noun incorporation is illustrated by the following examples from the Micronesian language Ponapean:

(1) a. I kanga-la wini-o
      I eat-COMP medicine-that
      'I took all that medicine'
   b. I keng-winih-la
      I eat-medicine-COMP
      'I completed my medicine-taking'   (source Mithun 1984: 850)

In sentence (1b) we see a case of noun incorporation. This sentence has another meaning than sentence (1a), which has a syntactically independent object *wini-o*. In (1b), with an incorporated object *winih-*, the sentence indicates completion of the action of medicine-taking, while there may be medicine left. Typically, incorporated nouns are unmarked for definiteness, number, and case, and the verbal compound behaves as an intransitive verb, whereas its verbal head is transitive. Thus, noun incorporation often has the effect of creating verbs with reduced syntactic valency: since the Patient-argument of the verb is expressed by the incorporated noun, this argument will no longer receive an independent syntactic expression.

In a number of cases, such combinations of a noun and a verb have been argued not to have the status of compounds *stricto sensu*, that is words, but rather that of units with phrasal status. For instance, in Hungarian we find the following possibilities for incorporation (Farkas 2006; Farkas and de Swart 2003):

(2) a. Mari olvas egy verset
      Mari read a   poem.ACC
      'Mari is reading a poem'
   b. Mari verset   olvas
      Mari poem.ACC read
      'Mari is reading a poem/poems/poetry'

---

[1] This is the type of incorporation referred to in Mithun (1984) as type I incorporation.

c. Mari verseket   olvas
   Mari poem.PL.ACC read
   'Mari is reading poems'

In sentence (2a), the object *egy verset* 'a poem' occurs after the verb, the regular word order of Hungarian being SVO. In sentence (2b), on the other hand, a bare noun *verset* precedes the verb. In this sentence, the NV combination denotes the act of reading one or more poems, that is, poetry. So this sentence does not mean that Mari is reading one, unspecified poem. In sentence (2c), the plural noun *verseket* is used, again without determiner, and with a generic interpretation for this plural noun.

   A clear indication of the phrasal status of the NV combinations in (2b) and (2c) is that the noun is case-marked. In morphological compounds, an incorporated N constituent does not bear its own marking for structural case. The noun and the verb are also separable, for instance by the word *nem* 'not' (Kiefer 1992). Note furthermore that in Hungarian the noun can be marked as a plural, and thus carries a specification for Number, as in (2c). Hence, the term 'incorporation' as used by Farkas and de Swart (2003) is meant to refer to both cases of morphological incorporation (compounding) and to syntactic structures with both specific formal properties and the semantics of incorporation. Dahl proposed the term 'quasi-incorporation' for constructions where elements enter into closely-knit units … but stop short of actually being incorporated' (Dahl 2004), and I will henceforth use this term. Quasi-incorporation has been reported to exist for a number of Germanic languages: Danish (Asudeh and Mikkelsen 2000), Dutch (Booij 1990; Kooij and Mous 2002), German (Zeller 2001), Norwegian (Carlson 2006), Swedish (Dahl 2004; Toivonen 2003), and for Japanese (Iida and Sells 2008). In these cases it is bare nouns that are quasi-incorporated. In some languages it is NPs rather than bare nouns that are incorporated since the nouns can co-occur with modifiers. This is the case for some Eastern-Indonesian languages (Klamer 2001), Hindi (Dayal 2007), and Niuean, an Oceanic language (Massam 2001). This is referred to by Massam (2001) as pseudo-incorporation.[2]

   In this chapter I argue that by making use of the notion 'construction' we obtain an insightful account of quasi-incorporation: combinations of N and V in quasi-incorporation are phrasal predicates that instantiate a specific construction with syntactic and semantic properties of its own. In my

---

[2] However, Ball (2005) argues for Tongan that what looks like incorporation of noun phrases is in fact incorporation of the noun only, with concomitant inheritance by the NV compound of the valence of the noun to co-occur with an adjectival modifier.

analysis, I will focus on Dutch data, but I will argue that a parallel analysis obtains for Japanese as well.

4.3 Noun + verb combinations in Dutch

In Dutch we find NV combinations that are sometimes referred to as (a subclass of) separable complex verbs. A number of such combinations is listed in (3):[3]

(3) *Noun Verb*   *Gloss*
    adem halen   breath take 'to take breath'
    auto rijden   car drive 'to drive a car'
    brand stichten   fire cause 'to set fire to'
    college lopen   lecture walk 'to attend lectures'
    deel nemen   part take 'to take part in'
    feest vieren   party celebrate 'to have a party'
    kaart lezen   map read 'to read maps'
    koffie zetten   coffee make 'to make coffee'
    komedie spelen   comedy play 'to play-act'
    les geven   lesson give 'to teach'
    piano spelen   piano play 'to play the piano'
    ruzie maken   quarrel make 'to quarrel'
    televisie kijken   television watch 'to watch television'
    thee drinken   tea drink 'to drink tea'

These NV combinations are given here in their citation form, the infinitival form of the verb (stem + -*en*). According to the rules of the *Woordenlijst Nederlandse Taal* (Renkema 1995), these NV combinations have to be written as one word, when there are no intervening words. However, in order not to prejudge the linguistic analysis of these NV combinations, I will write them with spacing. The nouns are all used as bare nouns.

---

[3] Similar combinations with bare nouns occur in Danish (Asudeh and Mikkelsen 2000), Norwegian (Carlson 2006), and Swedish (Dahl 2004: 217). An example from Swedish is *Vi har häst* 'lit. We have horse, we are horse-owners', in which sentence the bare noun *häst* 'horse' follows the verb, since Swedish is an SVO language. In Spanish we find sentences like:

(i) Busco   piso
    Look-1SG   flat
    'I am flat-hunting, I am looking for a flat'
(ii) Busco   asistente
    Look-1SG   assistant
    'I am assistant-hunting, I am looking for an assistant'

in which the bare noun also receives a generic interpretation (Teresa Vallès, pers. comm.). Hindi also has this type of noun incorporation (Mohanan 1995).

The NV combinations in (3) are special in that the nouns are bare singular nouns. In Dutch, singular nouns are normally preceded by a determiner, unless they are mass nouns such as *koffie* 'coffee' and *thee* 'tea'. There are also abstract nouns that can optionally occur without a determiner, such as the noun *brand* 'fire'. For most of the nouns in (3), the fact that they can be used as bare singulars is tied to their co-occurring with these verbs. The use of count nouns as bare singulars is tied to a number of specific constructions, and it is also lexically governed (De Swart and Zwarts 2009). The absence of the determiner implies a generic, non-specific use of these nouns. This use of bare singular nouns is also found in prepositional phrases, as illustrated by the following Dutch examples:

(4)   per trein 'by train'
       zonder bril 'without glasses'
       op school 'at school'

In these prepositional phrases, the bare noun receives a generic reading as well. There is a substantial set of such P + N expressions with generic interpretation in Dutch. Similarly, the nouns in (3) receive a generic interpretation, and consequently the NV combinations denote nameworthy and conventional activities. Even though these NV combinations are not complex words, they exhibit the semantics of noun incorporation.[4]

An additional property of some of these NV combinations is that the use of the verbs in this configuration is special. For instance, the verb *spelen* 'to play' does not take a direct object like *de piano* 'the piano', and the verb *kijken* 'to watch' selects a prepositional object; yet, these verbs combine with direct objects in the form of bare singular nouns in *piano spelen* and *televisie kijken*. The verb *lopen* 'to walk' is normally intransitive, but it can be used transitively in combination with *college* 'class', where it gets the meaning 'to attend classes'. Even in the case of mass nouns such as *koffie* 'coffee' we have to consider the combination with the verb as lexicalized since the use of the verb *zetten* 'lit. to put' with the meaning 'to make' is tied to its combination with the mass nouns *koffie* 'coffee' and *thee* 'tea'.

Since these bare singular nouns invoke a generic interpretation, the corresponding NV combinations are interpreted as referring to nameworthy activities. We might hypothesize that these special properties of the nouns

---

[4] Similar examples from English are the PN constructs *in prison, at work,* and *in hospital* (British English). Compare the ungrammaticality of the PNs **at restaurant* and **at toilet*, which shows that these PPs are lexicalized and must be stored in the lexicon (Adele Goldberg, Nijmegen lecture December 2008). French also features a number of constructions in which bare nouns receive a generic interpretation (Lambrecht 2004).

in these NV combinations follow from these combinations being morphological compounds of the type [NV]$_V$. However, this option is out because
these combinations can be split in certain syntactic contexts. This is why they
are traditionally classified as (a subclass of) separable complex verbs, and
must be phrasal in nature, in accordance with the principle of Lexical
Integrity that forbids syntactic manipulation of parts of words:

(5)   Principle of Lexical Integrity (Anderson 1992)
      'The syntax neither manipulates nor has access to the internal structure
      of words.'

This principle blocks the syntactic reordering of parts of words. The separability of the Dutch N + V combinations is illustrated here for *piano spelen* 'to
play the piano' in root clauses (6a), and verbal clusters (6b). It is usually
assumed that the underlying word order of Dutch is SOV (Koster 1975). This
is also the surface word order in embedded clauses, at least when the object is
a noun phrase. In root clauses, however, the finite form of the verb has to
appear in second position, after the first constituent, whereas non-finite parts
of the verbal predicate remain in situ, at the end of the clause. That is, there is
a syntactic reordering rule of Verb-Second that applies to finite verbal forms
in root clauses (6a,c). Verbal clusters can be seen as an effect of the syntactic
reordering process of Verb Raising: the verb of an embedded clause is raised to
a higher clause, and forms a complex verbal predicate with the verb of the
higher clause (6b). The separability of N and V can also be observed in
the form of the relevant past participles, as illustrated in sentence (6c): the
prefix *ge-* attaches to the verb constituent and does not appear before the
whole N + V combination:

(6)   a. Jan speelt$_i$ piano t$_i$ (*root clause with Verb-Second*)
          John plays piano
          'John plays the piano'
      b. dat Jan piano t$_i$ wilde spelen$_i$ (*embedded clause with Verb Raising*)
          that John piano wanted play
          'that John wanted to play the piano'
      c. Jan heeft$_i$ piano gespeeld t$_i$ (*root clause with Verb-Second*)
          John has piano played
          'John has played the piano'

In sentence (6a), the finite verb *speelt* occurs in second position, but the noun
piano occurs at the end of the sentence. In sentence (6b), the verb *wilde*
'wanted' forms a verb cluster with the verb *spelen*, and thus splits the
combination *piano spelen*. The past participle prefix *ge-* in (6c) appears before

the verbal stem, but after the noun *piano*. These facts show that we have to assign phrasal status (VP status) to *piano spelen*. We therefore conclude that these NV combinations are phrasal combinations, to be listed in the lexicon as lexical collocations in order to account for the fact that these verbs license bare singular nouns as arguments and, together with the noun, denote a conventional activity.

However, this is not the whole story of NV combinations like *piano spelen*, since there are two syntactic tests that show that these NV combinations can also form tighter syntactic constructs than VPs. This is what I will refer to as quasi-incorporation.

First, NV combinations such as *piano spelen* may occur as a constituent of the *aan het* INF-construction of Dutch. This is a construction with a progressive meaning (Chapter 6), found in a number of West-Germanic languages. Consider the use of *piano spelen* in sentence (7). The parenthesized part is the part of the sentence for which two alternatives are considered.

(7)   Jan is {piano aan het spel-en/aan het piano spel-en}
      John is {piano at the play-INF/at the piano play-INF}
      'John is playing the piano'

Normally, the object of a verbal infinitive in the *aan het* INF-construction has to appear before *aan het*, as illustrated in (8). The verb *bespelen* 'to play on something' is a regular transitive verb (with a transitivizing prefix *be-*) that requires its direct object, the singular noun *piano*, to be preceded by a determiner:

(8)   Jan is {de piano aan het bespelen/*aan het de piano bespelen}
      John is {the piano at the play-INF/at the the piano play-INF}
      'John is playing music on the piano'

In (8) the noun *piano* is preceded by the definite determiner *de* 'the', and hence it is not used as a bare noun. In contrast, in the case of NV combinations such as *piano spelen* the noun can appear either before the *aan het* INF-sequence (the regular position of objects), or right before the infinitive, after *aan het*, as shown in (7).

Second, the special nature of these NV combinations of being tight syntactic units also manifests itself in the verb raising construction mentioned above. Normally, direct objects of main verbs cannot be clustered in standard Dutch together with their verb, as shown in (9a), but bare nouns can form part of the verbal cluster created through verb raising, as shown in (9b):

(9) a. ... dat Jan {de piano wilde bespelen/*wilde de piano bespelen}
         '... that John {the piano wanted to play/wanted the piano play}'
     b. ... dat Jan {piano wilde spelen/wilde piano spelen}
         '... that John {piano wanted play/wanted piano play}'

Hence we have to conclude that such NV combinations have a special formal
status.

   This raises the question of the structure of such NV combinations. My
proposal is that they can receive two structural interpretations. One option
is that they are interpreted as VPs consisting of an NP (containing a bare N^0
only) and a V^0. The other structural option for such NV sequences is that of
a syntactic compound: the bare noun is adjoined as an N^0 to a V^0, resulting
in the structure $[N^0\ V^0]_{V0}$. This latter structure expresses that NVs with
noun incorporation are not words in the strict, morphological sense but
syntactic compounds dominated by an X^0 category symbol. The syntactic
compound structure allows for the NV sequence to occur as a V^0 unit in the
aan het INF construction and after raising verbs. This adjunction structure
is also proposed for noun incorporation in Hindi (Mohanan 1995), Persian
complex predicates (Ghomeshi and Massam 1994), for the Persian Ezafe-
construction (Ghomeshi 1997), for Swedish NV sequences (Toivonen 2003),
and for Japanese quasi-incorporation (Iida and Sells 2008).

   In sum, a combination of N and V can occur in three different structural
configurations, with the following structural properties, which will be discussed below:

(10) a. regular syntax: $[[\ldots N^0]_{NP}\ V^0]_{VP}$
         – N occurs before *aan het* in the *aan het* INF-construction;
         – N precedes the complex predicate created by raising of V^0;
         – N can be negated by negative word *geen*;
         – N can be preceded by an adjectival modifier;
         – N can be stranded in root clauses with V in second position;
         – the past participle is formed by prefixing *ge-* to the stem of the V in V^0.
     b. quasi-incorporation (syntactic compounding): $[N^0\ V^0]_{V^0}$
         – N occurs after *aan het* in the *aan het* INF-construction;
         – N can be raised with V to form a higher clause complex predicate;
         – N can be preceded by the negative word *niet*;
         – N cannot be preceded by an adjectival modifier;
         – N cannot be stranded in root clauses with V in second position;
         – the past participle is formed by prefixing *ge-* to the stem of the V in V^0.

c. morphological compounding: $[\text{N V}]_{V^0}$
  – the NV appears as a unit in second position in root clauses
  – N and V cannot be split by syntactic rules
  – the past participle is formed by prefixing *ge-* before the N

This means that quasi-incorporation is interpreted as syntactic compounding, different from morphological compounding in that in the latter case the whole compound is inserted into one syntactic V^0 position. The third structural type is marginal and unproductive in Dutch where quasi-incorporation is the preferred alternative.[5] The idea that $N^0 V^0$ combinations can receive two structural interpretations (regular VP structure or syntactic compound) is also defended for Hindi, by Mohanan (1995).

Structure (10b) is a structure for non-projecting nouns, that is, nouns that do not project a phrase. The non-projecting nature of the quasi-incorporated nouns of Dutch is confirmed by the observation that they cannot be modified by adjectives. For instance, Dutch does not allow for quasi-compounds like *klassieke piano spelen* 'to play classical piano', in which the (inflected) adjective *klassieke* 'classic' modifies the noun *piano* (11b). Modification of the noun is possible, however, when the NV sequence is interpreted as VP, even though it has the semantics of incorporation (11c):

(11) a. ... dat Jan klassieke piano speelt
       that John classical piano plays
       'that John plays classical piano music'

---

[5] Instead of considering the full phrases in which the bare nouns occur as NPs, one might also consider them DPs, but nothing hinges on this issue in the present analysis. See Payne (1993) and Matthews (2007) for a critical discussion of the DP-hypothesis.

  A similar analysis for similar cases of incorporation in German is proposed by Zeller (2001: 129), who makes crucial use of the distinction between NPs and DPs. A German quasi-compound like *Auto fahren* 'to drive a car' is proposed by Zeller to have the structure $[[N^0]_{NP} V^0]_{VP}$. That is, the noun *Auto* is an NP, but not a DP, and the functional projection for the determiner (the DP structure) is absent. Hence, this noun receives a generic interpretation. This proposal does justice to the phrasal nature of quasi-incorporation. It also expresses that the complex predicate can function as an intransitive predicate. However, in order to express that quasi-compounds may form a unit with respect to the progressive construction and verb raising, as shown above, in contrast to regular VPs, a Principle of Reanalysis has to be invoked (Zeller 2001: 273). This principle states that particles and bare nouns, when adjacent to a verb, can be reanalysed as being adjoined to a lexical head V^0 with which they form a V^0. That is, Zeller assumes the same adjunction structure as proposed above as an option for such complex predicates.

  In Booij (1990, 2002a,b) the phrasal nature of quasi-compounds (and particle verbs), and the non-projecting nature of these nouns is pointed out as well; quasi-compounds are considered as minimal projections of V, that is V'. In Chapter 5 I present an analysis of particle verbs in which they are analysed as either V' or, as a consequence of incorporation, as syntactic compounds (V^0).

   b. *Jan is aan het klassieke piano spelen
      John is at the classical piano play-INF
      'John is playing classical piano music'
   c. Jan is klassieke piano aan het spelen
      John is classical piano at the play-INF
      'John is playing classical piano music'

Structure (10b) is motivated for quasi-incorporation in Dutch by the special behaviour of NV combinations such as *piano spelen* in the *aan het* INF-construction and in verbal clustering. If we specify the infinitive position of the *aan het* INF-construction as V^0, we predict that not only simplex or complex verbs but also these NV combinations can be used in that construction (cf. 7). Similarly, if we formulate Verb Raising as applying to V^0 constituents, it is predicted that either the V^0 *spelen* (structure 10a) or the whole $[N^0V^0]_{V^0}$ combination *piano spelen* (structure 10b) is raised (cf. 9b).

The assumption that there are two syntactic interpretations for Dutch N + V combinations (VP or V^0) is corroborated by the behaviour of these combinations with respect to the selection of negative words. The negating word in Dutch is *niet* or *geen*. The difference between these two words is that *geen* forms a syntactic constituent with the following noun, that is, an NP (12a), unlike *niet*, that is used with intransitive predicates (12b) (Broekhuis et al. 2003):

(12)   a. Ik kan {*niet/geen} auto kopen
        I can NEG car buy.INF
        'I cannot buy a car'
     b. Ik kan {niet/*geen} fluiten
        I can NEG flute.INF
        'I cannot play the flute'
     c. Ik kan {niet/geen} piano spelen
        I can NEG piano play.INF
        'I cannot play the piano'

Note that in sentence (12c) both negative words can be used. This follows, if the sequence *piano spelen* can receive two structural interpretations. If it is interpreted as a regular VP (structure 10a), there is an NP and hence the negative word *geen* will be selected (and forms an NP with the noun). If it is interpreted as quasi-incorporation (structure 10b), it is an intransitive predicate that selects the negative word *niet*.

In root clauses the finite, tensed verb appears in second position. Non-finite verbal constituents (which form a complex predicate V^0 with the finite verb) are left behind:

(13)   a. Jan [heeft$_i$]$_{V^0}$ [de piano]$_{NP}$ [[bespeeld]$_{V^0}$ t$_i$]$_{V^0}$
         John has the piano played
         'John has played on the piano'
       b. Jan [heeft$_i$]$_{V^0}$ [[piano]$_{N^0}$]$_{NP}$ [[gespeeld]$_{V^0}$ t$_i$]$_{V^0}$
         John has the piano played
         'John has played the piano'

This means that only the finite verbal form of the V of an N + V combination is moved to second position (*bespeeld* is the part participle of the prefixed verb *bespelen*, and *gespeeld* that of the simplex verb *spelen*).

Consider now the following range of sentences with the negative words *niet* and *geen*, and their (un)grammaticality:

(14)   a. Jan speelt$_i$ {geen/*niet} piano t$_i$
         John plays NEG piano
         'John does not play the piano'
       b. Jan heeft$_i$ {geen/niet} piano gespeeld t$_i$
         John has NEG piano played
         'John has not played the piano'

In (14a), the finite verb *speelt* has moved to second position. The presence of *niet* implies the presence of the structure of quasi-incorporation since *niet* co-occurs with intransitive predicates. Therefore, we conclude that the finite verb cannot be moved out of quasi-compounds, thereby stranding the noun. In (14b), it is the auxiliary for perfect tense that is moved to second position. The grammatical variant with *niet* again implies quasi-incorporation. This quasi-compound is kept intact, and thus this variant is grammatical.

This does not mean that the negative word *niet* can never be used for negation with independent NPs. This is possible when the NP is in a position where it is stressed contrastively. This holds both for NPs with a determiner, and for NPs with a bare singular noun like *piano*:

(15)   a. Een bíer-tje drink ik niet
         A beer-DIM drink I not
         'I do not drink a beer'
       b. Piáno speel ik niet
         Piano play I not
         'I do not play the piano'

The difference between (14a) and (14b) requires a constraint that 'prohibits syntactic reordering into or out of lexical categories', the principle of Lexical Integrity in the formulation of Bresnan (1982: 54). Bresnan invoked this principle in the context of her discussion of incorporation of prepositions into verbs. For instance, in the English passive sentence *Everything was paid for twice*, the verb *pay* and the preposition *for* form a unit for the operation of the lexical rule of passive. This incorporation structure can also be observed in the NP *an unpaid for item* in which the passive form *paid for* has fed *un*-prefixation. Hence, Bresnan assumes the following incorporation structure for *pay for*: $[[pay]_V [for]_P]_V$. This complex predicate is a unit of which the two parts cannot be separated, as illustrated by the ungrammaticality of the sentence *Everything was paid twice for*. Bresnan considered this incorporation structure a morphological structure (Bresnan 1982: 51). However, I consider it a syntactic compound since in English morphological compounds are right-headed, whereas we have to do here with a left-headed structure. The inseparability of these complex predicates still follows from the principle of Lexical Integrity if we interpret the notion 'word' as used in Anderson's definition (5) as a unit dominated by X^0, since syntactic compounds are dominated by X^0. This interpretation[6] of the principle of Lexical Integrity will also block the movement of finite forms of the verb *spelen* 'to play' from the incorporation structure *(niet) piano spelen* in Dutch root clauses, as required. More examples of this pattern are given in (16):

(16) a. Jan zet {geen/*niet} koffie
          John makes NEG coffee
          'John does not make coffee'
      b. Morgen geef ik {geen/*niet} les
          Tomorrow give I NEG lesson
          'Tomorrow, I will not teach'
      c. Ik rijd helaas {geen/*niet} auto
          I ride, alas, NEG car
          'Alas, I do not drive a car'
      d. Hij haalt {geen/*niet} adem meer
          He takes NEG breath more
          'He does not breathe anymore'

What does this analysis predict as to the distribution of *niet* and *geen* in combination with incorporation and verb raising? Verb raising is the operation by which complex verbal predicates are formed. In classical generative grammar this operation is conceived of as a syntactic transformation but it is

---

[6] A more detailed discussion of the principle of Lexical Integrity is given in Chapter 7.

also possible to see it as a lexical rule (Bierwisch 1990). Consider now the following sentences with the complex predicate *kan spelen* 'can play':

(17) a. dat Jan geen piano kan spelen
         that John no piano can play
         'that John cannot play the piano'
    b. dat Jan niet kan piano spelen
         that John not can piano play
         'that John cannot play the piano'
    c. *dat Jan geen kan piano spelen
         that John no can piano play
         'that John cannot play the piano'
    d. dat Jan niet piano kan spelen
         that John not piano can play
         'that John cannot play the piano'

In sentence (17b) the verb *kan* is combined with the incorporation structure *piano spelen*. Sentence (17d) shows that the noun *piano* can also be incorporated into a complex predicate, in this case $[[kan]_{V^0}\ [spelen]_{V^0}]_{V^0}$. The resulting incorporation structure is $[[[piano]_{N^0}[[kan]_{V^0}]\ [spelen]_{V^0}]_{V^0}]_{V^0}$. Since this is a V^0 predicate it can be negated by the negative word *niet*. In sentence (17c), the noun *piano* is incorporated, and hence the use of *geen* is impossible.

    As pointed out above, in most cases the use of nouns as bare singulars implies a generic interpretation of these nouns, and hence the relevant predicates denote conventional actions. In the case of mass nouns like *koffie* 'coffee' and *bier* 'beer', the bare singular nouns can also be interpreted as indefinite nouns. Hence, there is a difference in the interpretation of the two structures for such NV sequences, which can be illustrated by the following sentences, both meaning 'John cannot make coffee':

(18) a. Jan kan geen koffie zetten
    b. Jan kan niet koffie zetten

Sentence (18a) is ambiguous, unlike sentence (18b). In (18a) *koffie zetten* denotes either an event or a conventional action, but in (18b), a case of quasi-incorporation (as proven by the use of *niet* as a negator), *koffie zetten* can only denote a conventional action. Hence, a sentence like *Jan kan vandaag niet koffie zetten* 'John cannot make coffee today' is semantically odd because *koffie zetten* is here a conventional activity, and hence *kunnen koffie zetten* 'to be able to make coffee' is interpreted as an individual, not a stage-level predicate. This means that it cannot be combined with the temporal adverbial *vandaag* 'today' that would coerce a stage-level interpretation. The quasi-compounds function as intransitive predicates that denote a conventional activity. Therefore, sentence (18a) may be uttered in a situation where there is no coffee available, whereas sentence (18b) may be used in a situation in which John has never learnt how to make coffee.

The structure and corresponding meaning that I therefore propose for quasi-incorporation is the following:

(19) $[[N^0_i][V^0_j]]_{V^0,k} \leftrightarrow$ [conventional action V_j in which N_i is involved]$_k$

This structure is a constructional schema that specifies the structure of quasi-incorporation, and (an approximation of) the semantic correlate of its formal structure. This structure is used for conventional actions that require a specific competence and are therefore nameworthy. Buying a car may be a conventional action but, since no specific competence is involved in that action, it is odd to use the Dutch NV combination *auto kopen* 'car buy' as a syntactic compound in the *aan het* INF-construction. Recall that constructions are pairings of form and meaning at different levels of abstractions. Individual lexicalized instantiations of these quasi-compounds are listed in the lexicon. In the lexicon both the abstract patterns and their instantiations are represented. This also applies to the phrasal construction (10a), and its instantiations. As we have seen, the NV combinations listed in (3) are instantiations of both V^0 construction (10b) and VP construction (10a). Since such phrasal patterns have to be listed, there is no sharp boundary between lexicon and grammar (Jackendoff 2002*a,b*, 2007, 2008). Schema (19) expresses the fact that quasi-incorporation is not only a formal structural operation but has a specific semantic effect as well: it expresses actions that are conventional and require a specific competence. A similar 'semantic incorporation' effect has to be specified for the lexical collocations mentioned in (10a).

As noted above, the use of count nouns as bare singulars is only available for a restricted set of nouns, in combination with specific verbs. (As we will see below, this is different for plural nouns which can freely occur as bare nouns.) Hence, the following condition must be added to schema (19): 'the N^0 position is filled by a bare noun that forms a lexical collocation with the verb'. In other words, these idiomatic collocations of a noun and a verb can be embedded in two structural configurations, a VP or a syntactic compound.

Quasi-incorporation thus creates intransitive syntactic compounds that license *niet* as a negative operator, can occur in the progressive *aan het* INF-construction, and can cluster with raising verbs such as *willen* 'want'. Quasi-incorporation is possible if the N + V combination is a lexical collocation for a conventional activity.

The lexically governed nature of the process is illustrated by the pair *adem halen* 'lit. to take breath, to breathe'/*adem krijgen* 'to get breath'. Note that *adem* 'breath' is a mass noun, and therefore its use as a bare singular does not depend on the presence of a specific verb. It is only the first NV, *adem halen*, that can denote the action of breathing with a certain duration, and can therefore exhibit the typical effects of quasi-incorporation discussed above, such as co-occurrence with the negative word *niet*:

(20)   ... omdat hij {*niet adem kreeg/niet adem haalde}
       ... because he {not breath got/not breath took}
       '... because he did not breathe'

This observation confirms that quasi-incorporation of bare singular nouns is restricted to lexical collocations of bare nouns and verbs.

4.4 Quasi-incorporation of bare plural nouns

In Dutch, quasi-incorporation of nouns also applies to plural nouns.[7] Again, the N + V combination denotes a nameworthy activity. However, since plural nouns can always occur without a determiner, there is no factor of lexical collocation involved. If a particular action is nameworthy, the N + V combination can be used:

(21)   a. aardappels schill-en
          potatoes peel-INF
          'to peel potatoes'
       b. appels plukk-en
          apples pick-INF
          'to pick apples'
       c. brieven schrijv-en
          letters write-INF
          'to write letters'
       d. kousen stopp-en
          stockings mend-INF
          'to mend stockings'

Unlike the cases of singular N incorporation, these combinations are not written as one word.

---

[7] This type of quasi-incorporation is also found in other Germanic dialects such as Low-Saxon and North-Frisian (Booij 2004; Ebert 2000).

The arguments for considering these word combinations as cases of (optional) quasi-incorporation are the same as for the cases of incorporation of singular nouns: the noun can occur right before the infinitive in the *aan het* INF-construction and in verb clusters, and the negative word *niet* can be used. This indicates that these N + V combinations may function as intransitive predicates, and that the object-argument must have been incorporated. As was the case for quasi-incorporation of bare singulars, these NV combinations may also function as transitive VPs in which the noun functions as an NP. In the sentences (22), the first variant of each sentence evokes an indefinite interpretation of the bare plural, and the second variant evokes a generic interpretation, due to quasi-incorporation:

(22) {full NP status of bare plural noun/quasi-incorporation of bare plural noun}
      a. Jan is {aardappels aan het schill-en/aan het aardappels schill-en}
         John is potatoes {at the peel-INF/at the potatoes peel-INF}
         'John is peeling potatoes'
      b. Jan is {de aardappels aan het schill-en/*aan het de aardappels schill-en}
         John is {the potatoes at the peel-INF/at the the potatoes peel-INF}
         'John is peeling the potatoes'
      c. Jan is {nieuwe aardappels aan het schill-en/*aan het nieuwe aardappels schill-en}
         John is {new potatoes at the peel-INF/at the new potatoes peel-INF}
         'John is peeling new potatoes'
      d. dat Jan {geen aardappels schilt/niet aardappels schilt}
         that John {no potatoes peels/that John not potatoes peels}
         'that John does not peel potatoes'
      e. Jan schilt {geen aardappels/*niet aardappels}
         John peels {no potatoes/not potatoes}
         'John does not peel potatoes'
      f. Jan is {geen aardappels aan het schill-en/niet aan het aardappels schill-en}
         John is {no potatoes at the peel-INF/not at the potatoes} peel-INF
         'John is not peeling the potatoes'
      g. dat Jan {aardappels moet schill-en/moet aardappels schill-en}
         that John {potatoes must peel-INF/must potatoes peel-INF}
         'that John must peel potatoes'

Again, we assume the quasi-incorporated plural nouns to have the syntactic status of N^0, and their occurrence as bare nouns is licensed by the adjacent verb in the $[N^0 \ V^0]_{V^0}$ structure.

Sentence (22g) shows the scopal effects of quasi-incorporation. In the first variant of (22g) the noun *aardappels* can have scope over *moet schillen*, hence the meaning 'there are potatoes for which it holds that John must peel them' (*aardappelen* is not within the scope of *moet schillen*). Another scopal interpretation is possible as well, with the meaning 'John must peel things that are potatoes'. That is, *aardappelen* is within the scope of the complex predicate *moet schillen*. This latter interpretation is the only possible one for the second, quasi-incorporating, variant of (20g): the obligation expressed by *must* cannot pertain to peeling only but scopes over the peeling of potatoes.

These scopal effects are not necessarily tied to the formal structure of quasi-incorporation, since they can also be observed in languages where full NPs can be incorporated. For instance, in Flemish (the variant of Dutch spoken in Belgium), NPs can be incorporated, as shown by Verb Raising. Consider now the following sentences (Haegeman and Van Riemsdijk 1986: 442):

(23)   da Jan {geen vlees hee willen eten/hee willen geen vlees eten}
        that John {no meat has want eat/has want no meat eat}
        'that John has not wanted to eat meat'

In the first variant it is either stated that there is no meat that John wants to eat, or that John does not want to eat any meat (with *willen* having scope over *geen vlees eten*), whereas in the second variant with incorporation, the sentence can only mean that John does not want to eat any meat (Haegeman and Van Riemsdijk 1986: 443). This is exactly parallel to what holds for quasi-incorporation in standard Northern Dutch, the variant of Dutch analysed here.

As pointed out above, the quasi-incorporation structure typically evokes the interpretation of these NV combinations as a nameworthy activity. The effect is the creation of intransitive predicates. The incorporation cannot be interpreted in terms of a syntactic derivation from a clause with a transitive VP because it is only the incorporation structure that forces the generic interpretation of these bare plurals, and thus creates the obligatory interpretation as a nameworthy activity. Therefore, this form of quasi-incorporation should be interpreted as a construction, a pairing of a particular phrasal configuration with a particular form, as given in (19). The productivity of this incorporation schema for bare plural nouns is higher than that for bare singulars because bare plurals can always be interpreted as generic, whereas bare singular count nouns with generic interpretation have a much more restricted, lexically governed distribution, as mentioned above.

Additional evidence for the syntactic compound status of this construction is that the quasi-incorporation structure must also be available in syntactic contexts where a full NP structure is impossible as underlying structure because the syntactic context requires intransitive predicates. That is the case for the *aan het* INF-complements of causative verbs such as *brengen* 'to bring', *krijgen* 'to get', and *maken* 'to make' (Haeseryn et al. 1997: 1052–1053). Note that *twijfelen* 'to doubt' is an intransitive verb, but *vertellen* 'to tell' a transitive one that becomes intransitive when the object argument is pseudo-incorporated:

(24)   a.   Hij brengt ons aan het twijfel-en   (*intransitive predicate*)
            He brings us at the doubt-INF
            'He makes us doubt'

       b.   *Hij brengt ons sprookjes aan het vertell-en   (*transitive predicate*)
            He brings us fairy tales at the tell-INF
            'He makes us tell fairy tales'

       c.   Hij brengt ons aan het sprookjes vertell-en   (*intransitive predicate*)
            He brings us at the fairy tales tell-INF
            'He makes us tell fairy tales'

Selecting the plural form of the incorporated noun is usually the only option since there is only a restricted, fixed set of bare singulars that combine with verbs, as pointed out above:

(25)   *Jan schilt aardappel/*Jan is aan het aardappel schill-en
       Jan peels potato.SG/John is at the potato.SG peel-INF
       'John is peeling potatoes'

The same holds for the conventional activity of collecting stamps, where a plural noun has to be selected:

(26)   {postzegel-s/*postzegel} verzamelen
       {stamp-PL /stamp.SG} collect
       'stamp collecting'

The verb *verzamelen* 'to collect' is one of the verbs that require a plural object, and example (26) shows that the feature [plural] is semantically active in quasi-incorporation.[8] This can be contrasted with real compounding in which noun stems standardly receive a generic interpretation without plural marking. For instance, in the compound *postzegelverzamelaar* 'stamp collector', the absence of plural marking on the noun *postzegel* 'stamp' does not block a generic reading: a *postzegelverzamelaar* certainly collects more than one stamp. That is, it is only in cases of real compounding that number neutrality is at stake.

---

[8] The non-neutrality of the plural marking in quasi-incorporation has also been observed for Hungarian (Farkas and de Swart 2003) and for Hindi (Dayal 2007).

4.5 Immobile verbs

There is another class of NV combinations in Dutch that differs from the NV combinations discussed above in that the noun has no argument role with respect to the verb. Examples are the following (more Dutch examples and similar examples for German can be found in Vikner (2005)):

(27)   *Noun Verb*
     buik spreken 'to stomach speak, ventriloquizing'
     koord dansen 'to rope dance, walking a tightrope'
     mast klimmen 'to pole climb, climbing the greasy pole'
     steen grillen 'to stone grill, stone-grilling'
     stijl dansen 'to style dance, ballroom-dancing'
     vinger verven 'to finger paint'
     zak lopen 'to bag walk, running a sack-race'
     zee zeilen 'to sea sail, ocean-sailing'

Again, in order not to prejudge the linguistic analysis, I write these word combinations as two words, although Dutch orthography requires them to be written as one word.

   These word combinations cannot be compounds because they do not occur in root clauses. In such clauses, they can only be used with the periphrastic progressive construction mentioned above. In non-root-clauses, however, they can be used in both their non-finite and their finite forms (Booij 2002*c*; Van Marle 2002):

(28)   a.   *Mijn vader zee zeilt vaak
        My father sea sails often
        'My father often sails at sea'
    b.   Mijn vader is vaak aan het zee zeil-en
        My father is often at the sea sail-INF
        'My father often sails at sea'
    c.   dat mijn vader vaak zee zeilt
        that my father often sea sails
        'that my father often sails at sea'

(29)   a.   *Mijn zuster stijl danst goed
        My sister style dances well
        'My sister is a good ballroom dancer'
    b.   Mijn zuster is vaak aan het stijl dans-en
        My sister is often at the style dance-INF
        'My sister does ballroom dancing often'

c. dat mijn zuster goed stijl danst
   that my sister well style dances
   'that my sister is good at ballroom dancing'

As mentioned in Vikner (2005), the same array of facts holds for German. Vikner (2005) refers to these NVs as immobile verbs because the finite verb cannot be moved into other syntactic positions such as the first position (questions) or second position (root clauses), cf. (28a, 29a).

The non-occurrence of these quasi-compounds in root clauses follows from assigning them phrasal status. A quasi-verbal compound cannot occur in second position in root clauses because this second position is for a single finite V only, not for a phrasal predicate. In this respect, quasi-compounds differ from converted nominal compounds such as *voetbal* 'to play soccer' (created through conversion of the nominal compound *voetbal* 'football'):

(30)   Mijn vader voetbal-t elke zaterdag
        My father football-s every Saturday
        'My father plays football every Saturday'

The analysis presented here answers the question why NV combinations such as *piano spelen* 'to play the piano' discussed in section 4.2 behave differently from NV combinations such as *zee zeilen* in which the noun does not function as an argument of the verb. The NV sequence *piano spelen* can be interpreted as a regular VP with a bare singular noun that functions as an NP. This structural interpretation is only possible with nouns that can function as an argument of the verb. In this respect, they are therefore different from NV combinations such as *zee zeilen* that only occur in the quasi-incorporation construction, since *zee* 'sea' is not an argument of *zeilen* 'to sail'.

In his discussion of the different types of NV compounds and pseudo-compounds of Dutch, Ackema (1999) proposed the following generalization:

(31)   If N is an argument of V, N-V is separable.

This generalization states the distributional differences between the NV combinations of the *piano spelen* type and those of the *zee zeilen* type. It follows directly from the analysis presented here because NV combinations when separated are regular VPs, and hence the N must be an argument. Yet, even the NV combinations that Ackema qualifies as inseparable complex verbs such as *zee zeilen* have to be considered as phrasal in nature, in order to explain why they do not occur in second position in root clauses, and why the participial prefix appears after the noun, before the verbal stem. In other words, none of the NV combinations has word status.[9]

The schema of quasi-incorporation $[N^0 V^0]_{V^0}$ requires the two words to be adjacent, and thus predicts the class of *zee zeilen* combinations to be non-separable, unlike the *piano spelen* class for which a structural interpretation as regular VP is available as well. This difference is also found in sentences with contrastive focus such as:

(32) a. Píano kan hij niet spelen
          Piano can he not play
          'He cannot play the píano'
      b. *Zée kan hij niet zeilen
          Séa can he not sail
          'He cannot do séa-sailing'

Since *zée* in (32b) cannot be interpreted as an NP, it cannot be topicalized, unlike *piano* in (32a).

It is obvious that NV combinations of the immobile type cannot be derived from VPs in which the N functions as an NP-argument, because the incorporated Ns are not arguments. Thus, these immobile verbs show again that lexical templates for syntactic combinations of words are necessary.[10]

---

[9] Vikner (2005) proposed another explanation for the immobility of these NVs than that proposed above. According to him, immobile verbs are simultaneously Vs and V*s, that is, both words and small phrases. The only syntactic position in which these NVs can fulfil the requirements of both structures is when N and V are adjacent. Hence, the verbal part cannot be moved. There are two problems with this proposal, however. One is that assigning them V-status implies that the participial prefix *ge*-cannot occur in the middle, right before the verbal stem. As we saw above, the prefix does occur in that position. Secondly, Vikner's analysis does not explain Ackema's correct generalization that only verbs with argumental nouns possess mobility. He has to stipulate for which NVs the double requirement holds. In my analysis this difference is accounted for by providing two different structural interpretations for combinations of verbs with argumental nouns only. A noun like *zee* 'sea' in *zee zeilen* 'sea-sailing' is not a argument but an adjunct. Hence, it can only occur as part of the syntactic compound construction.

[10] Individual cases of quasi-incorporation may be reanalysed as morphological compounds. In that case, they can occur in second position in root clauses. Examples from a Google search (15 January 2008) are *stijl-dansen* 'to style-dance' and *koek-happen* 'to cake-eat'. Both of these NV combinations are used in root clauses:

(i) De koning zelf koek-hapt
     'The king himself cake-eats'

(ii) en stijldanst hij met zijn nichtje
      'and style-dances he with his niece'

There is variation among speakers in this respect, and this is to be expected given the fact that NV sequences have potentially three different structural interpretations. My Google search data confirm that generally we do not find these NVs in second position in clauses, but it comes as no surprise that language users do not always find it easy to assign the proper structure to such word combinations.

Summing up our findings as to quasi-incorporation in Dutch, we have seen that there are three subtypes, all with the structure $[N^0\ V^0]_{V^0}$ given in (10b): (i) incorporation of argumental bare singular nouns, with verbs that are subcategorized for appearing with these bare singulars; (ii) incorporation of argumental bare plural nouns, and (iii) incorporation of non-argumental bare singular nouns. In the next section I will argue that this analysis of quasi-incorporation can also be used for the analysis of Japanese *suru*-compounds.

4.6 Quasi-incorporation in Japanese

Japanese features a class of verbal complex expressions that are usually referred to as *suru*-compounds (Kageyama 1982, 1999). These are right-headed compounds with the verb *suru* 'to do' as head; the non-head is a verbal noun. The following examples illustrate this type of compounding:

(33) a. yama-nobori-suru
       mountain-climbing-do
       'to do mountain-climbing'
     b. kenkyuu-suru
       research-do
       'to do research'

Hence, some language users impose a compound interpretation on NV sequences. For instance, I found the following numbers of tokens for the competing participle forms of NV combinations (Google search 15 January 2008):

pseudo-incorporation	*compounding*	*gloss*
buik-ge-sprok-en 23	ge-buik-spreek-t 3	ventriloquized
	ge-buik-sprok-en 0	
steen-ge-grild 9	ge-steen-gril-d 363	stonegrilled
stijl-ge-dans-t 35	ge-stijl-dans-t 355	ballroom-danced
vinger-ge-verf-d 3	ge-vinger-verf-d 257	finger-painted
wad-ge-lop-en 176	ge-wad-loop-t 40	walked across the shallows
zak-ge-lop-en 54	ge-zak-loop-t 3/ge-zak-lop-en 0	run a sack-race

The forms on the left are to be expected if a pseudo-incorporation interpretation is imposed on these NV sequences. The forms on the right are expected if these NVs are morphological compounds. Similar variation is observed for German speakers by Vikner (2005). The forms on the left have a higher token frequency when the participle is that of a strong verb. This reflects the fact that strong verbs such as *spreken* 'to talk' do not have a past participle that ends in the suffix -t (*ge-sprok-en*, not *ge-spreek-t*), which makes forms like *ge-buik-spreek-t* very marked.

The reinterpretation of phrasal combinations as NV compounds took place on a much larger scale in Frisian where we find sentences like (Dyk 1990):

(i) Hy noas-snutte wakker
    He nose-blew heavily
    'He blew his nose heavily'

  c. saikuringu-suru
     cycling-do
     'to do cycling'

Instead of *suru*, a number of other suppletive forms with a related meaning can be used: the potential form *dekiru*, the honorific form *nasaru*, and the humble form *itasimasu* (Kageyama 1999: 313).

One interesting feature of this kind of incorporation is that it is only productive with the verb *suru* and the related suppletive forms mentioned above. Therefore, we might qualify the schema for this kind of compound as a constructional idiom (Booij 2002*b*; Jackendoff 2002*a*), that is, a schema in which one of the positions is lexically filled with the verb *suru*, whereas the other (non-head) position is a variable, and can be filled with all sorts of verbal nouns (VN):

(34) $[[x]^i{}_{VN}\ [suru]^j{}_{V^0}]^k{}_{V^0} \leftrightarrow$ [perform action denoted by SEM^i]^k

As argued by several authors, these compounds are phrasal in nature because the constituents can be separated by certain morphemes such as focus particles (Iida and Sells 2008; Kageyama 1982, 1999; Matsumoto 1996*a*,*b*). Therefore, they might be interpreted as cases of quasi-incorporation.

(35)   a. sampo-sae suru
           walk-even do
       b. bidoo-dani si-nai
           budge-even do-not   (Kageyama 1999: 314)

Iida and Sells (2008: 964) show that there are in fact two structural options for the verb *suru*: either it takes a regular phrasal complement or it forms a syntactic compound with the verbal noun (a case of what they call 'subphrasal syntax'). That is, as in Dutch, a bare singular N complement of a V can be interpreted as either an NP (36a) or an N^0 (36b). Iida and Sells (2008) provide the following minimal pair:

(36)   a. benkyoo-o su-ru 'study-ACC do-NonPast' (phrasal)
       b. benkyoo su-ru 'study do-NonPast' (subphrasal)

In (36a) the VN *benkyoo* is marked with accusative case (regular verbal complementation), whereas in (36b) this verbal noun has no case marker.

When the VN is modified, and hence cannot be interpreted as an N^0, the case marker must be present; when the thematic object of VN does not modify VN and appears in the accusative, the VN itself cannot be case-marked. That is, modification implies a phrasal projection for the VN, whereas a subphrasal interpretation is possible when there is no modifier, with concomitant absence of case marking (Iida and Sells 2008: 964):

(37) a. kare-wa [nihongo-no benkyoo]-o si-ta
          he-TOP [Japanese-GEN study]-ACC do-PAST
          'He did study of Japanese'
      b. kare-wa nihongo-o [benkyoo si-ta]
          he-TOP Japanese-ACC [study do-PAST]
          'He studied Japanese'

In sum, as in Dutch, sequences of a bare noun and a verb can be interpreted in two ways, either as regular VPs or as cases of quasi-incorporation in which a noun (N^0) is adjoined to a V^0.

4.7 Conclusions

The facts of Dutch and Japanese discussed above have the same implications for a proper theory of the architecture of the grammar: word sequences that are not words in the morphological sense, but are compound-like, should be interpreted as syntactic compounds (besides having an interpretation as regular VPs). Such subphrasal, non-morphological patterns can be accounted for by constructional schemas in the lexicon, with a specification of both form and meaning, just like morphological patterns. Thus, both Dutch and Japanese quasi-incorporation provides evidence in support of a theory of grammar that does away with the sharp boundary between grammar and lexicon.

5

Separable complex verbs

5.1 Complex predicates

The notion 'construction' as used in the preceding chapters is a very useful and enlightening concept for the analysis of syntactic word combinations that form lexical units. The theoretical advantage of this approach is that we can keep the notions 'word' and 'lexical unit' formally distinct, and yet can do justice to the similarities between these two types of linguistic constructs, as was shown in Chapter 4 for quasi-compounds. Moreover, such an analysis will also contribute to our understanding of the emergence of morphology because some affixes are the historical descendants of words in such phrasal constructions. This chapter will focus on separable complex verbs, whereas the next chapter will deal with progressive constructions.

Separable complex verbs form a subcategory of the category of complex verb constructions or complex predicates: phrasal predicates in which verbs play a crucial role, and with specific formal properties (Ackerman 1995, 2003; Ackerman and Webelhuth 1998). Examples of such constructions are serial verbs, constructions with raising verbs, and constructions with light verbs (Bowern 2008). Another type of complex verb construction is quasi-noun incorporation, discussed in Chapter 4.

Serial verbs are found in many languages (Aikhenvald and Dixon 2006). An example is the Austronesian language Kambera, spoken on the island of Sumba in Indonesia. This language features many combinations of verbs that function as one predicate. The structural unity of the verb combinations is manifested in the marking of arguments. Consider the following sentence (Klamer 1998: 279):

(1) Na=ngàndi   maráu=ya$_j$ [na anakeda]$_j$
     3SG.NOM-take   be.far=3SG.ACC   the child
     'He takes the child far away'

The accusative clitic =*ya* attaches to the intransitive verb *maráu* 'be far' which shows that the two verbs behave structurally as a unit.

Functionally similar to serial verb constructions are cases of pseudo-coordination of verbs in which one of the verbs is a light verb. An example from Swedish is the following sentence (Hilpert and Koops 2008: 246):

(2)   Mona satt och sydde i det blå rummet
       Mona sat and sewed in the blue room
       'Mona was sewing in the blue room'

Verbs of posture like *sitta* 'to sit' are in the process of losing their lexical meaning and becoming aspectual verbs. In this example this verb expresses progressive meaning.

In verb raising constructions, verbs trigger the raising of the verb of the embedded clause to a higher clause. This results in clauses with complex predicates and the arguments of the raised verb appearing with the raising verb, as if they were arguments of the raising verb. An example is the Dutch raising verb *beloven* 'to promise' that allows both for regular complement clauses with an implicit subject and for the raising construction;

(3) a. dat Jan beloofde [een boek te kopen]   *complementation*
        that John promised [a book to buy]
        'that John promised to buy a book'
    b. dat Jan een boek [beloofde te kopen]   *raising*
        that John a book [promised to buy]
        'that John promised to buy a book'

In sentence (3b), the verb *kopen* 'to buy' of the embedded clause has been raised to the higher clause, and its object argument *een boek* 'a book' now precedes the main verb *beloofde*. Verb Raising is also characteristic of German, and it is considered by some linguists as a lexical process (Bierwisch 1990).

In many Australian languages an inflecting verb is combined with a non-inflecting 'preverb' to form a complex predicate. The preverbs form an open class whereas the inflecting verbs form a closed class. In the following example from the Northern Australian language Jaminjung the preverb for 'finish' is combined with the general impact verb for 'to hit' (Schultze-Berndt 2003: 150):

(4) ning=biji   yirri-ma   gurunyung barr
      break.off=only 1P.EXCL;3SG-hit.PAST head   smash
      'we just finished (= killed) it (a flying fox) smashing its head'

This combination of the preverb *ning* and the inflecting verb *yirri-ma* expresses the meaning of 'killed'.

Many languages have preverb–verb combinations in which the preverbs belong to a closed set, whereas the verbs form an open set. The preverb usually corresponds with an adposition, and adpositions used as preverbs are usually referred to as particles. This type of complex predicate is found in Indo-European languages (Watkins 1964), such as Germanic languages, but also Italian (Iacobini and Masini 2006), in Finno-Ugric languages such as Hungarian (Kiefer and Honti 2003) and Estonian (Ackerman 2003), and in the Caucasian languages Georgian and Udi (Harris 2003). Here are some examples from Hungarian, English, Norwegian, Dutch, and German respectively:

(5) a. Péter tegnap ki-ment az erdöbe
        Peter yesterday out-went the forest.in
        'Yesterday, Peter went to the forest'
     b. Péter tegnap ment ki az erdöbe
        Peter yesterday went out the forest.in
        'Yesterday, Peter went to the forest'   (Kiefer and Honti 2003: 142)

(6) a. John looked up the information
     b. John looked the information up

(7) a. Mannen har drikket opp vinnen
        Man.the has drunk up wine.the
        'The man has drunk up the wine'
     b. Mannen har drikket vinnen opp
        Man.the has drunk wine.the up
        'The man has drunk up the wine'   (Zeller 2002: 234)

(8) a. dat Hans zijn moeder op belde
        that Hans his mother up phoned
        'that Hans phoned up his mother'
     b. Hans belde zijn moeder op
        Hans phoned his mother up
        'Hans phoned up his mother'

(9) a. dass Hans seine Mutter an ruft
        that Hans his mother at calls
        'that Hans phoned up his mother'
     b. Hans ruft seine Mutter an
        Hans calls his mother at
        'Hans phoned up his mother'

These particle verbs have a number of properties that make them similar to words. Yet, they are phrasal in nature since the particle and the finite verb can be split, as shown in (5b)–(9b). These properties of particle verbs can be dealt with insightfully in a constructionist approach. In this chapter I will focus on the behaviour of Dutch particle verbs, which are quite similar to their German counterparts.[1] In section 5.2 I argue that the productive patterns of particle verb formation have to be accounted for by a set of constructional idioms in which the position of the particle is lexically fixed and the slot for the verb is a variable. In section 5.3 the interaction of particle verbs with word formation is discussed in more detail, and section 5.4 deals with particle verbs as a historical source of prefixes.

5.2 Dutch separable complex verbs

Separable complex verbs (SCVs) – also called *samenkoppelingen* 'combinations' in Dutch grammars – are combinations of a verb and some other word that have both word-like properties and properties of word combinations. The following sentences illustrate the use of SCVs, both with SOV word order (embedded clauses) in the a-sentences, and with SVO word order (main clauses) in the b-clauses. As pointed out in Chapter 4, the underlying word order of Dutch is SOV, and in root clauses the finite verb moves to second position (Koster 1975):

(10)   a. dat de leeuw het hert aan valt
          that the lion the deer at falls
          'that the lion attacks the deer'
       b. De leeuw valt het hert aan
          The lion falls the deer at
          'The lion attacks the deer'

(11)   a. dat Vader neer stortte
          that Father down fell
          'that Father fell down'
       b. Vader stortte neer
          Father fell down
          'Father fell down'

(12)   a. dat Jan het huis schoon maakte
          that John the house clean made
          'that John cleaned the house'

[1.] For analyses of German particle verbs, see Lüdeling (1999); Müller (2002, 2003, 2006); Zeller (2001, 2002, 2003); for Swedish, see Toivonen (2003).

    b. Jan maakte het huis schoon
      John made the house clean
      'John cleaned the house'

(13) a. dat Rebecca piano speelde
      that Rebecca piano played
      'that Rebecca played the piano'
    b. Rebecca speelde piano
      Rebecca played piano
      'Rebecca played the piano'

(14) a. dat Wim ons teleur stelde
      that Wim us sad put
      'that Wim disappointed us'
    b. Wim stelde ons teleur
      Wim put us sad
      'Wim disappointed us'

The spelling of the SCVs in the a-sentences violates a rule of Dutch orthography: SCVs have to be written as one word, without internal spacing, a rule which reflects the lexical unity of these word combinations. I will ignore this rule from time to time for expository reasons. In the first example, the word *aan* 'at' that combines with the verb is also used as an adposition. In that case, the non-verbal element is also referred to as a particle, and the SCV is then referred to as a particle verb. Particle verbs form a productive class of SCVs. In the second example, the word *neer* 'down' is an adverb. The next two examples show that adjectives (*schoon*) and nouns (*piano*) can also occur in SCVs. SCVs of the NV type are dealt with in detail in Chapter 4 under the heading of quasi-noun incorporation. The word *teleur* 'sad' in the last example does not occur as an independent word.

    The main reason why SCVs have to be considered as syntactic combinations, and not as prefixed words or compounds, is that they are separable: in root clauses, the tensed verbal form appears in second position, whereas the other part of the SCV is stranded in its underlying position. If we assumed SCVs to be words, we would violate the principle of Lexical Integrity which forbids syntactic rules to move parts of complex words.

    A second phenomenon in which we see the separability of SCVs is Verb Raising. Sentence (15a) represents the underlying SOV word order. The main verb *wilde* 'wanted' selects a sentential complement with a particle verb. When the verb of an embedded clause is raised to the matrix clause, the SCV can be split, as in (15b), but it can also be treated as a unit, as in (15c):

(15)   a. dat Hans [zijn moeder op bellen]$_S$ wilde
            that Hans his mother up phone wanted
            'that Hans wanted to phone up his mother'
       b. dat Hans zijn moeder op [wilde bellen]
            that Hans his mother up wanted phone
            'that Hans wanted to phone up his mother'
       c. dat Hans zijn moeder [wilde op bellen]
            that Hans his mother wanted up phone
            'that Hans wanted to phone up his mother'

Sentence (15c) shows that there is the possibility that the SCV forms a unit for
Verb Raising. This conclusion is supported by the behaviour of SCVs in the
progressive construction *aan het* + INFINITIVE 'at the V-INF, V-ing' mentioned in Chapter 4 and discussed in more detail in Chapter 6; compare:

(16)   a. Hans is zijn moeder aan het op bell-en
            Hans is his mother at the up phone-INF
            'Hans is phoning his mother'
       b. Hans is zijn moeder op aan het bell-en
            Hans is his mother up at the phone-INF
            'Hans is phoning his mother'
       c. *Hans is aan het zijn moeder bell-en
            Hans is at the his mother phone-INF
            'Hans is phoning his mother'
       d. Hans is zijn moeder aan het bellen
            Hans is his mother at the phone-INF
            'Hans is phoning his mother'

Whereas *op bellen* can appear after *aan het*, this is not the case for the VP *zijn
moeder bellen*. This shows that the phrase *op bellen* has a special syntactic
status.

The separability of Dutch SCVs can also be observed in the location of the
infinitival particle *te* that occurs between the two constituents of SCVs, as in
op te bellen, and in the form of the past participle, with the prefix *ge-* in
between the particle and the verbal stem: *op-ge-beld*. Past participles are
formed in Dutch by means of the simultaneous attachment of the prefix *ge-*
and the suffix *-t/-d/-en*. Ablauting verbs choose the suffix *-en*, regular verbs
select /t/ when the stem ends in a voiceless obstruent, and /d/ otherwise. In
derivational morphology, SCVs behave similarly; for instance, the *ge*-nomi-
nalization of *opbellen* is *opgebel*, with the nominalizing prefix *ge-* between
the particle and the verbal stem.

A number of these particles correspond with prefixes, i.e. bound morphemes that cannot be separated from the verb with which they co-occur.
These prefixed verbs carry main stress on the verbal stem, not on the prefix,
whereas the SCVs carry main stress on the non-verbal constituent. Thus, we
get minimal pairs like the following (the verbs are presented in their citation
form, the infinitive, which has the form stem + -(e)n)

(17) *SCV*   *prefixed verb*
      dóor boren 'to go on drilling'   door-bóren 'to perforate'
      óm blazen 'to blow down'   om-blázen 'to blow around'
      ónder gaan 'to go down'   onder-gáan 'to undergo'
      óver komen 'to come over'   over-kómen 'to happen to'
      vóor komen 'to occur'   voor-kómen 'to prevent'

The contrast between SCVs and prefixed verbs is illustrated by the following
sentences:

(18) a. Ongelukken komen voor
          Accidents come for
          'Accidents occur'
      b. Goede regels voor-komen ongelukken
          Good rules for-come accidents
          'Good rules prevent accidents'

The separability of the two constituents of SCVs has led a number of
linguists to propose a syntactic account of such complex predicates. The
syntactic account usually has the form of a so-called Small Clause-analysis:
the particle is considered as the predicate of a Small Clause (SC), a subject–
predicate combination without a copula, which is then raised to the matrix
clause, and Chomsky-adjoined to the verb of the matrix clause. In such an
analysis the following surface structure is assigned to the verb phrase *het
huiswerk afmaken* 'to finish one's homework' (*t* is the trace of the moved PP *af*
'finished'):

(19) [[het huiswerk]$_{NP}$[t_i]]$_{PP}$]$_{SC}$ [[af$_i$]$_{PP}$ [maken]$_V$]$_{VP}$

In (19) the SCV *af maken* is a structural unit, which can thus partake in Verb
Raising. The particle in this structure expresses the result of the action
expressed by the verb. In such an analysis, particle verbs are instantiations
of regular syntactic structures that express a resultative meaning.

Such a syntactic Small Clause analysis raises a number of problems, however, which are discussed briefly below. We will see why and how a constructional analysis of particle verbs is more adequate than a Small Clause analysis.

5.2.1 Lexical properties of particle verbs

Although the facts discussed above show that particle verbs are not morphological words, this does not mean that there is a straightforward syntactic
account for all of them. They clearly behave as lexical units in a number of
ways which I will focus on now. It is these word-like properties that have led a
number of linguists to take the opposite view that particle verbs are morphological constructions created by a pre-syntactic morphological component
(Ackema 1999*a*, *b*; Neeleman 1992; Neeleman and Weerman 1993). The basic
problem for this latter view is that it does not account in a principled manner
for the separability of particle verbs. Such analyses have to weaken the
principle of Lexical Integrity, allowing syntactic rules to move parts of complex words.

In many cases, the meaning of an SCV is not fully predictable. The semantic
unpredictability of SCVs is nicely illustrated by the different SCVs with the
verb *vallen* 'to fall' which exhibit a bewildering variety of meanings, in many
cases without a meaning constituent that corresponds to the meaning of the
verb *vallen*:

(20)   aan vallen 'to attack', af vallen 'to lose weight', bij vallen 'to applaud', in
        vallen 'to set in', mee vallen 'to turn out better than expected', om vallen
        'to fall down', op vallen 'to draw attention', tegen vallen 'to disappoint',
        toe vallen 'to come into the possession of'

This means that SCVs have to be stored in the lexicon. Lexical storage of SCVs
is also necessary for other reasons: in SCVs such as *teleur stellen* 'to disappoint' and *gade slaan* 'to watch' the first parts *teleur* and *gade* do not occur as
independent words (21a). Moreover, there are also verbal constituents of SCVs
that do not occur as independent verbs such as *bootsen, kukelen,* and *kalefa-
teren* (21b):

(21)   a. gade slaan 'to watch', teleur stellen 'to disappoint'
        b. na bootsen 'to imitate', om kukelen 'to fall down', op kalefateren 'to
           restore'

These idiosyncrasies show that many SCVs must be lexically stored; however,
since syntactic units can be stored as idioms, this fact does not necessarily
point to a morphological analysis of SCVs.

A second observation is that SCVs freely feed deverbal word formation.
Usually, derivation is fed by words as bases, not by phrases, and this is taken
by those linguists who advocate a morphological analysis of SCVs as evidence
for the word status of SCVs:

(22)   a. *deverbal suffixation*
        aan bied-en 'to offer'   aan-bied-er 'offerer'
        aan kom-en 'to arrive'   aan-kom-st 'arrival'
        aan ton-en 'to prove'   aan-toon-baar 'provable'
        aan trekk-en 'to attract'   aan-trekk-elijk 'attractive'
       b. *deverbal prefixation*
        in voer-en 'to introduce'   her-in-voer-en 'to reintroduce'
        uit gev-en 'to publish'   her-uit-gev-en 'to republish'
        uit zend-en 'to transmit'   her-uit-zend-en 'to retransmit'
       c. *compounding with verbal left constituent*
        door kiez-en 'to dial through' door-kies-nummer 'direct number'
        door kijk-en 'to see through'   door-kijk-bloes 'transparent blouse'
        op berg-en 'to store'   op-berg-doos 'store box'

However, it is not the case that syntactic constructs can never feed word
formation, which may be fed by units that are larger than one word (Booij
2007: 188–189). Hence, these observations do not imply word status for
particle verbs and similar SCVs.

There are two other important observations on SCVs that seem to speak in
favour of a morphological analysis. First, the addition of a particle may have
the effect of category change since particle verbs can also be formed productively on the bases of adjectives and nouns. The power to change category is
generally assumed to be a prerogative of morphological operations. The
following examples illustrate the seemingly category-determining power of
particle attachment (the particle verbs are presented here in their stem form):

(23)   a. *adjectival base*   *particle verb*
        helder 'clear'   op helder 'to clarify'
        hoog 'high'   op hoog 'to raise'
        knap 'tidy'   op knap 'to tidy up'
        leuk 'nice'   op leuk 'to make nicer'
       b. *nominal base*   *particle verb*
        hoop 'pile'   op hoop 'to pile up'
        luister 'lustre'   op luister 'to add lustre to'
        som 'sum'   op som 'to sum up'

In all these examples, the corresponding particle-less verb does not exist
independently, and hence it is the combination with the particle that makes
these adjectives and nouns function as verbs. Note that these formations differ
from verbalizing prefixation in that the adjectives and nouns themselves are
turned into verbs. This is clear from the fact that they occupy the verb second

position in main clauses, without the particle, as is shown by the following examples, with inflected forms of the verbs *hogen* and *hopen*:

(24)   a.   De fabrikant hoog-de de prijzen op
            The manufacturer high-PAST the prices up
            'The manufacturer raised the prices'
       b.   De problemen hop-en zich op
            The problems pile-3PL.PRES REFL3 up
            'The problems pile up'

These observations imply that the adjective *hoog* and the noun *hoop* have been converted into verbs. In other words, we have to assign the conversion structure $[[hoog]_A]_V$ to the second part of the particle verb *op hogen*, and the structure $[[hoop]_N]_V$ to the second part of the particle verb *op hopen*. Thus, the stem of the SCV *op hogen* has the structure $[op\ [[hoog]_A]_{V^0}]_V$. An additional relevant observation is that conversion of adjectives into verbs is normally not a productive process for Dutch adjectives (De Vries 1975: 165), and hence the occurrence of this type of conversion depends on the adjective appearing in the SCV construction.

A second, related argument for a morphological view of particle verbs is that the addition of a particle may change the syntactic valency of the verb. In many cases, the SCV is transitive, whereas the verb itself is intransitive. The following examples illustrate the valency change effect:

(25)   bellen (optionally transitive)   iemand op bellen 'to phone
       'to phone'   someone'
       juichen (intransitive) 'to cheer'   iemand toe juichen 'to cheer
                                                someone'
       lopen (intransitive) 'to walk'   de straten af lopen 'to tramp the
                                                streets'
       rijden (intransitive) 'to ride'   de auto in rijden 'to run in the car'
       wonen (intransitive) 'to live'   een vergadering bij wonen 'to
                                                attend a meeting'
       zitten (intransitive) 'to sit'   een straf uit zitten 'to serve one's
                                                time'

Morphological operations may have effects on the syntactic valency of words. Yet, the syntactic configuration in which a word occurs may also affect its syntactic valency. This is a basic insight of Construction Grammar: 'the main verb typically underdetermines the overall argument structure of a sentence' (Goldberg 2009: 95). It is the construction as a whole that determines the argument structure of a sentence.

In a syntactic account of these effects, the Small Clause analysis (Hoekstra 1988), the VP *de straten af lopen* 'to tramp the streets' receives the following deep structure analysis:

(26)   [de straten af]$_{SC}$ lopen

The verb *lopen* combines with a small clause, of which *af* forms the resultative predicate. Hence, the superficial object *de straten* originates as subject of the small clause. Thus, it is explained why *af lopen* is a transitive predicate, even though *lopen* is an intransitive verb. It is true that resultative constructions contain arguments that are not selected by the base verb, as illustrated by the following sentence with a resultative meaning (the verb *zingen* 'to sing' does not select an argument like *sterren* 'stars'):

(27)   Maria zong de sterren van de hemel
        Mary sang the stars from the heaven
        'Mary sang beautifully'

Semantically, however, it is odd to consider *af* as the predicate of *de straten* in (26) because it does not make sense to claim that *de straten* receive the property of being *af* 'finished'. Moreover, the small clauses do not behave as structural units under standard tests for phrasal status (Neeleman 1992). A sentence with a preposed small clause like *De straten af wilde hij niet lopen* 'He did not want to tramp the streets' is ungrammatical.

Another problem for a resultative small clause analysis is that it does not relate syntactic valency to the semantics of each individual particle verb. Argument structure, and hence syntactic valency, is the syntactic projection of the meaning of a linguistic unit. The crucial role of semantics can be seen in the following two sentences, in which the particle verb *af lopen* is used with two different meanings and has corresponding differences in syntactic valency:

(28)   a. De wekker loopt af   (*intransitive*)
           The alarm-clock walks off
           'The alarm-clock goes off'
        b. Hij liep de hele tentoonstelling af   (*transitive*)
           He walked the whole exposition off
           'He did the whole exposition'

Such differences in semantics and corresponding syntactic valency are not captured by assigning sentences with these particle verbs a uniform resultative small clause structure.

Particle verbs form a productive category, and thus cannot simply be qualified as idioms, as lexicalized syntactic constructions. For instance, in the variety of Dutch spoken in the Netherlands the particle *af* can be used productively to form telic verbs; witness recent coinages from *dansen* 'to dance' and *rijden* 'to drive' such as *af dansen* 'to do one's dancing examination' and *af rijden* 'to do one's driving examination'. Similarly, the particle *door* can be used to create new durative verbs such as *door vergaderen* 'to go on with a meeting' and *door drinken* 'to go on drinking'. The point to be noted here is that the words *af* and *door* have a specific (aspectual) meaning in their use as particles. We are dealing here with bound meanings, meanings of words tied to specific constructions, that is, heterosemy. In this respect particle verbs are parallel to compounds (section 3.2). This issue has also been discussed by Marchand (1969) in relation to the specific meanings of particles in English particle verbs. He argued therefore in favour of an interpretation of such morphemes as being part of compounds as well. 'I am not overlooking the fact that particles used in conjunction with verbs display other senses than the ones found in the independent words, which brings them nearer to prefixes. But as they do not have their dependent morphological status, a term such as semi-prefix would have had to be introduced. To avoid this, I have classed them as verbal compounds' (Marchand 1969: 112).

Productive use can also be observed for the particles *aan, in, op,* and *uit.* Remarkably, the meaning contribution of the particles is very vague, and sometimes fully absent, i.e. the particle verb has about the same meaning as the verb by itself. This use of SCVs is particularly popular in the language of politicians and managers. Examples of such pairs are the following (Van der Horst and Van der Horst 1999: 351):

(29) | *simplex verb* | *particle verb* |
|---|---|
| delen 'to divide' | op delen 'to divide' |
| huren 'to rent' | in huren 'to rent' |
| leveren 'to deliver' | aan leveren 'to deliver' |
| schatten 'to estimate' | in schatten 'to estimate' |
| splitsen 'to split' | op splitsen 'to split' |
| sturen 'to steer' | aan sturen 'to steer' |
| testen 'to test' | uit testen 'to test' |

The only general difference between such simplex verbs and their particle verb counterparts is that the particle verb is always obligatorily transitive, whereas the simplex verb may be used without an overt direct object. That is, these particles have primarily a syntactic valency determining function.

In conclusion, we need an analysis that can do justice to all the properties of SCVs discussed above. The notion that we can use for such an analysis is that of 'constructional idiom' introduced in section 1.3. The next section presents such an analysis.

5.3 SCVs as instantiations of constructional idioms

The debate on the proper analysis of SCVs as being either morphology or syntax reflects a limited and rather standard view of the lexicon. The lexicon is seen as the fund of existing words that can be extended by morphological operations. In addition, the lexicon will also contain idioms, that is, syntactic chunks with a non-compositional semantic interpretation. Productive syntactic constructions on the other hand are accounted for by the syntactic module.

This sharp boundary between lexicon and syntax has been challenged for good reasons in the theoretical framework of Construction Grammar. In particular the notion 'constructional idiom' can be used to do justice to both the phrasal and the word-like properties of SCVs. The claims that I will defend are the following:

- preverbs are words that are optionally projecting (Toivonen 2003). If they do not project a phrase of their own, they have the status X^0 (bare head); if they project a phrase, they can be modified and topicalized;
- many Dutch particles (adpositional preverbs) are standardly non-projecting, that is, they never project a full phrase since they can never be modified or topicalized;
- a restricted set of nouns, adjectives, and adverbs are optionally projecting. If they do not project a phrase, they form an SCV with a verb (see Chapter 4 for nouns with this property);
- non-projecting words optionally incorporate into a syntactic verbal compound of the form $[X^0 \, V^0]_{V^0}$, as argued for nouns in Chapter 4.

An example of a word that is optionally projecting is the word *af* as in *af maken* 'to finish'. It can function as part of an SCV given the criteria outlined above. However, it can also be modified and topicalized, as illustrated by the following examples:

(30)   a. Jan maakte zijn huiswerk helemaal af
         John made his homework completely ready
         'John finished his homework completely'
       b. Helemaal áf is het huiswerk nog niet
         Completely finished is the homework yet not
         'The homework is not yet completely ready'
       c. Áf maakte Jan zijn huiswerk nog niet
         Finished made John his homework yet not
         'John has not yet finished his homework'

Similar patterns of use can be observed for the word *op* with the meaning 'gone'. In other interpretations, however, the word *op* cannot be modified, as in the particle verb *opbellen* 'to phone', where *op* cannot be modified or topicalized:

(30)   e. *Hans belde zijn moeder helemaal op
           Hans phoned his mother completely up
           'Hans phoned his mother completely'
       f. *Óp belde Hans zijn moeder niet
           Up phoned Hans his mother not
           'Hans did not phóne his mother'

Hence, with this meaning the word *op* is non-projecting.

   This means that SCVs have the following syntactic structure:

(31)   [X^0 V^0]$_{V'}$ where X^0 = P, Adv, A or N

By assigning a V'-node to SCVs, we represent their phrasal nature, and hence their syntactic separability. The node V' indicates a first level of projection above the V-node. The left constituent is a single lexical category and does not project a phrase; it is a bare head. This correctly implies that the left constituent cannot be modified or topicalized.

   In structure (31), the verbal position is open and can in principle be filled by any verb. The non-verbal constituent, however, is specified. That is, there are at least as many different constructional idioms of this kind as there are words that can fill the left position (some particles may occur in more than one constructional idiom because they are polysemous). For instance, we will have the following constructional idioms:

(32)   [[*af*]$_{P^0}$ V^0]$_{V'}$, [[*door*]$_{P^0}$ V^0]$_{V'}$, [[*op*]$_{P^0}$ V^0]$_{V'}$

that both generalize over and give rise to particle verbs that begin with *af*, *door*, and *op* respectively, with a fixed terminal node for the particle constituent. Note that there are also cases where the verb only occurs in the SCV construction, cases like *na bootsen* 'to imitate' and *om kukelen* 'to fall down'. In these cases, we have lexical idioms, with all terminal nodes fixed. Those lexical idioms will be dominated in the hierarchical lexicon by the constructional idioms with *na* and *om* respectively that also dominate particle verbs such as *na volgen* 'after follow, to imitate' and *om vallen* 'down fall, to fall down'.

   For each constructional idiom of this kind, its meaning will be specified, in line with the basic assumption that constructions are pairings of form and meaning. For instance, the meaning of the constructional idiom *door-V* that expresses continuative aspect will be specified as 'to go on V-ing', and the constructional idiom *af-V* will be specified as 'to finish V-ing'. As pointed out by Blom (2004: 15), SCVs are thus compositional and conventionalized at the same time. The conventionalized aspect of the meaning of these SCVs is expressed as a property of the whole construction.

Note that the word *door* 'through' is also used as an adposition, and has a range of meanings when used as such. In addition, it can also be used as a predicate, as in *Die jas is helemaal door* 'That coat is completely through, that coat is threadbare'. The specific meaning of continuation, however, is tied to the occurrence of *door* in the particle verb construction. In this respect such constructional idioms are similar to the subpatterns of compounding discussed in section 3.2, where we also saw that words may have a specific conventional, yet productive meaning when part of a compound construction.

For the meaning contribution of a constructional idiom we may have to allow for subcases with specific meanings. These meanings may form a semantic chain, related by semantic extension mechanisms like metaphor and metonymy. For instance, the particle *op*, which is a locative adposition as well, shows up with the following meanings in particle verbs:

(33)   A semantic chain for *op* 'up' (Blom 2004: 14)
        a. to (cause to) move upward: op tillen 'to lift up', op gooien 'to throw up', op borrelen 'to bubble up', op graven 'to dig up', op duiken 'to dive up';
        b. to (cause to) surface: op borrelen 'to bubble up', op graven 'to dig up', op duiken 'to bring to the surface, to surface';
        c. to (cause to) appear/become visible: op duiken 'to turn up', op dienen 'to serve up', op vragen 'to ask for', op zoeken 'to look up';
        d. to (cause to) become perceptually/cognitively accessible: op vragen 'to ask for', op zoeken 'to look up', op bellen 'to phone up', op piepen 'to beep up'.

There are other meanings for the particle *op* as well, as illustrated by the particle verb *op binden* 'lit. up tie, tie together'. In a hierarchical lexicon with subgeneralizations for subsets of particle verbs, these patterns of regular polysemy can be expressed. In short, constructional idioms with particles such as *op* exhibit a high degree of semantic flexibility, and form a very productive category of complex predicates in Dutch.

What about those SCVs that do not take an existing verb in the open position but an adjective or a noun? The obvious step to take is to specify constructional idioms of the type

(34) $[[op]_{P^0}[[x]_{A^0}]_V]_{V'}$

This means that adjectives can be converted to verbs by inserting them in the slot after the particle *op*. This makes the conversion of adjectives dependent on their occurrence in SCVs, and this is correct since, except for the particle context, conversion of adjectives to verbs is not productive in Dutch, as pointed out above. Moreover, this approach enables us to express the dependency of A to V conversion on its occurrence with specific particles. It is indeed the case that the particle *op* is used productively in this construction, but this does not apply to all particles. It is in particular the particles *aan, af, in, op,* and *uit* that combine productively with adjectives; as for nouns, the corresponding verbs are used as verbs in combination with *af, in, na, op,* and *uit* (to see the conversion effect properly, the infinitive ending *-en* is omitted):

(35) a. *adjective*   *verb*
         sterk 'strong'   aan sterk 'to convalesce'
         zwak 'weak'   af zwak 'to weaken'
         dik 'thick'   in dik 'to thicken'
         fris 'fresh'   op fris 'to refresh'
         diep 'deep'   uit diep 'to deepen'
      b. *noun*
         beeld 'image'   af beeld 'to represent'
         polder 'id.'   in polder 'to drain, to impolder'
         aap 'monkey'   na aap 'to imitate'
         hype 'id.'   op hype 'to turn into a hype'
         huwelijk 'marriage' uit huwelijk 'to marry off '

Noun to verb conversion is productive in Dutch, but verbs like *apen, beelden,* and *huwelijken* do not exist on their own, and the N to V conversion *polderen* only exists with a different meaning 'to compromise'. These facts once more show the importance of low level schemas to represent the regions of productivity.

   What we see here is another case of schema unification, this time not the unification of two word formation schemas but of a word formation schema (zero-conversion) with a constructional schema for specific types of particle verbs. These unified schemas express the co-occurrence of these two ways of creating lexical constructs, conversion and particle verb formation. Conversion of nouns and adjectives into verbs is subject to the requirement that the input word is simplex. The formation of particle verbs conforms to this restriction as can be seen from the examples in (35). The only possible exception is *uithuwelijk*, since *huwelijk* 'marriage' might be seen as a complex word with the verbal base *huw* 'to marry' and the suffix *-elijk*. However, this word has lost its morphological transparency since words in *-elijk* are normally adjectives.

Schema unification thus serves to express what I refer to as embedded productivity: a particular word formation process may be only productive when embedded in other structures. The construction of NV compounding appeared to be dependent on these compounds being embedded in other compounds or derivational structures (section 2.4.1). Structure (34), for instance, can be labelled as productive even though conversion of As to Vs is not productive in isolation. The representation of particle verbs by schemas in the lexicon makes it possible to express this co-occurrence relationship with the lexical process of conversion.

5.3.1 Preverb incorporation

As illustrated by the sentences (15) and (16), repeated here for convenience, a particle can be raised with its verb to a higher clause (15c), and can appear after *aan het* in the *aan het* + INF construction (16a):

(15) a. dat Hans [zijn moeder op bellen]$_S$ wilde   *underlying structure*
         that Hans his mother up phone wanted
      b. dat Hans zijn moeder op [wilde bellen]   *raising without particle*
         that Hans his mother up wanted phone
      c. dat Hans zijn moeder [wilde op bellen]   *raising with particle*
         that Hans his mother wanted up phone

(16) a. Hans is zijn moeder aan het op bellen 'Hans is phoning his mother'
      b. Hans is zijn moeder op aan het bellen 'Hans is phoning his mother'
      c. *Hans is aan het zijn moeder bellen 'Hans is phoning his mother'
      d. Hans is zijn moeder aan het bellen 'Hans is phoning his mother'

For the progressive construction, incorporation of the particle is the preferred variant but both variants occur.

This ambiguous behaviour of particle verbs is accounted for by the incorporation structure proposed in Chapter 4: a bare element followed by a verb can be structurally interpreted as a syntactic compound. Hence, the second structure available for *op bellen* is the syntactic compound structure in (36):

(36) $[P^0 \ V^0]_{V^0}$

Verb Raising in standard Dutch raises V^0, not V', as shown by the ungrammaticality of (16c), and hence the variable behaviour of particle verbs follows from the availability of two structural interpretations for a particle verb combination. Similarly, the progressive construction accepts only V^0-infinitives (Chapters 4 and 6).

As argued in Chapter 4, preverb incorporation is not to be interpreted as a syntactic transformation since there are SCVs like *zee zeilen* 'sea-sailing' which can only occur in incorporation structures. Incorporation can best be viewed as a paradigmatic relationship between two schemas:

(37) $[X^0 \ V^0]_{V'} \approx [X^0 \ V^0]_{V^0}$

Schema correlation (37) states that for every structure of the type on the left (a bare head plus a V), there is a corresponding structure of the type right of the $\approx$, the structure of a syntactic compound.

SCVs with adjectives and adverbs exhibit the same behaviour. For instance, the adjective *open* 'id.' functions as preverb. The difference with an adjective that is not a preverb, such as *groen* 'green', can be seen in the Verb Raising construction:

(38)   a. dat ik de deur {wilde open maken/open wilde maken}
           that I the door {wanted open make/open wanted make}
           'that I wanted to open the door'
      b. dat ik de deur {*wilde groen verven/groen wilde verven}
           that I the door {wanted green paint/green wanted paint}
           'that I wanted to paint the door green'

Since *groen* does not form a verbal constituent with *verven*, the modal verb *wilde* cannot be adjoined to the word sequence *groen verven* because it does not form a SCV. On the other hand, the grammaticality of the sequence *wilde open maken* shows that *open maken* is a verbal unit. Thus, we must assume a constructional idiom $[[open]_{A^0} \ [x]_{V^0}]_{V'}$, and a corresponding syntactic compound, with the left terminal node fixed. The constructional idiom approach enables us to account for the productivity of SCVs with the word *open*. This is indeed a productive category. The *Van Dale Woordenboek van het Hedendaags Nederlands* (1991^2) lists 36 SCVs with *open*, for example:

(39)   open barsten 'to burst open', open breken 'to break open', open scheu-ren 'to tear open', open schieten 'to burst open', open schoppen 'to kick open'

Actually, intuitions of native speakers of Dutch vary with respect to the SCV character of *open* + Verb combinations because there are two potential sources of such a combination: a regular syntactic construction with a secondary resultative predicate and the constructional idiom with *open*.

Both interpretations are possible when there is no semantic irregularity involved.

In many cases, the SCV nature of the adjective + verb sequence which can be determined on the basis of its behaviour under Verb Raising is also proven by its unpredictable meaning, and the fact that the adjective does not allow for modification:

(40)   bloot staan 'to be exposed to'   < bloot 'naked', staan 'to stand'
           goed keuren 'to approve of '   < goed 'well', keuren 'to judge'
           groot brengen 'to raise'   < groot 'big', brengen 'to bring'
           vreemd gaan 'to sleep around'   < vreemd 'strange', gaan 'to go'

In these SCVs, the adjectives cannot be modified. For instance, sentences such as:

(41)   a. *Hij ging heel vreemd
           He went very strange
           'He slept around a lot'
    b. *Hij bracht zijn kind heel groot
           He brought his child very big
           'He raised his child enormously'

are ungrammatical. This follows from the proposed structure since the left constituent of such SCVs is specified as a bare adjective, not as an AP. Hence, it is impossible to modify the adjective in that position.

Most of the SCVs with adjectives are cases of lexicalization; only a few patterns, such as the *open*-V combination, are productive and will therefore be represented as constructional idioms, with an open V-position.

There are quite a number of adverbs that can be used in Dutch SCVs, including complex locational and temporal adverbs such as *omlaag* 'down' and *achtereen* 'continuously'. The examples below are SVCs with simplex adverbs:

(42)   heen gaan 'to leave'   < heen 'away', gaan 'to go'
           neer komen 'to descend'   < neer 'down', komen 'to come'
           samen komen 'to convene'   < samen 'together', komen 'to come'
           terecht wijzen 'to reprimand'   < terecht 'right', wijzen 'to point'
           thuis brengen 'to identify'   < thuis 'home', brengen 'to bring'
           voort gaan 'to go on'   < voort 'further', gaan 'to go'
           weg gaan 'to go away'   < weg 'way', gaan 'to go'

When a bare adverb is used productively in this construction, a constructional SCV idiom for that adverb is justified.

5.3.2 Mismatches between form and meaning

Particle verbs, and SCVs in general, feed word formation processes, and are also subject to inflectional processes. The formation of past participles for particle verbs shows their phrasal nature, as pointed out above: the prefixal part *ge-* of the participial form appears in between the preverb and the verbal stem. This position of the participial prefix is explained if SCVs are phrasal in nature.

(43)　a.　op ge-bel-d
　　　　　up PREF-phone-SUFF
　　　　　'phoned up'
　　　b.　neer ge-daal-d
　　　　　down PREF-descend-SUFF
　　　　　'descended'
　　　c.　schoon ge-maak-t
　　　　　clean PREF-make-SUFF
　　　　　'cleaned'

The participial prefix *ge-* cannot be added before the particle because it requires a V as its base, not a V'. Yet, the semantic scope of the participial prefix–suffix combination is not the verb only but the particle verb combination as a whole. The same observation has been made by Stump (1991) who lists a number of such cases. For instance, in Sanskrit complex predicates with preverbs, the past tense prefix appears right before the verbal stem and after its preverb (Stump 1991: 687). Hence, there is a mismatch between the form and the meaning of inflected particle verbs.

A second example of such a mismatch concerns the conversion of particle verbs into nouns. Even here we are able to see that the formal aspect of this morphological operation applies to the head of the particle verb, although there is no overt morphology involved. There is a systematic correlation between the gender of the converted noun and the form of the corresponding verb: if a verb is simplex, the converted noun has common gender and selects the DEF.SG article *de*; if the verb is prefixed, the corresponding noun has neuter gender and selects the DEF.SG. article *het*:

(44)　a.　bouw-en 'to build'　　de bouw 'the construction'
　　　　　vall-en 'to fall'　　　de val 'the fall'
　　　　　lop-en 'to walk'　　　de loop 'the course'
　　　　　trapp-en 'to kick'　　de trap 'the kick'
　　　b.　be-stur-en 'to govern'　het bestuur 'the board, the governance'
　　　　　ge-bruik-en 'to use'　　het gebruik 'the use'
　　　　　ver-vall-en 'to decay'　het verval 'the decay'

Prefixed verbs correspond with *het*-nouns, but particle verbs with *de*-nouns. This is exactly what is expected since conversion operates on the head of the particle verb which is simplex in nature:

(45)   aan vall-en 'to attack'   de aanval 'the attack'
        af trapp-en 'to kick off '   de aftrap 'the kick-off '
        in gooi-en 'to throw in'   de ingooi 'the throw-in'

These facts are also interesting from a general constructionist point of view because they provide evidence for holistic properties of morphological constructions. The gender of these nouns cannot be assigned to an affix that functions as the head of the morphological construction because there is no affix. Hence, it is the conversion construction that assigns a gender feature to the complex word as a whole (section 2.3). Note that the prefixes in (44b) are not the heads of the converted nouns. Hence, we need morphological schemas for conversion that specify the gender of the converted noun:

(46)   a. $[[x]_{Vi}]_{Nj[-neuter]} \leftrightarrow [\text{event of SEM}_i]_j$
        b. $[[\text{Prefix } [x]_V]_{Vi}]_{Nj[+neuter]} \leftrightarrow [\text{event of SEM}_i]_j$

Since (46b) is more specific than (46a), it will take precedence in the case of prefixed verbs and hence predict that the corresponding nouns are neuter. Schema (46b) also shows that morphological schemas may need access to the internal morphological structure of words.

Dutch SCVs feed word formation processes with overt affixation:

(47)   *particle verb*   *prefixed noun*
        a. rond spring-en 'to jump around' rond-ge-spring 'jumping around'
           op bell-en 'to phone'   op-ge-bel '(repeated) phoning'
           schoon mak-en 'to clean'   schoon-ge-maak 'cleaning'
                                            suffixed noun
        b. aan vall-en 'to attack'   aan-vall-er 'agressor'
           aan bied-en 'to offer'   aan-bied-ing 'offer'
           aan kom-en 'to arrive'   aan-kom-st 'arrival'
           aan ton-en 'to prove'   aan-toon-baar 'provable'
           aan trekk-en 'to attract'   aan-trekk-elijk 'attractive'

Again, we observe an asymmetry between form and meaning because the attached prefix or suffix formally attaches to the verb, whereas semantically it has scope over the SCV as a whole. How can we account for this asymmetry?

This problem has been discussed by Müller (2003) for similar facts of German. For instance, the derived noun of the SCV *herum hopsen* 'to jump around' is *Herum-ge-hopse*, and the past participle of German *an kommen* 'to arrive' is *an-ge-komm-en*. Müller's proposal is to assume a sublemma for the verbal part of SCVs which carries a subcategorization specification, requiring that verb to co-occur with a certain other word. It is to this sublemma that the morphological operations apply. In the case of the Dutch particle verb *aan vallen* 'to attack' this would mean that the verb *vallen* 'to fall' will have a sublemma with the meaning 'to attack' that is specified as obligatory co-occurring with the word *aan*. It is this sublemma that is converted to a noun *val* with the same subcategorization requirement. The drawback of this analysis is that the holistic meaning of the particle verb *aan vallen* is assigned in an artificial way to the verbal part *vallen* only.

This kind of mismatch is a much more general phenomenon, however. Classic examples are phrases like *transformational grammarian* related to *transformational grammar*, and *physical scientist* related to *physical science*. A transformational grammarian is not a grammarian who is transformational but a linguist who adheres to the theoretical framework of transformational grammar. Hence, the semantic scope of the suffix *-ian* is *transformational grammar*, whereas its formal scope is the noun *grammar* only. This phenomenon is usually referred to as a 'bracketing paradox' since two different bracketing structures seem to be necessary (Spencer 1988):

(48) *form*: $[[\text{transformational}]_A\ [\text{grammar-ian}]_N]_{NP}$
      meaning: $[[[\text{transformational grammar}]_{NP}\text{-ian}]_N]_{NP}$

The analysis proposed by Spencer is an essentially paradigmatic analysis of these facts since he invokes the notion 'proportional analogy' to account for this type of word formation (Spencer 1988: 675).

(49)   grammar   ↔   grammarian
                       ↕   ↕
      transformational grammar   ?

In this pattern, the question mark will be filled in as *transformational grammarian*. Note that in this case, the solution proposed by Müller for the German particle verbs would not work, unless one subcategorizes the word *grammar* for appearing with the adjective *transformational*.

A paradigmatic analysis can also do justice to the observation that, if a verb has an irregular corresponding nominalization, this irregular form will return in the nominalized particle verb. Consider the following data concerning the nominalization of Dutch particle verbs:

(50) a. kom-en 'to come'   kom-st 'coming'
         aan kom-en 'to arrive' aan-kom-st 'arrival'

b. bied-en 'to offer'   bod 'offer'
   aan bied-en 'to offer'   aan-bod 'offer'

In (50a), the deverbal noun contains an unproductive suffix -*st* (the suffix -*ing* is the productive suffix for deverbal nominalization), and the long vowel of the verbal stem *komen* /o:/ is shortened. The deverbal noun in (50b) is created by means of vowel change, another completely unproductive and lexicalized process. Yet, these forms return in the nominalizations of the particle verbs. In other words, from a formal point of view these nominalizations of particle verbs have to be considered compounds consisting of a particle and an existing lexicalized deverbal noun. The wider semantic scope of the nominalization involved is expressed by postulating a paradigmatic relationship between these two patterns (independent arguments for such relationships are presented in section 2.2):

(51) $< [\text{Part } V_k]_{V'_i} \leftrightarrow \text{SEM}_i > \approx < [\text{Part } [V_k\text{-suff}]_N]_{Nj} \leftrightarrow [\text{NOM } [\text{SEM}_i]]_j >$

The semantic operator NOM stands for the semantic effect of nominalization. SEM_i stands for the meaning of the particle verb as a whole, and since NOM has scope over SEM_i, it is expressed that compounds consisting of a particle and a deverbal noun are interpreted as nominalizations of the corresponding particle verbs. Thus, we see another argument here for the necessity of paradigmatic relationships in the lexicon.

In this analysis, we interpret nominalizations of particle verbs such as *aankomst* 'arrival' as nominal compounds since this is the only morphological structure available for combining a particle and a deverbal noun. We do not have 'separable complex nouns', and hence, when combined with a noun, a particle can only appear as the left constituent of a nominal compound.

This effect of the availability of morphological structures on the nominalization of particle verbs is even stronger in Norwegian and Swedish. In these languages, particles follow the verb, just as in English. However, in nouns derived from these particle verbs, the particle has to precede the deverbal noun because in these languages nominal compounds are right-headed:

(52)   a. *Norwegian*
          kjøre opp 'to take one's driving test'
          opp-kjør-ing 'driving test'
          opp-kjør-sel 'driveway'
       b. *Swedish*
          stiga upp 'ro rise'
          upp-stig-ning 'rising'

Thus, the paradigmatic relationship with the corresponding particle verb is preserved, but the order of the two words involved varies with the kind of structure that is available for accommodating the deverbal word.

In English, we expect the same effects since English compounds are also right-headed. Indeed, we find deverbal nouns like *on-looker* and *by-passer*, with the particle preceding the verb (compare *to look on, to pass by*). Yet, we also find cases where the particle appears after the deverbal noun, and cases where the derivational suffix is attached to the particle which reflects the lexical unit nature of particle verbs (53b). We even find cases where *-er* is attached to both verb and particle (53c). This variation may be seen as a reflexion of the uncertainty of the language user as to the proper structure to be assigned to denominal derivatives of English particle verbs:

(53)   a. These determined *lookers-on* are not likely to leave before dawn (Elenbaas 2007: 9)
      b. This book is *unputdownable* (on the cover of a book)
      c. I had really believed that I was going to live in Hastings and become a *putter-upper* of giant bowling pins or a *lifter-upper* of old people who needed to climb a lot of stairs (Nick Hornby, *Slam*, p. 125)

Other examples of the three types of *-er*-nouns are: *bystander, stander-by*, and *washer-upper* (Ryder 1999*b*).

We thus conclude that the structure of words like Dutch *rondgespring* 'jumping around' and the other derived words mentioned in (47) is that of compounds. This correctly predicts that they have the stress patterns of compounds. The Dutch rule for compound stress is that there is main stress on the first constituent if the compound is nominal. As to adjectival compounds, there is variation. Adjectival compounds with a complex head carry main stress on the second constituent, such as *milieu-belást-end* 'environment-unfriendly' and *tijd-gebónden* 'time-bound, dated' (De Haas and Trommelen 1993: 426).[2] In words like *aan-tóon-baar* and *aan-trékk-elijk*, the adjectives for the particle verbs *aan tonen* 'to demonstrate' and *aan trekken* 'to attract', main stress is on the adjectival heads *toon-baar* and *trekk-elijk*, as expected, since these are complex heads.

Complex adjectives for particle verbs thus exhibit a systematic difference in main stress location with adjectives derived from other types of complex verbs:

[2.] Such adjectival compounds with complex heads tend to have variation in stress location in that the main accent can also appear on the first constituent in non-predicative position. In the case of adjectives derived from particle verbs, however, main stress is fixed on the second constituent.

(54)   a. *base = particle verb*
  ín zet 'to employ'   in-zét-baar 'employable'
  wáar neem 'to observe' waar-néem-baar 'observable'
  úit steek 'to excel'   uit-sték-end 'excellent'
  b. *base = complex verb*
  be-ín-vloed 'to influence' be-ín-vloed-baar 'influenceable'
  ver-wáar-loos 'to neglect' ver-wáar-loos-baar 'negligible'

The suffix *-baar* is normally a stress-neutral suffix that does not shift the main stress of the word rightward, as illustrated in (54b). In the cases shown in (54a), however, main stress shifts from the particle to the verbal stem. This follows from the fact that these adjectives can only be interpreted as adjectival compounds, with the following structure:

(55) $[[in]_P [[zet]_V baar]_A]_A$
  $[[waar]_A[[neem]_V baar]_A]_A$
  $[[uit]_P [[stek]_V end]_A]_A$

Hence, they get the prosodic properties of adjectival compounds with complex heads (main stress on the second prosodic word), and not the stress patterns of derived adjectives.

 In conclusion, the assumption of paradigmatic relationships between different constructional schemas for lexical units such as particle verbs and compounds is crucial for understanding how phrasal lexical units interact with word formation processes. It is only by means of a paradigmatic analysis that we can make sense of how particle verbs feed word formation processes.

5.4 Diachrony and grammaticalization

The emergence of particles as parts of complex verbal predicates can be seen as a form of grammaticalization, 'the process whereby lexical items and constructions come in certain linguistic contexts to serve grammatical functions, and, once grammaticalized, continue to develop new grammatical functions' (Hopper and Traugott 2003: xv). This is indeed what we observe for particles: they occur in phrasal constructs that function as complex verbs, and have acquired specific grammatical and semantic properties. Thus, a set of constructional idioms came into being, since the particles have acquired specific properties and can be used productively with that meaning. It is an important insight of grammaticalization theory that grammaticalization of lexical morphemes always takes place in particular constructions (Bybee et al. 1994; Traugott 2003), and the emergence of particles with specific grammatical meanings in verbal constructions is a perfect illustration of this insight.

As far as Dutch is concerned, two patterns of grammaticalization should be distinguished (Blom 2004). One pattern is the development of resultative predicates into aspectual particles such as *af* in *af maken* 'to finish'. The other pattern is the reanalysis of non-predicative predicates such as adverbs and adpositions into particles. An example of the latter type of reanalysis is given in (56):

(56)   [[het publiek]$_{NP}$ [toe]$_P$]$_{PP}$ [spreken]$_V$ >   [het publiek]$_{NP}$ [toe spreken]$_{V'}$
      the public to speak   the public to speak
      'speak to the public'   'address the public'

The particle verb *toe spreken* 'to address' is a transitive verbal predicate that selects an object that denotes an audience.

Additional evidence for the structural reanalysis involved here is that the form of the particle is identical to the postpositional allomorph *toe* 'to', whereas the corresponding prepositional allomorph is *tot* 'to'. The particle *toe* hence clearly derives from a postposition.

Some of these non-predicative particles form intermediate stages in the development of words into prefixes. The following minimal pairs (with different locations of main stress) illustrate this:

(57)   *particle verb*   *prefixed verb*
      dóor breken 'to break through'   door-bréken 'to break'
      dóor lopen 'to walk on'   door-lópen 'to pass'
      ónder gaan 'to go down'   onder-gáan 'to undergo'
      óver komen 'to come over'   over-kómen 'to happen to someone'

The change from non-predicative particle to prefix implies a further loss of lexical meaning: the prefixes have an abstract, aspectual meaning with a spatial flavour, whereas the corresponding particles tend to have a more concrete, spatial meaning. The verbs are subject to a similar type of change: their meanings are more abstract in combination with the prefixes, as a comparison of the glosses in (57) will reveal, and hence these prefixed verbs all have lexicalized meanings.

This difference between more abstract meanings for prefixes and more concrete meanings for particles is found for other Dutch prefixes as well. The Dutch verbalizing prefixes *be-* and *ver-* that contribute a relatively abstract, grammatical meaning to the relevant complex verbs derive historically from the words *bi* (modern Dutch *bij* 'at') and *fair/fair/fra* (modern Dutch *voor* 'for') respectively, whereas the modern Dutch counterparts *bij* and *voor* function as prepositions and particles.

The hypothesis that SCVs may function as an intermediate stage in the grammaticalization of syntactic constructs into morphological constructs is supported by the observation that some verbs which were still SCVs in Middle Dutch have developed into prefixed verbs in modern Dutch. This applies to, for instance, the following verbs:[3]

(58)   achter-vólgen 'to run after', om-ríngen 'to surround', om-síngelen 'to surround', over-brúggen 'to bridge', over-vállen 'to attack suddenly' (Van Loey 1976)

As the glosses of these examples show, the preverbal elements, originally locational adpositions, contribute a more abstract meaning in their use as prefixes. The following examples serve to illustrate the use of the more concrete, spatial interpretation of these verbs in Middle Dutch, which correlates with separability, of *over bruggen* 'over bridge, to bridge across' and *om ringen* 'around ring, to surround':

(59)   a. Voort gheven wy hem oorloff [...] die over te brugghen
            Furthermore give we him permission that across to bridge
            'Furthermore, we give him permission to put a bridge across it'
       b. Mettien hebben si=se omme-geringhet
            Immediately have they=her around-ringed
            'Immediately they surrounded her'

The SCVs in (59) have a holistic meaning: they denote an action through which the object is completely affected. The holistic meaning of these SCVs is the basis for such SCVs to change into prefixed verbs, as is the case in present-day Dutch, where we find the inseparable prefixed verbs *over-brúggen* 'to bridge' and *om-ríngen* 'to surround'. Some such verbs were used as separable verbs in 18th- and 19th-century Dutch, and are now inseparable, thus instantiating the same development as took place in Middle Dutch, verbs such as *voor-kómen* 'to prevent' and *door-stáan* 'to endure' (Van der Horst and Van der Horst 1999: 348).

The rise of a large set of constructional idioms of this type in Germanic languages explains why verbal prefixation is not very productive in these languages. There are many particles available for the expression of various grammatical meanings (aspectual, locational, etc.), and particles combine with verbs to form lexical units, just like verbal prefixes. It is noteworthy that these constructional idioms are quite stable: the particles involved do not exhibit a massive tendency to become prefixes. Hence, they strongly compete with verbal prefixation. Such competition is understandable if we consider SCVs as lexical units, just like prefixed verbs.

[3.] See Blom (2004, 2005a,b) and Blom and Booij (2003) for more detailed analyses of these developments.

5.5 Conclusions

Complex predicates may have both phrasal and lexical properties. This is the case for the specific subtype of complex predicates known as particle verbs discussed in this chapter. By looking in detail at particle verbs in one language, Dutch, we see that the notion of constructional idiom provides the right analytic tool for dealing with the apparently paradoxical properties of phrasal complex predicates. The interaction of particle verbs with word formation patterns has provided new evidence for the necessity of assuming paradigmatic relationships between constructional schemas in the lexicon. It is clear that the historical origins and diachronic developments of SCVs find motivation in a constructional approach. This suggests that a constructional approach is not only insightful with respect to the inventories of synchronic constructions but that the same basic assumptions are crucial to understanding how these patterns arise and develop.

6

Progressive constructions

6.1 Periphrastic progressives

In many languages we find multi-word expressions that serve to express progressive aspect. English is an example of such a language since it expresses progressive aspect on verbs by means of a form of the verb *to be* and the *-ing*-form of the verb. Hence, we have to assume a constructional idiom for English of the following type:

(1) $[\text{be } V_i\text{-ing}]_{V^0j} \leftrightarrow [\text{PROGR } [\text{SEM}_i]]_j$

The progressive meaning is not a property of the individual words but of the construction as a whole (Lee 2007). The constructional schema in (1) is a constructional idiom because certain positions in this schema are lexically filled, whereas the position of the verb is variable and open. That is, all kinds of verbs can be inserted into that schema, subject to certain semantic constraints.

The rise of this constructional idiom is a form of grammaticalization in which the verb *to be* has acquired the grammatical role of progressive auxiliary. It is an essential insight of grammaticalization theory that grammaticalization does not affect words in isolation but words in specific syntactic constructions (Bybee et al. 1994; Heine 1993; Heine et al. 1991; Kuteva 2001; Petré and Cuyckens 2008; Traugott 2003). For instance, the developments of postural verbs into auxiliaries of progressive aspect takes place in constructions of the type verb + complement that develop into constructions of the type progressive marker + main verb.

In this chapter I focus on one particular progressive construction in Dutch, the *aan het* + INFINITIVE 'at the V-ing' construction, and I will argue that a detailed analysis of this construction will give us more insight into the nature of constructional idioms.

In European languages we mainly find two sources of progressive constructions: combinations of a postural verb with a main verb and locative constructions (Bertinetto et al. 2000).

Instantiations of the first type of construction in Dutch are combinations of the verb *zitten* 'to sit' with an action verb, as in (2):

(2) a. Jan zit te zeur-en/*Jan zit zeur-en
     John sits to nag-INF/John sits nag-INF
     'John is nagging'
  b. Jan heeft zitt-en te zeur-en/Jan heeft zitt-en zeur-en
     John has sit-INF to nag-INF/John has sit-INF nag-INF
     'John has been nagging'
  c. Jan begint te zitt-en zeur-en/*Jan begint te zitt-en te zeur-en
     John begins to sit-INF nag-INF/John begins to sit-INF to nag-INF
     'John starts nagging'

As the examples in (2) illustrate, the meaning of *zitten* has bleached into a more abstract meaning: it does not imply that John is actually sitting. These examples also serve to illustrate the formal complexities of such constructions: in the present tense (2a) and in combination with verbs such as *beginnen* 'to begin' (2c), the particle *te* must be present, whereas it is optional in the perfect tense (2b). In (2b) we also see the Infinitivus-Pro-Participio-effect: instead of the expected perfect participle *gezeten*, the infinitive *zitten* has to be used. Finally, a second appearance of *te* after *zitten* in (2c), a sentence with two infinitives, leads to ungrammaticality, even though this is grammatical in sentence (2b).

Postural verbs are used as progressive markers in languages across the world (Newman 2002), for instance in a number of Germanic languages (Ebert 2000), among them Afrikaans, Middle Dutch, Standard Modern Dutch (Lemmens 2002, 2005; Leys 1985; Pottelberge 2002), and Swedish (Hilpert and Koops 2008).

The other type of progressive marking, the locative construction, is illustrated by the following example from Dutch:

(3) Julian is aan het fiets-en
     Julian is at the cycle-INF
     'Julian is cycling'

The word sequence *aan het fietsen* has the form of a PP: the preposition *aan* 'at', followed by the DEF.SG. determiner for neuter nouns *het* and the infinitive, a verbal form with nominal properties such as having neuter gender and being able to function as the head of an NP. This is therefore another case of grammaticalization of a particular construction: the sequence *aan het* has developed into a progressive marker for the verb, which is functioning as the main verb, as we will see below. In present-day Dutch the preposition *aan* 'at' can be used as a locative preposition in restricted contexts only. For instance, unlike English *at* and German *an* (contracted with the determiner to *am*), it cannot be used unrestrictedly in a simple locative expression:

(4)   Dutch: Jan is *aan/op het station
         English: John is at the station
         German: Johann ist am Bahnhof

The preposition *aan* can be used for expressing some types of location and combines with some process nouns, such as *werk* 'work', as in:

(5)   a. Jan zit aan de tafel
       John sits at the table
       'John is sitting at the table'
     b. Jan is aan het werk
       John is at the work
       'John is working'

However, most process nouns do not allow for *aan* as their governing preposition, as illustrated by the ungrammaticality of (6a):

(6)   a. *Jan is aan de bespreking van het probleem
       John is at the discussion of the problem
       'John is discussing the problem'
     b. Jan is bezig met de bespreking van het probleem
       John is busy with the discussion of the problem
       'John is discussing the problem'

These observations show that the occurrence of *aan* in present-day standard Dutch is bound to PPs with specific types of NPs, such as NPs of the type *het* + INFINITIVE. This use of *aan* is a reflex of an earlier stage of Dutch in which the preposition *aan* had a more elaborated use as locative preposition. For instance, in 17th-century Dutch it was possible to say *aan deze plaats* 'at this place', whereas nowadays the phrase *op deze plaats* has to be used instead, with the preposition *op* 'on'. These facts are obviously in line with the status of constructional idiom of the *aan het* + INF-construction. Combined with the observation that the progressive meaning of such constructions is not a compositional one that derives completely from the meaning of its constituent parts, this justifies the classification of this syntactic pattern as a (progressive) construction.

    The use of the verb *to be* plus a PP with an originally locative meaning for the expression of action in progress is widespread cross-linguistically (Bybee and Dahl 1989; Bybee et al. 1994). As was the case for postural verbs, the locative construction is used for progressive aspect in quite a range of genetically related and unrelated languages. For instance, it is found in a vast number of African languages (Heine 1993), in French (*être en train de*), and in a number of Germanic languages such as Dutch, the Low-Saxon dialect of Ruinen (Sassen 1953), Frisian (Dyk 1997), Afrikaans (Ponelis 1979), and certain dialects of German (Krause 2002) such as the Cologne dialect, where it is a relatively recent innovation (Kuteva 2001). In standard Dutch, this use of *aan het* + INFINITIVE dates back to at least the 17th century (as a search of the historical dictionary of Dutch, the *Woordenboek der Nederlandse Taal* reveals), and it belongs to the standard language, whereas it is not considered as standard language for High German yet. The following two examples are from Afrikaans (Ponelis 1979: 224–225) and Cologne German (Kuteva 2001: 30–35) respectively:

(7)   a.   Sy is aan die weg-gaan/Sy is an-et weg-gaan
           She is at the away-go.INF/She is at-the away-go.INF
           'She is leaving'
      b.   Ich bin am schlaf-en
           I am at.the sleep-INF
           'I am sleeping'

The word combination *an-et* 'at the' in Afrikaans has developed into a progressive marker, and the bound determiner *-et* 'the' only occurs in this context (Jac Coenradi, pers. comm.). The English progressive construction also derives from a locative construction, of the type *be on hunting* (Smith 2007).

The rise of this type of progressive marker can be explained by means of the method of reconstruction, based on two types of evidence: cross-linguistic comparison and the study of related expressions within individual languages. First, the fact that this type of grammaticalization occurs in so many not necessarily genetically related languages makes it plausible that a general cognitive mechanism is involved: the metaphorical use of spatial expressions for referring to temporal notions. Secondly, in a language like Dutch we have prepositional phrases of the form *aan het N* with a regular, compositional interpretation, besides prepositional phrases beginning with the progressive marker *aan het*, although we should observe that this use of *aan* in present-day Dutch is restricted, as we have seen above. A simple example of such a locative use of *aan* is a sentence like *Het huis staat aan de gracht* 'lit. The house stands at the canal, the house is situated on the canal'. If we want to make sense of these two uses of the *aan het*-PP we should relate them in terms of grammaticalization.

Strictly speaking, this type of evidence is not diachronic evidence. The reconstructed development should be checked by careful inspection of the available historical data. In this chapter, however, I will not present such evidence concerning the rise of the Dutch progressive constructions because I want to focus on another aspect of grammaticalization: how does the rise of such a construction affect the synchronic grammar of a language, and what does its existence imply for our conception of the architecture of the grammar? In particular, I will argue that the notion 'constructional idiom' is essential for a proper account of the impact of grammaticalization on the grammar.

In a number of recent publications (Fillmore, Kay, and O'Connor 1988; Jackendoff 1997*b*, 2002*a*; Kay and Fillmore 1999; Nattinger and De Carrico 1992; Wray 2002), and in the preceding chapters of this book, attention has been drawn to the existence and theoretical implications of multi-word expressions that are idiomatic in nature but not completely fixed because some of the positions in these expressions are variable. For instance, in the English idiomatic expression *a* + Noun (time) *ago* the position of the noun can be filled by all nouns with a temporal interpretation, words such as *minute, hour,* and *day*. Such expressions with variable positions must be stored and are referred to as 'constructional idioms' (Jackendoff 1997*b*, 2002*a*) or as 'lexical phrases with a generalized frame' (Nattinger and De Carrico 1992: 36). This construction also allows for nouns that are not inherently temporal, for instance *grief* as in Dylan Thomas' *a grief ago* (an example provided to me by Nigel Vincent). There is even a poem by Michael Sheperd with that title (Elizabeth Traugott, pers. comm.). In this latter case we see the effect of type coercion: in this construction the word *grief* has to be interpreted as a time expression because it occurs in the position of the time noun.

In this chapter I will discuss one specific constructional idiom of Dutch, the progressive construction for verbs of the form *aan het* + INF introduced above. In section 6.2 I present an outline of the properties of this construction. It will be made clear there that the *aan het* + INF sequences occur with a number of verbs besides *zijn* 'to be'. Section 6.3 deals with the role of the progressive construction in triggering quasi-incorporation. In section 6.4 it is shown how the regular aspects of this particular construction and its instantiations can be accounted for. In section 6.5 I argue that the *aan het* + INF-construction may be seen as a case of periphrasis since it interacts with the use of morphological means to express progressive aspect. Section 6.6 concludes that the rise of this progressive construction is a clear case of grammaticalization.

6.2 The *aan het* + INFINITIVE construction

Let us have another look at example (3), repeated here for convenience:

(3)   Julian is aan het fiets-en
      Julian is at the cycle-INF
      'Julian is cycling'

The formal structure of the part *aan het fietsen* is that of a PP headed by the preposition *aan* and followed by an NP complement, consisting of the neuter singular determiner *het* 'the' followed by the infinitive *fietsen* 'to cycle'. This type of constructional idiom is thus canonical in that it follows the rules of Dutch syntax: it has the form of a PP, and PPs can be used as predicates in sentences with the verb *zijn* 'to be' as their main verb. Nevertheless, the *aan*-PP needs to be listed as such because the progressive meaning of this *zijn* + *PP* sequence cannot be derived compositionally from the meaning of its parts. There is no general principle of interpretation that predicts the progressive interpretation of locative prepositions combined with durational or process nouns. For instance, a sentence like *We zijn aan de wandel-ing* 'We are at the walk-ing' (with the well-formed deverbal process noun *wandel-ing* 'walk') does not allow for a progressive interpretation (and cannot be used in Dutch anyway), unlike *We zijn aan het wandelen* 'We are walking'.

As the gloss of sentence (3) indicates, the *aan*-PP in combination with *zijn* 'to be' functions as the equivalent of the English progressive form. The Dutch progressive construction is restricted as to the kind of verbs it allows: the verb should be an activity or an accomplishment verb (that is, a durational verb); stative and achievement verbs are excluded:

(8)   a. *Rebecca is aan het won-en in Amsterdam   *(state)*
          Rebecca is at the live-INF in Amsterdam
          'Rebecca is living in Amsterdam'
      b. Julian is aan het fiets-en   *(durational event, activity)*
          Julian is at the cycle-INF
          'Julian is cycling'
      c. Wouter is de appel aan het et-en   *(telic event, accomplishment)*
          Wouter is the apple at the eat-INF
          'Walter is eating the apple'
      d. *Jan is de finish aan het bereik-en   *(punctual event, achievement)*
          John is the finish at the reach-INF
          'John is reaching the finish'

In fact, the classical division of four aspectual classes in Vendler (1967) is partially based on their (in)compatibility with the progressive construction.

The progressive construction requires verbs with a durational interpretation. As noted by Boogaart (1999: 175), there is a difference between Dutch and English in that Dutch completely excludes the use of stative verbs in its progressive construction, whereas English allows for stative stage-level predicates, as in:

(9)   She was living in London at the time

Additional restrictions on the Dutch progressive, observed by Boogaart (1999: 187ff.) that do not hold for English are that it cannot be used in the passive voice nor with a habitual meaning:

(10)   a. *De krant was aan het lez-en geworden
           The paper was at the read-INF been
           'The paper was being read'
       b. *Vroeger waren ze altijd aan het ontbijt-en in de keuken
           Formerly were they always at the breakfast-INF in the kitchen
           'Formerly, they were always having breakfast in the kitchen'

There is no incompatibility between the use of the progressive form and telic events, that is, events with an inherent endpoint (Boogaart 1999). Telicity has to do with the presence of potential endpoints, and is a case of Aktionsart, whereas (un)boundedness, which has to do with the presence of actual temporal boundaries, is a matter of aspect. Telic Aktionsart combines well with an unbounded aspect (progressive reading), as illustrated by sentence (3).

The use of the *aan het* + INF-construction is not restricted to combinations with the verb *zijn* 'to be'. In fact, it combines with a number of other verbs. The data presented here are taken partially from the Dutch reference grammar *Algemene Nederlandse Spraakkunst* (Haeseryn et al. 1997: 1050ff.), and partially constructed by myself as a native speaker of Dutch. First, the *aan het* + INF-construction functions as a predicate with a progressive meaning in combination with (A) verbs of appearance, (B) accusativus-cum-infinitivo-verbs, (C) verbs that take a secondary predicate, (D) inchoative and continuative verbs, and (E) causative verbs.

A. With verbs of appearance such as *blijken* 'to appear', *lijken* 'to seem', *schijnen* 'to seem':

(11)   Indriaas *bleek* aan het schilder-en
       Indriaas appeared at the paint-INF
       'Indriaas appeared to be painting'

(12)   Suzanne *lijkt* aan het verander-en
       Suzanne seems at the change-INF
       'Suzanne seems to be changing'

(13)   Herry *scheen* weer aan het strijk-en
       Herry seemed again at the iron-INF
       'Herry seemed to be ironing again'

The use of the *aan het* + INF-construction with verbs of appearance indicates that the construction functions as a predicate; it follows the rules of Dutch syntax in that such verbs combine with similar kinds of PPs that attribute a property, that is, PPs with a non-locational interpretation; compare:

(14)   Geert bleek in de war
       Geert appeared in the knot
       'Geert appeared to be confused'

B. With the accusativus-cum-infinitivo-verbs (aci-verbs) *horen* 'to hear', *zien* 'to see', *vinden* 'to find':

(15)   We *hoorden* hem aan het rommel-en op zolder
       We heard him at the potter-INF in the attic
       'We heard him pottering around in the attic'

(16)   Ik *zag* haar aan het wied-en in de tuin
       I saw her at the weed-INF in the garden
       'I saw her weeding in the garden'

(17)   Ze *vonden* hem aan het debatter-en met zijn vrienden
       They found him at the debate-INF with his friends
       'They found him debating with his friends'

The latter three examples show that the *aan het* + INF-construction can function as the predicate of the complement of aci-verbs.

C. With the verbs *hebben* 'to have' and *houden* 'to keep', which take secondary predicates:

(18)   Ik *heb* de motor weer aan het lop-en
       I have the engine again at the run-INF
       'I have the engine running again'

(19)   Kun jij die machine aan het draai-en *houden*?
       Can you that engine at the run-INF hold?
       'Can you keep that engine running?'

D. With the inchoative verbs *gaan* 'to go', *raken* 'to get', *slaan* 'to hit', and the continuative verb *blijven* 'lit. to remain, to continue':

(20)   Ze *gaan* aan het discussiër-en
       They go at the discuss-INF
       'They start discussing'

(21)   De twee partijen *raakten* aan het vecht-en
       The two parties got at the fight-INF
       'The two parties started fighting'

(22) De matrozen *sloegen* aan het muit-en
      The sailors hit at the mutiny-INF
      'The sailors started mutinying'

(23) De soldaten *bleven* aan het vecht-en
      The soldiers kept at the fight-INF
      'The soldiers kept fighting'

E. With the causative verbs *brengen* 'to bring', *maken* 'to make', *krijgen* 'to get', *zetten* 'to put':

(24) Jan *bracht* hem {aan het twijfel-en/*twijfel-en}
      John brought him {at the doubt-INF/doubt-INF}
      'John made him doubt'

(25) Dat *maakte* hem {aan het lach-en/*lach-en}
      That made him {at the laugh-INF/laugh-INF}
      'That made him laugh'

(26) De politie *kreeg* hem {aan het prat-en/*prat-en}
      The police got him {at the talk-INF/talk-INF}
      'The police got him talking'

(27) Deze gebeurtenis *zette* hem {aan het denk-en/*denk-en}
      This event put him {at the think-INF/think-INF}
      'This event made him think'

The combinability of the verbs listed under D and E with PPs is idiomatically restricted. Compare the following sentences with the sentences (20–27) above:

(28) a. *Ze gaan in de war
         They go in the knot
         'They get confused'
      b. Ze gaan aan het werk
         They go at the work
         'They start working'

(29) a. *De matrozen sloegen in de war
         The sailors hit in the knot
         'The sailors got confused'
      b. De matrozen sloegen op de vlucht
         The sailors hit on the flight
         'The sailors fled'

(30) a. *De partijen raakten op de vlucht
          The parties got on the flight
          'The parties fled'
      b. De partijen raakten in de war
          The parties got in the knot
          'The parties got confused'

(31) a. *Dat maakte hem op de vlucht
          That made him on the flight
          'That made him flee'
      b. Dat maakte hem in de war
          That made him in the knot
          'That made him confused'

This means that the co-occurrence of these verbs with the *aan het* + INF-construction does not follow from a general phrasal schema [PP V], since this co-occurrence has to be specified for individual lexically specified PPs.

   On the basis of these observations, I conclude that Dutch has a constructional idiom *aan het* + INF with the meaning of progressive aspect. This constructional idiom in its turn forms part of a number of idioms of the type *aan het* INF Verb (the position of the verb after the infinitive in this schema reflects the underlying SOV-order of Dutch), in which the Verb slot is filled by one of a closed set of verbs, such as *gaan* and *slaan*. This shows that the notion construction has to be conceived of as a recursive pattern with a hierarchical organization. It therefore has to be specified that, for instance, the polysemous verbs *gaan* 'to go' and *slaan* 'to hit' have an inchoative meaning in this specific combination. This is another example of heterosemy, the phenomenon that words may have specific meanings in specific constructions, as discussed in Chapter 3. The most straightforward way of representing this information is the assumption of constructional idioms such as '*aan het* INF *gaan*' and '*aan het* INF *slaan*'. Thus, it is accounted for that, for instance, *slaan* has an inchoative meaning in combination with the *aan het* + INF-construction. This means that constructional idioms may form part of larger idiomatic constructions.

   The verb *gaan* 'to go' can also be used as an inchoative verb in combination with an infinitive, as in:

(32) Zij gaan discussiër-en
      They go discuss-INF
      'They start a discussion'

There is a subtle semantic difference between this sentence and sentence (20). Sentence (20) expresses the start of an event with some duration, whereas sentence (32) only expresses that an event will begin. More generally, the progressive construction does not have the same distribution as a simple infinitive, since most of the verbs mentioned above that combine with the *aan het* + INF-construction do not combine with a verbal infinitive, unlike *gaan*:

(33)   a. De twee partijen raakten {*vecht-en/aan het vecht-en}
        The two parties got {fight-INF/at the fight-INF}
        'The two parties started fighting'
       b. De matrozen sloegen {*muit-en/aan het muit-en}
        The sailors hit {mutiny-INF/at the mutiny-INF}
        'The sailors started mutinying'
       c. Jan bracht hem {*twijfel-en/aan het twijfel-en}
        John brought him {doubt-INF/at the doubt-INF}
        'John made him doubt'
       d. Dat maakte hem {*lach-en/aan het lach-en}
        That made him {laugh-INF/at the laugh-INF}
        'That made him laugh'
       e. De politie kreeg hem {*prat-en/aan het prat-en}
        The police got him {talk-INF/at the talk-INF}
        'The police got him talking'
       f. Deze gebeurtenis zette hem {*denk-en/aan het denk-en}
        This event put him {think-INF/at the think-INF}
        'This event made him thinking'
       g. Ik heb de motor weer {*lop-en/aan het lop-en}
        I have the engine again {run-INF/at the run-INF}
        'I have the engine running again'
       h. Kun jij die machine {*draai-en/aan het draai-en} houden?
        Can you that engine {run-INF/at the run-INF} keep?
        'Can you keep that engine running?'

There are two ways of accounting for the specific use of these verbs in this progressive construction. One option is providing these verbs with a subcategorization frame for the *aan het* + INF-construction, and assigning the inchoative meaning of, for instance, the verb *gaan* to the relevant subcategorization frame for *gaan*. The alternative is listing constructional idioms such as *aan het* INF *gaan* in the lexicon. The advantage of the latter approach is that it directly expresses that the use of *gaan* as an inchoative verb is linked to the use of an *aan*-PP as a progressive construction. This problem is similar to that discussed in Chapter 5 for particle verbs, since particles also have specific meanings in combination with a verb. In both cases, the second option is

preferable because it gives direct expression to the meaning of the construction as a whole.

A remarkable property of the *aan het* + INF-construction with *zijn* and some
other verbs is that it inherits the syntactic valence of the verb that appears in the
infinitival form. This property shows very clearly that this construction functions as a verbal lexical unit. For instance, if the verb selects a direct or
prepositional object, this is also possible with the *aan het* + INF-construction,
but these complements cannot appear directly in front of the verb:

(34)   a. Jan is {de aardappels aan het schill-en/*aan het de aardappelen
           schill-en}
           John is {the potatoes at the peel-INF/at the the potatoes peel-INF}
           'John is peeling the potatoes'
       b. De kinderen zijn {de boeken aan het lez-en/*aan het de boeken lez-en}
           The children are {the books at the read-INF/at the the books read-INF}
           'The children are reading the books'
       c. Hij is zijn geld aan het op-mak-en/*aan het zijn geld op-mak-en
           He is {his money at the up-make-INF/at the his money up-make-INF}
           'He is using up his money'
       d. Jan is {naar de papieren aan het zoek-en/*aan het naar de papieren
           zoek-en}
           John is {for the papers at the look-INF/at the for the papers look-INF}
           'John is looking for the papers'
       e. Jan is {op zijn vader aan het wacht-en/*aan het op zijn vader
           wacht-en}
           John is {for his father at the wait-INF/at the for his father wait-INF}
           'John is waiting for his father'

The relevant observation here is that the direct and prepositional objects do
not appear directly before the verb to which they belong, as is normally the
case in Dutch infinitival clauses, but before the *aan*-PP. There is a similarity
here with the infinitival particle *te* 'to' that also separates objects from the verb:

(35)   Jan belooft de aardappels te schill-en
       John promises the potatoes to peel-INF
       'John promises to peel the potatoes'

The *aan het* + INF-construction has this external valence in combination
with the verb *zijn* 'to be', but also with the other verbs that induce a
progressive interpretation such as the verbs of appearance (36a), the verb
blijven 'to keep' (36b), and the *aci*-verbs (36c). The use of inchoative verbs in
combination with a direct or prepositional object, on the other hand, as in
(36d,e), leads to ungrammatical sentences:

(36)   a. Jan bleek de appels aan het schill-en
          John appeared the apple at the peel-INF
          'John appeared peeling the apples'
       b. Hij bleef de boeren aan het bedrieg-en
          He kept the farmers at the cheat-INF
          'He kept cheating the farmers'
       c. Ik zag hem naar de papieren aan het zoek-en
          I saw him for the papers at the look-INF
          'I saw him looking for the papers'
       d. *Hij ging de kinderen aan het wass-en
          He went the children at the wash-INF
          'He started washing the children'
       e. *Hij kreeg de kinderen fruit aan het et-en
          He got the children fruit at the eat-INF
          'He got the children eating fruit'

The ungrammaticality of (36d,e) shows that the inchoative and causative
verbs involved require an intransitive predicate in their complement.

   The infinitival verb in the *aan het* + INF-construction does not exhibit the
normal projection potential of a verbal infinitive within the *aan het*-PP. Verbal
infinitives in Dutch can either be preceded by an NP or a PP argument, which
reflects their verbal nature, or followed by a PP-complement, which shows
that the verbal infinitive is simultaneously nominal in nature (cf. 38).
However, this syntactic valence of verbal infinitives is not available in the
aan het + INF-construction. For instance, of the following sentences, only the
first is grammatical:

(37)   a. Hij is de appel aan het et-en
          He is the apple at the eat-INF
          'He is eating the apple'
       b. *Hij is aan het de appel et-en
          He is at the the apple eat-INF
          'He is eating the apple'
       c. *Hij is aan het et-en van de appel
          He is at the eat-INF of the apple
          'He is eating the apple'

Compare other cases of the use of infinitives as the heads of NPs; in these cases
the infinitive does allow for a preverbal or a postverbal complement:

(38)   a. Het naar de oplossing zoek-en kostte veel tijd
          The for the solution search-INF took much time
          'Searching for the solution took a lot of time'

  b. Het et-en van appels is gezond
     The eat-INF of apples is healthy
     'Eating apples is healthy'

These observations prove that in the *aan het* + INF-construction the infinitive has become a main verb, and the word sequence *aan het* functions as a grammatical marker of progressive aspect. This conclusion is supported by the observations that adverbs also appear before *aan het*, not directly before the verb:

(39)   De jongens waren {hard aan het fiets-en/*aan het hard fiets-en}
        The boys were {fast at the cycle-INF/at the fast cycle-INF}
        'The boys were cycling fast'

Thus, the *aan het* + INF form functions as the progressive form of the verb, and arguments and modifiers cannot come in between *aan het* and the infinitive.

6.3 Quasi-incorporation

The INF-position in the *aan het* + INF-construction can be occupied by the infinitive of a separable complex verb, that is, a verb preceded by a particle, a generic noun, or a bare adjective that functions as a lexical unit, as discussed in Chapters 4 and 5. Therefore, this progressive construction can be used to determine whether a word combination is a separable complex verb. The generalization is that verbs with incorporated elements can appear in the INF-position of this construction since they can be structurally interpreted as syntactic V^0-compounds, that is, as cases of quasi-incorporation. Thus, such sentences are licensed by the unification of two constructional schemas, $[aan\ het\ V_{inf}^0]_{PP}$ and $[N^0\ V^0]_V^0$ into the complex schema $[aan\ het\ [N^0\ V^0]_{Vinf}^0]_{PP}$. The relevant facts are presented below, the infinitive may be separated from the *aan het* sequence by a generic noun (40–42), an adjective (43–44), or a particle (45–46):

(40)   Ik ben aan het thee zett-en[1]
        I am at the tea make-INF
        'I am making tea'

---

[1] A reminder on the orthography of complex predicates is in order here. In Dutch orthography, complex predicates such as *thee zetten* 'to make tea', *schoon maken* 'to clean', *wit wassen* 'to white-wash', and *op bellen* 'to phone' are written as one word, without internal spacing, which reflects their status as established lexical units. In the sentences above, I did not follow this orthographical convention in order not to prejudge the analysis.

(41)   De kinderen waren aan het sneeuwballen gooi-en
       The children were at the snowballs throw-INF
       'The children were throwing snowballs'

(42)   a. Ze zijn aan het brieven schrijv-en
          They are at the letters write-INF
          'They are writing letters'
       b. *Ze zijn aan het lange brieven schrijv-en
          They are at the long letters write-INF
          'They are writing long letters'
       c. Ze zijn lange brieven aan het schrijv-en
          They are long letters at the write-INF
          'They are writing long letters'

In these examples, the nouns *thee*, *sneeuwballen*, and *brieven* function as the
left, non-verbal constituents of syntactic verbal compounds. The NV combinations mention nameworthy activities such as making tea, throwing snow-
balls, and writing letters. In the case of *thee zetten* 'tea make, make tea' the
noun is a mass noun, in the other two examples the noun appears in the
plural form, and these plural forms receive a generic interpretation. In this
use, these nouns are non-projecting, in line with what we observed above for
the verb in the *aan het* + INF-construction: as soon as we modify such nouns,
they have to appear before the *aan het* + INF-construction. Similar observations can be made for AV combinations such as *schoon maken* 'to clean' and
wit wassen 'lit. to white-wash, to launder':

(43)   a. Ze was fruit aan het schoon mak-en
          She was fruit at the clean make-INF
          'She was cleaning fruit'
       b. *Ze was aan het fruit schoon mak-en
          She was at the fruit clean-make-INF
          'She was cleaning fruit'
       c. *Ze was aan het schoon mak-en van fruit
          She was at the clean make-INF of fruit
          'She was cleaning fruit'

(44)   a. Jan was geld aan het wit wass-en
          John was money at the white wash-INF
          'John was laundering money'
       b. *Jan was geld wit aan het wass-en
          John was money white at the wash-INF
          'John was laundering money'

   c. *Jan was aan het geld wit wass-en
      John was at the money white wash-INF
      'John was laundering money'
   d. *Jan was aan het wit wass-en van geld
      John was at the white wash-INF of money
      'John was laundering money'

In the case of *wit wassen* it is the metaphorical meaning 'money laundering' that is the only possible one, since this is the conventionalized meaning of this word sequence. Therefore, it is interpreted structurally as a syntactic compound, hence the ungrammaticality of *Jan was geld wit aan het wassen.*

   The third category of word combinations that appear after *aan het* in the progressive construction are particle verbs:

(45) a. Hij is zijn moeder aan het op bell-en
       He is his mother at the up call-INF
       'He is phoning up his mother'
     b. Hij is zijn moeder op aan het bell-en
       He is his mother up at the call-INF
       'He is phoning up his mother'
     c. *Hij is aan het zijn moeder op bell-en
       He is at the his mother up call-INF
       'He is phoning up his mother'
     d. *Hij is aan het op bell-en van zijn moeder
       He is at the up call-INF of his mother
       'He is phoning up his mother'

(46) a. Ze was de kinderen aan het uit lach-en
       She was the children at the out laugh-INF
       'She was laughing at the children'
     b. Ze was de kinderen uit aan het lach-en
       She was the children out at the laugh-INF
       'She was laughing at the children'
     c. *Ze was aan het de kinderen uit lach-en
       She was at the the children out laugh-INF
       'She was laughing at the children'
     d. *Ze was aan het uit lach-en van de kinderen
       She was at the out laugh-INF of the children
       'She was laughing at the children'

In conclusion, verbs do not take normal syntactic complements when they occur in the INF position of the *aan het* + INF-construction. However, the

verb may combine with a particle, an adjective, or a generic noun into a
syntactic compound that is allowed in the INF position. Thus, we can use the
aan het + INF-construction as a test for the status of word combinations as
syntactic compounds.

The potential of the progressive construction as a test for quasi-
incorporation manifests itself also in the fact that plural nouns can also be
incorporated, as long as they have a generic, non-referential interpretation, as
in *brieven schrijven* 'lit. letters write', *aardappels schillen* 'lit. potatoes peel', and
bonen plukken 'lit. beans pick':

(47)   Wij zijn aan het {brieven schrijv-en/aardappels schill-en/bonen plukk-en}
       We are at the {letters-write-INF/potatoes peel-INF/beans pick-INF}
       'We are {letter-writing/potato-peeling/bean-picking}'

These cases of incorporation mention nameworthy actions, and the plural
nouns receive a generic interpretation.

As argued in Chapter 5, these word sequences allow for more than one
structural interpretation because the preverbal element can be optionally
projecting and optionally incorporated. For instance, in the word sequence
af maken 'to finish' the predicate *af* 'ready' can be analysed as a phrase, a
non-projecting word, or as part of a syntactic compound. The first option is
possible because the word *af* can function as an independent predicate, as
in *Het boek is helemaal af* 'The book is completely ready'. This explains why
we can have *af* either before or within the *aan het* + INF-construction:

(48)   a. *phrasal* or *non-projecting word interpretation:*
          Ze was het boek (helemaal) af aan het mak-en
          She was the book (completely) ready at the make-INF
          'She was finishing the book (completely)'
       b. *syntactic compound interpretation:*
          Ze was het boek aan het (*helemaal) af mak-en
          She was the book at the (*completely) ready make-INF
          'She was finishing the book'

Words such as *na* 'after' and *door* 'through' do not denote a property, unlike *af*
'ready'. Hence, they do not allow for modification and a syntactic analysis
with phrasal status for the particle (49–50). If the generic noun is not an
argument of the verb, as in *zee zeilen* 'to do sea-sailing', the noun cannot
appear before the *aan het* + INF-construction (51):

(49)   Ze waren {aan het na-denk-en / (*helemaal) na aan het denk-en}
       They were {at the after-think-INF / (completely) after at the think-INF}
       'They were reflecting'

(50) Ze waren {aan het door-werk-en/door aan het werk-en}
      They were {at the through-work-INF/through at the work-INF}
      'They were working on'

(51) Mijn vader is {aan het zee zeil-en/*zee aan het zeil-en}
      My father is {at the sea sail-INF/sea at the sail-INF}
      'My father is sailing at sea'

These observations once more show that the *aan het* + INF-construction can be used for determining the structural interpretation of a word sequence.

6.4 Schema unification

As we saw above, the *aan het* + INF-construction, and this construction combined with an additional verb such as *zijn* 'to be' or *gaan* 'to go', are constructional idioms with a number of unpredictable properties. Yet, they also have a number of canonical properties since they reflect more general phrasal schemas of Dutch. For instance, the phrasal construct *aan het et-en* 'eating' is an instantiation of the pattern *aan het* + INF obtained through the unification of this pattern and the lexical information that *eten* is an infinitive. The three words *aan*, *het*, and *eten* exhibit a part-of relation with respect to the word sequence *aan het eten*. This PP can be unified with the phrasal schema [PP V], and hence be combined with various verbs, as discussed in section 6.2. So the following unification steps predict the occurrence of the VP construct *aan het eten zijn* 'to be eating':

(52) a. $[\text{P NP}]_{\text{PP}}$
      b. $[[\text{P } [\text{Det N}]_{\text{NP}}]_{\text{PP}}$ through unification with $[\text{Det N}]_{\text{NP}}$
      c. $[[\textit{aan}]_{\text{P}} [[\textit{het}]_{\text{Det}} \text{N}]_{\text{NP}}]_{\text{PP}}$ through unification with $[\textit{aan}]_{\text{P}}, [\textit{het}]_{\text{Det}}$
      d. $[[\textit{aan}]_{\text{P}} [[\textit{het}]_{\text{Det}} [\text{V-INF}]_{\text{N}}]_{\text{NP}}]_{\text{PP}}$ through unification with $[\text{V-INF}]_{\text{N}}$
      e. $[[\textit{aan}]_{\text{P}} [[\textit{het}]_{\text{Det}} [\text{V-INF}]_{\text{N}}]_{\text{PP}} \text{V}]_{\text{VP}}$ through unification with $[\text{PP V}]_{\text{VP}}$
      f. $[[\textit{aan} [\textit{het} [\textit{eten}]_{\text{INF}}]_{\text{NP}}]_{\text{PP}} [\textit{zijn}]_{\text{V}}]_{\text{VP}}$ through unification with $[\textit{eten}]_{\text{V-INF}}$
                                                  and $[\textit{zijn}]_{\text{V}}$

The structures in (52) are the formal parts of schemas of which the meaning is not specified here. For instance, the general meaning of the PP schema is something like 'with relation R to NP' in which the preposition specifies the specific nature of relation R. I will not discuss the meaning correlates of these schemas in detail because the focus here is on the specific meaning of the constructional idiom *aan het* + INF. The additional idiosyncratic semantic information that we need at level (d) is the specific progressive interpretation of this type of PP. Level (e) is also a relevant level for the specification of idiosyncratic properties: as discussed in section 6.2, verbs have to be specified for being able to occur with the *aan het* + INF-construction.

An additional idiosyncratic property of the *aan het* + INF-construction is the transfer of the Predicate Argument Structure of the verb used in this construction to that of the progressive construction as a whole, when used in combination with *zijn*, verbs of appearance, and *aci*-verbs. Recall that direct and prepositional objects of the verb (in its infinitival form) do not appear right before the verb, as expected for a language with underlying SOV structure, but appear before the word sequence *aan het*. This transfer of syntactic valence does not take place with the inchoative and causative verbs mentioned in (20–23) and (24–27) respectively, and must be expressed in a proper account of this progressive construction. This kind of transfer is well known from studies of derivational morphology, and often referred to as 'inheritance'. For instance, deverbal nouns in English and Dutch may inherit the Predicate Argument Structure of their verbal base, as in *the destruction of the city by the Romans*, an NP in which the Agent and the Theme of the verbal base *destroy* are realized within the NP headed by the deverbal noun *destruction*. Hence, we specify the following paradigmatic relation between the constructional schema for the Dutch progressive construction and that for verb phrases:

(53) $< [(NP/PP_j)\ aan\ het\ V_i\text{-}INF]_k \leftrightarrow [PROGR\ [(ARGUMENT_j)\ PRED_i]_m]_k > \approx$
        $< [(NP/PP_j)\ V_i]_{VP,\ m} \leftrightarrow [(ARGUMENT_j)\ PRED_i]_m$

In (53) we express the paradigmatic relationship between the general schema for verbs and their arguments on the one hand, and the schema for the progressive construction on the other hand. Through co-indexation we can express that the arguments of the verb in regular VPs appear before *aan het* in the progressive construction.

As shown above, the progressive construction mentioned in the first line of (53) can combine with several types of verbs whose semantic interpretation depends on their occurrence with the progressive construction. This is the case for, for instance, the verb *slaan* 'lit. to hit' that expresses inchoative meaning when combined with the progressive construction. Thus, the lexicon of Dutch will contain subconstructions of the following type, with the main verb lexically specified:

(54) $[[aan\ het\ V_i\text{-}INF]_{PP,m}\ [slaan]_{Vj}]_k \leftrightarrow [INCHOATIVE_j\ [PROGR\ [PRED_i]_m]_k$

The verb *slaan* does not allow for the transitive version of the progressive construction, hence the relevant part of the schema in (53) is omitted. The combination of the verb *gaan* with a PP is quite regular, but it is the combination with the progressive PP-construction that licenses this inchoative interpretation.

Construction (54) is thus an illustration of the two basic mechanisms of constructional approaches, the unification of constructional schemas, and the possibility of subconstructions, that is, instantiations with specific properties.

6.5 The periphrastic role of the *aan het* + INF-construction

The existence of multi-word lexical units has a blocking effect on the use of morphological constructions. For instance, as shown in Chapter 7, the existence of phrasal names of the type A + N may block the coining of NN compounds or AN compounds with the same meaning. Constructional idioms may also have this blocking effect on the use of competing morphological constructions. That is, such phrasal constructional idioms have acquired a periphrastic function, since they function as an alternative to morphological expression.

In the inflectional domain, it is quite clear that we need the theoretical concept of periphrasis, that is, the expression of inflectional information by means of a combination of words in case there is no synthetic word form available to fill a cell of an inflectional paradigm. Periphrastic constructions are the prototypical cases of analytic lexical expressions.

The notion 'periphrasis' can also be used in a looser sense, namely for the analytic expression of information in a language that is expressed morphologically in other languages (Haspelmath 2000). This applies to the expression of information with respect to voice, aspect, Aktionsart, etc. This kind of analytic expression is found in many languages, as is also clear from the grammaticalization studies in Bybee and Dahl (1989) and Bybee et al. (1994). It is the very phenomenon of grammaticalization that makes us expect to find such patterns of analytic expression of grammatical information: lexical words can develop into grammatical words (and these in their turn may subsequently develop into bound grammatical morphemes).

The Dutch *aan het* + INF-construction appears to be periphrastic in this latter sense, since there are no synthetic verbal forms available that express progressive aspect and can be used in predicative position. This is clear from the division of labour between this progressive construction and the use of present participles. Dutch has present participles that receive a progressive interpretation, but these present participles can only be used in attributive position:

(55)   a.   De fiets-end-e man
            The cycle-PRES.PTCP-INFL man
            'The cycling man'

    b. De man is {*fiets-end/aan het fiets-en}
       The man is {cycle-PRES.PTCP/at the cycle-INF}
       'The man is cycling'

The data in (55) show that the *aan het* + INF-construction functions as a periphrastic form of verbs, in order to express progressive aspect in predicate position. This also applies to the other verbs with which the *aan het* + INF-construction can be combined:

(56) a. Mijn moeder blijkt {*fietsend/aan het fietsen}
       My mother appears {cycle-PRES.PTCP/at the cycle-INF}
       'My mother appears to be cycling'
    b. We zagen hem {*fietsend/aan het fietsen}
       We saw him {cycle-PRES.PTCP/at the cycle-INF}
       'We saw him cycling'
    c. We gingen {*fietsend/aan het fietsen}
       We went {cycle-PRES.PTCP/at the cycle-INF}
       'We started cycling'

Present participles in Dutch (with the form verbal stem + suffix *-end*) still have a full verbal potential even when used as adjectives in attributive position (with an inflectional ending *-e* added in attributive position). In predicate position, however, present participles cannot be used, but the *aan het* + INF-construction can be used as an alternative, at least for durational verbs:

(57) a. de zijn vader beledig-end-e jongen
       the his father insult-PRES.PTCP-INFL boy
       'the boy who insults his father'
    b. *De jongen is zijn vader beledig-end
       The boy is his father insult-PRES.PTCP
       'The boy is insulting his father'
    c. De jongen is zijn vader aan het beledig-en
       The boy is his father at the insult-INF
       'The boy is insulting his father'

Note that there are adjectives with the form of present participles that can be used in predicative position such as *schokk-end* 'shocking', *woed-end* 'lit. raging, angry', and *lop-end* 'lit. walking, on foot', as in:

(58) a. Deze opmerking is schokk-end
       This remark is shock-PRES.PTCP
       'This remark is shocking'
    b. Mijn moeder was woed-end
       My mother was rage-PRES.PTCP
       'My mother was angry'

   c. Ze zijn lop-end
      They are walk-PRES.PTCP
      'They are on foot'

However, these are all lexicalized cases of present participles with idiosyncratic meanings that belong to the class of adjectives. They cannot be used in predicative position in their literal interpretation, and hence cannot express progressive aspect.

The periphrastic role of the *aan het* + INF-construction extends to the verbal compounds with quasi-incorporation such as *mast klimmen* 'to pole-climb' and *zee zeilen* 'to sea-sail'. As noted in Chapter 4, such syntactic compounds cannot occur in second position in root clauses. Instead, it is possible to use a finite form of the verb *zijn* 'to be' in second position, in combination with the *aan het* + INF-construction. The progressive interpretation imposed by this construction is in accordance with the fact that these verbs are all activity verbs.

(59) a. Jan {*mast-klim-t/is aan het mast-klimm-en}
       John {pole-climb-s/is at the pole-climb-INF}
       'John is pole-climbing'
    b. Mijn vader {*zee-zeil-t/is aan het zee-zeil-en}
       My father {sea-sail-s/is at the sea-sail-INF}
       'My father is sea-sailing'

These observations on the *aan het* + INF-construction show its function as a periphrastic expression. Thus, this construction affects morphology in the sense that it functions as an alternative to the morphological expression of a particular semantic content. In sum, constructional idioms with a periphrastic potential may affect the use of the morphological constructions of a language. In the case of verbal compounds with quasi-incorporation, the existence of a periphrastic progressive construction in combination with the verb *zijn* 'to be' has made it possible to use these quasi-compounds in root clauses.

6.6 Grammaticalization

This detailed analysis of the Dutch progressive *aan het* + INF-construction demonstrates that the notion 'constructional idiom' enables us to give a proper account of a productive multi-word combination pattern that serves as an alternative to the morphological expression of lexical and/or grammatical content. Such constructional idioms arise through grammaticalization. The Dutch *aan het* + INF-construction functions as a marker of progressive aspect, and hence as a grammatical marker, and has become productive in that role. Once more we see that grammaticalization is always the grammaticalization of constructions, in which particular words change from lexical morphemes to grammatical morphemes, or in which grammatical morphemes become even more grammatical. The latter variety applies to the grammatical words *aan* and *het*, which in this construction have shifted from their normal grammatical meaning of preposition and definite determiner respectively to the grammatical meaning of progressive aspect.

7

Phrasal names

7.1 Demarcating morphological and syntactic constructs

Some types of phrases share the naming function with complex words. Hence both phrases and words are stored as lexical units in the lexicon. This chapter discusses how the functional equivalence and formal similarities between words and phrasal lexical units with a naming function can be accounted for without ignoring their formal differences. Such types of phrases can be characterized in terms of syntactic schemas with specific properties, that is, as constructions. In this chapter I focus on the formal properties of adjective + noun constructs with naming function, in particular in Modern Greek and Dutch. I will argue that the constructionist approach enables us to do justice to the lexical properties of these phrasal names.

7.2 Naming and description

Words[1] are the linguistic expressions par excellence for the function of naming. Words function as names for concepts. This holds for both underived and derived words. However, the naming function is not restricted to words: certain types of phrases can also function as names. This functional equivalence between words and phrases is a challenge for linguistic theory because we should maintain the formal distinction between words and phrases, and yet do justice to their common properties.

The following definition of naming is the starting point of this chapter: 'Naming is creating a link between an expression and a concept. The expression is often a word, but can also consist of more than one word' (Koefoed 1993) [my translation].[2] As an example of a phrase with a naming function,

---

[1.] The term 'word' is to be understood here in the sense of 'lexeme', the abstract lexical unit which is realized by one or more concrete words (or word forms).

[2.] The original Dutch text reads as follows: 'Benoemen is het tot stand brengen van een verbinding tussen een talige uitdrukking en een begrip (bewustzijnsinhoud). De uitdrukking is vaak een woord, maar kan ook uit meerdere woorden bestaan' (Koefoed 1993: 3).

Koefoed mentions the Dutch noun phrase *vaderlandse geschiedenis* 'national history', which is the conventional name for a particular form of history, namely that from the perspective of one's native country. This phrase can be opposed to the phrase *geschiedenis van het vaderland* 'history of the native country', a descriptive phrase that refers to the history of one's native country.

These two different functions of phrases are important from the perspective of a theory of the architecture of the grammar. Phrases used as names are often conventional expressions, and hence lexical units. However, when a linguistic expression is a lexical unit, this does not imply that it is a word. Words and phrases need to be distinguished carefully in an adequate linguistic theory. On the other hand, the functional similarity or even equivalence between words and certain types of phrases as names has the effect that such phrases may have specific formal properties, as will be discussed below. Hence, a proper theory of the relation between morphological and syntactic naming constructions is called for.

The role of word formation as an alternative to phrasal expression has been discussed in detail by Kastovsky (1988), who refers to this use of morphology as 'recategorization'. It applies to both compounding and derivation, and sometimes it has to do with the need for stylistic variation in texts. In the following examples, the use of *ringer-up* is a means of avoiding the clumsy phrase 'the person who rang up'. In the second example, repetition of the word *civil* is avoided in the root clause by not using the phrase *make civil* but the complex word *civilize*:

(1)   Miss Pride is convinced that the *ringer-up* was Miss Cost
      If that's not *civil, civilize* it and tell me   (Kastovsky 1988: 595)

Nominal compounds are often used as short alternatives to syntactic descriptions. This is found in particular in the headlines of newspapers, to such an extent that one might speak of 'headline-morphology'. Here are some examples of such descriptive compounds, the first two from Dutch newspaper headlines:

(2)   a. zwemles-regeling 'swimming lessons arrangement'
      b. het Cruyf-interview 'the Cruyf-interview'
      c. Schelde-verdieping 'lit. Schelde-deepening, deepening of the river Schelde'.[3]

These compounds show that complex words can also be used for both naming and description.

[3.] Source: C. Paulus (2008), *Met hart en ziel. 15 passionante jaren als gouverneur*. Antwerpen: Provincie Antwerpen.

The formation of new names for concepts can take place through a number of mechanisms (De Caluwe 1990): word formation, the construction of phrases, borrowing of names from other languages, the creation of new simplex words (brand names), the formation of acronyms which turns descriptions into names, as in *sms* 'short message service', semantic extension mechanism (for instance, metaphor and metonymy), and clippings from phrases (for instance Dutch *mobiel*, often used in its diminutive form *mobiel-tje*, clipped from *mobiele telefoon* 'mobile phone').[4]

Phrasal names, once conventionalized, belong to the class of fixed expressions (Wray 2002). Fixed expressions may be qualified as follows:

(3) Fixed expressions (FEs) refer to specific combinations of two or more words that are typically used to express a specific concept. Typical examples of FEs that are referred to in the literature often have an opaque meaning or a deficient syntactic structure, for example, *by and large* or *kick the bucket*. However, these properties are not essential. The defining feature of a FE is that it is *a word combination, stored in the Mental Lexicon of native speakers, that as a whole refers to a (linguistic) concept*. This makes FEs 'non-compositional' in the sense that the combination and structure of their elements need not be computed afresh, but can be retrieved from the Mental Lexicon. However, the degree of lexical and syntactic fixedness can vary. (Sprenger 2003: 4)

In this quotation, it is rightly stressed that the notion 'fixed expression' encompasses more than idioms. Idiomatic expressions have one or more non-compositional properties, whereas a fixed expression may be completely compositional, but nevertheless lexically stored, because it is a conventional name for a particular concept. Thus, this quotation reminds us of the fact that knowledge of a language encompasses both knowledge of the grammatical system of a language, and knowledge of the conventions involved in using that language (Coseriu 1952/1975). The lexicon is the place where the conventional use of linguistic expressions is encoded, and hence, the lexicon is the meeting point of the systematic and conventional properties of language constructs.

As mentioned above, the notion 'lexical unit' is not to be identified with the notion 'word' (in the sense of 'lexeme' or in the sense of 'syntactic atom'). Lexical units can be constructed by means of syntactic rules. In European languages we find the following types of names with phrasal appearance:

[4.] The same process is found in Russian *mobil'nyj telefon* > *mobil'niki* (Francesca Masini, pers. comm.)

(4)   a. A + N or N + A: Spanish *media luna* 'half moon', *luna nueva* 'new
         moon';
      b. N + PP: French *moulin à vent* 'windmill';
      c. N-GEN + N or N + N-GEN: English *women's magazine*, Greek *zona
         asfalias* 'belt safety.GEN, safety belt';
      d. N + NP (apposition): Dutch *directeur artistieke zaken* 'director of
         artistic affairs'.

Such constructs are sometimes referred to as loose compounds. In an expression like Spanish *media luna* in (4a), we observe that the syntactic rule of gender agreement has applied: the form of the adjective is *medi-a* because it has to agree with the feminine gender of *luna*. Therefore, *media luna* cannot be interpreted as a morphological compound, if complex words are subject to the principle of Lexical Integrity which states that 'the syntax neither manipulates nor has access to the internal structure of words' (Anderson 1992: 84).[5] In section 7.3, the issue of the analysis of loose compounds and the proper definition of the principle of Lexical Integrity will be broached again.

Expressions of the type (4b) are used a lot in Romance languages. For instance, Fradin (2003: 199) provides the following French examples (and many more) that can all be used as names:

(5)   a. N de N: fil de fer 'lit. wire of iron, iron wire'
      b. N à N : moulin à vent 'lit. mill on wind, windmill'
      c. N à Det N : sauce à l'ail 'lit. sauce with garlic, garlic sauce'
      d. A N : moyen âge 'lit. middle period, Middle Ages'
      e. N A : poids lourd 'lit. weight heavy, heavyweight'

The patterns in (5) have a certain degree of productivity. In particular the construction *N à N* is very productive for coining names in French, as illustrated in (6):

(6)   moulin à poivre 'pepper mill'
      verre à vin 'wine glass'
      bois à feu 'firewood'
      fruit à confiture 'jam fruit'
      moteur à essence 'petrol engine'

[5.] However, this principle is too strong in that syntactic rules may have access to word-internal structure but should not be allowed to manipulate parts of words, which is the essential point here (Booij 2009a).

Note also the difference between *verre à vin* 'wine glass' and *verre de vin* 'glass of wine'. The construct with *à* has typically a classifying role, whereas the variant with *de* can be used for descriptive purposes.

N + PP complement (with a bare noun in the PP) that function as names are also found in Spanish and Italian:

(7) *Spanish* (Rainer and Varela 1992)
     telón de acero 'lit. curtain of iron, iron curtain (between Western and Eastern Europe)'
     piano de cola 'lit. piano of tail, grand piano'
     gafas de sol 'lit. glasses of sun, sun glasses'

(8) *Italian* (Bisetto and Scalise 1999)
     permesso di pesca 'lit. licence of fishing, fishing licence'
     mulino a vento 'lit. mill on wind, windmill'
     occhiali da sole 'lit. glasses for sun, sun glasses'

The Spanish examples are traditionally classified as *compuestos improprios* 'improper compounds'. However, Rainer and Varela (1992) rightly point out that they are phrases, albeit with specific formal properties:

The naming function of such phrases can be attributed to the pragmatic component in a modular conception of the grammar. Global pluralization, accental unity and opacity to syntactic rules like adjectival / adverbial modification, properties which some of these formations – among them *media luna* – share with simple words, should be viewed as what they are, namely consequences of the naming function or lexicalization which one also finds in idioms. (Rainer and Varela 1992: 120)

These formal effects of the naming function of phrasal lexical units are the focus of this chapter, in particular as far as A + N combinations are concerned.

Examples of the genitive construction mentioned in (4c) can be found in English. The genitive noun is in prenominal position and has a classifying role: *a boy's hat, a woman's/women's magazine*. These genitive constructions function like compounds, and the modifying noun is marked by a morpheme that is historically a genitive case ending (Rosenbach 2007). Note that the *-s* can also be used in determiner phrases, as in *the boy's hat* 'the hat of the boy'.

Modern Greek features N + N constructions with a genitive marker as well. The second noun is marked with genitive case, and the whole expression functions as a name (Ralli 2007):

(9) oikos anoxi-s 'lit. house tolerance-GEN, brothel'
     zoni asfalia-s 'lit. belt safety-GEN, safety belt'
     oikos evigiria-s 'lit. house old-PL.GEN, old people's home'

The fact that both words and phrases can function as names creates a problem of demarcation for languages with left-headed compounds: left-headed N + N sequences (the class of expressions (4d)) can be interpreted either as left-headed compounds or as phrases in which the head noun is followed by an appositive noun. For instance, French and Italian feature N + N/NP sequences that look like left-headed compounds but may also be analysed as phrases with appositional Ns (Arnaud 2003):

(10)   *French*
        cigarette filtre 'filter cigarette'
        sortie piétons 'pedestrians' exit'
        impression laser 'laser printing'
        cuisinière quatre feux 'four-burner stove'
        assurance tous risques 'all risks insurance'

        Italian
        effetto serra 'greenhouse effect'
        smaltimento rifiuti 'garbage disposal'

An argument for interpreting these N + N/NP sequences as phrases is that the second constituent can be modified, as in the last two French examples. However, phrases in the non-head position of compounds cannot be excluded by a universal constraint (Booij 2007: 188), and hence this observation does not exclude the word combinations in (10) to be interpreted as left-headed compounds.

When we pluralize these expressions, it is the left noun that is pluralized: *cigarettes filtre* 'filter cigarettes', *effetti serra* 'greenhouse effects'. If we require inflection to be always at word edges, these constructs must be phrases. However, one may argue that the inflection of compounds is a morphological head operation (Stump 2005). Word-internal operation of morphological rules is not excluded by the principle of Lexical Integrity. That is, in such an analysis, these constructs can still be considered compound words, with plural inflection on the left constituent.

Additional examples of Italian N + N expressions with a compound-like function are the following (Bisetto and Scalise 1999: 39):

(11)   a. produzione scarpe 'lit. production shoes, shoe production'
        b. caduta massi 'lit. fall rocks, rock fall'

Baroni et al. (2008) argue that these N + N sequences are phrases, subject to specific principles of 'headline syntax', a specific style or register in which

determiners and prepositions are omitted.[6] The complement of such
N-headed phrases can also be a phrase (12a,b), and the complement is
sometimes even used in a non-generic manner (12b):

(12) a. approvazione nuovi parametri 'checking of new parameters'
      b. accertamento posti disponibili 'checking for some/the available seats'

The use of appositional constructions without determiners and prepositions as names can also be observed in Dutch personnel advertisements.
Dutch compounds are right-headed, and hence the following left-headed
expressions must be seen as phrases with a special syntax used for coining
names for particular jobs (source *NRC-Handelsblad* 28 Sept. 2008):

(13) senior-adviseur installatietechniek 'senior adviser equipment technics'
      manager kredietrisicomanagement 'manager credit risk management'
      lid raad van commissarissen 'member board of supervisory directors'
      sectormanager infrastructuur 'sector manager infrastructure'
      hoofd communicatie 'head communication'
      adjunct-directeur artistieke zaken 'deputy director artistic affairs'

In conclusion, certain types of syntactic word combinations can function as
names, and there is no simple one-to-one correlation between the form of a
linguistic expression and its function as name or description. Yet, there are
specific correlations between the form and the naming function of these
syntactic word combinations. In section 6.3 these formal properties are discussed for A + N constructs, in particular those of Greek and Dutch, and I
will argue in favour of a constructionist account of these A + N names. We
will see that there is a gradient of expression types from synthetic morphological expressions to standard syntactic phrases.

7.3 A + N combinations as names for concepts

The use of A + N / N + A combinations as names for concepts or categories is
widespread in European languages. The following examples of A + N phrases
illustrate this for Dutch:

(14) dikke darm 'lit. thick intestine, large intestine', dood spoor 'lit. dead
      trail, deadlock', hoge hoed 'lit. high hat, top hat', magere yoghurt 'lit.
      lean yoghurt, fat-free yoghurt', open haard 'lit. open hearth, fireplace',

---

[6.] As argued by Östman (2005), the form of constructions may be sensitive to specific styles or
registers. Östman therefore argues that the principles of Construction Grammar must be extended to
the discourse level. These Italian facts support this conclusion.

rode kaart 'red card', vaste benoeming 'lit. fixed appointment, tenure', zure regen 'acid rain', vrije trap 'free kick', witte was 'white laundry', zwarte doos 'black box'

We are certain that these A + N sequences are not words in the morphological sense because the adjectives are inflected and agree with the head noun with respect to the features gender, number, and (in)definiteness. In Dutch, a pre-nominal adjective ends in -e, unless the NP is indefinite and the head noun is singular and neuter. According to the principle of Lexical Integrity, the syntactic rule of agreement cannot affect parts of words, and hence these A + N sequences cannot be morphological compounds. In morphological compounds of the AN-type, there is no inflection of the adjective.

The functional similarity between such lexical phrases and compounds is nicely shown by the comparison between German compounds (source *Die Welt* 31 May 2008) and their Dutch glosses:

(15) | *Dutch AN phrase* | *German A-N compound* | *gloss* |
|---|---|---|
| bijzonder-e zitting | Sonder-sitzung | 'special session' |
| gebruikt-e batterijen | Alt-batterien | 'used batteries' |
| geheim-e nummer | Geheim-nummer | 'secret number' |
| mobiel-e telefoon | Mobil-telefon | 'mobile phone' |
| nieuw-e auto | Neu-auto | 'new car' |

This comparison between Dutch and German should not be taken to imply that Dutch does not have A-N compounds. Examples of such compounds are *fijn-stof* 'lit. fine dust, fine-grained dust' and *vroeg-geboorte* 'lit. early-birth, premature birth' in which the A is not inflected (otherwise, we would get *vroege-geboorte* and *fijne-stof* respectively). However, they are far less frequent than A-N compounds in German. The A in the Dutch A-N compounds has to be simplex; German also imposes that restriction, but with some exceptions such as adjectives in -*al* (*National-staat* 'nation state'), -*iv* (*Suggestiv-frage* 'suggestive question'), and -*ig* (*Niedrig-wasser* 'low tide'). This implies a certain division of labour between the phrasal and the compound coining of such names: in Dutch, and partially also in German, these two different A + N constructions only compete when A is simplex.[7]

The adjective in these Dutch A + N phrases cannot be modified. That is, it does not project a phrase of its own, and can therefore be qualified as a non-projecting category (Toivonen 2003). Hence, it is an A^0 and not an AP since an

---

[7.] In German A-N compounding is far more productive than in Dutch. Hüning (2010) has proposed an explanation for this difference which reads as follows: 'In German AN phrases, the form of the adjective is highly variable due to the rich inflectional system of German. Using compounds avoids this variability in the form of the adjective, which always appears in the stem form.'

AP can contain modifiers in addition to the head. Moreover, A and N cannot be split by an intervening word, they must be adjacent. There are therefore two structural interpretations for these A + N syntactic constructs: that of a syntactic compound or that of a regular noun phrase:[8]

(16) a. [[donker-e]$_{A^0}$ [kamer]$_{N^0}$]$_{N^0}$ 'dark room'   (*syntactic compound*)
      b. [[donker-e]$_{A^0}$ [kamer]$_{N^0}$]$_{N'}$ 'dark room'   (*regular noun phrase*)

The structure in (16a) is that of a syntactic compound, as opposed to the morphological compound structure [A N]$_N$ which can be inserted as a whole in a syntactic N^0 position, and in which agreement between A and N does not apply. Hence, this syntactic compound structure predicts that no other word can intervene between the A and the N. This structure has also been proposed for similar English A + N constructs (Sadler and Arnold 1994). Alternative (16b) will be discussed below.

How does the principle of Lexical Integrity relate to the distinction between syntactic compounds (a special type of phrases) and morphological compounds (words in the morphological sense)? Recall from Chapter 4 that the notion 'syntactic compound' is used for denoting syntactic units created by means of incorporation that cannot be subject to syntactic reordering. That is, the two constituents of a syntactic compound must be adjacent. Examples of such syntactic compounds were given in Chapters 4 and 5. I assume morphological compounds to be subject to the stronger constraint that rules like agreement and case assignment cannot apply internally. Therefore, we should decompose the constraint of Lexical Integrity into at least two subconstraints:[9]

(i)   both morphologically complex words and syntactic compounds are subject to the prohibition on syntactic reordering;

(ii) morphologically complex words do not allow for the internal application of syntactic rules of agreement and case assignment, whereas syntactic compounds, being (minimal) syntactic units, do.

[8.] The phenomenon of non-projecting words (Toivonen 2003) is also discussed in detail under the heading of *légèreté* (lite-ness) in recent work by Abeillé and Godard (2004, 2006), and this notion is also relevant for the analysis of syntactic forms of noun incorporation (Abeillé and Godard 2004), and the analysis of particle verbs (Blom 2005*a*; Booij 2002*c*; Elenbaas 2007; Los et al. 2010).

[9.] In Booij (2009a) I argue that Anderson's definition of the principle of Lexical Integrity is too strong: syntactic rules that only require access to parts of words, without affecting their form, should be allowed to apply within morphologically complex words. That is, another refinement of this principle is necessary.

These two constraints give empirical substance to the different formal structures used in this book, in particular to the formal distinction between morphological words, which are dominated by one X^0-node only, versus syntactic compounds, which have the shape $[X^0\ Y^0]_{Y^0}$ or $[X^0\ Y^0]_{X^0}$. These structural differences are given empirical substance and predictive power by means of the interpretation of Lexical Integrity given above, and make predictions as to how syntactic rules apply to these two types of lexical units. In other words, the principle of Lexical Integrity is not an independent empirical hypothesis but specifies what it means to assign a linguistic construct the label 'complex word', 'syntactic compound', or 'phrase'. These labels indicate that word combinations may exhibit various degrees of tightness and predict how rules will apply to them.

Let us now return to the analysis of Dutch A + N combinations. Qualifying adjectives such as *rood* 'red' and *geel* 'yellow' cannot be modified when used in A + N sequences that function as names, and hence they are non-projecting adjectives in this use:

(17) a. *erg rode kool 'very red cabbage'
      b. *heel gele koorts 'very yellow fever'

The phrase *rode kool* 'red cabbage' does not denote the intersection of the class of cabbages, and that of red things, but denotes a particular type of cabbage, and therefore it has a non-intersective reading. The same applies to *gele koorts* 'yellow fever'. The non-projectivity of the adjective is a reflection of this semantic property. The phrase (17a) is a grammatical expression, but not when *rode kool* is meant to refer to a specific conventional subtype of cabbage, red cabbage (note that the actual colour of red cabbage is more purple than red). In (17b), the use of the degree adverb *heel* 'very' forces the adjective *gele* to be interpreted as referring to the set of yellow things, resulting in an uninterpretable reading.

Relational adjectives, that is, adjectives (often denominal) that express a relation between the head noun and a nominal entity such as *Nederland* 'Netherlands' in *Nederland-se regering* 'Dutch government', and *burger* 'civilian' in *burger-lijke vrijheid* 'civilian liberty', always function as non-projecting adjectives (Heynderickx 2001), and only occur in NPs with a naming function.

The use of A + N syntactic constructs as names is widespread in European languages; examples are given in (18):

(18) a. Dutch (Booij 2002*b*; Hüning 2010): *dikke darm* 'large intestine', *magere yoghurt* 'lit. meagre yoghurt, fat-free yoghurt', *zwarte dood* 'black death, pest';

    b. English (Jackendoff 1997*b*, 2002; Sadler and Arnold 1994): *Arabian horse, blue cheese, electrical outlet, modern art, natural childbirth*;

    c. German (Hüning 2010): *saure Sahne* 'sour cream', *saurer Regen* 'acid rain', *grüne Welle* 'phased traffic lights';

    d. French (Fradin 2003): *moyen âge* 'Middle Ages', *poids lourd* 'heavyweight';

    e. Italian (Semenza and Mondini 2006): NA: *febbre gialla* 'yellow fever', *natura morta* 'still life'; AN: *alta moda* 'haute couture', *mezza luna* 'half moon';

    f. Spanish (Rainer and Varela 1992): NA: *luna nueva* 'new moon'; AN: *media luna* 'half moon';

    g. Catalan: AN *llibre blanc* 'white book', *peix blau* 'bluefish', AN *belles arts* 'fine arts';

    h. Greek (Ralli and Stavrou 1998): *psixros polemos* 'cold war', *tritos kosmos* 'Third World'.

A short survey of such 'tight' A + N phrases in Celtic and Romance languages is given by Dahl (2004: 228–230). In some cases, the semantic tightness of these phrases manifests itself in the prenominal position of the adjective in languages where the default position of the adjective is postnominal, as in Spanish *un gran hombre* 'a great man' versus *un hombre grande* 'a big man' (Dahl 2004: 229).[10]

In the next subsection, I will discuss Greek AN combinations in more detail, and the properties of Dutch AN units are discussed in section 7.3.2. Section 7.3.3 deals with the way in which these phrasal names interact with word formation.

7.3.1 Greek A + N combinations

Ralli and Stavrou (1998) distinguish two types of A + N combinations for Greek: A + N compounds and A + N constructs. Note that the term 'compound' is used by these authors in the sense of 'lexical unit', in contrast with our use of the term compound as referring to a morphological class of words.[11]

[10.] Similar prenominal adjectives of French are analysed as 'lite', non-projecting adjectives by Abeillé and Godard (2004).

[11.] The Latin transcription of the Greek words is that given in Ralli and Stavrou (1998).

(19)   a. *A + N 'compounds'*:
          psixr-os polemos 'cold war'
          trit-os kozmos 'third world'
          mavr-i lista 'black list'
          mikr-i othoni 'small screen'
       b. *A + N 'constructs'*
          atomik-i vomva 'atomic bomb'
          musik-i kritiki 'musical review, music review'
          odhik-o dhiktio 'road network'
          pirinik-i dhokimi 'nuclear testing'

The difference between (19a) and (19b) is that in (19b) relational adjectives are used, whereas (19a) contains qualifying adjectives. In both constructions, the As are non-projecting, and they cannot be separated from the head N by the definite determiner nor follow the head noun, unlike what is the case for descriptive A + N phrases in Greek, where double marking of definiteness is possible:

(20)   a. *o polemos o psixros
          the war the cold
          'the cold war'
       b. o kafes o zestos
          the coffee the hot
          'the hot coffee'

According to Ralli and Stavrou (1998), the difference between the two types of A + N combinations is that (i) A + N 'compounds' are idiosyncratic in meaning whereas A + N 'constructs' are semantically regular, and (ii) in the A + N constructs (21b), but not in the A + N compounds (21a), the order of A and N may be reversed in indefinite phrases:

(21)   a. mia pedh-iki xara >   *mia xhara phed-iki
          a child-ADJ delight   a delight child-ADJ
          'a playground'
       b. atom-iki vomva   >   vomva atom-iki
          'atom-ic bomb'

Moreover, the Greek A + N 'constructs' can be split by parenthetical expressions, unlike A + N 'compounds'.

(22)   i   viomixaniki,   opos   oli   borite   na   dhite,   zoni
          the industrial,   as   all   you   can   see,   area

For these reasons, Ralli and Stavrou consider the first class of A + N combinations as created by a morphological rule of compounding, whereas A + N constructs are considered to be phrasal and hence syntactic in nature.

Ralli and Stavrou note that not only the A + N 'compounds' but also the A + N combinations classified as 'constructs' behave as units with respect to qualifying adjectives, since they can follow or precede the qualifying adjective as a whole as shown in (23):[12]

(23)   a.   sinexis psixros polemos
             continuous cold war
             'continuous cold war'
             *psixros sinexis polemos
       b.   mia theatriki kritiki kali
             a drama review good
             'a good drama review'
             *mia theatriki kali kritiki

The main problem for a morphological analysis of the Greek A + N 'compounds', as proposed by Ralli and Stavrou (1998), is that there are formal indications that these units are phrasal: the adjectives are inflected, and they agree with the head noun in gender, number, and case. Hence, interpreting these A + N sequences as morphological compounds is in conflict with the principle of Lexical Integrity which forbids syntactic rules such as agreement to apply within complex words. Therefore, I opt for a syntactic interpretation of both subsets of A + N combinations. The two classes can be distinguished by considering the A + N compounds as syntactic N^0 compounds, and the A + N constructs as phrasal. These structures contrast with those of Greek morphological compounds such as *nixtopuli* 'night bird', which has structure (24c):

(24)   a.   constructs: $[A^0 \ N^0]_{N'}$ e.g. $[[\text{atomiki}]_{A^0} \ [\text{vomva}]_{N^0}]_{N'}$
       b.   syntactic compounds: $[A^0 \ N^0]_{N^0}$ e.g. $[[\text{psixros}]_A \ [\text{polemos}]_{N^0}]_{N^0}$
       c.   morphological compounds: $[A \ N]_N$ e.g. $[[\text{nixt}]_A o [\text{puli}]_N]_N$

Morphological A + N compounds in Greek are different from the other two types of construction: the first constituent is a stem, followed by a linking

---

[12.] This observation concerning the order in which adjectives appear applies to such A + N combinations in many European languages (Heynderickx 2001).

element -o, and the compound as a whole forms one phonological word (Ralli 2007). A morphological compound headed by the category label N can occupy an N^0 position in a syntactic structure. This structural differentiation can be used to account for the differences in syntactic behaviour of the different types of A + N sequences.

The structure proposed here for the A + N syntactic compounds is the same as that proposed for similar A + N constructs in English by Sadler and Arnold (1994). A similar structure has been proposed for verbs with quasi-noun incorporation in Japanese (Iida and Sells 2008) and Dutch (see Chapter 4). These verbal units are tight N + V sequences that behave as very tight syntactic units. Hence, their structure can be assumed to be $[N^0 \ V^0]_{V^0}$.[13]

Ralli and Stavrou (1998) point out that a morphological compound analysis of the Greek A + N 'constructs' is also out of the question because they cannot be used as the nominal bases of relational adjectives, as we would expect under a morphological compound interpretation of these A + N sequences. This is one of the reasons why Ralli and Stavrou do not qualify them as compounds but give them phrasal status (constructs). It is only the corresponding stems without the inflectional endings that can form the basis of such relational adjectives, as illustrated in (25):

(25)   psixr-os polem-os 'cold war' psixr-o-polem-ikos 'cold-war-like'

This is to be expected if derivation is restricted to taking words (in their stem form) as bases, as is the default case. Word-based derivation excludes the phrasal name *psixros polemos* from functioning as a base for complex adjectives. The base *psixr-o-polem-* in *psixropolemikos* has the form of a compound: its first constituent is the adjectival stem *psixr-* followed by the standard linking element -o- and the nominal stem *polem-*. What we therefore observe here is a paradigmatic relationship between an A + N syntactic compound and a denominal relational adjective with the corresponding morphological compound as its base. The meaning of the complex adjective is a compositional function of that of the paradigmatically related phrasal name *psixros polemos* and that of the suffix -ik-os. The morphological schema for such Greek relational adjectives with a compound base is:

(26) $[[A-o-N]_N \ ik-os]_A$

This schema is a unification of the schema for denominal relational adjectives with the schema for Greek AN morphological compounds.

[13.] For a similar analysis, cf. Abeillé and Godard (2004).

7.3.2 Dutch A + N phrases with naming function

Let us now have a more detailed look at how the naming function of A + N phrases affects the form and behaviour of such phrases in Dutch.

A. A first relevant observation is that of a blocking effect: the coining of NN compounds is often blocked by the existence of a competing A + N phrase, and vice versa (Booij 2002a):

(27) A + N phrase   NN compound
      academisch jaar 'academic year'   ?academie-jaar 'academy year'
      ?academisch lid 'academic member'   academie-lid 'academy member'
      koninklijk besluit 'royal decision'   ?konings-besluit 'king decision'
      koninklijk huis 'royal family'   konings-huis 'king-house, royal
                                                 family'
      ?koninklijk blauw 'royal blue'   konings-blauw 'king blue'
      muzikale scholing 'musical training'   ?muziek-scholing 'music training'
      muzikaal talent 'musical talent'   muziek-talent 'music talent'
      ?muzikale school 'musical school'   muziek-school 'music school'

The adjectives in these A + N phrases are denominal relational adjectives. That is why they form an alternative to modifying a noun by means of another noun in NN compounds. Some of the phrases and compounds are marked with a question mark. This does not mean that these word combinations are ungrammatical but that they are infelicitous because of the existence of a conventionalized synonymous (and hence competing) expression. This type of blocking is the effect of competition between synonymous lexical units and may therefore be called 'lexical blocking' (Ackerman and Webelhuth 1998). It is not a formal principle that qualifies constructs as ungrammatical. We also find individual variation, which is to be expected since language users differ in which lexical units they have stored. The blocking effects observed in (27) show that coining such A + N phrases is coining names which therefore, as lexical units, compete with synonymous compounds.

B. A + N phrases with a classifying role can appear in the non-head-position of compounds and as bases of certain types of derived words. In this position, they function as names for categories and hence receive a generic interpretation:

(28) oude-mannen-huis 'old men's home'
      vaste-schijf-module 'hard disk module'
      volle-maans-gezicht 'lit. full moon face, moonface'

(29)   jonge-mensen-achtig 'young people-like'
        kleine-meisjes-achtig 'little girls-like'
        geiten-wollen-sokken-achtig 'goats' wool socks-like'

C. In Dutch A + N phrases that form lexical collocations the adjective may appear without the expected inflectional ending -e (Booij 2002b: 47–48; Tummers 2005). In the following examples, the nouns have common gender. An adjective in a definite NP headed by a common gender noun normally ends in a schwa. Yet, in the following examples, this ending is missing:

(30)   een/de geheim-ø agent 'a/the secret agent'
        een/de taalkundig-ø onderzoeker 'a/the linguistic investigator'

The absence of the expected inflectional schwa strengthens the naming function of these NPs: 'the common meaning of the construction resides in the fact that the uninflected adjective in these constructions focuses less on the individual properties of the person or thing referred to, and more on general or categorial properties or stereotypes deducible from certain specialized usages of the substantives' (Blom 1994: 81). The effect of the absence of the inflectional schwa is that they look more like AN compounds. Yet, they are still different from morphological compounds since they have main stress on the noun (in AN compounds, main stress is on the adjective).

    There are also A + N phrases with a neuter noun as head that function as names. In that case, the inflectional ending -e tends to be omitted in the singular form only, but some speakers use uninflected adjectives before plural neuter nouns as well:[14]

(31)   het oudheidkundig(e) museum 'the archeological museum'/?de oud-heidkundig musea 'the archeological museums'
        het koninklijk(e) paleis 'the royal palace'/?de koninklijk paleizen 'the royal palaces'

The phrasal nature of these A + N names is clear from their stress pattern (stress on the last constituent), and the optionality of the absence of the inflectional ending of the adjective.

D. A + N phrasal names can occasionally be modified as if they are the heads of complex words, with a modifying word or prefix in the non-head position. The head of a compound or a prefixed word in Dutch is not expected to be phrasal: Dutch compounds are right-headed and hence a phrasal head would imply phrasal status for the construction as a whole. Yet, we do find A + N

[14.] As Matthias Hüning (pers. comm.) observed, Dutch speakers sometimes also use plural neuter nouns with uninflected adjectives.

sequences with naming function, preceded by a noun with modifying function, or preceded by a prefix that normally attaches to nouns. Thus, these A +
N sequences function as heads of complex words. The following examples,
some of them from Ackema and Neeleman (2004: 125), illustrate this
phenomenon:

(32)   *compounds*
       namaak [mobiele telefoon] 'imitation mobile phone'
       wereld [rode wijn] 'world red wine, superb red wine'
       deeltijd [pastoraal medewerker] 'part-time pastoral assistant'

       prefixed words
       ex-aanstormend talent 'ex up-and-coming talent'
       pseudo-taalkundig onderzoeker 'pseudo-linguistic researcher'
       pseudo-epileptische aanval 'pseudo-epileptic attack'

These examples suggest that A + N phrasal names are sorts of words and
hence usable as heads of the constructs in (32). However, the A + N heads of
these constructs still exhibit inflection of the adjective, an effect of the
syntactic rule of agreement. This suggests interpreting these A + N heads as
cases of syntactic compounds dominated by N^0.

E. Classifying A + N phrases (i.e. phrasal names) can be coordinated with
compounds but not with descriptive phrases (Heynderickx 2001); the common constituent of the coordinated constituents can be gapped. This gapping
involves the deletion of a prosodic word constituent under identity with
another one (Booij 1985):

(33)   a. *classifying phrase + compound*
          Amerikaanse (talen) en Papoeatalen
          'American (languages) and Papua-languages'
       b. **descriptive + classifying phrase*
          *het grote (paleis) en koninklijke paleis
          'the large and royal palace'
       c. *compound + classifying phrase*
          ijs(beren) en bruine beren
          'ice bears and brown bears'
       d. **classifying phrase + descriptive phrase*
          *Amerikaanse (talen) en moeilijke talen
          'American languages and difficult languages'

These observations show that classifying phrases behave like compounds as to
their coordination possibilities, and differ in this respect from descriptive
phrases. That is, we need a specific semantic category 'name' that generalizes

across morphological compounds and these phrasal lexical units, in order to express the constraint on coordination that the two non-heads must exhibit semantic parallelism.

F. The order of adjectives in Dutch is such that descriptive adjectives precede classifying adjectives:

(34)   vieze rode kool 'filthy red cabbage'/*rode vieze kool
        goedkope witte wijn 'cheap white wine'/*witte goedkope wijn
        dure mobiele telefoon 'expensive mobile phone'/*mobiele dure telefoon

Thus, descriptive adjectives are peripheral to the A + N unit that functions as a name. These distributional facts follow from the status of Dutch A + N phrasal names being interpreted either as syntactic compounds with the structure $[A^0 \ N^0]_{N^0}$ or as phrases of the type $[A^0 \ N^0]_{N'}$. Both structures require the adjective to be adjacent to the noun.

   The same observation as to the order of adjectives can be made for adjective noun combinations in other languages, as mentioned in section 7.3.1 for Greek. It also holds for the other type of phrases with naming function listed in (4), as illustrated here for the Italian [N *a* N] name *sedia a rotelle* 'wheel chair' (Semenza and Mondini 2006: 92):

(35)   sedia a rotelle rotta/*sedia rotta a rotelle 'broken wheel chair'

G. A + N phrasal names behave like compounds in allowing for a particular type of semantic reanalysis, that of semantic concentration, in which the meaning of a whole compound is projected onto its first constituent (Meesters 2004). The notion of semantic concentration can be illustrated by the following example. In Dutch, the verbal stem *scharrel* 'to scratch, to potter around' acquired the meaning 'free-range, eco-' starting from the compound *scharrel-kip*:

(36)   scharrel-kip 'scratch chicken, free range chicken > scharrel-ei 'free-range egg'
        scharrel-vlees 'free-range meat, eco-meat', scharrel-wijn 'eco-wine'

Whereas chickens can potter around, this is not the case for eggs or meat. This shows that a process of semantic reinterpretation has been in effect here. Such semantic concentration effects may lead to the rise of new affixes from compound constituents, as discussed in section 3.4. The semantic concentration effect can also be observed in A + N phrasal names, as illustrated here for the adjective *onbespoten* 'unsprayed' that acquired the meaning 'eco-':

(37)   onbespoten groente 'unsprayed vegetables, eco-vegetables'
       onbespoten restaurants 'lit. unsprayed restaurants, eco-restaurants'
       onbespoten mensen 'lit. unsprayed people, eco-minded people' (daily
       newspaper *Trouw*, 14 June 2008)
       onbespoten idealen 'lit. unsprayed ideals, ecological ideals'

This use of *onbespoten* in A + N names has led to the meaning 'environment-friendly'. This phenomenon shows that we have to distinguish a semantic class of tight A + N phrasal constructs in order to explain why, like compounds, these constructs may exhibit these semantic concentration effects.

In sum, we have seen a number of phenomena in which A + N phrasal names in Dutch behave as tight syntactic units. Their formal and corresponding semantic structure should therefore be represented in such a way that their parallelism with morphological AN and NN compounds as names for categories is made clear. A first, admittedly rather informal approach to the semantics of these construction types is the following:

(38)   a. syntactic constructs with qualifying adjectives:
          $[A^0_i \ N^0_j]_k \leftrightarrow [NAME \ for \ SEM_j \ with \ some \ relation \ R \ to \ SEM_i]_k$
       b. syntactic constructs with denominal relational adjectives:
          $[A^0_i \ N^0_j]_k \leftrightarrow [NAME \ for \ SEM_j \ with \ some \ relation \ R \ to \ entity \ E \ of \ SEM_i]_k$

The name interpretation of these constructional schemas is specified to the right of the double arrow, which stands for the correspondence between form and meaning. SEM stands for the meaning of the constituents, and co-indexation specifies the relation between formal constituents and corresponding meanings. In (38b), the meaning of the relational adjective involves a relation with some entity which may have a corresponding base noun in this relational adjective. In a relational adjective like *academ-isch* 'academic' the evoked entity *academie* 'academy' corresponds with a base noun, *academie*. In the case of the adjective *jurid-isch* 'legal' there is no identifiable base noun that corresponds with the entity 'law' but the meaning of *juridisch* implies the existence of such an entity.

Just as in morphological compounds, the semantic relation R between the head and the modifier is not predictable from the linguistic structure as such, and has to be filled in for each individual expression on the basis of contextual and world knowledge (Downing 1977). For instance, in *gele koorts* 'yellow fever' the fever has the effect of a yellow skin, whereas in *het Rode leger* 'the Red army', the army adheres to principles symbolized by the colour red.

The representations (38) are constructional schemas in which a particular structural configuration is linked to a particular semantic interpretation. The distinguishing formal property of these constructional phrasal schemas for names is the non-projecting A, which does not project a full phrase with modifiers.

We may ask now whether these Dutch A + N constructs have the syntactic status of N' (phrases) or N^0 (syntactic compounds). Unlike what was the case for Greek, I do not know of clear evidence for the necessity of two different structures. The crucial property of these constructs is that the adjective is non-projecting and strictly adjacent to the head noun. Since the adjectives in these constructs are inflected, the principle of Lexical Integrity predicts them to be non-morphological, that is, syntactic in nature. If there is a principled reason why adjectives in N' phrases cannot be excluded from projecting, the syntactic compound status is the correct one, as suggested for English by Sadler and Arnold (1994). Moreover, Chapter 4 presents clear evidence for syntactic compounding in Dutch, the formation of compound verbs like *zeezeilen* 'to sea-sail' in which the N is not an argument of the verb and hence cannot form a V'. I will leave the choice between these two structural interpretations open for further investigation.

7.3.3 Syntactic lexical units and word formation

Let us now look at the interaction of phrasal A + N names with word formation. A + N phrases can function as modifiers in compounds, as mentioned above. There are a few Dutch denominal suffixes that accept phrases as bases: the denominal suffixes -*er* 'id.' and -*achtig* '-like' with A + N phrases as bases:

(39)   derde-klass-er 'third class-er, member of the third class'
        zeventiende-eeuw-er '17th century-er, someone living in the 17th century'
        zwarte-band-er 'black belt-er, judoka with a black belt'
        jonge-meisjes-achtig 'young girls-like, like young girls'
        gele-koorts-achtig 'yellow fever-like'

The Dutch diminutive suffix, on the other hand, does not accept phrasal bases. Yet, we can diminutivize phrasal A + N names. The diminutive suffix has semantic scope over the whole phrase, but formally attaches to its head N only:

(40)   hog-e hoed   'high hat, top hat'   hoog hoed-je   *hoge-hoed-je
        voll-e maan   'full moon'   vol maan-tje   *volle-maan-tje
        rod-e wijn   'red wine'   rood wijn-tje   *rode-wijn-tje
        witt-e was   'white laundry'   wit was-je   *witte-was-je

In the example *rood wijntje*, the diminutive is used either as a suffix of endearment or individuation (in order to express the meaning 'a glass of'). The scope of the diminutive suffix in all examples is clearly the whole A + N. For instance, *een hoog hoedje* is 'a small top hat', not 'a small hat that is high', and *een rood wijntje* is 'a nice red wine' or 'a glass of red wine', not 'a red nice wine' or 'a glass of wine that is red'.[15] This kind of mismatch is a general phenomenon, as discussed in section 5.3.2.

The interaction of lexical phrasal expressions with word formation can be observed in many other cases. Particle verbs in Germanic languages are phrasal in nature, even though they are lexical units (Chapter 5). The same applies to Italian phrasal verbs (Iacobini and Masini 2006). Some examples of this kind of mismatch between form and meaning are listed in (41):

(41) a. English particle verbs may carry the suffixes *-er* and *-ing* on their verbal head: *look-er-on, runn-er-up, digg-ing up, switch-ing off the lights*;

   b. the past participle of Dutch particle verbs is formed by prefixing *ge-* and suffixing *-t/-d/-en* to the stem form of the verbal head: *aan-val* 'to attack' – *aan-ge-vall-en, op-bellen* 'to phone up' – *op-ge-bel-d*); *ge*-nominalization also applies to the head: *rond-spring* 'jump around' – *rond-ge-spring* 'jumping around';

   c. when German particle verbs undergo nominalization with the affix combination *ge-e*, this affix combination is attached to the verbal head of the particle verb: *herum-hops-en* 'to jump around' – *Herum-ge-hops-e* 'jumping around' (Müller 2003, 2006);

   d. in Italian, nominalizing suffixes are attached to the verbal head (Masini, pers. comm.): *venire giù* 'to come down' – *la venuta giù* 'the coming down', *mangiare fuori* 'to eat out' – *la mangiata fuori* 'the meal at a restaurant';

   e. French *mettre en scène* 'to direct a play' has the corresponding agent noun *metteur en scène* 'director'.

We can also observe this difference between the semantic scope and the formal scope of affixes in the following Dutch noun phrases:

[15.] AN phrases may lexicalize into words. This is the case for expressions like Dutch *wittebrood* 'white bread' in which the inflectional ending *-e* is still there. Its diminutive is *wittebroodje* which shows that synchronically it is one word, otherwise we would get *wit broodje* since *broodje* is a neuter noun. For some speakers of Dutch the same applies to *rode kool* 'red cabbage' which has to be written as one word according to the Dutch rules of orthography. Yet, *rood kooltje* 'small red cabbage' is the usual diminutive form of *rode kool* for Dutch language users, as a Google search shows. Other examples of the development of such A + N phrases into words are *jongeman* 'young man' and *blindedarm* 'blind gut'.

(42)   a. muzikal-e vaardig-heid 'musical ability'
        b. digital-e competent-ie 'digital competence'

In example (42a), the suffix -*heid* '-ity' has semantic scope over *muzikaal vaardig* 'lit. musically able, being musical'. In (42b), the suffix -*ie* has scope over *digitaal competent* 'digitally competent'. Yet, the adjectives are not part of the base of the suffixes, as we can see from their being inflected.

These cases form additional evidence for the existence of paradigmatic relationships between constructional schemas, as discussed in section 5.3.2. For instance, the schema for syntactic constructs of the type (38) is paradigmatically related to the schema for diminutive nouns. This relation, symbolized by the sign ≈, may be expressed as follows (recall that the brackets < and > demarcate the boundaries of a constructional schema):

(43) $< [A^0_i \, N^0_j]_k \leftrightarrow SEM_k> \approx < [A^0_i \, [N_j\text{-}tje]_N^0]_m \leftrightarrow [SMALL \, [SEM_k]]_m >$

This paradigmatic correlation between two constructional schemas expresses that the diminutive suffixes attached to the head noun have semantic scope over the whole A + N combination: the semantic operator SMALL of the diminutive suffix has as its scope SEM_k, which stands for the meaning of the A + N phrasal name construction.

The paradigmatic analysis must be extended to the other types of phrasal expressions mentioned in (4). For example, if we pluralize the Italian *N di N* expression *coda di cavallo* 'pony tail', this will have the result *code di cavallo*, not *coda di cavalli*. That is, it is the head noun that is formally pluralized. Yet, the pluralization operation has semantic scope over the whole expression.

7.4 Theoretical implications: lexical phrasal constructions

The Greek and Dutch A + N phrasal names discussed above need to be listed in the lexicon, even though they are formed according to non-morphological, that is, syntactic schemas, since they are the conventional names for certain concepts. Hence, these schemas may function as redundancy statements with respect to conventionalized A + N sequences. In this respect, syntactic schemas are not different from morphological ones. Recall that morphological schemas function as redundancy statements with respect to existing, listed complex words (Chapter 2), and can also be used to coin new words. The same holds for syntactic schemas. This implies that the lexicon contains syntactic schemas.

In the case of A + N phrases with naming function, the schemas (38) are instantiations of the more general schema for N' or N^0 in the grammar of Dutch. The specific meaning contribution of these subconstructions is that they are used for making names for concepts. This correlates with the adjective being non-projecting.

The implication of this analysis is in line with our findings in the previous chapters that there is no strict boundary between syntactic and lexical constructs: syntax permeates the lexicon because syntactic units can be lexical. The grammar is a network of syntactic and morphological constructions, with conventionalized instantiations of both types of constructions listed in the lexicon. A similar conclusion was reached by Sadler and Arnold (1994) in their analysis of AN combinations in English as 'syntactic small constructions'.

The link between a specific syntactic pattern and the naming function can also be observed in the case of appositional names consisting of a head N followed by an N or NP without intervening grammatical words such as prepositions or determiners. It is only when such patterns are used as names that the omission of grammatical words is permitted (and, we should add, in the special register of headline syntax, as mentioned above). In Dutch, this appositional structure is used for coining job names; it can also be used for names of committees, and all kinds of notions in the domain of government administration, etc.:

(44) $[directeur]_{N^0}$ [$[artistieke]_{A^0}$ $[zaken]_{N^0}$] 'director (of) artistic affairs'
       $[[Commissie]_{N^0}$ $[Kok]_{N^0}]$ 'committee Kok, committee chaired by Mr Kok'
       $[[Wet]_{N^0}$ $[Arbeids-Ongeschiktheid]_{N^0}]$ (WAO) 'law labour-disabledness, law for people being unable to work'

These names are syntactic constructs. The first example shows that the expression following the head noun can also be complex; it can be a phrasal name itself: *artistieke zaken* 'artistic affairs'. Such names are not necessarily lexicalized phrases since these patterns are very productive for coining new (job) names.

Nice examples of the possible complexity of the postnominal modifier in appositional names are found in Italian: naming expressions with coordinated nouns in the postnominal position:

(45)   a. un marito pipa e pantofole   (Bisetto and Scalise 1999: 32)
          a husband pipe and slippers
          'the type of husband characterized by smoking a pipe and wearing slippers'

b. un marito tutto pipa e pantofole   (Bisetto and Scalise 1999: 32)
   a husband entirely pipe and slippers
   'a type of husband very much characterized by smoking a pipe and
   wearing slippers'
c. una ragazza acqua e sapone   (Masini, pers. comm.)
   a girl water and soap
   'a girl who does not use make-up'

These expressions are obviously phrasal names for specific concepts.[16]

In sum, (i) using the notion 'construction' (a pairing of form and meaning), (ii) modelling the grammar of natural languages as a network of constructions of various degrees of abstractness, and (iii) assuming paradigmatic
relationships between constructions, are essential ingredients for coping with
the relation between the form and function of phrasal names. The lexical
constructs used for naming exhibit various degrees of tightness. Their similarities and differences which are often qualified as the grey area between
morphology and syntax can be done justice to in a constructionist framework
as outlined above.

[16.] The construction of names by means of phrasal expressions is not restricted to the domain of
nominal entities. Several languages have a similar mechanism for creating names for events, quasi-
incorporation, as discussed in Chapter 4.

8

Numerals as lexical constructions

8.1 Numerals: morphology or syntax?

Numerals form a challenge for the proper demarcation of morphology and syntax. Some of them are clearly complex words. A word like English *seventy* can be decomposed straightforwardly as consisting of a stem *seven* and a suffix *-ty*. Hence, it is a derived word. But what about the number name *seventy-six*? Is this a compound or a phrase? In English number names higher than 100, we connect the two number words by means of a conjunction: *hundred and three*. This suggests that such expressions are cases of syntactic coordination and not of word formation. The spelling of such numerals (with internal spacing) also suggests that they might be phrases. Yet, the order of the constituents in this type of coordination is fixed; a number name like *three and hundred* is ill-formed. So the use of syntactic coordination for numerals is subject to specific restrictions.

In this chapter I argue that the notion construction provides the right analytic tool for a proper analysis of numerals. Numerals may be analysed as either morphological or syntactic constructions, depending on the subtype involved. I focus on the various types of Dutch numerals since they form a nice illustration of the kind of analytical problems one encounters in deciding how numerals fit into the architecture of the grammar. This chapter provides a construction-based analysis of these types and confirms the conclusion of Chapters 4–7 that lexical units may be formed according to phrasal schemas with specific formal and semantic properties.

8.2 Dutch numerals

Consider the following numerals of Dutch and their glosses in English:

(1)   a. 5   vijf 'five'
       b. 15 vijf-tien 'fif-teen'

    c. 50   vijf-tig 'fif-ty'
    d. 51   een-en-vijf-tig 'one-and-fif-ty'
    e. 105 honderd (en) vijf 'one hundred (and) five'

Most numerals of Dutch and English are complex linguistic expressions, formed by a recursive system of rules that enables the language user to form in principle an infinite set of numerals. In Dutch, as in English and German, all numerals above the number 12 are such complex expressions. The numeral *vijf-tien* '15' in (1b) has the shape of a compound consisting of two lexeme constituents, *vijf* '5' and *tien* '10', whereas *vijftig* has the shape of a derived word with the suffix *-tig*. The next two examples (1d,e), on the other hand, have the appearance of phrases, formed by means of coordination with the conjunction *en* 'and'. The difference between (1d) and (1e) is that only in (1e) can the conjunction be omitted. Another difference between (1d) and (1e) is that in (1d) the conjunction *en* is pronounced as [ən], whereas in (1e) it must be pronounced as [ɛn].

   Even though (1d) and (1e) look like phrases, they can function as bases of word formation, for the formation of ordinal numerals by means of the suffixes *-ste* and *-de*:

(2)   a. een-en-vijf-tig-ste
          one-and-fif-ty-th
          'fifty-first'
       b. honderd (-en) vijf-de
          hundred (and) fif-th'
          'hundred and fifth'

One may therefore conclude that morphological operations can take phrasal lexical units as their bases, a position that is also defended in Chapter 7.

   Dutch numerals raise the question to what extent their construction is a matter of morphology, and to what extent it belongs to syntax. The reference grammar of Dutch, the *Algemene Nederlandse Spraakkunst* (Haeseryn et al. 1997) discusses the formation of numerals under the heading of word classes and word formation, whereas Hurford, in his studies of numerals (Hurford 1975, 1987, 2003, 2007) considers them as syntactic constructs (Hurford 2007: 777). In this chapter I will argue that Dutch numerals are a mixed bag of derived words, compounds, and syntactic idioms, and form a complex network of constructional schemas of varying degrees of abstractness. Thus, this chapter will provide additional evidence for a constructional analysis of lexical units.

Section 8.3 deals with the numerals that are usually referred to as cardinal numerals. Note, however, that such words that denote numbers have more functions than expressing the cardinality of sets. Wiese distinguishes three functions (Wiese 2007: 759–760):

(a) cardinal number assignment, as in *three books*; *I saw three of the students*;
(b) ordinal number assignment, as in *group 5*, *(the year) 2001*, *Downing Street 10*;
(c) nominal number assignment, as in *line 5* (name of one of a number of lines in public transport), *MasterCard # 6666 etc.* (number of credit card).

In addition, cardinal numerals can be used for counting: *one, two, three* ....

When used as cardinal numbers, these numerals function attributively, as in *three books*, or as heads of phrases, as in *I saw three of the students*. In the uses (b) and (c) the numeral follows the head noun of a phrasal name. They function as appositional modifiers to these head nouns, and are thus similar in structure to the type of phrasal names discussed in section 7.4.

In section 8.4 I deal with the morphological construction of ordinal numerals, and in section 8.5 with the construction of fraction names. Section 8.6 summarizes my findings and presents some conclusions concerning the architecture of the grammar.

8.3 Cardinal numerals

Let me first give a representative selection of the expressions that are used as cardinal numerals in Dutch:

(3) *a. numerals 1–9   b. numerals 11–19*   *c. numerals 10–90*

1 een /eːn/	11 elf /ɛlf/	10 tien /tin/
2 twee /tʋeː/	12 twaalf /tʋaːlf/	20 twin-tig /tʋɪn-təɣ/
3 drie/ driː/	13 der-tien /dɛr-tin/	30 der-tig /dɛr-təɣ/
4 vier /viːr/	14 veer-tien /veːr-tin/	40 veer-tig /veːr-təɣ/
5 vijf /vɛɪf/	15 vijf-tien /vɛɪf-tin/	50 vijf-tig /vɛɪf-təɣ/
6 zes /zɛs/	16 zes-tien /zɛs-tin/	60 zes-tig /sɛs-təɣ/
7 zeven /zeːvən/	17 zeven-tien /zeːvən-tin/	70 zeven-tig /seːvən-təɣ/
8 acht /ɑxt/	18 acht-tien /ɑxt-tin/	80 tach-tig /tɑx-təɣ/
9 negen /neːɣan/	19 negen-tien /neːɣən-tin/	90 negen-tig /neːɣən-təɣ/

d. numerals 21–99

22 twee-en-twin-tig
33 drie-en-der-tig
44 vier-en-veer-tig
55 vijf-en-vijf-tig
66 zes-en-zes-tig
77 zeven-en-zeven-tig
88 acht-en-tach-tig
99 negen-en-negen-tig

e. numerals 100 and higher

100	honderd
101	honderd (en) een
1,000	duizend
1,000,000	miljoen
1,000,000,000	miljard

The numeral *een* [eːn] has the same orthographic form as the indefinite singular determiner *een* [ən]. Historically, the determiner derives from the numeral. A characteristic difference between grammatical words and words of lexical categories is that only the former can have schwa [ə] as their only vowel (Booij 1995). The difference in phonetic form between the two lexemes *een* reflects this phonological constraint, since the numeral *een* has to be pronounced with a full vowel [eː].

There is some allomorphy to be observed in the bases of the numerals in (3b,c) in comparison with the forms in (3a): *drie* has the allomorph *der-*, and *vier* has the allomorph *veer-*. The suffix for the numerals 20–90, the multiples of 10, is *-tig* /təɣ/; it is affixed to the allomorphs *twin-* for *twee* 'two', *der-* for *drie* 'three', *veer* for *vier* 'four', and *tach-* for *acht* 'eight', as shown in (3c). Note that there is also allomorphy involved in the numerals *zestig* and *zeventig* even though this is not indicated in the orthography: these words begin with a voiceless consonant [s].

The suffix *-tig* has also been reanalysed as a word, as in *tig keer* 'for the umpteenth time'. In that case, the vowel letter is realized as [ɪ] because a word of a lexical category cannot have schwa [ə] as its only vowel.

The numerals listed in (3b) and (3c) are clear cases of complex words. The following morphological schemas express the commonalities of these closed sets of words:

(4) 13–19: $[[x]^i_{Num, [dig]} \text{ tien}]^j_{Num} \leftrightarrow [NUM^i + 10]^j$
     20–90: $[[x]^i_{Num, [dig]} \text{ tig}]^j_{Num} \leftrightarrow [NUM^i \times 10]^j$

(The feature [dig] denotes the set of digital numbers 1–9; for reasons of presentational clarity the indices are rendered as superscripts). The schemas (4) represent the correspondence between particular forms and particular meanings. The meaning of each numeral in *tien* is the addition of the numerical value of the digital numeral and 10; that of the numerals in *-tig* is 10 times the value of the digit number. The superscripts *i* and *j* identify the form and the corresponding meaning (= arithmetical value) of the base and the complex numeral. The indices *i* and *j* are variables for lexical indexes: each lexical unit in the lexicon carries its own lexical index. NUM stands for the arithmetical value of a numeral. Even though these types of word formation are unproductive since the number of bases is a closed set, I assume schemas in order to express the common and predictable properties of these sets of words. It is obvious that the numerals listed in (3b,c) are stored in the lexicon. Hence, the schemas are to be seen as redundancy statements that specify which information concerning the individual numerals in *-tig* is predictable. The words for 20, 30, 40, 60, 70, and 80 are exceptional in that their base has not exactly the same phonological shape as the corresponding digital numerals.

We might represent these numerals as follows in a hierarchical lexicon, linked to the schema (9), with (arbitrary) lexical indices such as 82.

(5) a. $[[\text{vijf}]^{82}_{\text{Num, [dig]}} \text{ tig}]^{83}_{\text{Num}} \leftrightarrow [5^{82} \times 10]^{83}$
     b. $[[\text{veer}]_{\text{Num, [dig]}} \text{ tig}]^{84}_{\text{Num}} \leftrightarrow [4 \times 10]^{84}$

The lexical index 82 indicates that the form and meaning of *vijf* (with the lexical index 82) recur in *vijf-tig*. Thus, co-indexation expresses the part-of-relation that exists between a complex word and its base. The base *veer* is not an existing numeral of Dutch, and hence it does not carry a lexical index that identifies it with an independently existing lexeme in the lexicon. Therefore, the meaning of *veer* '4' on the right of the arrow is information that has to be learned independently.

The arithmetical operations involved in the formation of complex numerals of Dutch are addition and multiplication. The default linguistic expression of addition is coordination, with at least one explicit conjunction such as *en* 'and'. The use of this universal syntactic mechanism can be seen in the formation of numerals, but in Dutch numerals it is grammaticalized into three specific subpatterns listed and exemplified in (6); these patterns impose specific restrictions on the presence of an overt conjunction and on the order of the subconstituents in numerals:

(6) a. 13–19: no overt conjunction, lower number before higher number: *vijf-tien* '15';

  b. 21–99: conjunction, lower number before higher number *een-en-vijf-tig* '51';

  c. > 100: optional conjunction before the last numeral, higher number before lower number: *honderd (en) vijf* '105', *twee-duizend acht-honderd (en) vijf* '2,805'.

These patterns are constructions that reflect the general syntactic principles of coordination of Dutch, but need to be stated separately as specific instantiations of the coordinating construction, with properties of their own. These numerals may contrast with the regular pattern of coordination, as illustrated by the following minimal pair:

(7) a. vijf-tien boeken 'fif-teen books'
  b. vijf en tien boeken 'five and ten books'

In (7a) the phrase denotes one set of books with cardinality 15, whereas (7b) denotes two different sets of books with the cardinalities 5 and 10 respectively.

A numeral such as *vijftien* '15' has the appearance of a compound word since it has the stress pattern of Dutch compounds, with main stress on the first constituent. Yet, it does not possess the property of regular compounds of Dutch of being right-headed. In *vijftien* the right constituent *tien* 'ten' has no semantic head properties with respect to the word as a whole. This is explained by this special type of compound word being derived historically from (asyndetic) coordination. It sides with regular compounds, however, in that main stress is on the first constituent and secondary stress on the second: *vijf-tien*. Hence, we consider these numerals as a subset of the class of Dutch compounds.

Dutch (and the closely related Germanic languages Frisian and German) differ from English as to the order of the number constituents below 100. In English, the higher number comes before the lower number after 20 (*twenty-one*, etc.), whereas in Dutch this switch of order takes place after 100. The exact locus of switch varies from language to language. In Italian, for instance, the switch takes place after 16: *se-dici* '16', but *dici-a-sette* '17'.

These facts all conform to the following universals:

(8) 26. If in a language, in any sum the smaller addend precedes the larger, then the same order holds for all smaller numbers expressed by addition.

27. If in a language, in any sum the larger addend precedes the smaller, then the same order holds for all larger numbers expressed by addition. (Greenberg 1978: 273)

The second arithmetical operation involved in the construction of Dutch numerals is that of multiplication, as in the following numerals:

(9) a. vijf-tig   5 × 10
     b. vijf-honderd   5 × 100
         vijf-duizend   5 × 1000
     c. vijf-miljoen   5 × 1,000,000
         vijf-miljard   5 × 1,000,000,000

The words of the type *vijftig* are discussed above. The words *honderd* 'hundred', *duizend* 'thousand', *miljoen* 'million', and *miljard* 'billion' can be considered a subset of the category of measure nouns. Hurford (1975, 1987) refers to these units that function as the basis of multiplication with the symbol M. They have properties of nouns, as shown by the fact that they can be pluralized, as in:

(10) a. honderd-en bezoeker-s
          hundred-PL visitor-PL
          'hundreds of visitors'
      b. duizend-en gulden-s
          thousand-PL guilder-PL
          'thousands of guilders'
      c. miljoen-en sterr-en
          million-PL star-PL
          'millions of stars'
      d. miljard-en boek-en
          billion-PL book-PL
          'billions of books'

Such phrases instantiate the pattern of Dutch appositional NPs of the type *flessen wijn* 'bottles of wine' and *kisten appels* 'boxes of apples', in which the container noun functions as a kind of classifier and is followed by an appositional noun that specifies the contents of the container.

In combination with numerals the multiplication bases have the singular form, just like other Dutch measure nouns such as *meter* 'metre' and *kilo* 'kilogram':

(11) a. drie meter
         three metre.SG
         'three metres'
     b. vijf kilo
         five kilo.SG
         'five kilograms'

The numerals *honderd* en *duizend* are noun-like in that they can be pluralized. However, they differ from *miljoen* and *miljard*, since they can be used without a preceding numeral, unlike *miljoen* and *miljard*:[1]

(12)   a. honderd/duizend boeken 'hundred/thousand books'
      b. *miljoen/een [eːn] miljoen boeken 'one million books'
          *miljard/een [eːn] miljard boeken 'one billion books'

Thus, we need the following specifications for these classes of words:

(13) a. honderd, duizend: [+N, + Num, +M]
     b. miljoen, miljard: [+N, +M]

The feature [+N] predicts that these words, being nouns, can be pluralized. The feature [+M] qualifies them as measure nouns that appear in their singular form after a numeral. The words in (13b) do not carry a lexical feature [+Numeral], and hence they cannot occur by themselves as numerals in noun phrases and must be preceded by the determiner *een* 'a' or a numeral.

   Numerals can project a phrase. Numeral phrases are a subcategory of quantifier phrases, but I will refrain from a detailed discussion of the complexities of the structure of noun/determiner phrases and their quantifier subparts. Suffice it to mention here that numerals can project phrases since they can be modified:

(14)   ongeveer twintig 'approximately 20'
      ruim twintig 'amply 20'
      om en nabij twintig 'lit. around and close to 20, about 20'
      meer dan twintig 'more than 20'

   The next issue is how to properly characterize the grammar of complex numerals. The productive schemas for Dutch are those for multiplication and addition. The multiplication schema is an instantiation of the general schema for constructions with a numeral followed by a measure noun that creates quantifying expressions such as *drie meter boeken* 'lit. three metre books, three metres of books'. The additional property of this multiplication schema is that

---

[1] Except in headlines of newspapers, which have a special syntax (cf. Chapter 7).

it specifies these expressions as numerals which can hence form part of larger complex numerals, as discussed below. The numeral *drie-honderd*, for example, can be embedded in a numeral coordination structure, as in *drie-honderd-en-vijf* '305', unlike other measure expressions such as *twee meter* (**twee meter en vijf*):

(15)   *Multiplication schema*
        $[\text{Num}^i \; \text{Num}^j_{[+M]}]^k_{\text{Num}} \leftrightarrow [\text{NUM}^i \times \text{NUM}^j]^k$

(where NUM stands for the arithmetical value of the corresponding formal constituents indexed as *i* and *j*). Numerals like *honderd, duizend, miljoen*, and *miljard* are specified as belonging to the subcategory M, and hence they form bases of multiplication. This schema will generate numerals like the following:[2]

(16) $[[\text{achttien}]_{\text{Num}}[\text{honderd}]_{\text{Num}}]_{\text{Num}}$ 'eighteen hundred'
        $[[\text{negen-en-negen-tig}]_{\text{Num}}[\text{honderd}]_{\text{Num}}]_{\text{Num}}$ 'ninety-nine hundred'
        $[[\text{honderd}]_{\text{Num}}[\text{duizend}]_{\text{Num}}]_{\text{Num}}$ 'hundred thousand'
        $[[[\text{twee}]_{\text{Num}} \; [\text{honderd}]_{\text{Num}}]_{\text{Num}} \; [\text{miljoen}]_{\text{Num}}]_{\text{Num}}$ 'two hundred million'

As the last example illustrates, schema (15) can be applied recursively: the numeral *tweehonderd* contains an M (*honderd*) and also modifies an M (*miljoen*).

An important constraint on the construction of these multiplication numerals is that the value of the modifying numeral must be lower than that of M. This constraint accounts for the differences in well-formedness in (17):

(17)   a.   [negen-en-negen-tig]-honderd/negen-duizend (en) negen-honderd '9,900'
        b.   *[honderd en twee]-honderd/tien-duizend twee-honderd '10,200'

The ill-formedness of the first option in (17b) reflects the universal global constraint on numeral formation referred to as the Packing Strategy principle. This principle, proposed in the work of Hurford on numerals, is meant to make a choice between different structural options that the language system provides (Hurford 2007: 774). It basically says that you must first use the highest measure noun possible, so that you cover the largest subset possible with one numeral constituent. As (17a) with its two well-formed options shows, the principle does not apply without exceptions. However, the numerals for multiples of 10 which end in -*tig* 'ten' cannot occur as modifiers of

---

[2] In Dutch, these numerals are spelled without internal spacing, as one word.

hundred unless they are preceded by a one digit numeral. So we get the following difference in expression possibilities for the numbers 9,900 and 9,000:

(18)   9,900: negen en negentig-honderd *or* negen-duizend (en) negen-honderd

9,000: *negentig-honderd/negen-duizend

Expressing the number 9,000 as *negenduizend* is clearly the most economical option, and in line with the Packing Strategy principle. In the case of 9,900 on the other hand, the two options do not differ substantially in terms of complexity although the first option violates the Packing Strategy principle. Hence, economy of expression is another factor in choosing between different structural options. According to Hurford (2007: 779), the Packing Strategy principle may be explained as the effect of two pragmatic principles applied in counting entities: 'Go as far as you can with the resources you have', and 'Minimize entities'.

As to the operation of addition for the formation of numerals, Dutch requires two schemas of coordination. The most general one is that for all numerals from 100 onwards

(19)   *Addition schema for numeral expressions* > 100

$$[\text{Num}_C{}^*((\text{en})\ \text{Num}_D)]^j{}_{\text{Num}} \leftrightarrow [\text{NUM}_C + \text{NUM}_D \ldots]^j$$

where NUM stands for the value of the corresponding Num. Num_C stands for numerals $\geq$ 100, and Num_D stands for numerals < 100. The asterisk indicates that this constituent is recursive and can be repeated.

Schema (19) is an instantiation for numerals of the Dutch coordination construction in which constituents of the same category can be conjoined, and thus create a constituent of the same category. In the case of numerals, the conjunction is absent between numerals $\geq$ 100, and optional before Num_D, and in this respect numerals differ from other conjoined categories. For instance, one cannot conjoin two Ns without an overt conjunction (compare *vader en moeder* 'father and mother' with *vader moeder* 'father mother').[3] This is why the subcase of numeral coordination requires a schema of its own. The semantics is that of addition, as specified in the schema. The schema generates numerals like the following:

---

[3] Proper names can be conjoined, however, without overt conjunction, as in *Jan-Peter* 'John Peter' and *Rijn-Schelde-kanaal* 'Rijn-Schelde canal', which suggest that we need a specific subschema of proper name conjunction.

(20)   [drie-miljoen] [vier-honderd-acht-duizend] [drie-honderd (en) twee] '3,408,302'

if Num$_D$ is $\geq$ 21, we might get two occurrences of the conjunction *en* (compare 21a and 21b), but there is a preference for having *en* only before the last number constituent. Thus, in coining the numeral for the number 399, of the following two options, the first one is usually taken:

(21)   a. driehonderd negen-en-negentig '399'
       b. driehonderd en negen-en-negentig '399'

The order of the numeral constituents under addition (coordination) as specified by schema (19) must be such that a coordinated numeral constituent with a higher value precedes a coordinated numeral constituent with a lower value within the addition scheme, in line with the Packing Strategy principle. This is illustrated in (22):

(22)   5,002,600   *zes-honderd twee-duizend vijf-miljoen
                   vijf-miljoen twee-duizend zes-honderd
       9,900   *negen-honderd en negen-duizend
                   negen-duizend (en) negen-honderd

Fixation of word order in coordinated structures as illustrated above is not an exclusive property of numerals. It is also found in English binomial expressions like *salt and pepper* or *father and son*, and similar binomial expressions in many languages.

A second schema of addition is needed for the numerals 21–99 because there is a special order for such numerals in languages like Dutch and German, in which they differ from English. As mentioned above, these numerals are special in that the digit numeral for 1–9 precedes the numeral for the (multiple of) ten. In addition, the conjunction *en* is obligatorily present – unlike what is the case for numerals > 100 – and it is not pronounced as [ɛn] but as [ən]. This syllable forms one prosodic word with the preceding numeral, and if the first numeral ends in a vowel, this prosodic structure (two adjacent vowels within the same prosodic word) triggers homorganic glide insertion in order to avoid vowel hiatus (Booij 1995). Hence, we get the following prosodic structures for the Dutch numerals 23, 24, and 62:

(23)   23: drie-en-twintig (dri.jən)$_\omega$(tʊɪn.təx)$_\omega$
       24: vier-en-twintig (vi:.rən)$_\omega$(tʊɪn.təx)$_\omega$
       62: twee-en-zestig (tʊe:jən)$_\omega$(sɛs.təx)$_\omega$

The relevant schema for the construction of these numerals is:

(24) *Schema for numerals between 21 and 99*
      $[\text{Num}^i{}_{\text{Dig}} \text{ ən } \text{Num}^j{}_{\text{D}}]^k{}_{\text{Num}} \leftrightarrow [\text{NUM}^i + \text{NUM}^j]^k$

$(\text{Num}_{\text{Dig}} = \text{1--9}, \text{Num}_{\text{D}} = \text{20, 30 } \ldots \text{ 90}).$

The facts of Dutch numerals, as analysed above, thus confirm Hurford's general conclusion that 'numeral constructions in all languages tend to be [...] syntactic idioms' (Hurford 1987: 303). However, not all Dutch numerals are still syntactic in nature synchronically. The numerals for 1–20 and for the multiples of 10 listed in (3) are clearly words. The numerals formed according to schema (24) might be considered words as well. The full vowel [ɛ] of the conjunction *en* has been reduced to schwa. Thus, this *en* has become a linking element. In this respect they are now like other types of compound: Dutch compounds may have [ən] as a linking element, as in *boek-*[ən]*-plank* 'book shelf '. There is one subtle difference, however: many Dutch speakers drop the [n] of [ən] in compounds, but this does not apply to the [n] in numerals: pronouncing *drie-en-twintig* as [dri.jə.tʋɪn.təx] is odd. So these complex numerals still exhibit traces of being formed by means of a coordinating conjunction *en* 'and', and might therefore be considered phrases. Therefore, a choice between word status and phrasal status is hard to make, and not that important. Such numerals are lexical units with some relic phrasal properties.

As to numerals > 100, they are to be considered phrases because they allow for the appearance of the conjunction *en* in its unreduced form [ɛn] and hence have the standard form of syntactic coordination. The coordination pattern involved is lexicalized, however, in the sense that the conjunction can be omitted in numerals only. In addition, the order in which the constituents appear is fixed.

These properties of numerals illustrate how the grammar of a language can restrict the use of general principles of syntactic construction for specific subdomains. Grammaticalized conventions can also be observed in the use of numerals for specific purposes, such as naming years. Both in English and in Dutch the word *hundred/honderd* can be omitted in names of years, if there is no overt conjunction:

(25) 1654: zestien-honderd (en) vier-en-vijf-tig/zestien (*en) vier-en-vijf-tig
             'sixteen hundred fifty-four/sixteen fifty-four'

Moreover, we cannot use the alternative well-formed expression *duizend zeshonderd vier-en-vijf-tig* for denoting the year 1654. This shows how discourse-specific conventions may regulate and restrict the use of structural options offered by the language system (Östman 2005).

8.4 Ordinal numerals

Ordinal numerals in Dutch are created in a regular fashion by adding the suffix *-ste* or the suffix *-de*. The suffix *-ste* [stə] is added after the ordinal allomorph for *een* 'one', *eer-* (*eer-ste* 'first'), after *acht* 'eight' (*acht-ste* 'eighth'), after the suffix *-tig* (*twintig-ste*, *dertig-ste*, etc.), and after the numerals *honderd, duizend, miljoen,* and *miljard*. In all other cases (after 2–7, 9–10, and numerals ending in these numerals), the suffix *-de* [də] is used.

(26)   *Dutch ordinals 1–10*

    1   eer-ste
    2   twee-de
    3   der-de
    4   vier-de
    5   vijf-de
    6   zes-de
    7   zeven-de
    8   acht-ste
    9   negen-de
    10 tien-de

The final schwa of the ordinal suffixes is not the schwa of prenominal adjectival inflection; it is always present, including before singular neuter nouns in indefinite phrases where regular adjectives have no final schwa:

(27)   a. een {mooi/*mooi-e} huis 'a nice house'
       b. een {tweede/*tweed} huis 'a second house'

The word *eerste* is not a regular ordinal numeral but a superlative form used as an ordinal (Barbiers 2007). Dutch superlatives are formed by means of suffixation with *-ste*, and the word *eerste* can occur in the contexts in which superlatives occur. For instance, superlatives can be preceded by the intensifying prefix *aller-* 'most', as in *aller-mooi-st* 'most beautiful', and *aller-* can also precede *eerst*: *aller-eerst* 'very first'. On the other hand, the word *eerste* behaves as an ordinal in that the final schwa of the suffix is always present, even in indefinite neuter NPs where adjectives have no ending, and thus differs from regular adjectives:

(28)   a. een eerst-e/*eerst huis 'a first house'
       b. een *mooi-e/mooi huis 'a nice house'

Ordinals for complex numerals are created by using the ordinal form of the last numeral only. This applies to both Dutch and English.

(29) a. honderd en {eerste/*een-de} '101th'
     b. honderd en {derde/*drie-de} '103rd'
     c. honderd-twee-en-twintig-ste '122th'
     d. drie-duizend-drie-honderd-ste '3300th'

In both Dutch and English, irregular forms of digit ordinals such as *eer-ste* 'first' and *der-de* 'third' recur in the ordinals for complex numerals. This shows that the formal operation of ordinal formation applies to the first constituent only. Otherwise, we would get ordinals like [*honderd-en-een*]-*de* and [*honderd-en-drie*]-*de* since -*de* is the default ordinal suffix. This is the kind of mismatch discussed in sections 5.3.2 and 7.3.3 as well: the formal scope of the morphological operation is the last constituent only, whereas the semantic scope is that of the whole expression. Hence, we need the following two schemas for Dutch ordinals (that can be unified into one schema):

(30) a. $[\text{Num}^i \text{-de/ste}]^j_{\text{Ord}} \leftrightarrow [\text{ORD} [\text{NUM}^i]]^j$
     b. $[\text{Num}^k (\text{en}) \text{Ord}^j]^l_{\text{Ord}} \leftrightarrow [\text{ORD} [\text{NUM}^k + \text{NUM}^j]]^l$

(where ORD is the semantic operator of Ordinality). The Numeral base in (30a) is a word, simplex or complex (for instance, *tien, vijftien, twintig*); in the default case it is words that form the bases of morphological operations. The ordinal affix has scope formally over the last numeral only, as proven by the selection of irregular forms, whereas semantically it has scope over the whole complex numeral expression. The mismatch between form and meaning in the ordinal forms of complex numerals can be straightforwardly expressed by schema (30b), which refers to the NUM value of the ordinal (NUM^i). Such mismatches between form and meaning thus form an argument in favour of the use of constructional schemas.

8.5 Fraction numerals

In Dutch, as in many other European languages, cardinal and ordinal numerals are combined in the formation of names for fractions:

(31) a. drie-acht-ste
       three-eight-SUFFIX '3/8'
     b. twaalf-honderd-ste
       twelve-hundred-SUFFIX '12/100'

These fraction numerals can be seen as instantiations of the multiplication schema (15), since ordinals can function as measure nouns with a fractional meaning.[4] Ordinals can be used to denote parts in combination with determiners as in:

(32) a. een acht-ste
          a.SG eight-th.SG.NEUT
          'an eighth'
      b. het acht-ste
          the.SG.NEUT eight-th.SG.NEUT
          'the eighth part'
      c. vier vijf-de van de toeristen
          four fifth-SG.NEUT of the tourists
          '4/5 of the tourists'

These derived nouns have neuter gender, as shown by the choice of the definite determiner *het* in (32b). The following schema expresses the relevant generalization:

(33) [Ordinal^i]^j$_{\mathrm{N,\ [+M],\ [+\ neut]}}$ ↔ [1/NUM^i]^j
      (where NUM^i is the arithmetical value of the corresponding numeral, and N carries the feature [+neuter])

This schema specifies the specific fractional meaning of converted ordinals. The creation of such fraction numerals is thus a case of conversion of particular types of adjectives, ordinals, into nouns of neuter gender. The predictable semantic properties of these fraction numerals cannot be derived from their morphological constituents. Hence, these properties are holistic properties of the conversion construction as such. Such fraction nouns can be pluralized as in *de achtsten* 'the eighth parts', but when preceded by a numeral they are used as measure nouns, hence in their singular form.

Ordinals, like other adjectives, can also be converted to nouns by means of the overt nominalizing suffix *-e*. This creates names for persons (with common gender) or for inanimate entities (Booij 2002b):

(34) a. de zeven-d-e en de acht-st-e
          the seven-th-NOM and the eight-th-NOM
          'the seventh and eighth (person)'
      b. Derde-n veroorzaakten de schade
          Third-PL caused the damage
          'A third party caused the damage'

_____

[4] Note that in French, fraction names are also substantivized ordinals, and are always pluralized after numerals > 1, as in *trois huitièmes* '3/8'.

When used as the basis of multiplication, the fraction interpretation of the converted ordinals is the only possible interpretation, and the noun is used as a measure noun, in its singular form. The following schema for fraction numbers expresses the fractional interpretation of multiplication structures with ordinals:

(35)   *Multiplication schema for fraction numerals*
       $[\text{Num}^i\ [\text{Ordinal}^j]_{N,\ [+M]}]^k{}_{\text{Num}} \leftrightarrow [\text{NUM}^i \times 1/\text{NUM}^j]^k$

Schema (35) is not an independent schema but the unification of schemas (15) and (33), the schema for the conversion of ordinals into measure nouns with fractional meaning. When used in schema (35), the fraction nouns are measure nouns, and have the singular form.[5]

Fraction numerals can be added to cardinal numerals by means of coordination, thus expressing addition. The coordination is usually asyndetic, as in:

(36)   twee drie-vier-de '2¾'
       zeventig drie-vier-de '70¾'

The numerals with addition in (36) can thus be seen as instantiations of a schema that generalizes over fraction numerals and the addition schema (19) for number names > 100, in which numerals with a higher value precede numerals with a lower value. In this subcase of numeral construction with fractions the conjunction *en* is obligatorily absent, which is different from what is the case for numerals > 100. Once more, we observe that the construction of numerical expressions in Dutch reflects the syntax of Dutch, but is also subject to more specific restrictions as to the order of the numerals and the presence and form of conjunctions for various subcategories of numerical expressions. This necessitates the assumption of specific schemas for the various subsets of numeral expressions.

To complete our discussion of the intricacies of Dutch fraction numerals, we will have a look at the expression of the fraction number '1/2'. The simplex word *half* '1/2' can also be used as part of a numerical expression. The word *half* is an adjective; the noun for 'half' in Dutch is *helft*. In complex numerals the word *half* can be preceded by the indefinite determiner *een* [ən]. In such numerals, the fraction phrase *een half* 'a half' follows the numeral with the higher value, just as in the cases in (36). However, the conjunction *en* is optional here, as illustrated by the expression for 3½, for which two options are available:

---

[5]   The fraction numeral for ½ is the non-derived lexical item *half* 'half'. It is only in mathematical contexts that one will use the regular expression *een-twee-de*.

(37) a. drie-[ən]-half   (dri.jən)$_\omega$(hɑlf)$_\omega$
       b. drie-[ɛn]-[ən]-half   (dri)$_\omega$(ɛ.nən)$_\omega$(hɑlf)$_\omega$

The prosodic structure is predictable: each constituent forms a prosodic word of its own, except that the constituent -[ən]- has a schwa as its only vowel. Hence, it cannot form a prosodic word of its own, and will take the preceding word as its prosodic host. Therefore, in (37a) homorganic glide insertion takes place obligatorily before the schwa. In (37b), on the other hand, there is no vowel hiatus before the schwa.[6] In sum, the prosodic structure of such complex numeral expressions follows from general constraints on the construction of prosodic forms of Dutch words and phrases.

For complex fraction numerals of the type exemplified in (37) we need to assume a constructional idiom, that is, a pattern in which some positions are lexically filled whereas others are variable (Jackendoff 2002*a*; Booij 2002*a*). The constructional idiom, in which the non-initial constituents are specified lexically, will have the following form:[7]

(38)   [Num^i –([ɛn])$_{\text{Conj}}$ [ən] [half]$_A$]$^j_{\text{Num}}$ ↔ [NUM^i + ½]^j

This schema specifies how numerals with the fraction ½ can be formed productively, notwithstanding the idiosyncratic form of their fraction part. This type of numeral is inflected as an adjective, as illustrated by the following examples:

(39) a. drie-en-halv-e boterham
          three-and-half-SUFFIX sandwich.SG
          '3½ sandwiches'
       b. twee-en-half brood
          two-and-half loaf.SG
          '2½ loaves'

An additional, syntactic effect of the use of fraction numerals that can be observed in (39) is that, even when their numerical value is > 1, the noun in head position does not receive a plural marking, unlike what is the case after cardinal numerals. The forms of the adjective *half* are the regular ones of an adjective before a singular noun in an indefinite noun phrase (*halv-e* before non-neuter nouns, *half-ø* before neuter nouns). Thus, this instantiation of the fraction numeral construction with *half* exhibits another mismatch between morpho-syntactic form and meaning: morpho-syntactically, only *half* agrees

---

[6] There is a vowel hiatus between the [i] and the [ɛ] which may be filled optionally by a homorganic glide in connected speech (Booij 1995).
[7] The numeral for 1½ is a lexicalized compound, *ander-half* 'lit. other half '.

with the head noun, whereas semantically it is the whole numeral that modifies the head noun.

8.6 Numerals and the architecture of the grammar

In this chapter I have argued that a detailed analysis of the construction of Dutch numerical expressions throws light on the architecture of the grammar. Numerical expressions may be created by both syntactic and morphological means, and both play a role in the construction of Dutch numerals. The construction of Dutch numerals is partially a matter of conventionalized forms of syntactic coordination, subject to specific constraints. In the case of the numerals 21–99, the specific word order and the appearance of a linking element [ən] that derives historically from the conjunction *en* [ɛn], suggested the existence of a specific lexical schema for cardinal numeral compounds. Similarly, the construction of numerals > 100 by means of coordination also appeared to be subject to specific constraints as to constituent order and use of overt conjunctions. These restrictions on the use of the structural options provided by the syntactic constructions of Dutch reflect the Packing Strategy principle.

The analysis of ordinals showed how mismatches between form and meaning in complex expressions can be accounted for by means of constructional schemas. Moreover, the construction of numerical expressions with *half* illustrates the necessity of constructional idioms, schemas in which one or more of the constituents is lexically fixed. This latter type of complex numeral exhibits specific mismatches between form and meaning as well.

Thus, the detailed analysis of the numeral system of Dutch provides additional evidence for an architecture of the grammar in which constructional schemas (both syntactic and morphological ones) of different degrees of abstraction play a crucial role in accounting for the structure and creation of lexical expressions.

9

Construction-dependent morphology

9.1 Recycling morphology

In this chapter the utility and necessity of the notion 'construction' will be argued for from a perspective that differs from that of the previous chapters. Here, I will argue that language change may produce specific constructions that constitute core portions of the grammar. The constructions discussed here are marked by bound morphemes and thus instantiate construction-dependent morphology.

In many languages, the relations between words in a syntactic construction are marked by means of morphology. In languages with dependent-marking, for instance, one will find case markers on words that signal the relationship between the dependent word and the head of the construction. This kind of morphology can be qualified as contextual inflection (Booij 1996). A morphological marker may thus form part of a construction and hence function as a 'construction marker' (Koptjevskaja-Tamm 2003a).

Constructions are also a locus of language change (Bybee et al. 1994; Heine 1993; Heine et al. 1991; Traugott 2003). What happens to morphological markers when a language changes? They may disappear due to the erosion of the inflectional system, or because they get trapped inside a word (Harris and Faarlund 2006), but there are also cases where the morphological marker is preserved but receives a new function.

This phenomenon may be looked at from an evolutionary point of view. The re-use of morphological markers may be qualified as 'exaptation' (Lass 1990), a term introduced in 1982 by the biologists Gould and Vrba to denote the phenomenon that a trait of an organism receives a new function. This idea of recycling was already present in Charles Darwin's *The origin of species* (1859) under the name 'readaptation'. Greenberg refers to it as 'regrammaticalization' (Greenberg 1991).

A well-known case of such recycling of morphological markers is that of the genitive case markers in Germanic languages such as Dutch and German. The phrasal construction [N-GEN N]$_{NP}$ in which the N-GEN functions as the specifier of the noun phrase has been reinterpreted as an NN compound, with the genitive marker receiving a new function, that of linking element; cf. Booij (2002b) for Dutch, and Fuhrhop (1998) for German. The NN sequence is no longer a phrase but a complex word. What we observe then is that the genitive marker is reinterpreted as a linking element (in Dutch either -s or -en). The same development took place in Swedish where the genitive marker -s also became a linking element in compounds (Delsing 2008).

An interesting variant of this reinterpretation of the genitive marker -s can be found in so-called genitive compounds in Frisian, which are strikingly similar to the descriptive genitive of English (cf. 9b below). According to Hoekstra (2002), Frisian has NN sequences in which the first part is marked by an element that is historically a genitive marker. Note that Frisian has lost its case system. The following word sequences exemplify this construction:

(1)   a. koken-s doar
          kitchen-GEN door
          'door of the kitchen'
      b. húske-(e) rútsje
          toilet-GEN window
          'window of the toilet'

Hoekstra argued that these NN sequences are lexical phrases with main stress on the rightmost element and that they are different from regular NN compounds. NN compounding is the dominant form of compounding, with an optional linking element and main stress on the left constituent. The first N of genitive compounds ends in -s or -e /ə/, as exemplified in (1): 'The 'strong' ending -s appears after first elements ending in a consonant or a full vowel whereas the 'weak' ending -e is assumed to have been added to first elements that end in -e already' (Hoekstra 2002: 230). This weak ending will not surface because Frisian does not allow for a sequence of schwas. Nevertheless, such an ending should be assumed to be present in the underlying form of these words because it explains why such nouns never appear in a shortened form without schwa, unlike the weak nouns that are the first part of NN compounds. These genitive compounds have a specific semantic interpretation: 'There is always a part–whole relation between the two component nouns, in the sense that the object denoted by the second element is an integral (inalienable) part of the object denoted by the first element' (Hoekstra 2002: 232). The nouns involved are always concrete non-animate nouns. Finally, they have a specific referential property: the first element refers to a specific entity. Hence, we get minimal pairs like the following:

(2)   a. koken-tafel 'kitchen table'
      b. koken-s-tafel 'table of/in the kitchen'

Thus, we have to assume the following lexical schemas for Frisian phrasal NN-combinations with a morphological marker that was a case ending historically:

(3) $[N_i$-s $N_j]_{N'_ik} \leftrightarrow [SEM_j$ that is part of $SEM_i]_k$ (N_i ends in full vowel or consonant)

(4) $[N_i$-ə $N_j]_{N'_ik} \leftrightarrow [SEM_j$ that is part of $SEM_i]_k$ (N_i ends in schwa)

Since these word sequences are to be considered small phrases (Hoekstra 2002), I assume that they are lexical phrases dominated by the phrasal node N'.

   Another form of preservation of contextual inflection can be found in Afrikaans (Lass 1990). Afrikaans is a daughter language of Dutch. Originally, it had the same form of morphological marking of attributive adjectives as Dutch. This means that attributive adjectives were marked with an inflectional ending *-e* (pronounced as schwa), unless the NP is indefinite and headed by a singular neuter noun. Hence, Afrikaans adjectives had two forms, as is still the case in Dutch. For instance, the adjective *klein* 'small' used to have two forms, *klein* and *kleine* (*paard* is a neuter noun):

(5)   a. Het   paard   is klein
          the.DEF.NEUT.SG horse.NEUT.SG   is small
          'The horse is small'
      b. Een   klein   paard
          a.INDEF.SG   small.INDEF.NEUT.SG   horse.NEUT.SG
          'A small horse'
      c. Het   klein-e   paard
          the.DEF.NEUT.SG small-DEF.NEUT.SG   horse.NEUT.SG
          'The small horse'
      d. De klein-e   paard-en
          the small-PL   horse.NEUT-PL
          'The small horses'

This form of inflectional marking disappeared in Afrikaans. Instead, the following system emerged (Lass 1990):

(6)   *Afrikaans inflection of adjectives in attributive position*
          – all morphologically complex adjectives end in *-e*;
          – simplex adjectives with stem allomorphy end in *-e*;
          – in all other cases, there is a zero-ending.

The stem allomorphy of the simplex adjectives has to do with three phonological processes: word-final cluster simplification, medial syncope, and
word-final final devoicing of obstruents. These three types of allomorphy
are illustrated in (7):

(7) sag [sɑx] – sagte [sɑxtə] 'soft'
     droog [dro:x] – droë [dro:ə] 'dry'
     hard [hɑrt] – harde [hɑrdə] 'hard'

It is obvious that preserving the ending -e is essential for maintaining the stem
allomorphy: if there were no ending -e, the adjectives in (7) would have one
form only, the left one. It is the presence or absence of the final schwa that
determines the application of the relevant phonological processes.

   Lass concluded that these morpho-phonemic alternations in Afrikaans are
now lexically coded and that 'the inflectional locus has shifted from syntax to
lexicon' (Lass 1990: 95). Note, however, that the occurrence of forms ending in
-e is still confined to the attributive AN construction: in predicate position, all
adjectives appear without -e.

   Lass observed another form of preservation as well: in some cases the
absence versus presence of the inflectional schwa signals a semantic difference,
as in the following example: 'n enkel man 'a solitary man' versus 'n enkele man
'a single (unmarried) man'. This alternation is used for similar semantic
purposes in present-day Dutch, as illustrated by the contrast between een
goed-e vader 'a good father' and een goed vader 'a good father' (Booij 2002a:
48). In the absence of -e, the adjective goed receives an adverbial interpretation, and the phrase means 'someone who performs his fatherly duties well'. If
the ending is present, both an intersective reading (one who is good and is a
father) and an adverbial reading (one who 'fathers' well) are possible. Thus, a
morphological marking (or its absence) can receive a new semantic function.

   In Balanta, a language spoken in Senegal, the adjectival agreement prefix -a
has been reinterpreted. Instead of being one of the two adjectival agreement
prefixes for singular human nouns, with u- being the other one, it became a
prefix on singular human nouns with an adverbial meaning (u- is the only
agreement prefix for non-human nouns). Thus, the following contrast could
become expressed (Fudeman 2004: 106):

(8) a. Sibow gi   añirɛ   u-bɔntsɛ
        Sibow cop   dancer   U-beautiful
        'Sibow is a beautiful dancer' [Sibow is a dancer and is beautiful]
     b. Sibow gi   añirɛ   a-bɔntsɛ
        Sibow cop   dancer   A-beautiful
        'Sibow is a beautiful dancer' [Sibow dances beautifully]

Thus, the morphological marker *a-* received a new function in the grammar of Balanta.

Another form of reinterpretation of a morphological marker is the reinterpretation of the genitive case marker *-s* as the marker of specific constructions, as happened in English (Allen 1997), in Danish, Norwegian, and Swedish (Norde 1997, 1998, 2006), in German (Lanouette 1996), and in Dutch. In English we find two *s*-constructions, the determiner genitive and the descriptive or classifying genitive respectively (Rosenbach 2002, 2006, 2007):

(9) a. determiner genitive: John's book, the young girl's eyes
     b. descriptive (classifying) genitive: a man's suit, the lawyer's fees

In the determiner genitive construction, the word or phrase that is marked with *-s* functions as a definite determiner. For instance, the phrase *the young girl's eyes* means '**the** eyes of the young girl'. In many languages the use of a possessor imposes this definite interpretation on noun phrases (Haspelmath 1999). The descriptive genitive has a different function, which is comparable to that of the modifier noun in a right-headed Noun-Noun compound. In that case, the noun with *-s* can be preceded by a definite or indefinite determiner, as illustrated in (9b). These two uses of nouns with a genitive marker are also found in Swedish (Koptjevskaja-Tamm 2003*b*: 515, 539).

The term 'genitive construction' is often used in the literature as a convenient label for such constructions. Strictly speaking, however, this is not appropriate since in most of these languages regular case marking has been lost, and thus the term 'genitive construction' is an etymological label only. Therefore, Koptjevskaja-Tamm (2003*a*: 628) refers to them as 'deformed genitives'. The genitive case marker on nouns in prenominal position in Dutch has been reanalysed as the marker of a determiner construction. This also applies to German, a language where genitive case marking is still in use, but is not used anymore for nouns in prenominal position. In section 9.2 this phenomenon is discussed in more detail.

In sum, morphological markers may get tied to specific constructions. Hence, the distribution of such morphological markers is governed by such constructions. I refer to such phenomena as 'construction-dependent morphology'. They are the result of reanalysis of syntactic constructions. Croft qualifies this kind of reanalysis as 'hypoanalysis': 'In hypoanalysis, the listener reanalyzes a contextual semantic/functional property as an inherent property of the syntactic unit. In the reanalysis, the inherent property of the context [...] is then attributed to the syntactic unit, and so the syntactic unit in question gains a new meaning or function' (Croft 2000: 126–127).

In the next sections I will discuss a number of such constructions as they occur in modern standard Dutch, in all of which case markers have been subject to reanalysis. These analyses will show that the notions 'construction' and 'constructional idiom' are indispensable for a proper account of the distribution of bound morphological elements. Moreover, they show how the complexity of languages may increase due to the preservation of old case endings, thus supporting Dahl's finding that '[a]n important source of linguistic complexity lies in the retainment of properties from earlier stages of the life cycles of constructions' (Dahl 2004: 221).

9.2 The Definite -s Construction

Dutch nouns – except pronouns – do not exhibit case marking; this system disappeared in the transition from Middle Dutch to present-day Dutch. There are relics of the case system in idiomatic phrases, and in the occurrence of the bound morpheme -s on certain nouns in specifier position. The following examples illustrate this phenomenon:

(10)   a. *specifier = proper name*
          Jan-s hoed 'John's hat'
          Amsterdam-s rijke verleden 'Amsterdam's rich history'
       b. *specifier = form of address*
          vader-s fiets 'father's bicycle'
          moeder-s kamer 'mother's room'
          dominee-s studeerkamer 'reverend's study'
       c. *specifier = quantifier*
          ieder-s huis 'everybody's house'
          iemand-s vriend 'someone's friend'
          niemand-s schuld 'nobody's fault'
       d. *specifier = complex proper name*
          koning Salomo-s reputatie 'king Solomon's reputation'
          prins Bernhard-s brief 'Prince Bernhard's letter'
          Geert Booij-s recente boek 'Geert Booij's recent book'
          mijn moeder-s naaidoos 'my mother's sewing box'

Such noun phrases ending in -s can only be used in prenominal position: a sentence like *Deze hoed is Jans* 'This hat is John's' is ungrammatical. They function as definite determiners of the noun phrases they form part of. For instance, *Jan-s hoed* means '**the** hat of John'.

The morphological marking of such prenominal NPs is sometimes referred to as possessor marking. However, such NPs may also have other semantic functions than that of possessor, as in *Jan-s antwoord op de vraag* 'John's answer to the question', where *Jan* is the subject of the action denoted by *antwoord* 'answer'. Hence, a more general term than 'possessor', such as 'specifier', is more appropriate.

In Middle Dutch, NPs marked with a genitive case ending were used attributively, both in prenominal and postnominal position (Van Es 1938); in 17th-century Dutch one still finds genitive marking on all constituents of a postnominal phrase:

(11)   *prenominal*
    a. Symon-s Dankard-s son-s huse
        Symon-GEN Dankard-GEN son-GEN house.NOM.SG
        'the house of the son of Symon Dankard'
    b. De-r duechd-en moedere
        the-GEN.PL virtue-GEN.PL mother.SG.NOM
        'the mother of the virtues'
   postnominal
    c. t-gebot syn-s her-en
        the-order.NOM.SG his-GEN lord-GEN.SG
        'the order of his lord'
    d. In het huis mijn-s Vader-s zijn vele woningen
        In the house my-GEN Father-GEN are many dwellings
        'There are many dwellings in the house of my Father'
        (from the Dutch Bible Translation, 1637)

Historically, the -*s* is the genitive case ending of masculine and neuter singular nouns. In the modern Dutch -*s*-construction discussed here, however, the -*s* can also be used for feminine nouns. In Middle Dutch, modifiers had to agree in case marking with the head noun, as is illustrated by the examples in (11). This is no longer the case in modern Dutch. So there are two changes in the use of the ending -*s* in Dutch prenominal phrases: it is generalized to all nouns and it appears only once in a phrase, on the noun. Moreover, in modern Dutch the -*s* is not used elsewhere (there is no genitive marking on nouns governed by verbs or prepositions), and there is no morphological marking for other cases, except in some lexicalized expressions. Hence, there is only a subset of nouns (exemplified in 10) that have an *s*-marked form when used prenominally. This leads to the conclusion that there is no longer a morphological case system in Dutch. Similar changes took place in English (Koike 2006), German (Lanouette 1996), and Swedish (Norde 1997, 2006; Börjars

2003): in these languages the bound morpheme -s can be used for transform-
ing an NP into a definite determiner.[1]

The Dutch nouns and noun phrases that end in -s function as definite
determiners, and cannot be preceded by a determiner in the noun phrase: *de
Jan-s huis 'the John's house' is ungrammatical, as is *een Jan-s huis 'a house of
John'. The definiteness of the whole NP is also manifested by the form of a
prenominal adjective in this construction: Peter-s {nieuw-e/*nieuw} boek
'Peter's new book': the definite nature of this NP headed by the neuter
noun boek 'book' requires the definite form of the adjective with a final -e,
the inflectional ending that appears in prenominal position (see 5c).

The nouns that can be used prenominally are proper names, mainly but not
exclusively for human beings, and nouns that can be used as forms of address,
like vader and dominee. Instead of a single noun we also find noun sequences
with a function name or a possessive pronoun preceding a proper name.
There is a trend to also use specifier noun phrases with a definite determiner
and a singular noun denoting a human being, as in de auteur-s grootvader 'the
author's grandfather', with the noun auteur denoting a human being that is
not used as a form of address. In the latter case, the presence of the determiner
de is required since auteur is not a proper name (Van der Horst and Van der
Horst 1999: 320). However, this construction is still considered substandard.

As illustrated in (10d), complex names that consist of two words can also
appear in this construction. The -s always appears on the final noun only, even
though it may not be the head. For instance, in the phrase prins Bernhard it is
the second noun that hosts the -s even though the first noun prins is the head.
The generalization that this -s is always phrase-final is confirmed by the fact
that this is also the case when the possessor phrase is a case of coordination:

(12)   a. Jan en Piet-s vader
          'John and Pete's father'
       b. Pa, Ma, en de kinderen-s verjaardag
          'Dad, Mum, and the children's birthday'

These examples belong to more informal registers of language use. Some
speakers of Dutch even mark plural nouns as possessor (data from a Google
search):

(13)   de kinderen-s {belangen/naam/toekomst}
       'the children's {interests/name/future}'

---

[1] See Koptjevskaja-Tamm (2003a) for a survey of possessive marking in European languages.

Compared to the bound morpheme -*s* in English genitive constructions, the Dutch -*s* in prenominal position has a much more restricted distribution. A phrase like *De koning van Engeland's kroon* 'The king of England's crown' is impossible in Dutch. Instead of the bound morpheme -*s*, the possessive pronoun *zijn* has to be used in such cases: *de koning van Engeland zijn kroon* 'the king of England his crown'. Thus, there is a difference with languages such as English and Swedish, where -*s* can be attached to nouns that are not the phrasal head and to phrase-final words of other categories than nouns, such as verbs, as illustrated in (14):

(14) *English* (Weerman and De Wit 1998: 33)
      a. the man that I saw's friend
      b. a friend of mine's house

      Swedish (Norde 2006: 205)
      c. den som jobbar-s halva lön
         [the.one who works]s half salary
         'half the salary of the one who has a job'

This means that in English, and perhaps also in Swedish – judgements of native speakers vary as to whether verbs can carry this -*s* (Östen Dahl, pers. comm.) – the genitive case marker has evolved into a bound morpheme that makes the NP to which it attaches function as a determiner.

There is some debate as to the status of this -*s* in Swedish (Norde 1997, 2006; Börjars 2003). It is a characteristic of clitics that they exhibit a low degree of selectivity with respect to the word they attach to, unlike affixes. As to Dutch, it is clear that the -*s* cannot be seen as a straightforward clitic since it can only be attached to (pro)nouns, not to whatever word appears at the end of the phrase. The status of the -*s* in Swedish and English is in between that of a clitic and a phrasal affix since, as Börjars et al. (2008) observe, there are many cases in which the -*s* does not attach phrase-finally but to the nominal head of the prenominal phrase:

(15) *Swedish*
      den självständiga Evangeliska kyrkan-s i Kongo förste generalsekreterare
      the independent Evangelical church.DEF-s in Congo first general
      secretary
      'the first General Secretary of the Evangelical Church of the Congo'

      English
      the woman's bedroom who I lived with
      'the bedroom of the woman with whom I lived'

Thus, we conclude that the term 'genitive construction' is only appropriate as a convenient etymological label. In line with this conclusion, Weerman and De Wit (1998, 1999) speak of the Dutch 's-construction'. This then raises the question of the formal status of this -s in Dutch. It is neither a regular inflectional morpheme nor a canonical clitic. It is furthermore obvious that it cannot be interpreted as a derivational affix.

Weerman and De Wit (1998: 29) proposed the following structure for *Jans* in *Jan-s boek* 'John's book':

(16)

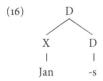

where X can stand for a noun or a noun phrase (of a certain type). In this structure, the -s must be assumed to have a feature [+definite] that percolates to the dominating D-node. Unless one allows for bound morphemes to occupy syntactic positions of their own – which violates the lexicalist hypothesis that parts of words cannot be distributed across syntactic nodes – this structure implies that -s qualifies as a clitic, a definite determiner that has a clitic form only, and hence will attach to the preceding word as far as prosodic structure is concerned. The problem for this analysis is that, as we have seen above, the Dutch -s is not a canonical clitic since it can attach to nouns only, reflecting its historical origin as a genitive case marker, and therefore this morpheme does not have the lack of selectivity with respect to word class of the host that is characteristic of clitics.

An alternative approach, proposed in Börjars (2003: 145) for Swedish, is the assumption of a feature [+POSS], which is an abstract morpho-syntactic marker on the specifier. This feature is then spelled out as /s/ on the last word of the specifier phrase:

(17)   NP [+ POSS]

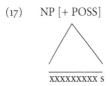

This analysis presupposes a realizational model of morphology in which (combinations of) morpho-syntactic features are spelled out phonologically (Anderson 1992).

This analysis is in accordance with lexicalist morphology and expresses the important basic insight that the suffix is a right edge phrasal affix. It does not yet express the semantic restrictions on the kind of noun phrases that can appear in this position. This may be achieved by putting semantic conditions on the kind of NP that can be assigned the feature [+POSS]. Moreover, it does not directly express that the *s*-marked specifier NP functions as a definite determiner and hence excludes the presence of a determiner, unlike post-nominal complements (as in *het boek van Jan/het boek van de kinderen* 'the book of John/the book of the children') discussed above. Finally, as far as Dutch is concerned we have to express the generalization that it is always a noun that carries the phrasal affix.

These considerations lead me to the following elaboration of Börjar's model for the Dutch grammatical pattern discussed here: it is best qualified as a construction in which a prenominal NP with certain semantic properties functions as a definite determiner. It is a pattern that is productive, since the slots for the noun and the preceding determiner are open ones, but with semantic restrictions on the kind of noun that can be inserted. The presence of a suffix -*s* on the noun, and the definiteness interpretation can be specified as parts of the construction, which is a pairing of form and meaning:[2]

(18) *The Definite -s Construction*
   $[[\ldots [x\text{-}s]_N]_{NPi} \ldots N_j]_{NPk} \leftrightarrow [\text{the} \ldots N_j \text{ of } NP_i]_k$

   NP$_i$ has one of the following forms:
   (i) a (simplex or complex) proper name, or a coordination of in-stances of such expression; (10a), (10d) (12a);
   (ii) a quantifying (pro)noun denoting human beings (10c);
   (iii) nouns that can function as forms of address, optionally preceded by a possessive pronoun (10b, 10d);
   (iv) (substandard): NPs that denote human beings (12b), (13).

These conditions define subconstructions of construction (18). The variable *x* stands for the stem of the rightmost noun. We thus express that the -*s* is a bound morpheme that is phonologically part of the phrase-final noun. The specifications of the specifier NP in (18) make clear that there exist a number of subconstructions that share the defining properties of this construction.

This constructional schema directly expresses under what conditions a Dutch NP can function as the definite determiner of a noun phrase. There is no general Dutch NP construction with an embedded NP functioning as specifier: such specifier NPs normally have to appear as part of a PP following

---

[2] This structure can easily be translated into a DP analysis of noun phrases. In that case the NP specifier will be co-indexed with an empty D, as illustrated here for *Jans boek* 'John's book': $[[\text{Jan-s}]_{\text{Spec-i}} [[e]_{\text{D-i}} [\text{boek}]_{N'}]_{D'}]_{DP}$

the head noun of the NP, in the default case preceded by the preposition *van* 'of'. The only pre-nominal specifiers with nouns are the *-s*-construction discussed here, and the construction with the specifier NP followed by 3rd person possessive pronouns, as in *Jan zijn boek* 'lit. John his book, John's book'.[3]

The implication of this schema is that syntactic constructions may refer directly to the presence of a specific morpheme: the *-s* is no longer an inflectional morpheme but marks an NP as having a determiner function. It is therefore not surprising that one finds the label '*s*-construction' in the literature. Since the *-s* is 'trapped' in this construction, it leads to construction-dependent morphology: the distribution of nouns ending in *-s* is no longer regulated by general principles of inflectional marking but is determined by a specific syntactic construction. Such facts show that the notion 'construction' is indispensable for a correct account of the distribution of bound morphological elements.

Similar constructions are used in a number of other languages besides Dutch, English, and Swedish: Frisian, German, Romani, Finnish, Latvian, and Scottish Gaelic (Koptjevskaja-Tamm 2003*b*: 550–551). In German, genitive case marking still exists, but it cannot apply generally to all sorts of nouns in prenominal position, only to proper names and names for close relatives, comparable to what is the case in Dutch.

In Hungarian, the possessor noun in an NP also has the role of definiteness marker. The head of the NP is marked as possessed (with features of the possessor), a case of head marking (Moravcsik 2003: 425–427):

(19)   a. az udvar kerítés-e
           the yard fence-3SG.POSSESSOR
           'the fence of the yard'
       b. a fiú könyv-e
           the boy book-3SG.POSSESSOR
           'the book of the boy'

Moravcsik (2003) qualifies this construction as a case of 'non-compositional definiteness marking': there is no specific definite determiner, and it is the construction as such that invokes a definite interpretation, just as is the case for Dutch. This non-compositionality supports the constructional interpretation of this syntactic configuration: there is an element of meaning that can only be attributed to the construction as a whole.

---

[3] The structure of such phrases may be the following: [[Jan]$_{Spec-i}$ [[zijn]$_{D-i}$ [boek]$_N$]$_{D'}$]$_{DP}$.In this case, the D position is not empty. There is again co-indexation of the Spec and the D position.

9.3 The Partitive -s Construction

A second remnant of the Dutch genitive marker -*s* originates from the use of this morpheme as marker of a partitive genitive, as in *iets groen-s* 'something green' and *een heleboel lekker-s* 'a lot of sweets' where -*s* is attached to an adjective. In Middle Dutch, nouns and adjectives after a quantifying expression were marked as (partitive) genitives (Stoett 1923). This system has disappeared, although there are idioms where the partitive genitive has been preserved, as in the idiomatic expression (20a):

(20)   *Modern Dutch*
    a. niet veel soep-s
       not much soup-s
       'without quality'
    b. niet veel soep
       not much soup
       'not much soup'

    Middle Dutch
    c. een lepel honich-s
       a spoon honey-GEN
       'a spoon of honey'
    d. iet lief-s
       something sweet-GEN
       'something sweet'

This development in Dutch is thus parallel to that in English that also lost its partitive genitive construction and replaced it with a PP-construction, as in *a spoon of honey*, or simply omitted the -*s* after quantifiers (as in *something sweet*). In German, there is also erosion of the partitive genitive: a phrase like *ein Glas Wein-es* 'a glass wine-GEN' has been replaced with *ein Glas Wein* 'a glass of wine' (Hentschel 1993). However, unlike English, standard Dutch still has a productive construction with a partitive marker -*s* (Broekhuis and Strang 1996; Hoeksema 1998*b*; Booij 2002*a*: 52–54). Noun phrases can have the surface form Quantifier Adjective+*s*, as is illustrated by the following examples (Van Marle 1996: 73):

(21)   a. iets groen-s 'something green'
       niets waar-s 'nothing true'
       wat leuk-s 'something nice'
       allerlei heerlijk-s 'all sorts of lovely (things)'
       een heleboel lief-s 'a lot of sweet (things)'
       een massa goed-s 'a lot of good (things)'

b. veel mooi-s 'a lot of nice (things)'
weinig prachtig-s 'few splendid (things)'
meer fraai-s 'more fine (things)'

In (21a), the first word or word combination is a noun that expresses an indefinite quantity. The quantifiers in (21b) *veel* 'a lot of', *weinig* 'few', and *meer* 'more' can be used either as nouns or as adjectives, as illustrated here for *veel*:

(22) a. Ik bezit veel
        I possess much (*veel* = Noun)
        'I possess a lot'
      b. Jan heeft veel geld
        John has much money (*veel* = Adjective)
        'John has a lot of money'

This makes it possible to interpret the quantifiers in (21b) as nouns, thus allowing for a unified structural analysis of (21a) and (21b). The difference between Dutch and English is illustrated by the first example *iets groens* and its English gloss *something green*: in (standard) Dutch the presence of the -*s* is obligatory, whereas in English there is no morphological marking on the adjective. However, southern Dutch as spoken in Belgium is similar to English in this respect and thus exhibits phrases such as *iets groen*.

Besides quantifying expressions, the *wat voor* 'what kind of' construction also requires this kind of morphological marking of the adjective:

(23) Wat voor mooi-s heb je gezien?
      What for beautiful-s have you seen?
      'What kind of beautiful things did you see?'

This construction is productive: it applies to adjectives that can be used as prenominal predicating adjectives. As observed in Broekhuis and Strang (1996) and Hoeksema (1998b), there are some classes of adjectives that can be used prenominally but yet cannot be used in this construction: relational adjectives (including geographic adjectives in -*er*), temporal adjectives, material adjectives ending in -*en*, and adjectives ending in schwa:

(24) *iets Groninger-s 'something from Groningen'
      *iets zaterdag-s 'something Saturday-like'
      *iets ijzer-en 'something iron'
      * iets oranje-s 'something orange'

The appearance of the -*s* on the adjectives in (21) looks like a case of contextual inflection in which the quantifier requires the adjective to carry the genitive ending -*s*. However, this interpretation raises the question why in present-day Dutch nouns are not subject to contextual inflection when used with a partitive meaning, as shown in (20b).

What is the categorial status of the adjective+*s* words? Van Marle (1996) argued that they are nouns and that the presence of the suffix -*s* hence has a category-changing effect. Arguments for that position are that Dutch has deadjectival nouns in -*s* that can be used as the head of an NP, without a quantifying determiner being present:

(25)   a. Het nieuw-s verbaasde ons
           The new-*s* surprised us
           'The news surprised us'
       b. Wie zoet is, krijgt lekker-s
           Who sweet is, gets sweet-*s*
           'Sweets for the sweet'

The noun status of these [adjective+*s*] words is in harmony with the fact that most indefinite quantifiers can modify (mass) nouns:

(26)   a. wat soep
           what soup
           'some soup'
       b. allerlei rommel
           variety rubbish
           'all sorts of rubbish'
       c. een massa snoep
           a mass confectionery
           'a lot of sweets'

However, the nouns *iets* 'something', *niets/niks* 'nothing' do not occur with nouns in a partitive construction, only with the *s*- marked adjectives:

(27)   *iets soep 'some soup', *niets soep 'no soup', *niks soep 'no soup'

The other option to be considered is that the *s*-marked words are adjectives. This is the position taken by Schultink (1962: 79–80) who states that the only function of -*s* is to mark this specific construction. Evidence for this interpretation is that the -*s*-marked words can head an adjectival phrase with adverbs and verbal/adjectival complements that occur before the head; such modifiers do not occur before nouns (Paardekooper 1958: 161–170; Broekhuis and Strang 1996; Hoeksema 1998*b*):

(28) a. iets heel lastig-s
          something very difficult-*s*
          'something very difficult'
       b. iets volgens mij ongelofelijk-s
          something according.to me unbelievable-*s*
          'something that is unbelievable according to me'
       c. niets in het oog vallend-s
          nothing in the eye falling-*s*
          'nothing that catches the eye'
       d. iets op ons doel afgestemd-s
          something on our goal tuned-s
          'something tuned to our goal'

The word *heel* 'very' in (28a) is an adverb, which suggests that the next word is an adjective. In (28b) the PP *volgens mij* 'according to me' functions as an adverbial modifier. In (28c) the word *vallend* is a present participle used as an adjective, as is the past participle *afgestemd* in (28d). Hence, *vallends* and *afgestemds* allow for verbal complements. The occurrence of such specifiers and complements that are typical for adjectives and participles is a problem for assigning the *s*-marked adjective the status of noun, unless one can show that deadjectival nouns systematically inherit the syntactic valency of their adjectival bases. This is not the case, however. For instance, the deadjectival noun *nieuw-s* 'news' cannot be modified by adverbs, only by adjectives, as illustrated by the contrast between *het goed-e nieuws* 'the good news' and **het goed nieuws* (*goed* is the adverbial form) versus *iets heel nieuws* 'something that is very new', with the adverb *heel* 'very'.

Another problem for Van Marle's hypothesis that the suffix -*s* used here is, at least synchronically, a suffix that creates nouns is that many of these words in -*s* cannot occur in other nominal syntactic slots, except for some lexicalized nouns in -*s* such as *nieuws* 'news': noun phrases such as **het lastigs* 'the difficulty' or **het in het oog vallends* 'that what catches the eye' are impossible. Yet, the construction as a whole is an NP, hence there must be a noun that can function as the head of an NP. Van Marle was aware of this problem, and therefore proposed a rule that makes this category shift from adjective to noun dependent on the specific syntactic context discussed here.

Kester (1996) and Hoeksema (1998*b*) proposed analysing this construction in a different way, as a determiner phrase with a quantifier in the determiner position and an empty head noun. Thus, the phrase *iets lastigs* would receive the following structural analysis (with a DP analysis of noun phrases):

(29)   [[iets]$_D$ [[lastig-s]$_{AP}$ [e]$_N$]$_{NP}$]$_{DP}$

where e stands for 'empty element'. The -s is then considered a case of contextual inflection of adjectives, and will be interpreted as licensing an empty noun in the head position of the NP. This analysis has the advantage of explaining why these words in -s do not have the normal distribution of nouns. Those cases where the adjective+s combination clearly behaves as a noun, as is the case for *nieuws* 'news' can then be seen as lexicalized cases of a nominal reinterpretation of the adjective on the basis of the surface structure in which an overt noun is lacking.

The drawback of this analysis is that the appearance of the -s is not a normal case of contextual inflection since it is restricted to NPs with empty nouns. The normal contextual inflection of adjectives in pronominal position is by means of the suffix -e [ə] or Ø, cf. (5).

Therefore, I will follow the analysis proposed by Broekhuis and Strang (1996) in which the quantifier noun is the head of the NP and is followed by an AP. Hence, the -s is a bound morpheme attached at the right edge of an AP in postnominal position. This AP is a modifier of the head noun that denotes an indefinite quantity. This analysis captures the insight that in modern Dutch APs cannot appear as postnominal modifiers, with the exception of these APs when marked by -s. Thus, there is a parallel with the Definite Construction where the -s licenses the use of NPs as prenominal modifiers.

(30)   *The Partitive -s Construction*
       [NP$_i$ [... [x-s]$_A$]$_{APj}$]$_{NPk}$ ↔ [Quantity$_i$ with Property$_j$]$_k$

Construction (30) has an open slot x for adjectival stems. All qualifying adjectives can be inserted into this slot, except those of the few subclasses mentioned in (24). This analysis correctly predicts that nouns like *iets* and *niets* can co-occur in this construction even though they cannot occur before nouns, as observed in (27–28). The variable x stands for the phonological form of the stem of the adjective. We thus express that the -s is a bound morpheme that is phonologically part of a phrase-final adjective.

The interpretation of the partitive -s as an affix of an adjective is confirmed by the observation that in this construction the -s can only appear on the adjective:

(31)   a. We zoeken iets [op ons doel afgestemd-s]$_{AP}$
          We search something to our goal tuned-s
          'We look for something tuned to our goal'

    b. *We zoeken iets [afgestemd op ons doel-s]_{AP}
       We search something tuned to our goal-*s*
    c. *We zoeken iets [afgestemd-s op ons doel]_{AP}

In (31b), the -*s* is affixed to the final noun, which leads to ungrammaticality. In (31c) the adjective is not at the right edge of the AP, which also leads to ungrammaticality.

    Quantifying expressions can also be derived from quantifying adjectives by means of the nominalizing suffix -*e*. Hence, noun phrases such as the following can be constructed for Dutch:

(32)   a. [het vel-e]_{NP} mooi-s
       the much-NOM beautiful-s
       'the many beautiful things'
     b. [het weinig-e]_{NP} opwindend-s
       The not.much-NOM exciting-s
       'the few exciting things'

In sum, the Partitive -*s* Construction is similar to the Definite -*s* Construction in that in both cases a bound morpheme -*s* that is a relic of the genitive case marker functions as the morphological marker of a specific syntactic construction.

9.4 Constructional idioms with -*s*

The old genitive suffix -*s* also appears in some constructions of Dutch in which one or more of the slots is lexically fixed. These constructions are therefore constructional idioms. The first one to be discussed is the construction exemplified by phrases like the following:

(33)   a. tot sterv-en-s toe
       to die-INF-s to
       'in such a manner that it leads to dying'
     b. tot brak-en-s toe
       to vomit-INF-s to
       'in such a manner that it leads to vomiting'
     c. tot schreeuw-en-s toe
       to shout-INF-s to
       'in such a manner that it leads to shouting'

These are prepositional phrases of the form [Preposition Infinitive-*s* Postposition]. The adposition *toe* is an allomorph of *tot* used when this word is used postpositionally.

This construction is an instantiation of the type of prepositional phrase of Dutch in which a PP is followed by a postposition, that is [[PP] P]$_{PP}$ (Van Riemsdijk 1978). The adpositions involved denote particular forms of motion, either in the spatial or in the temporal sense. The following examples illustrate this use of motional adpositions:

(34) a. van het dak af
          from the roof down
          'down the roof'
      b. met de muziek mee
          with the music with
          'along with the music'
      c. tot het kerkhof toe
          to the churchyard to
          'until the churchyard'

Infinitives, being verbal nouns (of neuter gender) with the infinitival suffix -*en*, can be used in this construction, either without morphological marker or marked with the suffix -*s* (the latter variety appears to have the higher token frequency in a Google search); an additional postposition *aan* is also possible:

(35) tot brak-en(s) (aan) toe 'in such a manner that it leads to vomiting'
      tot schreeuw-en(s) (aan) toe 'in such a manner that it leads to shouting'
      tot sterv-en(s) (aan) toe 'in such a manner that it leads to dying'
      tot vervel-en(s) (aan) toe 'in such a manner that it leads to being bored'

Historically, the -*s* is the genitive marker of singular masculine and neuter nouns, and infinitives are singular neuter nouns. In modern Dutch, adpositions do not assign morphological case to their nominal complements. Hence, the occurrence of the -*s* is linked to this specific instantiation of the [PP P]$_{PP}$ construction:

(36) [[*tot* [V-INF-(*s*)]$_{Ni}$]$_{PP}$ (*aan*) *toe*]$_{PPj}$ ↔ [in a manner leading to SEM$_i$]$_j$

The infinitive, being simultaneously a verb and a noun, has the external valency of a noun and the internal valency of a verb. As a noun, it can occur in a PP, and as a verb, it allows for preverbal complements, and thus combines with resultative APs. For instance, verbal projections of the type [AP *worden*] 'to become AP' occur in this construction:

(37)   a. tot gek word-en-s toe
         until mad become-INF-s to
         'in such a manner that one becomes mad'
       b. tot misselijk word-en-s toe
         until sick become-INF-s to
         'in such a manner that one becomes sick'

Thus, this -s is again a phrasal affix, located at the right edge of a nominal phrase and attached to the infinitive. Therefore, schema (36) has to be slightly modified in order to allow for preverbal complements as well:

(36')   [[tot [[(AP) V-INF-(s)]_N]_{NPi}]_PP (aan) toe]_{PPj} ↔ [in a manner leading to SEM_i]_j

This -s is therefore similar in nature to that in the two -s-constructions discussed above in functioning as a phrasal suffix. It is more restricted in its use, however, in that it only occurs in combinations with two specific adpositions, *tot* and (*aan*) *toe*.[4]

In this construction, infinitives cannot be preceded by a definite determiner, even though infinitives are neuter nouns. Marking with -s is moreover unique for the infinitive and does not occur with deverbal nouns such as -*ing*-nouns:

(38)   a. *tot het walg-en-s toe
         to the nauseate-INF-s to
         'in a nauseating manner'
       b. * tot walg-ing-s toe
         to nauseat-ing-s to
         'in a nauseating manner'

Both the lexical and the formal constraints on this type of PP and its specific semantic interpretation make it clear that it has to be considered a constructional idiom, an instantiation of the more abstract construction [PP P]_PP.

A final example of a trapped old genitive -s in Dutch is its use in cases like the following (Hoeksema 1998*a*):

(39)   Construction *des* N-*s* 'characteristic of all Ns'
       a. Cocooning is niet de-s schrijver-s, maar de-s Belg-s
         Cocooning is not the-*s* writer-*s*, but the-*s* Belg-*s*
         'Cocooning is not characteristic of writers but of Belgians'

---

[4] The *s*-marked infinitive also occurs in the fixed phrase *tot zie-n-s* 'lit. to see-INF-s, see you later', and analogical formations like *tot hor-en-s* 'hear you later', and *tot bell-en-s* 'phone you later'.

b. Agressie is niet de-s vrouw-s
   Aggression is not the-*s* vrouw-*s*
   'Aggression is not characteristic of women'

What we observe here is the use of the construction [*des* N-*s*]$_{NP}$ with the constructional meaning 'characteristic of N'. This NP can only be used as a predicate and often in combination with the negative adverb *niet* 'not'. The article *des* is the old GEN.SG form of the masculine and neuter definite articles *de* and *het*. The use of *des* in present-day Dutch is restricted to idioms. What is remarkable here is that the use of the genitive marker -*s* on the noun and the use of the definite article *des* have been extended to feminine nouns, as shown in (39b), and that this constructional idiom is productive in modern Dutch. Again, the old genitive marker has been reinterpreted as a marker of that construction.

9.5 Collective constructions

Dutch features a number of collective constructions, exemplified in (40):

(40)   a. *appositive collective*
          {wij/ons} drie-en
          {we/us} three-*en*
          'the three of us {SUBJ./OBJ.}'
       b. *collective adverbial I*
          met {ons/jullie/hun} drie-en
          with {our/your/their} three-*en*
          'the three of {us/you/them}'
       c. *collective adverbial II*
          met zijn [zən] drie-en
          with his three-*en*
          'the three of us/you/them'

The common property of these three constructions is that the cardinal must be marked by the ending -*en*.

In Middle Dutch the appositive collective had the form of a personal pronoun followed by a cardinal that could be used predicatively, as illustrated by the following examples:

(41)   a. Wi waren vier-e   (Duinhoven 1988: 81)
          We were four-NOM.PL
          'We were four in number'

  b. dat gi ons vier-en hebt gesien   (Van Helten 1887: 443)
     that you us four-ACC.PL have seen
     'that you saw the four of us'

Such NPs with a numeral could also be preceded by the preposition *met* 'with'
that assigns dative case:

(42) Alexander ginc inwaert met hem drie-en   (Duinhoven 1988: 87)
      Alexander went in with them three-DAT.PL
      'Alexander went in together with the three of them'

These constructions underwent both semantic and structural reinterpretation
(Duinhoven 1988; Heeroma 1948; Tinbergen 1949; Van Haeringen 1949*a*). The
preposition *met*, like its English counterpart *with*, also carries the meaning of
circumstance, as in *met Jan als directeur* 'with John as director'. Thus, a PP like
met hem seven-en could also be re-interpreted as 'the seven of them, seven in
total'. This is the interpretation of the *met*-construction in present-day Dutch,
as exemplified in (40b,c). The structural re-interpretation was made possible
by the fact that some case forms of the personal pronouns were homophonous with possessive pronouns. This is the case for:

(43) ons 'us, our'
      jullie 'you.PL, your.PL.'
      hun 'them, their'
      haar 'them.FEM, their.FEM'

This made the following structural reinterpretation of phrases like *met ons
drie-en* possible:

(44) [Preposition – Personal pronoun – Numeral-*en*] >
      [Preposition – Possessive pronoun – Numeral-*en*]

This led to the construction exemplified in (40b). Although the pronouns *ons
en jullie* function both as personal pronouns and possessive pronouns, in
modern Dutch the pronoun *hun* preceded by a preposition is a possessive
pronoun only (the form of the 3PL personal pronoun after a preposition is
hen). This possessive pronoun reinterpretation can also be observed in the
third type of construction, exemplified in (40c), with a fixed 3SG possessive
pronoun *zijn* that does not agree with another NP, as shown by the following
example with a 1PL subject:

(45) Wij kwamen met zijn drie-en
      We came with his three-*en*
      'We came the three of us'

The phonological form of this *zijn* is always the weak form [zən], which underlines the special nature of this PP-construction.

The effect of these historical developments is that Modern Dutch has three collective constructions that are marked by the suffix *-en*. What is the status of this suffix? Historically it is a case ending, but Dutch no longer has a morphological case system. It appears that the case ending *-en* has been reinterpreted as a plural suffix. Its presence is obligatory, since phrases like *wij vier* 'we four' and *met ons vier* 'the four of us' are ungrammatical. Dutch has two plural suffixes, *-s* and *-en* (the choice between these two suffixes is determined by an array of prosodic, morphological, and lexical factors). Evidence that the case ending was reinterpreted as a plural ending is the replacement of the form *twee-n* 'two-DAT.PL' by the form *twee-en*, with a clear plural ending *-en* (Van Loey 1959: 154).

Additional evidence for this ending being interpreted as a plural suffix comes from the use of diminutive forms. Let us first note that in the collective appositive construction besides numerals some other quantifier nouns and the adverb *samen* can be used:

(46)   Zij {allen/beiden/samen} komen
       They {all/both/together} come
       'They will come {all/both/together}'

Plural diminutives are formed by suffixing a word with (the correct allomorph of) the diminutive suffix followed by the plural suffix *-s* (the choice of *-s* is determined by the diminutive suffix); note that Dutch has two competing plural endings, *-s* and *-en*:

(47) | *noun* | *plural form* | *diminutive plural form* |
       |---|---|---|
       | appel 'apple' | appel-s | appel-tje-s |
       | paard 'horse' | paard-en | paard-je-s |
       | kind 'child' | kinder-en | kinder-tje-s/kind-je-s |

This diminutive-plural marking is also found on cardinals and other quantifiers when used in the collective constructions; the diminutive suffix expresses intimacy or cosiness. The formation of such plural diminutives is best interpreted as a case of paradigmatic word formation in which the plural suffix of the noun is replaced with the diminutive + plural suffix combination, because there are no base words *beid* and *saam* in Dutch, only *beiden* 'both' and *samen* 'together'. This replacement interpretation is confirmed by the form *kindertjes* in (47), which cannot be derived from *kindertje* since this word is ill-formed: the allomorph *kinder* of *kind* only shows up in plural forms and complex words:

(48) a. {wij drie-tje-s/wij beid-je-s/wij saam-pje-s}
        {we three-DIM-PL/we both-DIM-PL/we together-DIM-PL}
        '{the three of us/both of us/we together}'
      b. met ons {drie-tje-s/beid-je-s}
        with us {three-DIM-PL/beid-DIM-PL}
        '{the three/both} of us'
      c. met z'n {drie-tje-s/beid-je-s}
        with his {drie-DIM-PL/both-DIM-PL}
        '{the three/both} of us'

The diminutive form of the adverb *samen* 'together' can only be used in the
first construction since it is an adverb. Yet, the plural interpretation of the
word after the pronoun is so strong that the final *-en* of the simplex word
samen is interpreted as a plural ending that can be replaced with the DIM-PL
sequence *-pjes*.

   In sum, there is clear evidence that the Middle Dutch case ending *-en* has
been reinterpreted as a plural marker in collective constructions. This is an
example of exaptation, the use of a morphological marker for new purposes
(Lass 1990). Such exaptation of case markers as number markers also occurred
in Romance (Vincent 1995).

   There is an interesting complication in this recycling of case markers as
plural markers: in describing these collective constructions as part of the
grammar of present-day Dutch it does not suffice to mark the cardinal
numeral with the feature [+plural], since it is the specific ending *-en* that
is required. The basic division of labour between the two competing suffixes *-s*
and *-en* is that *-s* occurs after stems ending in an unstressed syllable, whereas
-en occurs after stems ending in a stressed syllable (this simple picture is
blurred by the behaviour of loan words, complex words with certain suffixes,
and simplex words ending in a full vowel (Booij 2002b: 28–32). The effect of
the prosodic conditioning is that a plural form always ends in a trochee.
Hence, we find the following forms for numerals when used as nouns:

(49) een 'one'   en-en [eːnən]
      twee 'two'   twee-en [tweːjən]
      zeven 'seven' zeven-s [zeːvəns]
      negen 'nine'   negen-s [neːɣəns]

However, in the collective constructions, the plural forms for the numerals
7 and 9 are *zeven-en* and *negen-en* respectively. That is, it is the specific suffix
-en that is the marker of these constructions.

   The conclusion that we have to refer to a specific suffix in accounting for
these constructions is confirmed by other PP-constructions in which cardinal

numbers were once case-marked by a preposition, temporal and partitive expressions that also require the presence of the suffix *-en*:

(50) a. Het is bij en-en
       It is at one-*en*
       'It is almost one o'clock'
   b. Het is nu na zeven-en
       It is now after seven-*en*
       'It is now past seven o'clock'
   c. Hij kocht het in en-en
       He bought it in one-*en*
       'He bought it as one piece'
   d. Het schip brak in drie-en
       The ship broke in three-*en*
       'The ship broke into three pieces'

These facts show that the suffix *-en* has become the morphological marker of a number of Dutch (mainly PP) constructions. We cannot consider this suffix as the exponence of the morpho-syntactic feature [plural], and hence we have to refer directly to this morphological marker in describing the various collective constructions, the temporal, and the partitive construction.

    This raises a problem for overly strict versions of the hypothesis of Lexical Integrity (Booij 2009*a*). In particular, it shows that in some cases syntax must be given access to the internal morphological structure of words, not only to the abstract morpho-syntactic features that they carry, as assumed by Anderson (1992).

9.6 Affixes as construction markers

The general conclusion of this chapter is that inflectional markers that form part of syntactic constructions may be preserved as markers of these constructions, even though the inflectional system in which it had an identifiable morpho-syntactic role has disappeared. The distribution of bound morphological elements may be linked to specific constructions. In Dutch, the old genitive case marker *-s* has been preserved as a marker of the Definite *-s* Construction and the Partitive *-s* Construction.[5] Thus, this morphological marker made it possible for Dutch to preserve certain syntactic structures: the prenominal use of NPs as determiner phrases, and the postnominal use of APs as modifiers of (quantifier) nouns. In addition, this *-s* also survives in a few

---

[5] A similar view is defended by Hoeksema (1998*b*: 164).

more restricted constructional idioms. These facts therefore support Lass' observation (Lass 1990, 1997) that language change exhibits *bricolage*: pieces of the old (morphological) system may be put to new uses. This recycling led to the growth of linguistic complexity since one has to learn the specific morphological markers of certain constructions that are preserved in restricted form, in some cases besides the productive analytic constructions that replaced them. This confirms Dahl's claim (Dahl 2004) that the preservation and reinterpretation of older constructions is one of the sources of linguistic complexity.

These preservation patterns imply the necessity of viewing the grammar of natural languages as a set of constructions of varying degrees of specificity, a finding that converges with the results of syntactic research in the framework of Construction Grammar. In other words, it is impossible to account for these changes in the morphology of Dutch and the distributional regularities of certain bound morphemes without making use of the notion 'construction'.

10

Stem allomorphy
and morphological relatedness

10.1 Underlying forms and lexical representations

In this chapter I will discuss some consequences of the view of morphology
and the lexicon developed in the preceding chapters for the way in which
phonological information concerning words is stored in the lexicon. Construction Morphology is output-oriented: it considers morphological
schemas as based on listed words. This raises the question how we should
conceive of the phonological representation of words in the lexicon. Given the
output orientation of Construction Morphology, words are expected to be
stored in their surface phonological forms, that is, with the phonetic forms
that they have when spoken in isolation.[1] This goes against the position of
classical generative phonology that words are listed with their underlying
phonological form, which may differ from the phonetic form of words as
spoken in isolation. The concept of underlying form serves to account for the
variation in the phonological form of a morpheme which depends on the
morphological and phonological context in which that morpheme occurs.
Phonological rules derive the various surface phonetic forms from the underlying form of a morpheme.

This classical generative approach implies that the phonological representation of a word used by itself is identical to that of the same word used as a
constituent of a complex word. For instance, the phonetic form of the English
adjective *sane* [seɪn] is different from the phonetic form of this word when
embedded in the complex word *sanity* [sænɪtɪ], in which the base noun *sane*
has the form [sæn]. This difference is due to the phonological rule of Trisyllabic Laxing. In standard generative phonology, the phonological form of *sane*
will be /seːn/, and *sanity* is represented as /seːn-ɪtɪ/. The phonetic form of the
deadjectival noun is then derived by means of the rule of Trisyllabic Laxing.

---

[1] The question to what extent phonetic details of the pronunciation of words are stored in the
lexicon is very interesting (Bybee 2001; Steriade 2000), but is not broached here. This chapter focuses
on one issue only, the lexical representation of phonological alternations.

The phonological identity of these two uses of *sane* will allow for a co-indexation relation to be established between the phonological form of a constituent of a complex word and that of the corresponding word (Chapter 1). However, it is not a priori clear that for a complex word and its base word to be recognized as being morphologically related it is necessary that they share a phonologically completely identical string. Below, evidence is presented that this is not the case. If morphological relatedness does not crucially depend on sharing a constituent in exactly the same phonological form, a consistent output-oriented approach to the representation of words is possible.

The question whether we need abstract underlying forms as stored lexical representations may also be approached from an acquisition point of view. Consider the Dutch word *paard* 'horse' that is pronounced as [paːrt]. When a child has acquired this word, it will be stored with this phonetic form. The plural form of this noun is *paard-en* pronounced as [paːr.dən], in which the stem *paard* is realized with a final [d]. The alternation is due to the constraint Final Devoicing: obstruents are voiceless in coda position (Booij 1995). If this plural form is not stored in the lexicon because it is completely regular from a morphological point of view – the standard assumption of classical generative phonology – the only way of computing the correct plural form is that the child restructures the lexical representation of the word *paard* from /paːrt/ to /paːrd/. Such a restructuring is not necessary, however, if the child stores the plural form *paarden* in its mental lexicon: *paard* is stored as [paːrt], and *paarden* as [paːr.dən]. It is only when a new word has to be derived from the lexeme PAARD that an underlying form /paːrd/ is needed. Suppose, for instance, that a speaker wants to coin the adjective *paard-ig* 'horsy' (this word is not listed in Dutch dictionaries, but can be found on the internet). Since its phonetic form is [paːr.dəx], with a stem-final [d], it is essential to use the underlying form /paːrd/. This underlying form can be computed on the basis of the phonetic forms of the word pair *paard – paarden*. This is an easy task to perform, since there is a wealth of psycholinguistic evidence that morphologically related words are co-activated in the mental lexicon (De Jong et al. 2000). Hence, when the language user deals with the word *paard*, its plural form will be readily available for the computation of its underlying form. Since Construction Morphology assumes that regular morphologically complex words can be stored in the mental lexicon, we do not need the concept of 'restructuring of the underlying form of a word'. Instead, we need a theory of how to select the proper phonological form of a base word that serves as a basis for the computation of the phonological form of words derived from that base word.

In this chapter I provide synchronic and diachronic evidence for concrete phonological representations, that is, for the claim that words are stored in their surface forms (section 10.3), and I argue that phonological differences do not impede the recognition of relations between a complex word and its base word (section 10.4). This discussion will take place against the background of some general assumptions concerning the relation between morphology and phonology (section 10.2). Section 10.5 discusses the selection of stem allomorphs in the construction of complex words, and section 10.6 summarizes my conclusions concerning the representation of allomorphy in the lexicon.

10.2 The relation between morphology and phonology

The formal representation of a complex word comprises two structures, its morphological structure and its phonological structure, as shown for the deverbal noun *baker* in Figure 1.3 of Chapter 1. These two representations are related in a systematic fashion, and the grammar contains an interface module that specifies these systematic correspondences between the phonological structure and the morpho-syntactic structure of a complex word.

The well-formedness of phonological representations is defined by the 'phonological grammar', a set of phonological schemas and constraints. This phonological grammar comprises a definition of the set of segments of a language and their phonological features, and the principles and constraints concerning the prosodic structure (syllables, feet, phonological words, etc.) of linguistic constructs. For instance, the phonological grammar of Dutch will state that the division of the segmental string of a word into syllables and feet takes place within the domain of the phonological word. The phonological constraint of Final Devoicing mentioned above will ensure that in the phonological representations of words, obstruents in coda position will be voiceless.

The morphological make-up of a word may co-determine the phonological representation of a word since there are systematic correspondences between morphological and phonological properties. An example of such a systematic correspondence is the relation between morphological constituent boundaries and phonological constituent boundaries. The morphological structure and the prosodic structure of a complex word are not necessarily isomorphic. In the word *baker*, for example, the internal morphological boundary is located after the *k*, whereas the phonological division of this word is *ba.ker*, with a syllable boundary before the *k*. The syllabification of *baker* is determined by a purely phonological constraint, the Maximal Onset Principle, which requires an intervocalic consonant to form a syllable with the following vowel. Hence, the internal morphological boundary of *baker* is ignored in syllabification. However, the word edges of *baker* do coincide with syllable boundaries.

The principles for the mapping of morphological constituent boundaries onto phonological constituent boundaries can be conceived of as alignment conditions, that is, as conditions on the alignment of these two types of boundaries (McCarthy and Prince 1994). In many languages, the edges of the constituents of a compound align with phonological word boundaries. This implies that in such languages each constituent of a compound is a separate domain of syllabification (the phonological word). Hence, each constituent boundary is aligned with a phonological word boundary. An example is the Dutch compound [[*hand*]$_N$[*appel*]$_N$]$_N$ 'lit. hand apple, eating apple', which is syllabified as [hɑnt.ɑ.pəl]. The prosodic structure of this word is therefore:

(1) $(((\text{hɑnt})_\sigma)_F)_\omega(((\text{ɑ})_\sigma(\text{pəl})_\sigma)_F)_\omega$

This structure presupposes that sounds of a word are combined into syllables (σ), syllables into feet (F), and feet into phonological words (ω). The correctness of the prosodic structure in (1) for the word *hand-appel* is confirmed by the fact that the final consonant of *hand* which is /d/ underlyingly (compare the plural form *hand-en* [hɑn.dən] 'hands') is realized as [t], in conformity with the phonological constraint of Final Devoicing.

The contrast in syllabification between the compound *hand-appel* and the suffixed word *hand-en* shows that the assignment of prosodic structure to words may differ depending on the subset of complex words involved. This also holds for stress assignment. Dutch nominal compounds carry main stress on their first constituent, whereas the location of main stress in Dutch suffixed words varies, and depends on the type of suffix (inflectional versus derivational, native versus non-native, cohering versus non-cohering[2]). Hence, we may need a number of 'co-phonologies' (Inkelas and Zoll 2005) linked to specific morphological constructions. The notion 'co-phonology' is partially a reflex of the fact that the morphological structure of complex words co-determines the phonetic realization of their morphological constituents.

This interface between morphology and phonology can be accounted for by means of various formalisms, for instance by phonological rules that refer to morphological information, as in classical generative phonology (Chomsky and Halle 1968), or by means of a set of ranked output constraints some of which refer to morphological information, as in Optimality Theory (Kager

---

[2] A cohering suffix forms one prosodic word with its stem, a non-cohering suffix forms a prosodic word of its own (Booij 1995).

1999). In this chapter I will not discuss the choice between these different formalisms since the focus is here on other issues.

The idea of co-phonologies can also be used in accounting for forms of non-concatenative morphology. For instance, in many languages nicknames and terms of endearment are formed by truncating the phonological forms of proper names. In English, this may be combined with the addition of the suffix *-y/-ie* which expresses endearment (Lappe 2007):

(2) Alfreda   Alf   Alf-y
     Camille   Cam   Camm-ie
     Elizabeth   Liz   Lizz-y

The morphological operation involved is that of the addition of a semantic feature [nickname] or [endearment] to the base word, a proper name. That is, there is a morphological construction schema for proper names in which the semantic representation is enriched with a semantic or pragmatic property, without an additional corresponding overt affix. This construction will then trigger the phonological operation of truncation, which may be modelled as the mapping of the phonological form of the input name onto a specific prosodic template, that of a heavy syllable (nickname) or that of a trochaic foot ending in [i] (endearment).

Partial reduplication can be accounted for in a similar way. In reduplication constructions, two constituents are combined, and in the case of total reduplication, one constituent has to be a full copy of the other. The meaning of a reduplication construction is specified in the relevant morphological construction schema. If partial reduplication is at stake, the reduplication structure will trigger a phonological operation that deletes part of the copy. That is, in partial reduplication there is a special co-phonology for the morphological construction at stake (Inkelas and Zoll 2005).

Ablaut (vowel alternation or apophony) is a well-known type of non-concatenative morphology. Such vowel alternations are readily expressed by paradigmatically related schemas with different vowels. For instance, the relation between the present stem *sing* and the past tense stem *sang* of the verb 'to sing' can be expressed by the following schema pair:

(3) $[\text{X i Y}]_{\text{V, [−past]}} \approx [\text{X a Y}]_{\text{V, [+past]}}$

This type of representation of morphological categories is discussed in detail in the literature (Bybee 1988, 1995), and will not be discussed any further in this chapter. These inflectional schemas are another case of the need for paradigmatically related morphological schemas, argued for in the domain of word formation in preceding chapters.

10.3 Lexical phonological representations

How are the phonological properties of words specified in the lexicon? As pointed out in section 10.1, the answer of classical generative phonology is that words are specified as strings of segments, and in their underlying form, which may differ from their surface form. Consider the Dutch noun *maand* [ma:nt] 'month'. The underlying form of this word is traditionally assumed to be /ma:nd/, with a final /d/, because its plural form is *maand-en* [ma:n.dən]. We need this underlying form in order to predict that the plural form is not [ma:n.tən], the expected form if the surface form of the singular noun is taken as a starting point for computing the plural form. The phonetic form of the singular form of this noun is derived from the underlying form /ma:nd/ by applying the constraint of Final Devoicing that neutralizes the opposition between voiced and voiceless obstruents in coda position. This form of abstraction is motivated by the fact that we cannot assume the form /ma:nt/ as the starting point of the computation of the phonetic form of the plural. Such an analysis requires a rule of voicing in order to derive phonetic forms like [ma:ndən]. However, assuming such a rule is incorrect since it would also voice the stem-final /t/ of words like *maat* [ma:t] 'mate, measure' with the plural form *maten* [ma:.tən]. Note that in this standard generative phonological approach the conceptually different notions 'underlying form of a word' and 'stored form of a word' are equated. The basic assumption underlying this analysis is the adage that what can be computed should not be stored. For instance, Kenstowicz motivates the claim that predictable information is not stored lexically as follows:

Generative grammar's answer to this question is based on the hypothesis that the human capacity for language is designed in such a way as to minimize the amount of information that must be stored in the speaker's mental lexicon. (Kenstowicz 1994: 60)

However, a few pages later in the same book, Kenstowicz points out that this point of view is no longer self-evident: 'with the advent of neural science and more accurate estimates of the capacity of the human brain, this "economy of storage" argument is not compelling in and of itself ' (Kenstowicz 1994: 69–70).

In this book I defend the position there is no contradiction between assuming rules or schemas and at the same time storing predictable information about words and phrases in the lexicon. This also applies to the phonological properties of language constructs. Consider once more the pair of word forms *maand – maanden* 'month(s)'. Even though the plural form is regular, it is stored in the lexicon since it has a certain frequency of use. In lexical decision tasks, there are frequency effects for regular inflectional word forms such as *maanden*, and hence such word forms must be stored in lexical memory (Baayen et al. 1997). Since a speaker of Dutch does not have to compute this plural form and can retrieve it directly from lexical memory, (s)he can also store the singular form in its lexical phonetic form with a final [t]: [maːnt]. The Dutch language user only needs the underlying form /maːnd/ when (s)he wants to derive a new word from the noun *maand*. In this view, an underlying form is not the form that is stored in the lexicon but the form that can be computed on the basis of sets of paradigmatically related words in the lexicon. The lexicon of speakers of Dutch comprises the word pair *maand* [maːnt] 'month' – *maanden* [maːn.dən] 'months', and related derived words belonging to the same word family, such as *maand-elijks* [maːn.də.ləks] 'monthly'. This will enable them to compute the underlying form /maːnd/ if necessary for the formation of a new word. The phonological constraint of Final Devoicing is used actively only when new words are coined or when words are borrowed, that is, in loanword adaptation. For example, the English loanword *pad* is pronounced [pɛt] in Dutch. For stored words, this phonological constraint expresses a regularity about their phonetic forms. This constraint also serves to distinguish the allomorphy in the lexeme *paard* 'horse' from suppletion. In the latter case, there is no systematic phonological relationship between the different allomorphs of the lexeme.

Psycholinguistic evidence for this position is that in lexical decision tasks Dutch listeners perform better on a phonetic form like [hɑnt] than a phonetic form like [hɑnd] which makes an abstract representation like /hɑnd/ unlikely as the lexical form of representation (Ernestus and Baayen 2007: 19).

Evidence for the storage of predictable phonological information can also be obtained from the formation of the past tense form of Dutch verbs. The past tense suffix is either *-te* (when the stem ends in a voiceless segment) or *-de* (in all other cases).

(4)   verb   past tense singular form
       a. klop 'to knock'   klop-te [klɔp.tə]
          stop 'to stop'   stop-te [stɔp.tə]
          werk 'to work'   werk-te [vɛrk.tə]
       b. tob 'to toil'   tob-de [tɔb.də]
          eb 'to recede'   eb-de [ɛb.də]
          zaag 'to saw'   zaag-de [zaːɣ.də]
          roer 'to stir'   roer-de [ruːr.də]

Given this alternation between *-te* /tə/ and *-de* /də/, we might conclude that there is an abstract representation of the past tense suffix with an initial alveolar stop not specified for [voice], since the feature value for [voice] of this consonant can always be computed on the basis of the [voice] specification of the stem-final segment (Booij 1995). Yet, some language users appear to determine the phonetic form of the past tense suffix by looking at the phonetic form of stored past tense forms. For instance, the regular past tense form for the verb *tobben* 'to toil', with the stem *tob-* /tɔb/ is *tob-de*, as expected. Yet, many speakers of Dutch use the form *top-te* [tɔp.tə] because most Dutch verbs with a stem ending in a labial stop have a past tense form [Xp-tə] (X is the variable for the preceding phonological segments), as shown by Ernestus and Baayen (2003*b*). That is, even though the [b] is maintained in the form *tobben* [tɔbən], the pattern [X pt] ≈ [X ptə] is extended to the verb *tobben*, thus resulting in the past tense form *top-te*.

These facts tell us once more that (i) inflected forms of words, even though they are regular, can be stored in the mental lexicon, (ii) that past tense suffixes of Dutch may be stored with a fully specified initial consonant, and (ii) that low-level schemas (generalizations about sets of words with similar make-up and a relatively high density) play a role in computing the properties of complex words.[3]

Linguistic evidence in favour of encoding the effect of Final Devoicing in lexical representations can be found in the set of morphologically related words in Dutch that exhibit vowel lengthening in open syllables. In present-day Dutch, this alternation, the relic of a once productive process of Open Syllable Lengthening, holds for a closed set of words, and therefore this length difference must be encoded in the phonological lexical representations of the relevant words. Vowel length plays a role in the distribution of fricative consonants. The generalization for all Dutch words is that /v/ and /z/ only occur after long vowels, the *v/z*-constraint. Consider now the following alternations:

(5)   a. *nouns, sg/pl*

graf [ɣrɑf]	grav-en [ɣraːvən]	'grave, SG/PL'
hof [hɔf]	hov-en [hoːvən]	'court, SG/PL'
glas [ɣlɑs]	glaz-en [ɣlaːzən]	'glass, SG/PL'
staf [stɑf]	stav-en [staːvən]	'staff, SG/PL'

   b. *verbs, past tense, sg/pl*

las [lɑs]	laz-en [laːzən]	'read'
genas [ɣənɑs]	genaz-en [ɣənaːzən]	'cured'
gaf [ɣɑf]	gav-en [ɣaːvən]	'gave'

---

[3] Similar facts concerning Polish inflection are discussed in Dąbrowska (2006, 2008).

c. *noun-verb conversion pairs*
   draf [drɑf] 'trot'   drav-en [drɑːvən]   'to trot'
   lof [lɔf] 'praise"   lov-en [loːvən]   'to praise'

In all words in (5), short vowels are followed by a voiceless fricative, whereas long vowels are followed by a voiced fricative. That is, the vowel length alternation conspires with Final Devoicing in order to comply with the *v/z* constraint. Thus, all allomorphs obey the constraint on the distribution of /v/ and /z/ mentioned above. In these cases, the voicelessness of the final obstruent in the words in the left column must therefore be part of the lexical representation, even though this information is predictable, and even though these obstruents alternate with voiced ones: an underlying form like /ɣrɑv/ would violate the *v/z-* constraint.

Confirmation of this conclusion is provided by observing the forms of complex words derived from words with these alternations. Such words are derived either from a stem with short vowel + voiceless obstruent or from a stem with long vowel + voiced obstruent; allomorphs of stems ending in a short vowel + voiced obstruent never occur in derived words: a word like *bestavving* [bəstɑvɪŋ] 'staff' is impossible.

(6) bestaff-ing [bəstɑfɪŋ] 'staff '   stav-en [stɑːvən] 'to prove'
     glass-ex   [ɣlɑsɛks]   'glass   glaz-enier [ɣlɑːzəniːr] 'stained-glass
     cleaner'   artist'
     hoff-elijk [hɔfələk] 'courteous'   hov-eling [hoːvəlɪŋ] 'courtier'
     loff-elijk [lɔfələk]   lov-en [loːvən] 'to praise'
     'praiseworthy'

If the noun ends in a stop or a velar fricative, this restriction does not apply, and morphology can apply to stems with a voiced stop:

(7) *singular*   *plural*   *derived word*
     god [ɣɔt]   goːd-en [ɣoːdən] 'god(s)'   godd-elijk [ɣɔdələk] 'divine'
     bad [bɑt]   bad-en [bɑːdən] 'bath(s)'   badd-eren [bɑdərən] 'to bathe'
     weg [ʋɛx]   weg-en [ʋeːɣən] 'road(s)'   wegg-etje [ʋɛɣətjə] 'small road'

Thus, it is only when the effect of Final Devoicing on the relevant words is encoded in the lexical representation that the right generalizations are made. If, for instance, the lexical representation of *glas* 'glass' did not encode the effect of Final Devoicing, it would have the form /ɣlɑz/, and so nothing would exclude ill-formed words like *glazzex* [ɣlɑzɛks].

For some words with alternation between stem-final voiced and voiceless obstruents, the stem allomorph that ends in a voiceless obstruent appears before certain schwa-initial suffixes, where the stem-final obstruent surfaces in onset position (Fehringer 2003):

(8) a. bederv-en 'to perish'   bederf-elijk 'perishable' [bədɛrfələk]
         [bədɛrvən]
         erv-en 'to inherit' [ɛrvən]   erf-elijk 'hereditary' [ɛrfələk]
     b. erv-en 'to inherit' [ɛrvən]   erf-enis 'inheritance' [ɛrfənɪs]
         begrav-en [bəɣra:vən] 'to bury' begraf-enis 'burial' [bəɣra:fənɪs]

In these cases the voicelessness of the stem-final obstruent does not follow from Final Devoicing because the obstruent is not in coda position. Thus, once more we have to conclude that the allomorphs with voiceless obstruent must be lexically stored, and the relevant suffixes must be subcategorized for appearing with that allomorph.

The phenomenon of vowel lengthening mentioned above is an example of lexicalization of a phonological rule. The rule disappears from the language, but its effects are maintained in a number of words. A classical example of such a lexicalization pattern is German Umlaut, the fronting of vowels in stems triggered by the presence of a front vowel in the next syllable. For instance, the diminutive suffix -*chen*, which once contained a front vowel /i/, triggered Umlaut in the diminutive form of *Vater* 'father', *Väter-chen*. The vowel of the diminutive suffix which was the trigger of the fronting process then changed to [ə]. Yet, its fronting effect has been maintained in *Väter-chen*. The only way in which effects of a phonological rule can survive after the loss of its trigger is by these effects being encoded in the phonological representations of words in the lexicon at the time that the trigger is still present (Booij 2002e, 2009b). Therefore, lexicalization of phonological alternations presupposes lexical storage of the surface forms of words. This conclusion has also been drawn by Croft (2000: 35) with respect to the voicing alternation in *life* – *lives*: 'at least at the time of the loss of the voicing alternation, *lives* was a single unit lingueme including specification of the voicing of the fricative'.

The application of optional phonological rules may also be lexically governed. Consider, for example, the phenomenon of vowel reduction in unstressed syllables in Dutch (Booij 1995, 2002e):

(9) juwéel [jyʋe:l] 'jewel'   juwel-íer [jyʋəli:r] 'jeweller'
     miníster [minɪstər] 'minister'   ministér-ie [minəste:ri] 'ministry'
     geníe [zjəni] 'genius'   geni-ál [ɣe:nija:l] 'brilliant'

In these examples a full vowel in a stressed syllable corresponds with a reduced vowel schwa in an unstressed syllable of a paradigmatically related word. The

differences in stress location between base words and derived words follow
from the rules for Dutch word stress. Vowel reduction is an optional process
in Dutch, but in the words in (9) vowel reduction is obligatory. In other
words, these schwas must be present in the lexical phonological representation of these words. These are interesting facts in relation to the rule versus list
fallacy because they show that storage and computation go together. Even
though vowel reduction is a productive process of Dutch, its effect has to be
encoded in the phonological representations of these words because reduction is obligatory here.

Another example of a lexically governed optional phonological process of
Dutch is the weakening of intervocalic /d/ to either /j/ or /w/:

(10)   goed 'good' [ɣut]   goed-e (inflected form) [ɣudə] or [ɣujə]
        rood 'red' [ro:t]   rod-e (inflected form) [ro:də] or [ro:jə]
        goud 'gold' [ɣɔut]   goud-en 'golden'   [ɣɔudən] or [ɣɔuwən]
        but
        wreed 'cruel' [ʋre:t]   wred-e (inflected form) [ʋre:də], never *[ʋre:jə]

Weakening must once have been a productive process applying to all relevant
words, but in present-day Dutch it is lexically governed. Hence, we have to
encode the effects of this weakening process in the phonological lexical
representations of these words. The set of complex words involved comprises
both derived and inflected words. This implies that inflected forms of adjectives such as *goed-e* and *rod-e* have to be stored in the lexicon for phonological
reasons, even though they are completely regular from a morphological point
of view. In some words, the weakening is obligatory, as in *goei-erd* [ɣu.jərt]
'good person, kind soul' derived from *goed* 'good'. Thus, these facts provide
phonological evidence for the claim that morphologically regular complex
words may be listed.

Palatalization of consonants before the vowel /i/ in Italian has also become
a lexically governed rule, as illustrated by the following examples (Celata and
Bertinetto 2005):

(11)   ami[k]-o – ami[tš]-i 'friend(s)'   ami[tš]-izia 'friendship'
        mendi[k]-o – mendi[k]-i 'mendicant(s)'   mendi[tš]-izia 'mendicity'

In the first example, palatalization applies across the board, whereas in the
second example, the plural form of *mendico* has no palatalization. These facts
show once more that the effects of phonological processes must be encoded in

lexical representations, and also that plural forms of nouns may have to be stored even though they are regular from a morphological point of view.[4]

10.3.1 The role of 'derived properties' of words

In the examples discussed in this section so far, we have dealt with phonological alternations. There are also phonological rules for predictable non-segmental properties of words such as their stress pattern and their prosodic structure. Again, classical generative phonology assumes that such properties are not stored, whereas in the view of the lexicon defended here there is no problem in assuming that they are stored. For example, morphological processes may be sensitive to the prosodic properties of their base words. In German, the past participle of verbs is formed by prefixing *ge-* to the verbal stem if the first syllable of the stem carries primary stress; otherwise the prefix is ø (Wiese 1996: 90):

(12) *infinitive*   *past participle*
    a. árbeit-en 'to work'   ge-arbeit-et
       réd-en 'to talk'   ge-red-et
       súch-en 'to search'   ge-such-t
    b. applaudíer-en 'to applaud'   applaudier-t
       diskutíer-en 'to discuss'   diskutier-t
       versúch-en 'to try'   versuch-t

This shows that the schema for participle formation requires input on the stress properties of the verbal stem. This information is predictable, yet it must be available for a proper application of the morphological schema for German past participles. This dependence of morphological operations on predictable phonological properties is expected if these predictable stress properties of German verbs are lexically specified.

Lexical storage of predictable non-segmental properties such as syllable structure can also be concluded from tip-of-the-tongue phenomena. Speakers might find it hard to retrieve the segmental string of a word while they know the number of syllables and/or the location of its main stress. This implies that such prosodic information is stored even though it can normally be computed on the basis of its segmental string (Levelt 1989: 320ff.).

There are many other cases where the application of morphological processes is determined by predictable phonological properties of input words

---

[4] For Finnish there is extensive psycholinguistic evidence that stem allomorphs have separate representations in the mental lexicon (Järvikivi et al. 2006: 421).

(Booij 2000, 2002*b,d*; Wiese 1996). This type of evidence has always been used as evidence for the application of morphological and phonological rules being interwoven and for the cyclic application of phonological rules. These are essential building blocks of the model of Lexical Phonology. This form of interaction between phonology and morphology is predicted by the model of the grammar proposed in this book, in which predictable phonological information for words is stored in the lexical representation of words. The stipulation that rules apply in a cyclic fashion has thus been made superfluous.

This does not mean that all phonological information concerning a base word will be preserved when it is embedded in a complex word. For instance, in *bak-er* the /k/ is not in coda position, as it is in *bake*, but in onset position. Stored properties may be overruled by phonological constraints. For instance, the No Empty Onset principle will overrule preservation of prosodic structure. In the framework of Optimality Theory this can be expressed by ranking the No Empty Onset constraint higher than the Faithfulness constraint that requires preservation of existing information (Kager 1999).

Another important building block of the model of Lexical Phonology is the distinction between lexical and post-lexical phonology: lexical phonology has to precede post-lexical phonology (Booij 1997*b*; Kiparsky 2000; Rubach 2000). Again, this follows from having concrete lexical representations. For instance, the 1SG PRESENT form of the Dutch verb *hebben* [hɛbən] is *heb* [hɛp]. When the clitic *er* 'her' [ər] is encliticized to the verbal form, the resulting form is [hɛ.pər]. In this phonetic form the stem-final voiceless stop forms the onset of the second syllable. That is, it is not in coda position. Yet, this stop is voiceless, because it is in coda position if there is no enclitic attached. In other words, the resyllabification induced by encliticization does not bleed Final Devoicing. In a derivational, rule-based model of phonology this can be captured by ordering lexical rules (like Final Devoicing) before post-lexical rules. In the analysis defended here, the verbal form *heb* is stored as [hɛp], and this predicts that the voicelessness of the stem-final stop is preserved even when it surfaces in onset position. Thus, the required ordering of lexical phonology before post-lexical phonology is predicted, and need not be stipulated as an independent claim.[5]

---

[5] Other examples of the effects of lexical phonological rules that apply to segments in specific prosodic positions being preserved even though the prosodic position of the segments has changed at the phrasal level have been discussed for Spanish (Harris 1983), French (Booij 1984), German (Ito and Mester 2003), and English (Gussenhoven 1986). The issue is discussed from a speech production point of view in Baumann (1996) and Levelt (1989).

10.4 Stem allomorphy and relatedness of words

As discussed in the preceding sections, the segmental composition and prosodic properties of a word under morphological embedding may differ from
that of the same word in isolation. This kind of allomorphy is pervasive in the
non-native stratum of languages like English (Booij 2007: 168–175), as illustrated here by the English word set *drama, dramat-ic, dramat-ist*. The word
drama in isolation lacks the final /t/ that shows up when this word is
morphologically embedded. Obviously, this does not impede recognition of
a relation between these words. Hence, we can co-index the constituent
dramat of *dramat-ic* and *dramat-ist* with the noun *drama*, thus expressing
the semantic compositionality of the two derived words. That is, allomorphy
does not impede establishing relations between words.

This is an important insight in view of the claim that the effect of lexical
phonological processes can be encoded in lexical phonological representations. Assuming concrete lexical representations of words implies that related
words or word forms will differ in their phonological form. Hence, it is
important that we are justified in assuming that such phonological variation
does not block the recognition of morphological relatedness.

Psycholinguistic experiments have confirmed that allomorphy in related
words does not impede the establishment of paradigmatic relations. For
example, German diminutive forms have the same priming effect on the
recognition of their base nouns, regardless of whether or not they have a
stem vowel change (Clahsen et al. 2003: 140). The stem vowel change in
German diminutives (Umlaut) is not automatic, as shown by the following
pairs of related words:

(13)   Vater 'father' – Väter-chen 'father, diminutive'
        Onkel 'uncle' – Onkel-chen 'uncle, diminutive'

In the second pair, the full vowel in the first syllable of the base is not fronted
in the diminutive noun. Yet, *Onkelchen* does not differ significantly from
Väterchen in its priming effect with respect to its base word.

As for English, it has been argued that the strength of the priming effect is
not reduced for phonologically dissimilar pairs such as *decision/decide* or
vanity/vain (Marslen-Wilson et al. 1994; Marslen-Wilson and Zhou 1999;
Reid and Marslen-Wilson, 2003).

There is also no effect on priming of Italian stem allomorphy in
plural nouns with or without palatalization (*amico – amici* 'friend(s)' versus
buco – buchi 'hole(s)'). Celata and Bertinetto (2005) found no difference in
priming. For instance, if the target word is *drastic-o*, then the words *drasti*[k]*-i*
and *drastic*[tš]*-i* have the same priming effect.

In their study of the effects of morphological relatedness on word recognition (the family size effect) of Dutch language users, De Jong et al. (2000: 353) concluded that 'the effect of Family Size is not mediated by the exact form of the base word, but by a more abstract central morphological representation'. For instance, there are family size effects for a verb and its irregular participle, as in *bind* 'bind' – *ge-bond-en* 'bound' which differ in the phonological form of their stem.

To conclude, allomorphy does not impede establishing relations between words, and recognizing relationships between words is a robust process. Establishing a relationship between a complex word and its base word(s) is not impeded by phonological differences. Containing a word constituent in exactly the same phonological form as that of the word by itself is no precondition for establishing lexical relatedness between a complex word and its base(s). Hence, lexical phonological representations can be concrete, with the effects of phonological rules or constraints encoded.

Complex words may be completely regular from a morphological point of view, and yet they may have to be stored because of lexically governed phonological alternations they are subject to.

10.5 Stem allomorph selection

If different allomorphs of a word are lexically stored, the following question arises: how is the proper stem allomorph of a lexeme selected for inflectional and derivational processes? For a proper answer to this question, we have to realize that there are different types of stem allomorphy, and therefore different types of selection.

First, there is allomorphy that is completely morphological in nature: lexemes may have more than one stem, as in Latin (Matthews 1972; Aronoff 1994) and Romance (Vogel 1993) verbal conjugation. For instance, we have three stems for Latin verbs, exemplified here for the verb *laudare* 'to praise': *lauda-* (stem 1), *lauda-v-* (stem 2), and *laud-at-* (stem 3). The selection of one of these stems is governed by morphology. The first stem is used for present tense forms (*laud-a-mus* 'we praise'), the second for the perfect tense (*lauda-v-i* 'I have praised'), and the third stem for past participles (*laud-a-t-us*) and derived words like *laud-a-t-or* 'praiser'. That is, each stem is associated with a part of the verbal paradigm and one of them is the stem for derivation.

The example *drama – drama-tic, dramat-ist* mentioned in section 10.4 shows that the selection of a stem allomorph may be governed by the stratum to which the complex word belongs. If we were to coin a derived verb with the non-native suffix *-ize*, the allomorph *dramat-* has to be selected since this is the non-native stem allomorph. In the native stratum, on the other hand, the allomorph *drama* has to be selected, as in *dramas, drama-like,* or *drama-performer.* Thus, allomorphs may carry a stratum label.

Thirdly, we find a lot of lexicalized allomorphy, relics of phonological processes that are no longer active, or not in the same form, as discussed in section 10.3. Synchronically, the selection of the right allomorph may have to be restated in terms of morphological structure and analogical patterns. For instance, in Dutch we find relics of vowel lengthening in open syllable in word pairs like *sch*[ɪ]*p* – *sch*[e:]*p-en* 'ship/ships', as discussed in section 10.3. Most NN compounds with the lexeme SCHIP 'ship' in the non-head position select the allomorph *scheep*, even though the vowel is not in an open position:

(14)   scheep-s-beschuit 'ship's biscuit'
       scheep-s-kat 'ship's cat'
       scheep-s-arts 'ship's doctor'

Hence, when a new compound with the lexeme SCHIP 'ship' in the non-head position is coined, language users will very probably use *scheep* as the form of the left constituent of the new compound. Such facts thus suggest that there is a set of compounds with the common form [[*scheep*]$_N$ [x]$_N$]$_N$ that may function as a schema for new compounds of this type. As shown by Krott (2001), this kind of analogy to sets of existing complex words plays a dominant role in determining another form of stem allomorphy, the selection of one of the possible linking elements between the two parts of a Dutch compound. As argued in section 3.6, these kinds of regularities concerning stem allomorphy can be expressed by subschemas for specific classes of compounds.

In some cases of lexicalized allomorphy, the selection of an allomorph of a stem or an affix can be done by phonological output constraints. This holds for Dutch (Booij 1998), for Polish, (Rubach and Booij 2001), and for Italian (Van der Veer and Booij in press). One of the allomorphs provides the optimal output form of the complex word of which it forms a part. For instance, in the verbal paradigm of the Italian verb *sedere* 'to sit' there are two stem allomorphs, *sed-* and *sjed-*, as in the present tense forms:

(15)   siéd-o, siéd-i, siéd-e, sed-íomo, sed-éte, siéd-ono

This allomorphy is lexically governed, and must hence be lexically stored. When the stem syllable is stressed, we get the stem allomorph *sied-* [sjɛd]; when the stem is unstressed, we get *sed-* [sed]. This choice is regulated by the phonological output constraint that stressed syllables must have a bimoraic nucleus. In *sied-*, the glide and the vowel together form a bimoraic nucleus, and thus they can carry stress. In unstressed syllables, monomoraic nuclei are preferred, and hence *sed-* is selected when the stress is on the suffix, in the 1PL and the 2PL form.

Finally, let us consider the phonologically conditioned allomorphy triggered by transparent, automatic phonological constraints such as Final Devoicing in Dutch, as in *paard* [pa:rt] – *paard-en* [pa:rdən] 'hors(es)'. Since this is a neutralizing process, we cannot always[6] compute the underlying form on the basis of the phonetic form of the singular noun (compare the word pair *kaart* [ka:rt] – *kaart-en* [ka:rtən] 'map(s)'). Underlying forms can be computed with certainty on the basis of existing sets of morphologically related words stored in the lexicon. Consider once more how we might coin the Dutch adjective *paard-ig* [pa:rdəx] 'horse-like, horsy'. Coining this adjective means, as far as the phonological part of the derivation is concerned, the unification of a phonological representation (the underlying form) of the word *paard* with the word formation schema $[[x]_N \, ig]_A$. The correct underlying form can be computed on the basis of the stored plural form *paarden* [pa:rdən]. Albright has argued that when language users have to identify the base form of a paradigm, they will choose the base form that is the most informative (Albright 2005: 41). In the case of Dutch nouns, the plural form will be identified as the most informative because it has a stem form from which the phonetic form of the singular form and of complex words with the lexeme PAARD as a constituent can always be computed correctly. So for Dutch nouns, plural forms are 'islands of reliability' (Albright 2002).[7]

10.6 Stem allomorphy in the lexicon

Let me now summarize these findings concerning allomorphy. Words may have more than one phonological form in the lexicon. The selection of the right allomorph may be a matter of pure morphology, of 'morphology by itself' (Aronoff 1994), or a matter of analogy to sets of existing complex words, which can be expressed by subschemas in which stem allomorphs are specified. Thus, the concept of a hierarchical lexicon is essential for making the right generalizations concerning allomorph selection. Even in the case of purely phonologically conditioned allomorphy, listing the different surface forms of a word is possible, since the lexicon need not be redundancy-free. In the case of Final Devoicing in Dutch, there is substantial evidence for

---

[6] In some cases the voice specification of the final obstruent in the underlying form can be computed on the basis of the phonological form of the rhyme (Ernestus and Baayen 2003*a*).

[7] The role of specific forms of the paradigms as starting points for computation is also discussed in detail in Finkel and Stump (2007), who develop the notion of 'principal parts', defined as 'a minimal subset of the members of a paradigm from which all other members of the paradigm can be deduced'.

the view that the effects of this phonological constraint may be encoded in lexical representations.

Psycholinguistic research has shown that stem allomorphy does not impede the recognition of relatedness between words with a common constituent. Therefore, nothing speaks against a view of the lexicon in which constituents of complex words are co-indexed with corresponding independent words, notwithstanding the variation in phonological form.

11

Taking Stock

At the end of this book, it is appropriate to ask ourselves what new insights have been obtained in the previous chapters, which topics have not been dealt with in detail, and which perspectives for linguistic research can be identified.

To begin with, an important domain of morphological phenomena has hardly been discussed, inflection. This does not mean that *CM* has nothing of interest to say about inflection. On the contrary: inflectional phenomena provide excellent arguments for word-based morphology and for the constructional approach. The classical problem of inflectional morphology is the complicated relation between form and meaning (Spencer 2004). It is often impossible to assign a specific meaning to an inflectional suffix, because its actual value depends on the kind of stem it combines with and the properties of that stem, unless one allows for large sets of homonymous inflectional affixes. Consider, for instance, the paradigm of masculine and neuter nouns (declension I) in Russian (Gurevich 2006: 51):

(1)

	MASCULINE		NEUTER	
	SG	PL	SG	PL
NOM	stol	stol-y	bljud-o	bljud-a
ACC	stol-a	stol-y	bljud-a	bljud-a
GEN	stol-a	stol-ov	bljud-a	bljud
DAT	stol-u	stol-am	bljud-u	bljud-am
INST	stol-om	stol-ami	bljud-om	bljud-ami
LOC	stol-e	stol-ax	bljud-e	bljud-ax
	'table'		'dish'	

As these paradigms illustrate, the same ending, for instance *-a*, has different interpretations depending on the class of the noun. Moreover, the particular value expressed is a combination of properties such as [ACC.SG] or [NOM.PL]. That is, there is no one-to-one correspondence between form and morphosyntactic properties. One also finds elements in inflectional forms such as the thematic vowels of verbal conjugation in Latin and the Romance languages that do not contribute by themselves to the meaning of the inflected forms; they are 'morphomic' properties (Aronoff 1994). Hence, the morpho-syntactic properties of each word form in the paradigm are best considered as constructional properties, that is, as properties of the word form as a whole. This may be expressed by morphological schemas that abstract, for instance, over words of the same declension such as the Russian ACC/GEN.SG word forms *stola* and *bljuda* in (1):

(2) $(x\text{-}a)_{\omega i} \leftrightarrow [N]_{i, \text{ masc.sg, acc/gen}} \leftrightarrow SEM_i$

where *x* is a phonological variable for nominal stems. The meaning SEM_i mentioned here is that of the lexeme. The semantic interpretation of the morpho-syntactic features is not specified here since this interpretation partially depends on the syntactic contexts in which a word occurs.

A prototypical property of inflectional forms is that they are organized in paradigms. This means that the inflectional forms exhibit systematic paradigmatic relationships. How can we account for the relationship between related inflectional forms, for instance the relation between *ragazz-o* 'boy, sg.' and *ragazzi* 'boys' in Italian? The answer is that we then assume paradigmatic relationships of correspondence (recall that such paradigmatic relationships appeared to be necessary in the domain of word formation as well) between the constructional schemas for the different forms, as illustrated here for Italian nouns of the *ragazzo*-type:

(3) $< (x\text{-}o)_{\omega i} \leftrightarrow [N]_{i, \text{ sg}} \leftrightarrow SING[SEM_i]> \approx < (x\text{-}i)_{\omega i} \leftrightarrow [N]_{i, \text{ pl}} \leftrightarrow PL[SEM_i] >$

where SING is the semantic operator of singularity, and PL that of plurality. The form in the left schema is the anchor form from which the plural form on the right can be computed: singular nouns in -*o* have a plural form in -*i*.

This representation implies that concrete word forms such as the singular forms of nouns are stored in the mental lexicon. That is, we do not represent the stem *ragazz-* as a lexical entry, assigned to a particular declination class, but only as a building block of listed word forms.

As Blevins (2006) has argued, word-based morphology also provides the best starting point for dealing with formal complications in inflectional systems such as stem allomorphy. Blevins thus defends an 'abstractive perspective' in which surface forms are regarded as basic morphotactic units of a grammatical system, with roots, stems, and exponents treated as abstractions over a lexicon of word forms (Blevins 2006: 531).

Periphrasis is another type of inflectional phenomenon that fits in very naturally with the basic assumptions of Construction Grammar: the combinations of words used for periphrasis have holistic syntactic and semantic properties, which makes them fit for filling in cells of paradigms. Thus, periphrasis can be seen as a syntactic form of exponence (Ackerman and

Stump 2004; Blevins 2008*b*). Again, this topic has not been dealt with in this book in any serious detail.

Two basic assumptions are involved in this approach to inflection: (i) morphology is based on full words and word forms being stored in the mental lexicon, and (ii) morphological regularities are based on the network of paradigmatic relationships between these words and word forms. There is a wealth of psycholinguistic evidence for these two related assumptions (Hay and Baayen 2005), and the previous chapters have provided various forms of internal linguistic evidence from the domain of word formation for the correctness of these assumptions.

An important consequence of constructionist approaches to syntax and morphology is that there is no longer a neat division between grammar and lexicon. In classical generative grammar, the lexicon is the storage component, the place where all idiosyncracies of words and larger linguistic units are stored, whereas the grammar comprises a number of rule components that deal with the creative aspects of the construction of words and sentences. A constructionist grammar contains a set of interrelated constructions of various degrees of abstractions, from lexical idioms to general syntactic schemas and with default inheritance, based on the psychological operations of categorization and abstraction. The only operation that is left in language production is that of unification: a well-formed word or sentence is constructed by unifying pieces of information that are specified in the 'constructicon', the list of constructions and words of a language.

One clear advantage of constructionist approaches to syntax is that they can do justice to the fact that a large number of phrasal units are not words in the morphological sense, and yet may form open sets of lexical expressions. As argued in this book, this is the case for certain types of noun incorporation (quasi-incorporation), separable complex verbs, progressive expressions, phrasal names, and certain types of numeral expressions. Thus, the functional and semantic similarities between such phrasal lexical units and words can be accounted for without giving up the distinction between words and phrases, that is, between morphological and syntactic constructs. Moreover, this view enables us to provide an explanation for the competition and blocking effects between morphological and syntactic constructions and their instantiations. This does not mean, however, that it is always possible to draw a sharp line between phrasal and morphological lexical units: phrasal constructions may develop into compound constructions and hence the boundary may be blurred in specific cases of lexical constructs.

Another advantage of constructionist syntax for morphological analysis is that it makes it possible to account for the distribution of bound morphemes that are governed by specific syntactic constructions, as shown in Chapter 9: bound morphemes may be markers of syntactic constructions.

A constructionist approach provides an interesting perspective for the interpretation of neuro-psychological findings and the proper location of various linguistic tasks in the brain. The argumentation of this book is built on internal linguistic evidence concerning word formation and syntax – with just a few hints as to psycholinguistic evidence – since that is where the competence of this book's author lies. Nevertheless, it is an important asset of a theory of linguistic structure that it is compatible and convergent with psycho- and neuro-linguistic evidence. For instance, *CM*, as developed in this book, is in line with the massive evidence for the storage of complex words, even when they are regular.

The psycholinguistic implication of the tripartite parallel architecture of grammar assumed in this book is that linguistic expressions are built in all three components in parallel. The phonological, morpho-syntactic, and semantic structures of words are each combined to larger structures, in a parallel fashion, by means of unification (Jackendoff 2007). Hagoort (2005) argues that this architectural design of the grammar is a good starting point for the interpretation of neuro-imaging studies of language processing.[1]

The domain of morphology has functioned and is still functioning as a battlefield for the debate on the nature of linguistic 'rules': symbolic schemas, connectionist networks, or analogical patterns. The constructional schemas presented in this book are symbolic representations of linguistic knowledge of varying degrees of abstraction. The question thus arises to what extent such symbolic representations give a proper characterization of the linguistic knowledge of language users. It is impossible to discuss this issue here in any detail, let alone provide empirical evidence for specific psychological interpretations of constructional schemas. However, there is evidence that subschemas based on similarities between words stored in the lexicon play a role in the language user's computing of the properties of complex words. In a detailed study of stress assignment in English compounds, Plag et al. (2008)

---

[1] Hagoort (2005) distinguishes three functional components of language processing: Memory, Unification, and Control (the MUC model). The memory component denotes the information in long-term memory of linguistic information. Unification is the integration of various types of linguistic information for the production or parsing of sentences. The Control component 'relates language to action, and is invoked, for instance, when the correct target language has to be selected (in the case of bilingualism), or for handling turn taking during conversation' (Hagoort 2005: 415). Hagoort claims that these different tasks can be linked to specific parts of the brain. In particular, the left inferior frontal gyrus is the place where unification takes place: 'In short, the left interior frontal cortex recruits lexical information, mainly stored in temporal lobe structures that are known to be involved in lexical processing, and unifies them into overall representation that are multiword utterances' (Hagoort 2005: 419). The memory component is distributed over the left temporal cortex.

showed that the constituent families of a compound play a role in stress assignment. For instance, there is categorical leftward stress in all compounds that have *street* as their right constituent (*Mádison Street* versus *Madison Ávenue*). This word family effect suggests that there may be a compound subschema $[[x][street]_N]_N$ with the constituent x being marked as carrying main stress. Alternatively, the computation of the stress pattern for a new compound with *street* as its head is modelled as being determined on the basis of the degree of similarity with existing compounds, that is, based on analogy with existing words, as in the Memory-Based Learning (MBL) paradigm (Keuleers and Daelemans 2007). In this model there are no abstract schemas, that is, it is a 'lazy learning model'. It is not clear, however, whether such lazy learning models can do justice to all aspects of productive word formation (cf. section 3.7).

In sum, *CM* is a theory of the architecture of the grammar, of the role of lexical units of various degrees of abstraction, and of the relation of the grammar to facts of language use such as the storage and frequency of linguistic constructs of varying size. *CM* provides proper analytic tools for complex phenomena on the borderline between morphology and syntax. *CM* is in harmony with state-of-the-art theories of the balance between storage and computation, and the insight that paradigmatic relationships between words are fundamental in understanding morphological systems. Nevertheless, it is obvious that many issues as to the linguistic and psychological interpretation of the knowledge of complex words and other lexical constructs remain open for further research and debate.

References

Aarts, Bas (1998). Binominal noun phrases in English. *Transactions of the Philological Society* 96: 117–157.

Abeillé, Anne, and Godard, Danièle (2004). De la légèreté en syntaxe. *Bulletin de la Société de Linguistique de Paris* 99: 69–106.

——— (2006). La légèreté en français comme déficience de mobilité. *Linguisticae Investigationes* 29: 11–24.

Ackema, Peter (1999a). *Issues in morpho-syntax*. Amsterdam / Philadelphia: Benjamins.

—— (1999b). The non-uniform structure of Dutch N-V compounds. In *Yearbook of Morphology 1998*, eds. Geert Booij and Jaap van Marle, 127–158. Dordrecht: Kluwer.

—— and Neeleman, Ad (2004). *Beyond morphology: interface conditions on word formation*. Oxford: Oxford University Press.

Ackerman, Farrell (1995). Systemic patterns and lexical representations: analytic morphological words. In *Levels and structures*, ed. Istvan Kenesei, 289–305. Szeged: JATE.

—— (2003). Aspectual contrasts and lexeme derivation in Estonian: a realization-based morphological perspective. In *Yearbook of Morphology 2003*, eds. Geert Booij and Jaap Van Marle, 13–32. Dordrecht: Kluwer.

—— and Stump, Gregory S. (2004). Paradigms and periphrastic expression: a study in realization-based lexicalism. In *Projecting morphology*, eds. Louisa Sadler and Andrew Spencer, 111–157. Stanford: CSLI.

—— and Webelhuth, Gert (1998). *A theory of predicates*. Stanford: CSLI.

Aikhenvald, Alexandra Y. (2007). Typological distinctions in word formation. In *Language typology and syntactic description, Vol. III. Grammatical categories and the lexicon*, ed. Timothy Shopen, 1–65. Cambridge: Cambridge University Press.

—— and Dixon, R.M.W. eds. (2006). *Serial verb constructions: A cross-linguistic typology*. Oxford: Oxford University Press.

Albright, Adam (2002). Islands of reliability for regular morphology: evidence from Italian. *Language* 78: 684–709.

—— (2005). The morphological basis of paradigm leveling. In *Paradigms in phonological theory*, eds. Laura J. Downing, T. Alan Hall, and Renate Raffelsiefen, 17–43. Oxford: Oxford University Press.

—— and Hayes, Bruce (2003). Rules vs analogy in English past tenses: a computational/experimental study. *Cognition* 90: 119–161.

Allen, Cynthia. 1997. The origins of the 'group genitive' in English. *Transactions of the Philological Society* 95: 111–132.

Amha, Azeb (2001). *The Maale language*. Leiden: University of Leiden, Research School of Asian, African, and Amerindian Studies.

Anderson, Stephen (1992). *A-morphous morphology*. Cambridge: Cambridge University Press.

Arnaud, Pierre J. L. (2003). *Les composés timbre-poste*. Lyon: Presses Universitaires de Lyon.

Aronoff, Mark (1976). *Word formation in generative grammar*. Cambridge, MA: MIT Press.

—— (1994). *Morphology by itself: stems and inflectional classes*. Cambridge MA: MIT Press.

—— (2007). In the beginning was the word. *Language* 83: 803–830.

Ascoop, Kirstin (2005). Affixoidhungrig? Skitbra! Status und Gebrauch von Affixoiden im Deutschen und Schwedischen. *Germanistische Mitteilungen* 65: 17–28.

—— and Leuschner, Torsten (2006). Affixoidhungrig? Skitbra! Comparing affixoids in Swedish and German. *Sprachtypologie und Universalienforschung* 59: 241–252.

Asudeh, Ash and Mikkelsen, Line Hove (2000). Incorporation in Danish: implications for interfaces. In *Grammatical interfaces in HPSG*, eds. Ronnie Cann, Claire Grover, and Philip Miller, 1–15. Stanford, CA: Stanford University Press.

Baayen, R. Harald (1992). Quantitative aspects of morphological productivity. In *Yearbook of Morphology 1991*, eds. Geert Booij and Jaap van Marle, 109–150. Dordrecht: Kluwer.

—— (2003). Probabilistic approaches to morphology. In *Probabilistic linguistics*, eds. Rens Bod, Jennifer Hay, and Stefanie Jannedy, 229–287. Cambridge, MA / London: MIT Press.

——Dijkstra, Ton, and Schreuder, Robert (1997). Singulars and plurals in Dutch. Evidence for a parallel dual route model. *Journal of Memory and Language* 36: 94–117.

Baker, Brett J. (2008). *Word structure in Ngalakgan*. Stanford: CSLI.

Baker, Mark C. (1988). *Incorporation: a theory of grammatical function changing*. Chicago: Chicago University Press.

—— (1996). *The polysynthesis parameter*. Oxford studies in comparative syntax. New York / Oxford: Oxford University Press.

Baldwin, Timothy, Beavers, John, van der Beek, Leonoor, Bond, Francis, Flickinger, Daniel Paul, and Sag, Ivan A. (2003). In search of a systematic treatment of determinerless PPs. Paper presented at *the ACL-SIGSEM Workshop on the Linguistic Dimensions of Prepositions and their Use in Computational Linguistics Formalisms and Applications,* Toulouse, France.

Ball, Douglas (2005). Phrasal noun incorporation in Tongan. In *Proceedings of the 12th annual conference of the Austronesian Formal Linguistics Association (AFLA)*, eds. Jeffrey Heinz and Dimitrios Ntelitheos, 19–33. Los Angeles: UCLA Working Papers in Linguistics.

Barbiers, Sjef (2007). Indefinite numerals ONE and MANY and the cause of ordinal suppletion. *Lingua* 117: 859–880.

Baroni, Marco, Guevara, Emiliano, and Zamparelli, Roberto (2009). The dual nature of deverbal nominal constructions: evidence from acceptability ratings and corpus analysis. *Corpus Linguistics and Linguistic Theory* 5: 27–60.

Bauer, Laurie (2008). Exocentric compounds. *Morphology* 18: 51–74.

—— (2009). Typology of compounds. In *The Oxford handbook of compounding*, eds. Rochelle Lieber and Pavol Štekauer, 343–356. Oxford: Oxford University Press.

Bauer, Winifred (1993). *Maori*. London / New York: Routledge.

Baumann, Monika (1996). *The production of syllables in connected speech*. Nijmegen: Ph.D. dissertation, University of Nijmegen.

Beard, Robert (1995). *Lexeme morpheme base morphology*. Albany, NY: SUNY Press.

Becker, Thomas (1990). *Analogie und morphologische Theorie*. München: Wilhelm Fink Verlag.

—— (1994). Back-formation, cross-formation, and 'bracketing paradoxes'. In *Yearbook of Morphology 1993*, eds. Geert Booij and Jaap van Marle, 1–26. Dordrecht: Kluwer.

Bertinetto, Pier-Marco, Ebert, Karen H., and de Groot, Casper (2000). The progressive in Europe. In *Tense and aspect in the languages of Europe*, ed. Östen Dahl, 517–588. Berlin: Mouton de Gruyter.

Bierwisch, Manfred (1990). Verb cluster formation as a morphological process. In *Yearbook of Morphology 1990*, eds. Geert Booij and Jaap Van Marle, 173–200. Dordrecht: Foris.

Bisetto, Antonietta and Scalise, Sergio (1999). Compounding: Morphology and/or syntax? In *Boundaries of morphology and syntax*, ed. Lunella Mereu, 31–48. Amsterdam / Philadelphia: Benjamins.

Blevins, James P. (2006). Word-based morphology. *Journal of Linguistics* 42: 531–573.

—— (2008a). Feature-based grammar. In *Non-transformational syntax*, eds. Robert D. Borsley and Kersti Börjars. Oxford: Blackwell.

—— (2008b). Periphrasis as syntactic exponence. In *Patterns in paradigms*, eds. Farrell Ackerman, James P. Blevins, and Gregory S. Stump. Stanford: CSLI.

Blom, Alied (1994). Het ondoorgrondelijk bijvoeglijk naamwoord. *Forum der Letteren* 35: 81–94.

Blom, Corrien (2004). On the diachrony of complex predicates in Dutch: predicative and non-predicative preverbs. *Journal of Germanic Linguistics* 16: 1–75.

—— (2005a). *Complex predicates in Dutch. Synchrony and diachrony*. Utrecht: LOT.

—— (2005b). The demarcation of morphology and syntax: a diachronic perspective on particle verbs. In *Morphology and its demarcations*, eds. Wolfgang U. Dressler, Dieter Kastovsky, Oskar E. Pfeiffer, and Franz Rainer, 53–66. Amsterdam / Philadelphia: Benjamins.

—— and Booij, Geert (2003). The diachrony of complex predicates in Dutch: a case study in grammaticalization. *Acta Linguistica Hungarica* 50: 61–91.

Bloomfield, Leonard (1935). *Language*. London: Allen and Unwin.

Bochner, Harry (1993). *Simplicity in generative morphology*. Berlin / New York: Mouton de Gruyter.

Boogaart, Ronny (1999). *Aspect and temporal ordering*. Utrecht: LOT.

Booij, Geert (1977). *Dutch morphology: a study of word formation in generative grammar*. Lisse / Dordrecht: The Peter de Ridder Press / Foris Publications.

—— (1979). Semantic regularities in word formation. *Linguistics* 17: 985–1001.

—— (1984). French C/ø alternations, extrasyllabicity and Lexical Phonology. *The Linguistic Review* 3: 181–207.

—— (1985). Coordination reduction in complex words: a case for prosodic phonology. In *Advances in non-linear phonology*, eds. Harry van der Hulst and Norval Smith, 143–160. Dordrecht: Foris Publications.

—— (1986). Form and meaning in morphology: the case of Dutch 'agent' nouns. *Linguistics* 24: 503–518.

—— (1988). The relation between inheritance and argument structure: deverbal -er-nouns in Dutch. In *Morphology and modularity. In honour of Henk Schultink*, eds. Martin Everaert, Arnold Evers, Riny Huybregts, and Mieke Trommelen, 57–74. Dordrecht: Foris Publications.

—— (1990). The boundary between morphology and syntax: separable complex verbs in Dutch. In *Yearbook of Morphology 1990*, eds. Geert Booij and Jaap van Marle, 45–63. Dordrecht: Foris.

—— (1995). *The phonology of Dutch*. Oxford: Clarendon Press.

—— (1996). Inherent versus contextual inflection and the split morphology hypothesis. In *Yearbook of Morphology 1995*, eds. Geert Booij and Jaap van Marle, 1–16. Dordrecht / Boston: Kluwer.

—— (1997a). Autonomous morphology and paradigmatic relations. In *Yearbook of Morphology 1996*, eds. Geert Booij and Jaap van Marle, 35–53. Dordrecht: Kluwer.

—— (1997b). Non-derivational phonology meets Lexical Phonology. In *Derivations and constraints in phonology*, ed. Iggy Roca, 261–288. Oxford: Clarendon Press.

—— (1998). Prosodic output constraints in morphology. In *Phonology and morphology of the Germanic languages*, eds. Wolfgang Kehrein and Richard Wiese, 143–163. Tübingen: Niemeyer.

—— (2000). The phonology–morphology interface. In *The first Glot International state-of-the-article book. The latest in linguistics*, eds. Lisa Cheng and Rint Sybesma, 287–306. Berlin: Mouton de Gruyter.

—— (2002a). Constructional idioms, morphology, and the Dutch lexicon. *Journal of Germanic Linguistics* 14: 301–327.

—— (2002b). *The morphology of Dutch*. Oxford: Oxford University Press.

—— (2002c). Separable complex verbs in Dutch: a case of periphrastic word formation. In *Verb-particle explorations*, eds. Nicole Dehé, Ray Jackendoff, Andrew McIntyre, and Silke Urban, 21–42. Berlin: Mouton de Gruyter.

—— (2002d). Prosodic restrictions on affixation in Dutch. In *Yearbook of Morphology 2001*, eds. Geert Booij and Jaap van Marle, 183–202. Dordrecht: Kluwer.

—— (2002e). The balance between storage and computation in phonology. In *Storage and computation in the language faculty*, eds. Sieb Nooteboom, Fred Weerman, and Frank Wijnen, 115–138. Dordrecht: Kluwer.

—— (2004). De aan het infinitief-constructie in het Nederlands. In *Taeldeman, man van de taal, schatbewaarder van de taal*, eds. Johan de Caluwe, Magda Devos, Georges de Schutter, and Jacques van Keymeulen, 97–106. Gent: Academia Press.

—— (2007). *The grammar of words: An introduction to morphology*. 2nd edition. Oxford textbooks in linguistics. Oxford: Oxford University Press.

Booij, Geert (2008). Constructional idioms as products of language change: the *aan het* INFINITIVE construction in Dutch. In *Constructions and language change*, eds. Alexander Bergs and Gabriele Diewald, 79–104. Berlin / New York: Mouton de Gruyter.

—— (2009*a*). Lexical integrity as a morphological universal, a constructionist view. In *Universals of language today*, eds. Sergio Scalise, Elisabetta Magni, and Antonietta Bisetto, 83–100. Dordrecht: Springer Science + Business Media.

—— (2009*b*). Lexical storage and phonological change. In *The nature of the word. Essays in honor of Paul Kiparsky*, eds. Christine Hanson and Sharon Inkelas, 497–505. Cambridge, MA: MIT Press.

—— and Lieber, Rochelle (2004). On the paradigmatic nature of affixal semantics in English. *Linguistics* 42: 327–357.

Börjars, Kersti (2003). Morphological status and (de)grammaticalisation: the Swedish possessive. *Nordic Journal of Linguistics* 26: 133–163.

—— Denison, David, and Scott, Alan (2008). What makes clitics tick? Paper presented at the *11th International Morphology Meeting*. Vienna.

—— Vincent, Nigel, and Chapman, Carol (1997). Paradigms, periphrases, and pronominal inflection. In *Yearbook of Morphology 1996*, eds. Geert Booij and Jaap Van Marle, 155–180. Dordrecht: Kluwer.

Botha, Rudolf P. (1988). *Form and meaning in word formation: a study of Afrikaans reduplication*. Cambridge: Cambridge University Press.

Bowern, Claire (2008). The diachrony of complex predicates. *Diachronica* 25: 161–185.

Bresnan, Joan (1982). The passive in lexical theory. In *The mental representation of grammatical relations*, ed. Joan Bresnan, 3–86. Cambridge, MA: MIT Press.

Brinton, Laurel J. and Akimoto, Minoji eds. (1999). *Collocational and idiomatic aspects of composite predicates in the history of English*. Amsterdam / Philadelphia: Benjamins.

—— and Traugott, Elizabeth C. (2005). *Lexicalization and language change*. Cambridge: Cambridge University Press.

—— —— (2009). Lexicalization and grammaticalization all over again. In *Historical linguistics 2005. Papers from the 17th ICHL, University of Madison-Wisconsin, July 31th–August 5th*, eds. Joseph C. Salmons and Shannon Andrew Dubenion-Smith, 3–19. Amsterdam / Philadelphia: Benjamins.

Briscoe, Edward, Copestake, Ann, and de Paiva, Valeria eds. (1993). *Inheritance, defaults and the lexicon*. Cambridge: Cambridge University Press.

Broekhuis, Hans and Strang, Anke (1996). De partitieve genitiefconstructie. *Nederlandse Taalkunde* 1: 221–238.

—— Keizer, Evelien, and Den Dikken, Marcel (2003). *Modern grammar of Dutch, Vol. 4. Nouns and noun phrases*. Leiden: Leiden University Centre of Linguistics.

Bybee, Joan (1988). Morphology as lexical organization. In *Theoretical morphology*, eds. Michael Hammond and Michael Noonan, 119–141. San Diego: Academic Press.

—— (1995). Regular morphology and the lexicon. *Language and Cognitive Processes* 10: 425–455.

—— (2001). *Phonology and language use*. Cambridge: Cambridge University Press.

—— and Dahl, Östen (1989). The creation of tense and aspect systems in the languages of the world. *Studies in Language* 13: 51–104.

—— Perkins, Revere, and Pagliuca, William (1994). *The evolution of grammar: Tense, aspect, and modality in the languages of the world.* Chicago: Chicago University Press.

Carlson, Barry (1990). Compounding and lexical affixation in Spokane. *Anthropological Linguistics* 32: 69–82.

Carlson, Greg (2006). The meaningful bounds of incorporation. In *Non-definiteness and plurality*, eds. Svetlana Vogeleer and Liliane Tasmowski, 35–50. Amsterdam / Philadelphia: Benjamins.

Ceccagno, Antonella and Basciano, Bianca (2009). Sino-Tibetan: Mandarin Chinese. In *The Oxford handbook of compounding*, eds. Rochelle Lieber and Pavol Štekauer, 478–490. Oxford: Oxford University Press.

Celata, Chiara and Bertinetto, Pier Marco (2005). Lexical access in Italian: words with and without palatalization. *Lingue e Linguaggio* 2: 293–318.

Chomsky, Noam and Halle, Morris (1968). *The sound pattern of English.* New York: Harper and Row.

Clahsen, Harald, Sonnenstuhl, Ingrid, and Blevins, James P. (2003). Derivational morphology in the German mental lexicon: a dual mechanism account. In *Morphological structure in language processing*, eds. R. Harald Baayen and Robert Schreuder, 125–156. Berlin: Mouton de Gruyter.

Copestake, Ann (1993). Defaults in lexical representation. In *Inheritance, defaults, and the lexicon*, eds. Ted Briscoe, Valeria De Paiva, and Ann Copestake, 223–245. Cambridge: Cambridge University Press.

—— and Briscoe, Edward (1995). Semi-productive polysemy and sense extension. *Journal of Semantics* 12: 15–67.

Corbett, Greville G. (2006). *Agreement.* Cambridge: Cambridge University Press.

—— and Fraser, Norman M. (1993). Network Morphology, a DATR account. *Journal of Linguistics* 29: 113–142.

Coseriu, Engenio (1952/1975). Sysem, Norm und Rede. In *Sprachtheorie und allgemeine Sprachwissenschaft*, ed. Eugenio Coseriu, 11–101. München: Fink Verlag.

Creissels, Denis (2008). L'incorporation en mandinka. In *La composition dans une perspective typologique*, ed. Dany Amiot, 75–88. Artois: Artois Presses Université.

Croft, William (2000). *Explaining language change: an evolutionary approach.* London: Longman.

—— (2001). *Radical Construction Grammar: syntactic theory in typological perspective.* Oxford: Oxford University Press.

—— (2003). Lexical rules vs constructions: a false dichotomy. In *Motivation in language*, eds. Hubert Cuyckens, Thomas Berg, René Dirven, and Klaus-Uwe Panther, 49–68. Amsterdam / Philadelphia: Benjamins.

—— and Cruse, D. Alan (2004). *Cognitive linguistics.* Cambridge: Cambridge University Press.

Culicover, Peter W., and Jackendoff, Ray (2005). *Simpler syntax.* Oxford: Oxford University Press.

—— —— (2006). The simpler syntax hypothesis. *Trends in Cognitive Science* 10: 413–418.

Dąbrowska, Ewa (2006). Low-level schemas or general rules? The role of diminutives in the acquisition of Polish case inflections. *Language Sciences* 28: 120–135.

—— (2008). The effects of frequency and neighbourhood density on adult native speakers' productivity with Polish case inflections: an empirical test of usage-based approaches to morphology. *Journal of Memory and Language* 58: 931–951.

Daelemans, Walter (2002). A comparison of analogical modeling of language to memory-based language processing. In *Analogical modeling*, eds. Royal Skousen, Deryle Lonsdale, and Dilworth B. Parkinson, 157–179. Amsterdam / Philadelphia: Benjamins.

Dahl, Östen (2004). *The growth and maintenance of linguistic complexity*. Amsterdam / Philadelphia: Benjamins.

Dalton-Puffer, Christiane, and Plag, Ingo (2000). Category-wise, some compound-type morphemes seem to be rather suffix-like: on the status of *-ful, -type*, and *-wise* in present-day English. *Folia Linguistica* 34: 225–244.

Dayal, Veneeta (2007). Hindi Pseudo Incorporation. Ms. Rutgers University.

De Caluwe, Johan (1990). Complementariteit tussen morfologische en in oorsprong syntactische benoemingsprocédé's. In *Betekenis en produktiviteit. Gentse bijdragen tot de studie van de Nederlandse woordvorming*, ed. Johan De Caluwe, 9–24. Gent: Seminarie voor Duitse Taalkunde.

—— (1992). Deverbaal *-er* als polyseem suffix. *Spektator* 21: 137–148.

—— (1994). Open versus gesloten semantiek van woordvormingsregels. *Spektator* 23: 137–148.

De Haas, Wim and Trommelen, Mieke (1993). *Morfologisch handboek van het Nederlands. Een overzicht van de woordvorming*. 's Gravenhage: SDU Uitgeverij.

De Jong, Nivja, Schreuder, Rob, and Baayen, R. Harald (2000). The morphological family size effect and morphology. *Language and Cognitive Processes* 15: 329–365.

De Swart, Henriette and Zwarts, Joost (2009). Less form – more meaning. Why bare singular nouns are special. *Lingua* 119: 280–295.

De Vries, Jan (1975). *Lexicale morfologie van het werkwoord in modern Nederlands*. Leiden: Leiden University Press.

Delsing, Lars-Olof (2008). Swedish linking *-s*. Paper presented at the *11th International Morphology Meeting*. Vienna.

Downing, Pamela (1977). On the creation and use of English compound nouns. *Language* 53: 810–842.

Duinhoven, Anton M. (1988). *Middelnederlandse syntaxis. Synchroon en diachroon. Deel 1. De naamwoordsgroep*. Leiden: Martinus Nijhoff.

Dyk, Siebren (1997). *Noun incorporation in Frisian*. Leeuwarden: Fryske Akademy.

Ebert, Karin H. (2000). Progressive markers in Germanic languages. In *Tense and aspect in the languages of Europe*, ed. Östen Dahl, 605–653. Amsterdam / Philadelphia: Benjamins.

Elenbaas, Marion (2007). *The synchronic and diachronic syntax of the English verb-particle combination*. Utrecht: LOT.

Ernestus, Mirjam and Baayen, R. Harald (2003a). Predicting the unpredictable: interpreting neutralized segments in Dutch. *Language* 79: 5–38.

—— —— (2003*b*). Analogical effects in regular past tense production in Dutch. *Linguistics* 42: 879–903.

—— —— (2007). Paradigmatic efects in auditory word recognition: the case of alternating voice in Dutch. *Language and Cognitive Processes* 22: 1–24.

Evans, Roger. and Gazdar, Gerald (1996). DATR: a language for lexical knowledge representation. *Computational Linguistics* 22: 167–216.

Everaert, Martin (1993). Vaste verbindingen in woordenboeken. *Spektator* 23: 3–27.

Farkas, Donka (2006). The unmarked determiner. In *Non-definiteness and plurality*, eds. Svetlana Vogeleer and Liliane Tasmowski, 81–105. Amsterdam / Philadelphia: Benjamins.

—— and de Swart, Henriëtte (2003). *The semantics of incorporation: from argument structure to discourse transparency*. Stanford: CSLI.

Fehringer, Carol (2003). Prosodic conditions on allomorph selection in Dutch derivational morphology. *Journal of Germanic Linguistics* 15: 297–325.

Fillmore, Charles, Kay, Paul, and O'Connor, Mary C. (1988). Regularity and idiomaticity in grammatical constructions: the case of *let alone*. *Language* 64: 501–538.

Finkel, Raphael and Stump, Gregory S. (2007). Principal parts and morphological typology. *Morphology* 17: 39–75.

Fleck, David W. (2006). Body-part prefixes in Matses: derivation or noun incorporation? *International Journal of American Linguistics* 72: 59–96.

Flickinger, Daniel Paul (1987). *Lexical rules in the hierarchical lexicon*. Stanford: Stanford University dissertation.

Fradin, Bernard (2003). *Nouvelles approches en morphologie*. Paris: Presses Universitaires de France.

—— (2009). IE, Romance: French. In *The Oxford handbook of compounding*, eds. Rochelle Lieber and Pavol Štekauer, 417–435. Oxford: Oxford University Press.

Fried, Mirjam and Östman, Jan-Ola (2004). Construction grammar: a thumbnail sketch. In *Construction Grammar in a cross-linguistic perspective*, eds. Mirjam Fried and Jan-Ola Östman. Amsterdam / Philadelphia: Benjamins.

Fudeman, Kisten (2004). Adjectival agreement vs. adverbal inflection in Balanta. *Lingua* 114: 105–123.

Fuhrhop, Nanna (1998). *Grenzfälle morphologischer Einheiten*. Tübingen: Stauffenburg.

Gerdts, Donna B. (1998). Incorporation. In *The handbook of morphology*, eds. Andrew Spencer and Arnold Zwicky, 84–104. Oxford: Blackwell.

Ghomeshi, Jila (1997). Non-projecting nouns and the Ezafe construction in Persian. *Natural Language and Linguistic Theory* 15: 729–788.

—— and Massam, Diane (1994). Lexical/syntactic relations without projection. *Linguistic Analysis* 24: 175–217.

Goldberg, Adele (1995). *Constructions: a Construction Grammar approach to argument structure*. Chicago: Chicago University Press.

—— (2006). *Constructions at work: the nature of generalization in language*. Oxford: Oxford University Press.

Goldberg, Adele (2009). The nature of generalization in language. *Cognitive Linguistics* 20: 93–127.

Greenberg, Joseph H. (1978). Generalizations about numeral systems. In *Universals of human language, Vol. 3. Word structure*, ed. Joseph H. Greenberg, 249–295. Stanford, CA: Stanford University Press.

—— (1991). The last stage of grammatical elements: contractive and expansive desemanticization. In *Approaches to grammaticalization*, eds. Elisabeth C. Traugott and Bernd Heine, 301–314. Amsterdam / Philadelphia: Benjamins.

Guevara, Emiliano and Scalise, Sergio (2009). Searching for universals in compounding. In *Universals of language today*, eds. Sergio Scalise, Elisabetta Magni, and Antonietta Bisetto, 101–128. Dordrecht: Springer.

—— Forza, Francesca, and Scalise, Sergio (2009). Compounding adjectives. Ms. University of Bologna.

Gurevich, Olga (2006). *Constructional morphology: the Georgian version*. Stanford: Ph.D. dissertation, Stanford University.

Gussenhoven, Carlos (1986). English plosive allophones and ambisyllabicity. *Gramma* 10: 119–141.

Haegeman, Liliane and Van Riemsdijk, Henk C. (1986). Verb projection raising, scope, and the typology of rules. *Linguistic Inquiry* 17: 417–466.

Haeseryn, Walter, Romyn, Kirsten, Geerts, Guido, de Rooij, Jaap, and van den Toorn, Maarten (1997). *Algemene Nederlandse spraakkunst*. Groningen / Deurne: Martinus Nijhoff / Wolters Plantyn.

Hagoort, Peter (2005). On Broca, brain, and binding: a new framework. *Trends in Cognitive Science* 9: 416–423.

Harbert, Wayne (2007). *The Germanic languages*. Cambridge: Cambridge University Press.

Harley, Heidi (2007). *English words: a linguistic introduction*. Oxford: Blackwell.

Harris, Alice C. (2003). Preverbs and their origins in Georgian and Udi. In *Yearbook of Morphology 2003*, eds. Geert Booij and Jaap Van Marle, 61–78. Dordrecht: Kluwer.

—— and Faarlund, Jan Terje (2006). Trapped morphology. *Journal of Linguistics* 42: 289–315.

Harris, James W. (1983). *Syllable structure and stress in Spanish*. Cambridge, MA: MIT Press.

Haspelmath, Martin (1989). Schemas in Hausa plural formation: product-orientation and motivation vs source-orientation and generation. *Buffalo Working Papers in Linguistics* 89: 32–74.

—— (1999). Explaining article-possessor complementarity: economic motivation in noun phrase syntax. *Language* 75: 227–243.

—— (2000). Periphrasis. In *Morphology: an international handbook on inflection and word formation*. Vol. 1, eds. Geert Booij, Christian Lehmann, and Joachim Mugdan, 655–664. Berlin: De Gruyter.

Haugen, Jason D. (2008). *Morphology at the interfaces: reduplication and noun incorporation in Uto-Aztecan*. Amsterdam / Philadelphia: Benjamins.

Hay, Jennifer and Baayen, R. Harald (2005). Shifting paradigms: gradient structure in morphology. *Trends in Cognitive Sciences* 9: 342–348.

Heeroma, Klaas (1948). De telwoorden. *De Nieuwe Taalgids* 41: 84–95.

Heine, Bernd (1993). *Auxiliaries: cognitive forces and grammaticalization.* New York: Oxford University Press.

——Claudi, Ulrike, and Hünnemeyer, Friederike (1991). *Grammaticalization: a conceptual framework.* Chicago / London: University of Chicago Press.

Hentschel, Elke (1993). Flexionsverfall im Deutschen? Die Kasusmarkierung bei partitiven Genetiv-Attributen. *Zeitschrift für Germanistische Linguistik* 21: 320–333.

Heynderickx, Priscilla (2001). *Relationele adjectieven in het Nederlands.* Antwerpen: Lessius Hogeschool.

Heyvaert, Liesbet (2003). *A cognitive-functional approach to nominalization in English.* Berlin / New York: Mouton de Gruyter.

Hilpert, Martin and Koops, Christian (2008). The case of Swedish pseudo-coordination with *sitta* 'sit'. *Diachronica* 25: 242–261.

Himmelmann, Nikolaus P. (1998). Regularity in irregularity: article use in adpositional phrases. *Linguistic Typology* 2: 315–353.

Hippisley, Andrew (2001). Word formation rules in a default inheritance framework: a Network Morphology account of Russian personal names. In *Yearbook of Morphology 2000,* eds. Geert Booij and Jaap Van Marle, 221–261. Dordrecht: Kluwer.

Hoeksema, Jack (1988). Head-types in morpho-syntax. In *Yearbook of Morphology 1988,* eds. Geert Booij and Jaap van Marle, 123–138. Dordrecht: Foris.

——(1998a). Adjectivale inflectie op -s: geen geval van transpositie. In *Morfologiedagen 1996,* eds. Eric Hoekstra and Caroline Smits, 46–72. Amsterdam: Meertens-Instituut.

——(1998b). Een ondode kategorie: de genitief. *Tabu* 28: 162–167.

——(2000). Compositionality of meaning. In *Morphology: an international handbook on inflection and word formation,* eds. Geert Booij, Christian Lehmann, and Joachim Mugdan and in collaboration with Wolfgang Kesselheim and Stavros Skopeteas, 851–857. Berlin / New York: De Gruyter.

Hoekstra, Jarich (2002). Genitive compounds in Frisian as lexical phrases. *Journal of Comparative Germanic Linguistics* 6: 227–259.

Hoekstra, Teun (1988). Small clause results. *Lingua* 74: 101–139.

——and Van der Putten, Frans (1988). Inheritance phenomena. In *Morphology and modularity. In honor of Henk Schultink,* eds. Martin Everaert, Arnold Evers, Riny Huybregts, and Mieke Trommelen, 163–186. Dordrecht: Foris.

Hopper, Paul J. (1991). On some principles of grammaticalization. In *Approaches to grammaticalization,* Vol. I, eds. Elisabeth Closs Traugott and Bernd Heine, 17–35. Amsterdam / Philadelphia: Benjamins.

——and Traugott, Elisabeth C. (2003). *Grammaticalization.* Cambridge: Cambridge University Press.

Hulk, Aafke and Tellier, Christine (1999). Conflictual agreement in Romance nominals. In *Formal perspectives on Romance linguistics: Selected papers from the*

28th linguistics symposium on Romance languages, eds. J.-Marc Authier, Barbara E. Bullock, and Lisa Rees, 179–195. Amsterdam / Philadelphia: Benjamins.

Hüning, Matthias (1996). Metonymische Polysemie in der Wortbildung. In *Lexical structures and language use*, eds. Eda Weigand and Franz Hundsnurscher, 215–224. Tübingen: Niemeyer.

—— (1999). *Woordensmederij. De geschiedenis van het suffix -erij*. Utrecht: LOT.

—— (2000). Monica en andere gates. Het ontstaan van een morfologisch procédé. *Nederlandse Taalkunde* 5: 121–132.

—— (2010). Adjective + Noun constructions between syntax and word formation in Dutch and German. In *Cognitive approaches to word formation*, eds. Sascha Michel and Michael Onysko, 195–215. Berlin: Mouton de Gruyter.

Hurford, James R. (1975). *The linguistic theory of numerals*. Cambridge: Cambridge University Press.

—— (1987). *Language and number: the emergence of a cognitive system*. Oxford: Basil Blackwell.

—— (2003). The interaction between numerals and nouns. In *Noun phrase structure in the languages of Europe*, ed. Frans Plank, 561–620. Berlin / New York: Mouton de Gruyter.

—— (2007). A performed practice explains a linguistic universal: counting gives the Packing Strategy. *Lingua* 117: 773–783.

Iacobini, Claudio and Masini, Francesca (2006). The emergence of verb-particle constructions in Italian: locative and actional meanings. *Morphology* 16: 155–188.

Iida, Masayo and Sells, Peter (2008). Mismatches between morphology and syntax in Japanese complex predicates. *Lingua* 118: 947–968.

Inkelas, Sharon and Zoll, Cheryll (2005). *Reduplication: Doubling in morphology*. Cambridge: Cambridge University Press.

Ito, Junko and Mester, Armin (2003). On the sources of opacity in OT: coda processes in German. In *The syllable in Optimality Theory*, eds. Caroline Féry and Ruben Van de Vijver, 271–303. Cambridge: Cambridge University Press.

Jackendoff, Ray (1975). Semantic and morphological regularities in the lexicon. *Language* 51: 639–671.

—— (1997a). Twistin' the night away. *Language* 73: 534–559.

—— (1997b). *The architecture of the language faculty*. Cambridge, MA: MIT Press.

—— (2002a). *Foundations of language*. Oxford: Oxford University Press.

—— (2002b). What's in the lexicon? In *Storage and computation in the language faculty*, eds. Sieb Nooteboom, Fred Weerman, and Frank Wijnen, 3–40. Dordrecht: Kluwer.

—— (2007). A Parallel Architecture perspective on language processing. *Brain Research* 1146: 2–22.

—— (2008). *Construction after construction* and its theoretical challenge. *Language* 84: 8–28.

—— (2009). Compounding in the parallel architecture and conceptual semantics. In *The Oxford handbook of compounding*, eds. Rochelle Lieber and Pavol Štekauer, 105–129. Oxford: Oxford University Press.

Järvikivi, Juhani, Bertram, Raymond, and Niemi, Jussi (2006). Affixal salience and the processing of derivational morphology: the role of suffix allomorphy. *Language and Cognitive Processes* 21: 394–431.

Julien, Marit (2002). *Syntactic heads and word formation.* Oxford: Oxford University Press.

Kager, René (1999). *Optimality Theory.* Cambridge: Cambridge University Press.

Kageyama, Taro (1982). Word formation in Japanese. *Lingua* 57: 215–258.

—— (1999). Word formation. In *The handbook of Japanese linguistics*, ed. Natsuko Tsujimura, 297–325. Oxford: Blackwell.

—— (2009). Isolate: Japanese. In *The Oxford handbook of compounding*, eds. Rochelle Lieber and Pavol Štekauer, 512–526. Oxford: Oxford University Press.

Kastovsky, Dieter (1988). The problem of productivity in word formation. *Linguistics* 24: 585–600.

Kay, Paul and Fillmore, Charles (1999). Grammatical constructions and linguistic generalizations. *Language* 75: 1–33.

Kenstowicz, Michael (1994). *Phonology in generative grammar.* Cambridge, MA: Blackwell.

Kester, Ellen-Petra (1996). *The nature of adjectival inflection.* Utrecht: LOT.

Keuleers, Emmanuel and Daelemans, Walter (2007). Memory-based learning models of inflectional morphology: a methodological case study. *Lingue e Linguaggio* 6: 151–174.

—— Sandra, Dominiek, Daelemans, Walter, Gillis, Steven, Durieux, Gert, and Martens, Evelyn (2007). Dutch plural inflection: the exception that proves the analogy. *Cognitive Psychology* 54: 283–318.

Kiefer, Ferenc (1992). Compounding in Hungarian. *Rivista di Linguistica* 4: 61–78.

—— and Honti, László (2003). Verbal 'prefixation' in the Uralic languages. *Acta Linguistica Hungarica* 50: 137–153.

Kilbury, James, Petersen, Wiebke, and Rumpf, Christoph (2006). Inheritance-based models of the lexicon. In *Advances in the theory of the lexicon*, ed. Dieter Wunderlich, 429–480. Berlin: Mouton de Gruyter.

Kiparsky, Paul (2000). Opacity and cyclicity. *The Linguistic Review* 17: 351–365.

Klamer, Marian (1998). *A grammar of Kambera.* Berlin / New York: Mouton de Gruyter.

—— (2001). Phrasal emotion predicates in three languages of Eastern Indonesia. In *Yearbook of Morphology 2000*, eds. Geert Booij and Jaap van Marle, 97–122. Dordrecht: Kluwer.

Koefoed, Geert (1993). *Benoemen. een beschouwing over de faculté du langage.* Amsterdam: P.J. Meertens-Instituut.

—— and Van Marle, Jaap (1980). Over Humboldtiaanse taalveranderingen, morfologie en de creativiteit van taal. *Spektator* 10: 111–147.

Koike, Takeshi (2006). The history of the genitive case from the Old English period onwards. *English Language and Linguistics* 10: 49–75.

König, Jean-Pierre (1999). *Lexical relations.* Stanford: CSLI.

Kooij, Jan and Mous, Maarten (2002). Incorporation: a comparison between Iraqw and Dutch. *Linguistics* 40: 629–645.

Koptjevskaja-Tamm, Maria (2003a). Possessive noun phrases in the languages of Europe. In *Noun phrase structure in the languages of Europe*, ed. Frans Plank, 621–722. Berlin / New York: Mouton de Gruyter.

——(2003b). *A woman of sin, a man of duty, and a hell of a mess*: non-determiner genitives in Swedish. In *Noun phrase structure in the languages of Europe*, ed. Frans Plank, 515–558. Berlin / New York: Mouton de Gruyter.

Kornfeld, Laura Malena (2009). IE, Romance: Spanish. In *The Oxford handbook of compounding*, eds. Rochelle Lieber and Pavol Štekauer, 436–452. Oxford: Oxford University Press.

Koster, Jan (1975). Dutch as an SOV language. *Linguistic Analysis* 1: 111–136.

Krause, Olaf (2002). *Der Progressiv im Deutschen: eine empirische Untersuchung im Kontrast mit Niederländisch und Englisch*. Tübingen: Niemeyer.

Krieger, Hans-Ulrich and Nerbonne, John (1993). Feature-based inheritance networks for computational lexicons. In *Inheritance, defaults, and the lexicon*, eds. Ted Briscoe, Valeria De Paiva, and Ann Copestake, 90–136. Cambridge: Cambridge University Press.

Krott, Andrea (2001). *Analogy in morphology: the selection of linking elements in Dutch compounds*. Nijmegen: Max Planck Institut für Psycholinguistik.

Kuteva, Tania (2001). *Auxiliation: an enquiry into the nature of grammaticalization*. Oxford: Oxford University Press.

Kutsch Lojenga, Constance (1994). *Ngiti, a Central-Sudanic language of Zaire*. Köln: Rüdiger Köppe Verlag.

Lambrecht, Knud (2004). On the interaction of information structure and formal structure in constructions: the case of French right-detached comme-N. In *Construction grammar in a cross-language perspective*, eds. Mirjam Fried and Jan-Ola Östman, 157–199. Amsterdam / Philadelphia: Benjamins.

Langacker, Ronald (1987). *Foundations of Cognitive Grammar, Vol. 1. Theoretical prerequisites*. Stanford, CA: Stanford University Press.

——(1991). *Foundations of Cognitive Grammar, Vol. 2. Descriptive applications*. Stanford, CA: Stanford University Press.

——(1999). *Grammar and conceptualization*. Berlin: Mouton de Gruyter.

Lanouette, Ruth Lunt (1996). The attributive genitive in the history of German. In *Germanic linguistics: syntactic and diachronic*, eds. Rosina Lippi-Green and Joseph C. Salmons, 85–102. Amsterdam / Philadelphia: Benjamins.

Lappe, Sabine (2007). *English prosodic morphology*. Dordrecht: Springer.

Lascarides, Alex and Copestake, Ann (1999). Default representation in constraint-based frameworks. *Computational Linguistics* 25: 55–106.

Lass, Roger (1990). How to do things with junk: exaptation in language evolution. *Journal of Linguistics* 26: 79–102.

——(1997). *Historical linguistics and language change*. Cambridge: Cambridge University Press.

Lee, Seung-Ah (2007). *Ing* forms and the progressive puzzle: a construction-based approach to English progressives. *Journal of Linguistics* 43: 153–195.

Lemmens, Maarten (2002). The semantic network of Dutch posture verbs. In *The linguistics of sitting, standing, and lying*, ed. John Newman, 103–140. Amsterdam / Philadelphia: Benjamins.

—— (2005). Aspectual posture verbs in Dutch. *Journal of Germanic Linguistics* 17: 183–217.

Levelt, Willem J.M. (1989). *Speaking: from intention to articulation*. Cambridge, MA: MIT Press.

Leys, Odo (1985). De konstruktie *staan te* + infinitief en verwante konstrukties. *Verslagen en Mededelingen van de Koninklijke Akademie voor Nederlandse Taal- en Letterkunde* 13: 265–277.

—— (1997). Ein Engel von (einer) Frau. Emotionalität als konstruktionale Bedeutung. *Leuvense Bijdragen* 86: 27–52.

Lichtenberk, Frantisek (1991). Language change and heterosemy in grammaticalization. *Language* 67: 475–509.

Lieber, Rochelle (1983). Argument linking and compounds in English. *Linguistic Inquiry* 14: 251–286.

—— (2004). *Morphology and lexical semantics*. Cambridge: Cambridge University Press.

Los, Bettelou, Blom, Corrien, Booij, Geert, Elenbaas, Marion, and Van Kemenade, Ans (2010). *Scenarios of morpho-syntactic change: particles and prefixes in Dutch and English*. Cambridge: Cambridge University Press.

Lüdeling, Anke (1999). *On particle verbs and similar constructions in German*. Stanford: CSLI.

Malkiel, Yakov (1978). Derivational categories. In *Universals of human language, Vol. 3. Word structure*, ed. Joseph H. Greenberg, 125–149. Stanford, CA: Stanford University Press.

Marchand, Hans (1969). *The categories and types of present-day English word formation*. München: Beck.

Marslen-Wilson, William D., Tyler, Lorraine, Waksler, Rachelle, and Older, Lianne (1994). Morphology and meaning in the English mental lexicon. *Psychological Review* 101: 3–33.

—— William D., and Zhou, Xiaolin (1999). Abstractness, allomorphy, and lexical architecture. *Language and Cognitive Processes* 14: 321–352.

Masini, Francesca and Thornton, Anna M. (2008). Italian VeV lexical constructions. In *Morphology and dialectology. On-line proceedings of the Sixth Mediterranean Morphology Meeting*, eds. Angela Ralli, Geert Booij, Sergio Scalise, and Athanasios Karasimos, 146–193. Patras: University of Patras.

Massam, Diane (2001). Pseudo noun incorporation in Niuean. *Natural Language and Linguistic Theory* 19: 153–197.

Matsumoto, Yo (1996a). *Complex predicates in Japanese: a syntactic and semantic study of the notion 'word'*. Stanford / Tokyo: CSLI Publications / Kurosio Publishers.

Matsumoto, Yo (1996b). A syntactic account of light verb phenomena in Japanese. *Journal of East-Asian Linguistics* 5: 107–149.

Matthews, Peter H. (1972). *Inflectional morphology: a theoretical study based on aspects of Latin verb conjugation.* Cambridge: Cambridge University Press.

——(2007). *Syntactic relations: a critical survey.* Cambridge: Cambridge University Press.

Mayo, Bruce, Schepping, Marie-Therese, Schwarze, Christoph, and Zaffanella, Angela (1995). Semantics in the derivational morphology of Italian: implications for the structure of the lexicon. *Linguistics* 33: 883–938.

McCarthy, John J. and Prince, Alan (1994). Generalized alignment. In *Yearbook of Morphology 1993*, eds. Geert Booij and Jaap Van Marle, 79–154. Dordrecht: Kluwer.

McConnell-Ginet, Sally (2008). Words in the world: how and why meanings can matter. *Language* 84: 497–528.

Meesters, Gert (2004). *Marginale morfologie in het Nederlands. Paradigmatische samenstellingen, neo-klassieke composita en splintercomposita.* Gent: Koninklijke Academie voor Nederlandse Taal- en Letterkunde.

Meibauer, Jörg, Guttropf, Anja, and Scherer, Carmen (2004). Dynamic aspects of German -er nominals: a probe into the interrrelation of language change and language acquisition. *Linguistics* 42: 155–193.

Michaelis, Laura A. and Lambrecht, Knud (1996). Toward a construction-based theory of language function: the case of nominal extraposition. *Language* 72: 215–247.

Mithun, Marianne (1984). The evolution of noun incorporation. *Language* 60: 847–894.

——(1997). Lexical affixes and morphological typology. In *Essays on language function and language type*, eds. Joan Bybee, John Haiman, and Sandra Thompson, 357–372. Amsterdam / Philadelphia: Benjamins.

——(1999). *The languages of Native North America.* Cambridge: Cambridge University Press.

——(2000). Incorporation. In *Morphologie/Morphology. Ein internationales Handbuch zur Flexion und Wortbildung/An international handbook on inflection and word formation* eds. Geert Booij, Joachim Mugdan, and Christian Lehmann, 916–928. Berlin: De Gruyter.

——(2009). Mohawk. In *The Oxford handbook of compounding*, eds. Rochelle Lieber and Pavol Štekauer, 564–588. Oxford: Oxford University Press.

——(2010). Compounding and incorporation. In *Cross-disciplinary issues in compounding*, eds. Sergio Scalise and Irene Vogel, 37–56. Amsterdam / Philadelphia: Benjamins.

—— and Corbett, Greville G. (1999). The effect of noun incorporation on argument structure. In *Boundaries of morphology and syntax*, ed. Lunella Mereu, 49–71. Amsterdam / Philadelphia: Benjamins.

Mohanan, Tara (1995). Wordhood and lexicality: noun incorporation in Hindi. *Natural Language and Linguistic Theory* 13: 75–134.

Moravcsik, Edith (2003). Non-compositional definiteness marking in Hungarian noun phrases. In *Noun phrase structure in the languages of Europe*, ed. Frans Plank, 397–466. Berlin / New York: Mouton de Gruyter.

Müller, Stefan (2002). *Complex predicates: verbal complexes, resultative constructions and particle verbs in German.* Stanford: CSLI.

—— (2003). The morphology of German particle verbs: solving the bracketing paradox. *Journal of Linguistics* 39: 275–325.

—— (2006). Phrasal or lexical constructions? *Language* 82: 850–883.

Nattinger, James R. and De Carrico, Jeanette (1992). *Lexical phrases and language teaching.* Oxford: Oxford University Press.

Neeleman, Ad (1992). *Complex predicates.* Utrecht: Led/LOT.

—— and Weerman, Fred. (1993). The balance between morphology and syntax: separable complex verbs in Dutch. *Natural Language and Linguistic Theory* 11: 433–476.

Newman, John ed. (2002). *The linguistics of sitting, standing, and lying.* Amsterdam / Philadelphia: Benjamins.

Norde, Muriel (1997). *The history of the genitive in Swedish.* Ph.D. dissertation, University of Amsterdam, Scandinavian Department.

—— (1998). Grammaticalization versus reanalysis: the case of possessive constructions in Germanic. In *Historical Linguistics 1995.* Vol. 2, eds. Richard M. Hogg and Linda van Bergen, 211–222. Amsterdam / Philadelphia: Benjamins.

—— (2006). Demarcating degrammaticalization: the Swedish *s*-genitive revisited. *Nordic Journal of Linguistics* 29: 201–238.

Orgun, Cemil Orhan and Inkelas, Sharon (2002). Reconsidering Bracket Erasure. In *Yearbook of Morphology 2001*, eds. Geert Booij and Jaap Van Marle, 115–146. Dordrecht: Kluwer.

Östman, Jan-Ola (2005). Construction discourse: a prolegomenon. In *Construction grammars: cognitive grounding and theoretical extensions*, eds. Jan-Ola Östman and Mirjam Fried, 121–144. Amsterdam / Philadelphia: Benjamins.

Paardekooper, Piet. C. (1958). *ABN-Spraakkunst. Voorstudies, tweede deel.* Den Bosch: L.C.G. Malmberg.

Packard, Jerome (2000). *The morphology of Chinese: a linguistic and cognitive approach.* Cambridge: Cambridge University Press.

Panther, Klaus-Uwe and Thornburg, Linda L. (2003). The roles of metaphor and metonymy in English -*er* nominals. In *Metaphor and metonymy in comparison and contrast*, eds. René Dirven and Ralf Pörings, 279–319. Berlin / New York: Mouton de Gruyter.

Paul, Hermann (1880) [3rd edition 1898]. *Prinzipien der Sprachgeschichte.* Halle: Max Niemeyer.

Payne, John (1993). The headedness of noun phrases: slaying the nominal hydra. In *Heads in grammatical theory*, eds. Greville G. Corbett, Norman M. Fraser, and Scott McGlashan, 114–139. Cambridge: Cambridge University Press.

Pérez Saldanya, Manuel and Vallès, Teresa (2005). Catalan morphology and low-level patterns in a network model. *Catalan Journal of Linguistics* 4: 199–223.

Petré, Peter and Cuyckens, Hubert (2008). Bedusted, yet not beheaded: the role of *be-*'s constructional properties in its conservation. In *Constructions and language change*, eds. Alexander Bergs and Gabriele Diewald, 133–169. Berlin / New York: Mouton de Gruyter.

Pinker, Steven (1999). *Words and rules*. New York: Basic Books.

Pitt, David and Katz, Jerrold J. (2000). Compositional idioms. *Language* 76: 409–432.

Plag, Ingo (2006). The variability of compound stress in English: structural, semantic, and analogical factors. *English Language and Linguistics* 10: 143–172.

—— Kunter, Gero, Lappe, Sabine, and Braun, Maria (2008). The role of semantics, argument structure, and lexicalization in compound stress assignment in English. *Language* 84: 760–794.

Ponelis, Frits A. (1979). *Afrikaanse sintaksis*. Pretoria: J.L. van Schaik.

Pottelberge, Jeroen van (2002). Nederlandse progressiefconstructies met werkwoorden van lichaamshouding. *Nederlandse Taalkunde* 7: 142–174.

Rainer, Franz (2001). Compositionality and paradigmatically determined allomorphy in Italian word-formation. In *Naturally! Linguistic studies in honour of Wolfgang Ulrich Dressler on the occasion of his 60th birthday*, eds. Chris Schaner-Wolles, John Rennison, and Friedrich Neubarth, 383–392. Torino: Rosenberg & Selier.

—— (2003). Semantic fragmentation in word-formation: the case of Spanish *-azo*. In *Explorations in seamless morphology*, eds. Rajendra Singh and Sol Starosta, 197–211. New Delhi / London: Thousand Oaks / Sage.

—— (2005). Typology, diachrony, and universals of semantic change in word formation: a Romanist's look at the polysemy of agent nouns. In *Proceedings of the Fifth Mediterranean Morphology Meeting*, eds. Geert Booij, Angela Ralli, Sergio Scalise, and Salvatore Sgroi. Catania: University of Catania, Faculty of Letters.

—— and Varela, Soledad (1992). Compounding in Spanish. *Rivista di Linguistica* 4: 117–142.

Ralli, Angela (2007). *I sinthesi lekseon: Morfologiki diaglossiki prosengisi [Compounding: a morphological cross-linguistic approach]*. Athens: Patakis.

—— and Stavrou, Melita (1998). Morphology–syntax interface: A-N compounds vs. A-N constructs in Modern Greek. In *Yearbook of Morphology 1997*, eds. Geert Booij and Jaap Van Marle, 243–264. Dordrecht: Kluwer.

Ramat, Paolo (2001). Degrammaticalization or transcategorization? In *Naturally! Linguistic studies in honour of Wolfgang Ulrich Dressler presented on the occasion of his 60th birthday*, eds. Chris Schaner-Wolles, John Rennison, and Friedrich Neubarth, 393–401. Torino: Rosenberg & Sellier.

Rappaport Hovav, Malka, and Levin, Beth (1992). *Er*-nominals: implications for the theory of argument structure. In *Syntax and the lexicon*, eds. Tim Stowell and Eric Wehrli, 127–153. New York: Academic Press.

Reid, Agnieszka Anna and Marslen-Wilson, William D. (2003). Lexical representation of morphologically complex words: evidence from Polish. In *Morphological structure in language processing*, eds. R. Harald Baayen and Rob Schreuder, 287–336. Berlin: Mouton de Gruyter.

Renkema, Jan (1995). *Woordenlijst der Nederlandse Taal*. Den Haag / Antwerpen: SDU Uitgevers / Standaard Uitgeverij.

Rice, Keren (2009). Athapaskan: Slave. In *The Oxford handbook of compounding*, eds. Rochelle Lieber and Pavol Štekauer, 542–563. Oxford: Oxford University Press.

Riehemann, Suzanne Z. (1998). Type-based derivational morphology. *Journal of Comparative Germanic Linguistics* 2: 49–77.

—— (2001). *A constructional approach to idioms and word formation*. Stanford: Ph.D. dissertation, Stanford University.

Riehl, Claudia Maria and Kilian-Hatz, Christa (2005). Structure and function of incorporation processes in compounding. In *Studies in African linguistic typology*, ed. F.K. Erhard Voeltz, 361–376. Amsterdam / Philadelphia: Benjamins.

Rosenbach, Anette (2002). *Genitive variation in English: conceptual factors in synchronic and diachronic studies*. Berlin: Mouton de Gruyter.

—— (2006). Descriptive genitives in English: a case study on constructional gradience. *English Language and Linguistics* 10: 77–118.

—— (2007). Emerging variation: determiner genitives and noun-modifiers. *English Language and Linguistics* 11: 143–189.

Rubach, Jerzy (2000). Glide and glottal stop insertion in Slavic languages: a DOT analysis. *Linguistic Inquiry* 31: 271–317.

—— and Booij, Geert (2001). Allomorphy in Optimality Theory: Polish iotation. *Language* 77: 26–60.

Rumelhart, David E. (1980). Schemata: the building blocks of cognition. In *Theoretical issues in reading comprehension: perspectives from cognitive psychology, linguistics, artificial intelligence, and education*, eds. Rand J. Spiro, Bertram C. Bruce, and William F. Brewer, 33–58. Hillsdale, New Jersey: Lawrence Erlbaum Associates.

—— and McClelland, James (1986). On learning the past tenses of English verbs: implicit rules or parallel distributed processing? In *Parallel distributed processing: explorations in the micro-structure of cognition*, eds. James McClelland, David E. Rumelhart, and PDP Research Group, 216–271. Cambridge: Cambridge University Press.

Ryder, Mary Ellen (1999*a*). Complex -er-nominals. Where grammaticalization and lexicalization meet? In *Between grammar and lexicon*, eds. Ellen Contini-Morava and Yishai Tobin, 291–332. Amsterdam / Philadelphia: John Benjamins.

—— (1999*b*). *Bankers* and *blue-chippers*: an account of *er*-formations in present-day English. *English Language and Linguistics* 3: 269–297.

Sadler, Louisa and Arnold, Douglas J. (1994). Prenominal adjectives and the phrasal/lexical distinction. *Journal of Linguistics* 30: 187–226.

—— and Spencer, Andrew (2001). Syntax as an exponent of morphological features. In *Yearbook of Morphology 2000*, eds. Geert Booij and Jaap Van Marle, 71–96. Dordrecht: Kluwer.

Sag, Ivan A. (2007). Sign-based construction grammar: an informal synopsis. Ms. Stanford University, Stanford, CA.

Sag, Ivan A. Baldwin, Timothy, Bond, Francis, Copestake, Ann, and Flickinger, Daniel Paul (2002). Multiword expressions: a pain in the neck for NLP. In *Proceedings of CICLING 2002*, ed. Alexander Gelbukh. Dordrecht: Springer.

—— Wasow, Thomas, and Bender, Emily M. (2003). *Syntactic theory: a formal introduction*. Stanford: CSLI.

Sapir, Edward (1911). The problem of noun incorporation in American languages. *American Anthropologist* 13: 250–282.

Sassen, Albert (1953). *Het Drents van Ruinen*. Assen: Van Gorcum.

Saunders, Ross and Davis, Philip W. (1975). Bella Coola lexical suffixes. *Anthropological Linguistics* 17: 154–189.

Scalise, Sergio (1984). *Generative morphology*. Dordrecht: Foris.

—— (1988). The notion of 'head' in morphology. In *Yearbook of Morphology 1988*, eds. Geert Booij and Jaap Van Marle, 229–246. Dordrecht: Foris.

—— (1992). Compounding in Italian. *Rivista di Linguistica* 4: 175–199.

—— and Guevara, Emiliano (2006). Exocentric compounding in a typological framework. *Lingue e linguaggio* 5: 185–206.

Schreuder, Rob and Baayen, R. Harald (1997). How complex simplex words can be. *Journal of Memory and Language* 37: 118–139.

Schultink, Henk (1962). *De morfologische valentie van het ongelede adjectief in modern Nederlands*. Den Haag: Van Goor Zonen.

Schultze-Berndt, Eva (2003). Preverbs as an open word class in Northern Australian languages: synchronic and diachronic correlates. In *Yearbook of Morphology 2003*, eds. Geert Booij and Jaap Van Marle, 145–177. Dordrecht: Kluwer.

Schwarze, Christoph (2005). Grammatical and para-grammatical word formation. *Lingue e linguaggio* 2: 137–162.

Semenza, Carlo and Mondini, Sara (2006). The neuropsychology of compound words. In *The representation and processing of compound words*, eds. Gary Libben and Gonia Jarema, 71–95. New York / Oxford: Oxford University Press.

Smith, K. Aaron (2007). The development of the English progressive. *Journal of Germanic Linguistics* 19: 205–243.

Spencer, Andrew (1988). Bracketing paradoxes and the English lexicon. *Language* 64: 663–682.

—— (2004). Morphology – an overview of central concepts. In *Projecting morphology*, eds. Louisa Sadler and Andrew Spencer, 67–109. Stanford: CSLI.

Sprenger, Simone A. (2003). *Fixed expressions and the production of idioms*. Nijmegen: Max-Planck-Institut für Psycholinguistik.

Steriade, Donca (2000). Paradigm uniformity and the phonetics-phonology boundary. In *Papers in Laboratory Phonology V. Acquisition of the lexicon*, eds. Michael Broe and Janet Pierrehumbert, 313–334. Cambridge: Cambridge University Press.

Stoett, F.A. (1923). *Middelnederlandsche Spraakkunst. Syntaxis*. 's Gravenhage: Martinus Nijhoff.

Stump, Gregory T. (1991). A paradigm-based theory of morphosemantic mismatches. *Language* 67: 675–726.

——(2001). *Inflectional morphology: a theory of paradigm structure*. Cambridge: Cambridge University Press.

——(2005). Word-formation and inflectional morphology. In *Handbook of word-formation*, eds. Pavol Stekauer and Rochelle Lieber, 49–71. Dordrecht: Springer.

Szymanek, Bogdan (2009). IE, Slavonic: Polish. In *The Oxford handbook of compounding*, eds. Rochelle Lieber and Pavol Štekauer, 464–477. Oxford: Oxford University Press.

Taylor, John R. (2002). *Cognitive grammar*. Oxford: Oxford University Press.

Teleman, Ulf, Hellberg, Staffan, and Andersson, Erik (1999). *Svenska Akademiens grammatik*. Stockholm: Norstedts.

Tinbergen, D.C. (1949). Nog enkele opmerkingen over telwoorden. *De Nieuwe Taalgids* 42: 96–99.

Toivonen, Ida (2003). *Non-projecting words: a case study of Swedish*. Dordrecht: Kluwer.

Tomasello, Michael (2000). Do young children have adult syntactic competence? *Cognition* 74: 209–253.

Traugott, Elisabeth C. (2003). Constructions in grammaticalization. In *The handbook of historical linguistics*, eds. Brian Joseph and Richard Janda, 624–647. Oxford: Blackwell.

Tuggy, David (2005). Cognitive approach to word formation. In *Handbook of word-formation*, eds. Pavol Stekauer and Rochelle Lieber, 231–263. Dordrecht: Kluwer.

——(2007). Schematicity. In *The Oxford handbook of cognitive linguistics*, eds. Dirk Geeraerts and Hubert Cuyckens, 82–116. Oxford: Oxford University Press.

Tummers, José (2005). *Het naakt(e) adjectief. Kwantitatief-empirisch onderzoek naar de adjectivische buigingsalternantie bij neutra*. Leuven: Katholieke Universiteit Leuven, Departement Linguïstiek.

Uhlenbeck, Eugenius M. (1976). Taal en taalwetenschap. *Anniversary lecture Universiteit Leiden, 8 February 1976*.

Ungerer, Friedrich (2007). Word-formation. In *The Oxford handbook of cognitive linguistics*, eds. Dirk Geeraerts and Hubert Cuyckens, 650–675. Oxford: Oxford University Press.

Vallès, Teresa (2003). Lexical creativity and the organization of the lexicon. *Annual Review of Cognitive Linguistics* 1: 137–160.

Van den Heuvel, Wilco (2006). *Biak: description of an Austronesian language of Papua*. Utrecht: LOT.

Van der Horst, Joop and Van der Horst, Kees (1999). *Geschiedenis van het Nederlands in de twintigste eeuw*. Den Haag / Antwerpen: SDU Uitgevers / Standaard Uitgeverij.

Van der Sijs, Nicoline (2001). *Chronologisch woordenboek. De ouderdom en herkomst van onze woorden en betekenissen*. Amsterdam: L.J. Veen.

Van der Veer, Bart and Booij, Geert (in press). Allomorphy in OT: the Italian mobile diphthongs. In *Understanding allomorphy: perspectives from OT*, ed. Bernard Tranel. London: Equinox.

Van Es, Gustaaf A. (1938). *De attributieve genitief in het Middelnederlandsch*. Assen: Van Gorcum & Comp.

Van Goethem, Kristel (2008). *Oud-leerling* versus *ancien élève*. A comparative study of adjectives grammaticalizing into prefixes in Dutch and French. *Morphology* 18: 27–49.

Van Haeringen, Coenraad B. (1949*a*). Een paar aantekeningen bij telwoorden. *De Nieuwe Taalgids* 42: 255–258.

——(1949*b*). Participia praeverbalia. *De Nieuwe Taalgids* 42: 38–44.

Van Helten, W. L. (1887). *Middelnederlandsche spraakkunst*. Groningen: J.B. Wolters.

Van Loey, Adolphe (1959). *Schönfelds historische grammatica van het Nederlands*. Zutphen: Thieme.

——(1976). *Scheidbare en onscheidbare werkwoorden hoofdzakelijk in het Middelnederlands, analytische studiën*. Gent: Koninklijke Akademie voor Nederlandse Taal- en Letterkunde.

Van Marle, Jaap (1985). *On the paradigmatic dimension of morphological creativity*. Dordrecht: Foris.

——(1996). The unity of morphology: on the interwovenness of the derivational and the inflectional dimension of the word. In *Yearbook of Morphology 1995*, eds. Geert Booij and Jaap van Marle, 67–82. Dordrecht: Kluwer.

——(2000). Paradigmatic and syntagmatic relations. In *Morphology: an international handbook on inflection and word formation*. Vol. 1, eds. Geert Booij, Christian Lehmann, and Joachim Mugdan and in collaboration with Wolfgang Kesselheim and Stavros Skopeteas, 225–234. Berlin / New York: Mouton de Gruyter.

——(2002). Dutch separable compound verbs: words rather than phrases? In *Particle verb explorations*, eds. Nicole Dehé, Ray Jackendoff, Andrew MacIntyre, and Silke Urban, 211–232. Berlin: Mouton de Gruyter.

Van Riemsdijk, Henk C. (1978). *A case study in syntactic markedness: the binding nature of prepositional phrases*. Dordrecht: Foris.

Van Santen, Ariane (1992). *Produktiviteit in taal en taalgebruik*. Leiden: University of Leiden.

——and De Vries, Jan (1981). Vrouwelijke persoonsnamen op *-ster*. *Forum der Letteren* 22: 115–125.

Vendler, Zeno (1967). *Linguistics in philosophy*. Ithaca: Cornell University Press.

Vikner, Sten (2005). Immobile complex verbs in Germanic. *Journal of Comparative Germanic Linguistics* 8: 83–115.

Vincent, Nigel (1995). Exaptation and grammaticalization. In *Historical Linguistics 1993*, ed. Henning Andersen, 433–445. Amsterdam / Philadelphia: Benjamins.

Vogel, Irene (1993). Verbs in Italian morphology. In *Yearbook of Morphology 1993*, eds. Geert Booij and Jaap van Marle, 219–254. Dordrecht: Kluwer.

Watkins, Calvert (1964). Preliminaries to the reconstruction of Indo-European sentence structure. In *Proceedings of the 9th International Congress of Linguists*, ed. Horace D. Lunt, 1035–1044. Berlin / New York: Mouton de Gruyter.

Weerman, Fred and De Wit, Petra (1998). De ondergang van de genitief. *Nederlandse Taalkunde* 3: 18–46.

—— ——(1999). The decline of the genitive in Dutch. *Linguistics* 37: 1155–1192.

Wiese, Heike (2007). The co-evolution of number concepts and counting words. *Lingua* 117: 758–772.

Wiese, Richard (1996). *The phonology of German.* Oxford: Clarendon Press.

Williams, Edwin (1981). On the notions 'lexically related' and 'head of a word'. *Linguistic Inquiry* 12: 245–274.

Wray, Alison (2002). *Formulaic language and the lexicon.* Cambridge: Cambridge University Press.

Zeller, Jochen (2001). *Particle verbs and local domains.* Amsterdam / Philadelphia: Benjamins.

—— (2002). Particle verbs are heads and phrases. In *Verb-particle explorations*, eds. Nicole Dehé, Ray Jackendoff, Andrew McIntyre, and Silke Urban, 233–267. Berlin / New York: Mouton de Gruyter.

—— (2003). Moved preverbs in German: displaced or misplaced? In *Yearbook of Morphology 2003*, eds. Geert Booij and Jaap van Marle, 179–212. Dordrecht: Kluwer.

Index

Ingram Content Group UK Ltd.
Milton Keynes UK
UKHW051112250523
422194UK00032B/220